Songs
of
Experience

Songs
of
Experience

AN ANTHOLOGY OF LITERATURE ON GROWING OLD

Compiled and Edited by
MARGARET FOWLER
and
PRISCILLA McCUTCHEON

FOREWORD BY ROBERT N. BUTLER, M.D., SERIES EDITOR

Published with the cooperation and consultation of the
Gerald and May Ellen Ritter Department of Geriatrics and Adult Development,
Mount Sinai School of Medicine, Mount Sinai Hospital, New York

BALLANTINE BOOKS
NEW YORK

Library of Congress Catalog Card Number: 89-92601
ISBN: 0-345-36057-5

Cover design by James R. Harris
Cover photographs: Photo Researchers, Inc./© John Bova
Text design by Beth Tondreau Design/Mary A. Wirth

Manufactured in the United States of America
First Edition: May 1991
10 9 8 7 6 5 4 3 2 1

TO OUR MOTHERS
Marjorie Carter Brown
Virginia Alcock Williamson

CONTENTS

Contents

❧ FOREWORD ❧

Except for a few notable examples, such as *Ecclesiastes*, Cicero's *De Senectute*, several of Montaigne's *Essays*, some of Rousseau's contemplations, and a few others, there was little literary and philosophic output in Western civilization concerned with the rich and varied landscape of old age. In all fairness, however, it's easy to understand why this was so: in the past, life expectancy was short, and not many people made it to old age. But what about today, when an unprecedented number of people worldwide are living well into their later years—when the fastest growing group of people in the United States are *centenarians?* Have the writers and thinkers of our own time successfully detected and monitored this significant social trend? How perceptive have they been in detailing the possibilities and the challenges, the pleasures and the pains of old age?

Songs of Experience, this fascinating collection of stories, poems, diary entries, and letters, in which old age plays the central role, lets us be the judge. We owe a great debt to editors Margaret Fowler and Priscilla McCutcheon, first for bringing to our attention contemporary works on the subject, and second, for stimulating our thoughts and perhaps even plans for our own old age. This book is a major step toward the formulation of a complete understanding of old age, an understanding that becomes all the more essential at this point in human history when so many of us will experience both the joys and hardships that come with living longer than previous generations.

"The test of a first-rate intelligence," said F. Scott Fitzgerald, "is the ability to hold two opposed ideas in the mind at the same time, and still retain the ability to function." Much the same could be said about both the capacity to understand longevity and the thread that weaves the selections in this anthology together: there is an ambivalence about growing older, because with the welcome added years of life comes the dread of physical and intellectual decline. Yet, in the face of potential misfortune, few renounce the chance to live to a ripe, old age. Rather, we embrace it and are grateful for the opportunity to gain a new and fuller perspective on our lives.

Old age is a complex stage of life, with its own set of pleasures and demands. We look to our writers and philosophers to help us paint a complete picture of this time, including the reality of human finitude as well as the rich opportunities for growth unavailable at earlier stages of life. In reading their words about their own (or their characters') processes of aging, we may not only identify experiences and feelings common to growing older, we may also transcend our narcissism and denial, for none of us is immune from aging.

ROBERT N. BUTLER, M.D.
Chairman
Gerald and May Ellen Ritter
Department of Geriatrics and Adult Development
Mount Sinai Medical Center

ᴥ§ INTRODUCTION ᵋᴥ

Old age is full of death and full of life.
It is a tolerable achievement and it is a disaster.
It transcends desire and it taunts it.
It is long enough and it is far from being
long enough.

         RONALD BLYTHE
         The View in Winter

For the first time in our country's history, most of us are going to live a long time. Yet in our youth-oriented culture we avoid old age with great determination. But what is old age all about? How do we make sense of it? Is it a season of enjoyment, when we reap the rewards of a long life, or simply a final deterioration and disintegration? Does this period of life have a special meaning and value of its own? How does it fit into the grand scheme of things? It is imperative that we seriously explore answers to these questions if we are to cope with the fear that most of us feel as we approach and enter the largely uncharted waters of old age.

In his book *Modern Man in Search of a Soul,* Carl Jung says, "A human being would certainly not grow to be seventy or eighty years old if this longevity had no meaning for the species to which he belongs." We started the research for this book with the supposition that old age does have its own special meaning and we wanted to contribute to the process of discovering that meaning for individuals, families, and communities in the America of the 1990s and beyond. Our experience with older people through our professional work, our research on aging as well as close ties with family members, and, perhaps most important, the glimmerings of our own impending old age have given us some assumptions about the unique aspects of old age that we set out to validate through literature.

Our first assumption was that only in old age does one truly have the freedom to develop oneself to the fullest, to define the essence of one's own individuality. Freed from the responsibilities of previous life stages—career, child raising—there is time to set priorities, distill what is really important. We believe that wisdom, venerated in many cultures as a distinction of old age, is the natural outcome of this process. Helen Lukes, a noted psychologist writing in her eighties, says, "Now that the harvest is gathered and you stand in the autumn of your life, your oar is . . . a spirit of discriminating wisdom, separating moment by moment the wheat of life from the chaff, so that you may know in both the wheat and chaff their meaning and value in the pattern of the universe."

Lukes' words led us to another observation that we hoped to illuminate through literary works. With advanced years comes a heightened awareness that rarely develops in earlier years, but seems nearly universal in old age. Perhaps increasing leisure allows the time for reflection and appreciation of nature and its wonders; perhaps the slowing body which deters strenuous activity spurs an interior development that promotes a new dimension of perception. We looked to find new works to verify Plato's words, "The spiritual eyesight improves as the physical eyesight declines."

We also knew this anthology must address the inescapable truth that old age is the last stage of life. It is for this reason that many people avoid thinking about their own aging, and we felt we needed to search for positive reasons to embrace the finality of life. We looked for examples of people bringing their experiences together, accepting and making sense of their lives and all they've been and done. We looked for examples of people content in the completion of a life. We hoped to document the statement of Dr. Robert Butler and Myrna Lewis in their book *Aging and Mental Health,* "Old age, in its best sense, can mean enjoyment of the finished product—a completed human being." We wanted to be able to show the enormous contributions that are possible only when the experience of living is nearly complete. Finally, and perhaps most important, we wished to explore the many ways in which writers portray the spirit continuing to live on after death.

Though one can find a great deal of literature on aging throughout history, we have limited this anthology to twentieth-century writing. Advances in technology and medicine have given life in this century a dimension never imagined previously, and therefore have changed the expectation and the reality of old age. Never before have so many people reached their sixties with the expectation of at least twenty to twenty-five healthy years stretching ahead of them. Changes in job patterns and advances in transportation and communication have all contributed to the breaking of customs that previously tied old people to an extended family, and never before have there been so many new possibilities for growth and new experiences.

To be thorough, we have included a wide variety of literature. In poetry, short stories, excerpts from journals, diaries, novels, and essays, the writers give their own unique vision of what it is like to be old. Each singular experience, each idiosyncratic reflection is one highly individual aspect of the multifaceted subject whose common denominator is age. Only through many different literary genres could we hope to express the complexity and the variety inherent in the last years of life. These disparate selections join to shape a multifarious, aggregate image of old age. Working on this project, we found that all the voices of the old, whether real or fictional, were essential pieces in the picture of old age that was emerging—each individual completed life itself a work of art.

As they approach their later years many writers recognize that they are crossing an important threshold and life will never again be just as it was. Losses of loved ones, energy, life-as-it-was can never be regained. Something new must take their place. Still, the feeling inside doesn't age so much. Polly Francis writes, "I want to cry out that the invisible part of me is not old." And nearly all of the works illustrate that the self grows more intensely individual with the years. As May Sarton wrote, "I am more myself than ever before."

Songs of Experience does not attempt to expose every aspect of aging in America today. Reports of elder abuse, of discrimination, of isolation and hopelessness, of poverty and substandard living conditions are readily available. These states exist in other age groups as well. But add these often reported facts to the long-held negative stereotypes of aging as a time of diminishment and resignation and it is not hard to understand why old age is the period of life most feared and abhorred. As we've worked on this book over the past few years, we've been amazed at the number of people who could not understand why we would choose to read about old age, and were clearly uncomfortable talking about it. With this book we wished to balance commonly held narrow definitions by concentrating on the positive, fulfilling, and rewarding prospects of aging.

Songs of Experience, on the other hand, does not portray old age as a purely blissful, utopian time of life. The characters and writers we've selected for inclusion are coping with failing health, loss, approaching death, and the numerous challenges of age. But the collective spirit they exhibit is testament to the promise that old age can be abundant.

Our probing of the literature confirms that old age is definitely a time of supreme paradox. It can offer the greatest challenges and the most exquisite personal rewards. Indeed, old age has a distinct meaning and value of its own. Only after many years of collecting and distilling the experiences of life can we possess the wisdom to understand and forgive ourselves and others. Only in old age are we allowed the freedom or time to develop our inner resources to the fullest. Only when faced with the inevitable end of life, can we comprehend the meaning of the beginning.

—MWF
PBMc

*S*ongs
of
*E*xperience

The Country of Old Age

"To enter the country of old age is a new experience, different from what you supposed it to be. Nobody, man or woman, knows the country until he has lived in it and has taken out his citizenship papers."

MALCOLM COWLEY
The View from 80

"A human being would certainly not grow to be seventy or eighty years old if this longevity had no meaning for the species to which he belongs."

CARL JUNG
Modern Man in Search of a Soul

"In the past few years, I have made a thrilling discovery . . . that until one is over sixty, one can never really learn the secret of living. One can then begin to live, not simply with the intense part of oneself, but with one's entire being."

ELLEN GLASGOW
The Woman Within

"We who are old know that age is more than a disability. It is an intense and varied experience, almost beyond capacity at times, but something to be carried high. If it is a long defeat it is also a victory, meaningful for the initiates of time, if not for those who have come less far."

FLORIDA SCOTT-MAXWELL
The Measure of My Days

May Sarton (1912–   ), contemporary American poet, novelist, and essayist, and author of more than forty books, was born in Belgium, educated in the United States, and now lives in Maine. Expressing her interest in the human relationships of everyday people, a number of her novels feature aging heroes and heroines. The following selection is the first entry in her journal, *At Seventy,* written during her seventieth year. The journal articulates Sarton's positive outlook toward old age as a time of growth and power.

from
AT SEVENTY: A JOURNAL

MONDAY, MAY 3RD, 1982

Such a peaceful, windless morning here for my seventieth birthday—the sea is pale blue, and although the field is still brown, it is dotted with daffodils at last. It has seemed an endless winter. But now at night the peepers are in full fettle, peeping away. And I was awakened by the cardinal, who is back again with his two wives, and the raucous cries of the male pheasant. I lay there, breathing in spring, listening to the faint susurration of the waves and awfully glad to be alive.

The table is set downstairs, all blue and white, with a tiny bunch of miniature daffodils, blue starflowers, and, glory be, two fritillaries. They always seem unreal with their purple-and-white-checkered bells, and I have never succeeded with a real show of them.

Then at each corner of the square table I have put a miniature rose, two white and two pale yellow, part of a bounty of miniature roses that have come for my birthday and will go along the terrace wall when the nights are not quite so cold. They are from Edythe Haddaway, one of the blessings of the last five years, for she comes when I am away to take care of Tamas and Bramble, feels at peace in this house, she tells me, and makes it peaceful for me to know that she is in residence and all is well at home when I am off on poetry-reading trips.

What is it like to be seventy? If someone else had lived so long and could remember things sixty years ago with great clarity, she would seem very old to me. But I do not feel old at all, not as much a survivor as a person still on her way. I suppose real old age begins when one looks backward rather than forward, but I look forward with joy to the years ahead and especially to the surprises that any day may bring.

In the middle of the night things well up from the past that are not always cause for rejoicing—the unsolved, the painful encounters, the mistakes, the reasons for shame or woe. But all, good or bad, painful or delightful, weave themselves into a rich tapestry, and all give me food for thought, food to grow on.

I am just back from a month of poetry readings, in and out through all of April. At Hartford College in Connecticut I had been asked to talk about old age—"The View From Here," I called the reading—in a series on "The Seasons of Womanhood." In the course of it I said, "This is the best time of my life. I love being old." At that point a voice from the audience asked loudly, "Why is it good to be old?" I answered spontaneously and a little on the defensive, for I sensed incredulity in the questioner, "Because I am more myself than I have ever been. There is less conflict. I am happier, more balanced, and" (I heard myself say rather aggressively) "more powerful." I felt it was rather an odd word, "powerful," but I think it is true. It might have been more accurate to say "I am better able to use my powers." I am surer of what my life is all about, have less self-doubt to conquer, although it has to be admitted that I wrote my new novel *Anger* in an agony of self-doubt most of the year, the hardest subject I have attempted to deal with in a novel since *Mrs. Stevens Hears the Mermaids Singing.* There I was breaking new ground, giving myself away. I was fifty-three and I deliberately made Mrs. Stevens seventy, and now here I am at what then seemed eons away, safely "old."

I have always longed to be old, and that is because all my life I have had such great exemplars of old age, such marvelous models to contemplate. First of all, of course, was Marie Closset (her pen name, Jean Dominique), whom I celebrated in my first novel and with whom I exchanged lives through letters and meetings from my twenty-fifth year until her death. I turn to her bound volumes of poetry this minute and open to the line

Au silence léger des nuits près de la mer

but I am bound to look for and find the long lyric addressed to Poetry, and as I write it here, I hear very clearly her light, grave voice, and we are sitting in her study, side by side:

Poésie! Je t'ai portée à mes lèvres
Comme un caillou frais pour ma soif,
Je t'ai gardée dans ma bouche obscure et sèche
Comme une petite pierre qu'on remasse
Et que l'on mâche avec du sang sur les lèvres!

Poésie, ah! je t'ai donné l'Amour,
L'Amour avec sa face comme une aube d'argent
Sur la mer,—et mon âme, avec la mer dedans,
Et la tempête avec le ciel du petit jour
Livide et frais comme un coquillage luisant.*

How happy Jean-Do would be to know that at seventy I live by the sea, and all those images are newly minted for me today "like a cool pebble for my thirst," "and my soul with the sea in it, and the tempest at dawn, pale and fresh as a shining shell." (But where is the music in English?)

Then Lugné-Poë, my father in the theater, was a constant challenger and giver of courage during the theater years. I see his immense devouring smile and remember my pet name for him, "mon éléphant." So he always signed his letters with an elephant head and a long trunk waving triumphantly at the end of a page.

*To the gentle silence of nights close to the sea

Poetry! I brought you to my lips
Like a cool pebble for my thirst
I kept you in my dark and dry mouth
Like a little pebble one takes
And chews with blood on the lips!

Poetry, oh! I gave you love,
Love with her face like a silver dawn
On the sea,—and my soul with the sea in it,
And the tempest with the sky of the daybreak
Pale and fresh like a shining shell.

Translated by Regis Aubert

Basil de Selincourt, my father in poetry, fierce as a hawk (and he looked rather like a hawk), wrote the first really good review I ever had (in the London *Observer* on *Encounter in April,* my first book of poems) and that was before we became friends. He taught me many things, not least how to garden into very old age by working at an extremely slow tempo—but I never did really learn it. That is still to come when, like Basil, I hope to put in a vegetable garden in my late eighties.

Then there is Eva Le Gallienne, who was only thirty when I first knew her as the star and creator of the Civic Repertory Theatre, and who has again triumphed in her eighties and shown a whole new generation what great acting is. She is proof that one can be eighty-three and still young. She too is a great gardener, so perhaps a good old age has to do with being still a friend of the earth.

I think also of Camille Mayran, who has written a magnificent book in her nineties, *Portrait de Ma Mère en Son Grand Âge.* She tells me that now, well over ninety, she sees no change in herself except for a "slight slowing down." She is all soul and mind, not a gardener at all! So one cannot generalize. But Eleanor Blair has just telephoned to wish me a happy birthday, as I write, and she says her garden is flourishing. Her voice sounded so young on the phone!

Perhaps the answer is not detachment as I used to believe but rather to be deeply involved in something, to be attached. I am attached in a thousand ways—and one of them compels me now to leave this airy room high up in the house to go down and get ready for my guests.

American editor, poet, and essayist, Malcolm Cowley (1898–1989), was literary editor of *The New Republic* magazine from 1930 to 1940, and later was literary adviser and editor at Viking Press. He served as editor for a number of well-known writers—among them, Whitman, Hemingway, Faulkner, and Fitzgerald—and wrote numerous criticisms and essays on modern American literature. At the age of seventy he published his collected poems, and, in his eighties, he wrote *The View from 80,* a book about his impressions of old age.

from
THE VIEW FROM 80

The new octogenarian feels as strong as ever when he is sitting back in a comfortable chair. He ruminates, he dreams, he remembers. He doesn't want to be disturbed by others. It seems to him that old age is only a costume assumed for those others; the true, the essential self is ageless. In a moment he will rise and go for a ramble in the woods, taking a gun along, or a fishing rod, if it is spring. Then he creaks to his feet, bending forward to keep his balance, and realizes that he will do nothing of the sort. The body and its surroundings have their messages for him, or only one message: "You are old. . . ."

Even before he or she is 80, the aging person may undergo another identity crisis like that of adolescence. Perhaps there had also been a middle-aged crisis, the male or the female menopause, but for the rest of adult life he had taken himself for granted, with his capabilities and failings. Now, when he looks in the mirror, he asks himself, "Is this really me?"—or he avoids the mirror out of distress at what it reveals, those bags and wrinkles. In his new makeup he is called upon to play a new role in a play that must be improvised. André Gide, that long-lived man of letters, wrote in his journal, "My heart has remained so young that I have the continual feeling of playing a part, the part of the 70-year-old that I certainly am; and the infirmities and weaknesses that remind me of my age act like a prompter, reminding me of my lines when I tend to stray. Then, like the good actor I want to be, I go back into my role, and I pride myself on playing it well. . . . "

. . . the men and women I envy are those who accept old age as a series of challenges.

For such persons, every new infirmity is an enemy to be outwitted, an obstacle to be overcome by force of will. They enjoy each little victory over themselves, and sometimes they win a major success. Renoir was one of them. He continued painting, and magnificently, for years after he was crippled by arthritis; the brush had to be strapped to his arm. "You don't need your hand to paint," he said. Goya was another of the unvanquished. At 72 he retired as an official painter of the Spanish court and decided to work only for himself. His later years were those of the famous "black paintings" in which he let his imagination run (and also of the lithographs, then a new technique). At 78 he escaped a reign of terror in Spain by fleeing to Bordeaux. He was deaf and his eyes were failing; in order to work he had to wear several pairs of spectacles, one over another, and then use a magnifying glass; but he was producing splendid work in a totally new style. At 80 he drew an ancient man propped on two sticks, with a mass of white hair and beard hiding his face and with the inscription "I am still learning."

Giovanni Papini said when he was nearly blind, "I prefer martyrdom to imbecility." After writing sixty books, including his famous *Life of Christ,* he was at work on two huge projects when he was stricken with a form of muscular atrophy. He lost the use of his left leg, then of his fingers, so that he couldn't hold a pen. The two big books, though never to be finished, moved forward slowly by dictation; that in itself was a triumph. Toward the end, when his voice had become incomprehensible, he spelled out a word, tapping on the table to indicate letters of the alphabet. One hopes never to be faced with the need for such heroic measures.

"Eighty years old!" the great Catholic poet Paul Claudel wrote in his journal. "No eyes left, no ears, no teeth, no legs, no wind! And when all is said and done, how astonishingly well one does without them!"

Best known for her books about the pleasures of food, Mary
Frances Kennedy Fisher (1908–) has also written novels,
short stories, poetry, essays, and memoirs. She grew up in California, lived for years in France and Switzerland, and now lives
in the Sonoma Valley in California. In the foreword to her book
Sister Age, she writes that a painting of an old woman, Ursula
von Ott, that she had happened upon years before in a junk shop
in Zurich, had started her thinking about old age and collecting
clippings on that subject for a book. Eventually, she threw away
all the clippings and used her own stories for *Sister Age.* The
afterword follows.

Afterword from
SISTER AGE

Of course it was strange to send
away some forty years of accumulated clippings and notes and even lengthy
writings that I had kept since my first meeting with Ursula von Ott, Sister
Age, in Zurich. There were a lot of books by other people too, everything
from Simone de Beauvoir's lengthy documents about the aging process, to
slim tacky collections of written "thoughts" by therapy-groups of senior
citizens in small Texas towns. I felt surgically bewildered as the cartons
went off to their chosen resting-place, as if I'd had more than my limbs
amputated. I wondered why my breath still kept going in and out, why my
truncated mind still clicked. What had all these readings taught me? What
was left?

Surely, I kept saying with some doggedness, I had learned a truth or two
from my long ponderings and considerings about the condition most of us

animals and plants must bow to. Had I found nothing worth the decades of such compulsive study? I felt lost and somewhat foolish.

By now, several years after I turned my back on all this, I think that I know a few things more clearly than I did when I was young, long before Ursula helped pull my fumblings into focus.

I know, for instance, that I like old people, when they have aged well. And old houses with an accumulation of sweet honest living in them are good. And the timelessness that only the passing of Time itself can give to objects both inside and outside the spirit is a continuing reassurance.

I have formed a strong theory that there is no such thing as "turning into" a Nasty Old Man or an Old Witch. I believe that such people, and of course they are legion, were born nasty and witch-like, and that by the time they were about five years old they had hidden their rotten bitchiness and lived fairly decent lives until they no longer had to conform to rules of social behavior, and could revert to their original horrid natures.

This theory is hard to prove, because by the time a person begins to show his true-born nature, most of the people who knew him when he was little have either died or gone into more immediate shadows. I still believe that it is probable, however. I have lived long enough to keep a sharp eye on a few of my peers, and they bear out almost frighteningly the sad natures they first promised us to end with.

On the other hand, there are a lot of people who seem to be born merry or serene or very lively. They are happy vital little babies and children, whether they live in ghettos or in suburban villas surrounded by electronic security systems. They need only one thing in life besides food and shelter, and that is warm open love from some person or animal or thing in their surroundings. They often live until they are very old, through the same delights and sadnesses that everyone else does, but after all the years of social subterfuge and conniving they emerge as bright souls . . . not nasty, not bitchy, just *good*.

If I could choose, I would like that to happen to me, because in our culture it is difficult to be old, and still live with younger fellowmen, and it helps to be tolerably acceptable instead of boring or obnoxious. So far, myself, I think I am in luck, because I was a lively, healthy child who wanted and got a great share of affection. I notice that as I get rid of the protective covering of the middle years, I am more openly amused and incautious and less careful socially, and that all this makes for increasingly pleasant contacts with the world. (It also compensates for some of the plain annoyances of decrepitude, the gradual slowing down of physical things like muscles, eyes, bowels. In other words, old age is more bearable if it can be helped by an early acceptance of being loved and of loving.)

The physical hindrances are of course important, no matter how little an old person manages to admit their dominance. As I write this I am well into my seventies, and I think that I have aged faster than I meant to, whatever that means! (It means, for one thing, that I resent being stiff and full of creaks and twinges.) I did not plan to be the way I am, although I probably knew more than most of my peers about the inevitabilities of disintegration. Fortunately, though, because I met Sister Age so long ago, I can watch my own aging with a detachment she has taught me. I know about the dismays and delights of my condition, and wish that all of us could prepare ourselves for them as instinctively and with as much outside help as we do those of puberty, adolescence, pregnancy, menopausal and climacteric changes. . . .

The Aging Process is a part of most of our lives, and it remains one we try to ignore until it seems to pounce upon us. We evade all its signals. We stay blandly unprepared for some of its obnoxious effects, even though we have coped with the cracked voices and puzzling glands of our emerging natures, and have been guided no matter how clumsily through budding love-pains, morning-sickness, and hot flashes. We do what our mentors teach us to do, but few of us acknowledge that the last years of our lives, if we can survive to live them out, are as physically predictable as infancy's or those of our full flowering. This seems impossible, but it is true.

We are helped by wise parents and teachers and doctors to live through our first couple of decades, and then to behave more or less like creative, productive social creatures, and then to withdraw from the fray, if possible on our various kinds of laurels. And then what?

We are unprepared for the years that may come as our last ones. We are repelled and frightened by our physical changes, some of them hindering and boring, and we feel puzzled and cheated.

Plainly, I think that this clumsy modern pattern is a wrong one, an ignorant one, and I regret it and wish I could do more to change it. Ours is not a society that can accept with patience the presence of clumsy or inept or slow-spoken human beings, and just as untrained puzzled young people drift aimlessly through our slums, untrained puzzled old men and women wait to die in rest-homes everywhere. The statistics of a Beauvoir tome are as monotonous as the outcries of sensational journalism: there is no room, right now in our society, for the useless.

That does not mean, though, that some of us who seem meant to survive *need* do it blindly. I think we must use what wits we have, to admit things like the fact that it is harder to get up off the floor at seventy than at forty . . . or even fourteen. We must accept and agree with and then attend to with dispassion such things as arthritis, moles that may be cancerous, constipation that may lead to polyps and hernias, all the boring physical symptoms of our ultimate disintegration. (Old clocks tick more slowly than they did when young.)

What is important, though, is that our dispassionate acceptance of attrition be matched by a full use of everything that has ever happened in all the long wonderful-ghastly years to free a person's mind from his body . . . to use the experience, both great and evil, so that physical annoyances are surmountable in an alert and even mirthful appreciation of life itself.

This sounds mawkish and banal as I try to write it, but I believe it. I am glad that I have been able to live as long as I have, so that I can understand why Ursula von Ott did not weep as she stood by the funeral urn of her son, surrounded by all the vivid signs of his short silly life . . . the fat cupids, the fatter Venuses whose satiny knees he lolled against. She did not smile, but behind her deep monkey-eyes she surely felt a reassuring warmth of amusement, along with her pity that he never had tried to feel it too.

Parts of the Aging Process are scary, of course, but the more we know about them, the less they need be. That is why I wish we were more deliberately taught, in early years, to prepare for this condition. It would leave a lot of us freed to enjoy the obvious rewards of being old, when the sound of a child's laugh, or the catch of sunlight on a flower petal is as poignant as ever was a girl's voice to an adolescent ear, or the tap of a golf-ball into its cup to a balding banker's.

When I was about twelve, my grandmother died and we all relaxed, especially at table. She was puritanical by nature, and did not believe in the indulgences of the flesh, so that sitting lazily after a good meal was not our privilege until she left us. Then we were like mice, with the cat gone. One day, after a long Sunday lunch, my younger sister and I stayed at table with our parents in the cool dining room. We were quiet, full of sponge-cake and peace. Mother murmured toward the end of the table where her husband sat. They sipped glasses of port from the decanter that usually stood untouched on the sideboard. Mother said idly something about Old Mrs. Tolbert, the organist at church. "I do wish she would stop scratching herself," she said. Father said, just as lazily and with as little malice, "Maybe she doesn't take enough baths." His wife protested gently, with a soft shrug and a little grimace. I said, with some boldness because although Anne and I were invited to stay on at the table now and then, we still spoke only when spoken to, as in Grandmother's recent days, "No. It's because she itches."

My parents put down their glasses. Anne looked daringly at me, although with correct politeness because of where we were.

"No," I said again. "She is old, and old people itch."

"Ah?" Mother asked, and Father went on, "Is that so? What do you think you mean?"

I said, "Well, I think the skin gets drier when people start to wither. You can see old women's arms. And when the skin gets withery, it itches. And anyway, they don't know they are scratching. They aren't dirty. They may just need to be oiled."

Anne said, "Scratching is rude. It's disgusting."

"I think so too," Mother said. "Disgusting. Old Mrs. Tolbert is really . . ." She sipped the last of her wine, and Father tipped his glass back and stood up. "Now that we've had our little lesson in geriatrics," he said, "and know all about how we'll itch as we age, I suggest that our medical advisor and her sister clear the table and leave us to our own pursuits. I may rub a little lotion on my chin, or—"

Mother laughed and we all went our ways on that fine free Sunday afternoon. But I knew I was right about Mrs. Tolbert. I did not like her, because she had a strong smell, but it was plain that she could not help her scratching: she was drying up like an old shoe and needed to be waxed. She did not need soap and water. Anne and I went on talking about this, as we tidied the kitchen before the cook came back from her Sunday cavortings. We decided that baths are all right, even fun, but that old people need *oil* on their skins, just as new babies do . . . olive oil, or maybe Hinds' Honey and Almond Cream, our current dream of exotic ointments.

And I kept on thinking about old people, and writing notes about them, and readying my spirit to meet Ursula von Ott on that dank crooked street in Zurich. Then, for decades, I kept on clipping and writing some of the notes that are in this book, instead of in a weighty set of statistics on library reference shelves. In one way or another they are about *why* Ursula was not weeping as she held the notice of her son's brave death in her slack old hand, and perhaps of why Old Mrs. Tolbert would have been better off with oil instead of soap and water on her itchy skin.

The crux of it all, perhaps the real secret, is that there was nobody to rub the gentle oil into Mrs. Tolbert's itch. She was alone, and unprepared to be so. There are too many people like her, caught unready for their last days, unprepared to cope with the logistics of dignified acceptance. She forgot to bathe now and then, forgot that she was scratching herself in front of finicky observers . . . finally forgot to breathe. There was nobody in the world to help her.

Mrs. Tolbert possibly started me on my long ponderings about how hard it can be for lonely old people to stay sweet, much less give a small damn whether they are or not. And her common plight leads neatly into the saddest conclusion I have reached about the art of aging, which can and should be as graceful and generally beneficent a "condition" as any other in our lives.

Our housing is to blame. It is said that by the end of this century most citizens in the Western world will have adapted themselves to living as family units in allotted spaces no bigger than a modern compact car. There will be at least four people to each cubicle: two parents and, temporarily at least, two children. (This social phenomenon is already well developed in Japan, where too many active healthy humans manage to live highly disciplined lives in too little space. Westerners will take longer to accept such an inevitability, and learn to adapt to its paranoidal side effects.)

There will be well-designed patterns for our prospective quarters, at least for sleeping, and hygiene will perforce be almost as necessary as oxygen, to avoid epidemics of everything from disease to civil mayhem. Bathing will probably be in communal centers, as will most of the eating. Day schools will take care of the children almost from birth. But what about lovemaking, and such perquisites to procreation as a bit of privacy? Will that too be scheduled, by the hour or two, in appointed governmental love-nests? And perhaps most important of all, where will Grandfather Tom and Great-Aunt Bessie go when they no longer feel nimble enough to maintain their own cubicles and their factory jobs? (Dreadful footnote: will they even exist, as family members, once their productive days are over?)

Perhaps this trend toward one-generation living took firm shape only after World War II, when the first monolithic cities rose in dominoes from devastated farmland around places like Paris and Rome. The healthy young women who had survived bombs and invasions married what men were left, and delighted in the elevators and supermarkets and laundromats and day nurseries that had supplanted their childhood days of drawing well-water and knitting socks while they watched the sheep in the meadows. And more than almost anything they loved being free of their mothers-in-law, their demanding parents. Who needed to make room for a dotty old aunt, when the State would take care of new babies? Who wanted a cranky ancestor sitting by the television all day, taking up space at night? Who wanted to take care of them?

It was seldom mentioned in the newspapers, for a decade or so after the *"cités"* went up, that many dotards jumped from high windows rather than live without a patch of earth to plant, a couple of rabbits to feed. Gradually they disappeared from all the high-rise slums, into discreet hostels as well as their final graves, and by about 1965 it was rare to find anyone sixty-five in the supermarkets. There was no room for them in the high-rises. They were a displaced generation, and charitable churches and governments made it cheaper to send them into exile with their peers than to rent space for them with their offspring.

This new way of life, which I honestly believe was an accident of war to begin with, spread fast through Western cultures. In our homeland, who has room any longer to ask Grandfather to come live with his children after his dear wife has died? Who has a nice attic where dotty old Cousin Etta can be gently locked away during the full of the moon? Who has time, anymore, to see that Great-Uncle George's meat is discreetly chopped so that he does not have to take out his clickers and lay them nonchalantly beside his plate at dinner? Above all (and this is the crux of the crux, the secret of the whole sad secret!), who has children who accept not only their necessary parents but their grandparents as an intrinsic part of life?

Until I was almost twelve, my mother's mother was part of all our lives, like hot buttered toast for breakfast and clean hair on Saturdays. It has long amazed and even hurt me that when she died I never felt one pang of sorrow or regret, but only a general relief. By now I understand this, because I doubt that I would ever have loved her, the way I loved my parents and siblings and a few plain human beings. But Grandmother was essential. She shaped all of us, willy-nilly, so that we talked and ate more politely than we might have without her. We spent long good hours with her, while Mother devoted herself to another batch of new babies, and our conversations were full of thought and instruction. When she went off to her many religious convocations, we laughed more at table, and ate more exciting meals than her Nervous Stomach dictated when she was in residence, but when she came back we settled easily again into her decorous patterns. She was there the way books were, or spoons. I don't remember ever kissing her or even feeling her hand, but often I held a skein of new yarn for her while she wound the ball, and then leaned my head against her knees as she read good stories from the Bible. Somewhere there is a picture of my face when

I was perhaps five, standing in the stiff folds of her long proper alpaca dress. I look safe and trusting. And I wish that every child alive could be with the detached attention of old people, as I was.

Grandmother's farthest removed cousins were almost as constant as she, in our house. They came for a month, for the winter, for "a stay." And they expected to be treated with affection and thoughtful dignity, which they always were. Some of them were plainly mad, and one or two were religious fanatics or uplifted birdwatchers or such-like, but they warmed all of us, and perhaps especially us little people, with their pleasure at being there.

Probably Mother and Father had their moments of exasperation and ennui at this constant flow of Grandmother's peers, but Anne and I loved every minute of it, from dissertations about the significance of every moment of Jesus Christ's Crucifixion to how to make paper furniture for the fairies who, one ancient cousin told us over Grandmother's pious protests, came Midsummer's Eve to a certain rosebush in the back yard.

Yes, housing is to blame. Children and old people and the parents in between should be able to live together, in order to learn how to die with grace, together. And I fear that this is purely utopian fantasy, for a few more centuries perhaps. I am sad, that we cannot try again. . . . I would have rubbed oil on my grandmother's dry old skin if she had asked me to, and now I would let a child ask to, if there were one nearby. But the course is set, temporarily as History hurtles on, for us to grow up fast, work hard while we are strong, and then die in a premature limbo. I cannot do anything to stop this.

But Sister Age still looks far past us all (Grandmother, little sister Anne, Mrs. Tolbert, her own spoiled brat called something like Johann Wilhelm Sebastian von Ott . . .), and her monkey-sad eyes are brighter than ever, and the letter of information remains open but unread in her bony hand.

Pulitzer prize–winning poet Stanley Kunitz (1905–   ) taught poetry for many years at Columbia University and served two years as the Consultant to the Library of Congress. Kunitz's poetic style changed as he grew older until he developed the open style used in "The Layers," a poem confronting life changes, written in his seventies.

THE LAYERS

I have walked through many lives,
some of them my own,
and I am not who I was,
though some principle of being
abides, from which I struggle
not to stray.
When I look behind,
as I am compelled to look
before I can gather strength
to proceed on my journey,
I see the milestones dwindling
toward the horizon
and the slow fires trailing
from the abandoned camp-sites,
over which scavenger angels
wheel on heavy wings.
Oh, I have made myself a tribe
out of my true affections,
and my tribe is scattered!
How shall the heart be reconciled

to its feast of losses?
In a rising wind
the manic dust of my friends,
those who fell along the way,
bitterly stings my face.
Yet I turn, I turn,
exulting somewhat,
with my will intact to go
wherever I need to go,
and every stone on the road
precious to me.
In my darkest night,
when the moon was covered
and I roamed through wreckage,
a nimbus-clouded voice
directed me:
"Live in the layers,
not on the litter."
Though I lack the art
to decipher it,
no doubt the next chapter
in my book of transformations
is already written.
I am not done with my changes.

Throughout his long writing career, John Hall Wheelock (1886–1978) held a number of administrative posts with Charles Scribner's Sons, the Poetry Society of America, and the Library of Congress. His poetry has been noted for its "simple directness." His later work shows an increasing wonder and veneration of life's mysteries. Wheelock wrote that poetry is "the compulsion to rediscover the essence of reality for oneself."

SONG ON REACHING SEVENTY

Shall not a man sing as the night comes on?
He would be braver than that bird
Which shrieks for terror and is gone
Into the gathering dark, and he has heard
Often, at evening's hush,
Upon some towering sunset bough
A belated thrush
Lift up his heart against the menacing night,
Till silence covered all. Oh, now
Before the coming of a greater night
How bitterly sweet and dear
All things have grown! How shall we bear the brunt,
The fury and joy of every sound and sight,
Now almost cruelly fierce with all delight:
The clouds of dawn that blunt
The spearhead of the sun; the clouds that stand,
Raging with light, around his burial;
The rain-pocked pool
At the wood's edge; a bat's skittering flight
Over the sunset-colored land;

Or, heard toward morning, the cock pheasant's call!
Oh, every sight and sound
Has meaning now! Now, also, love has laid
Upon us her old chains of tenderness,
So that to think of the belovèd one,
Love is so great, is to be half afraid—
It is like looking at the sun,
That blinds the eye with truth.
Yet longing remains unstilled,
Age will look into the face of youth
With longing, over a gulf not to be crossed.
Oh, joy that is almost pain, pain that is joy,
Unimaginable to the younger man or boy—
Nothing is quite fulfilled,
Nothing is lost;
But all is multiplied till the heart almost
Aches with its burden: there and here
Become as one, the present and the past;
The dead, who were content to lie
Far from us, have consented to draw near—
We are thronged with memories,
Move amid two societies,
And learn at last
The dead are the only ones who never die.

Great night, hold back
A little longer yet your mountainous, black
Waters of darkness from this shore,
This island garden, this paradisal spot,
The haunt of love and pain,
Which we must leave, whether we would or not,
And where we shall not come again.
More time—oh, but a little more,
Till, stretched to the limits of being, the taut heart break,
Bursting the bonds of breath,
Shattering the wall
Between us and our world, and we awake
Out of the dream of self into the truth of all,
The price for which is death.

Florida Scott-Maxwell (1883–1978) was born in Florida, but
moved, at the time of her marriage, to Scotland where she worked
for women's suffrage and wrote plays and novels. At fifty years
of age, she entered training with Carl Jung, became an analytical
psychologist, and practiced in clinics in Scotland and England.
At the age of eighty-two, she began to keep a journal, later
published as *The Measure of My Days,* in which she wrote of
her thoughts and feelings about being old.

from

THE MEASURE OF MY DAYS

A*ge puzzles me.* I thought it was a
quiet time. My seventies were interesting, and fairly serene, but my eighties
are passionate. I grow more intense as I age. To my own surprise I burst
out with hot conviction. Only a few years ago I enjoyed my tranquillity;
now I am so disturbed by the outer world and by human quality in general
that I want to put things right, as though I still owed a debt to life. I must
calm down. I am far too frail to indulge in moral fervour. . . .

Age is truly a time of heroic helplessness. One is confronted by one's own
incorrigibility. I am always saying to myself, "Look at you, and after a
lifetime of trying." I still have the vices that I have known and struggled
with—well it seems like since birth. Many of them are modified, but not
much. I can neither order nor command the hubbub of my mind. Or is it
my nervous sensibility? This is not the effect of age; age only defines one's
boundaries. Life has changed me greatly, it has improved me greatly, but
it has also left me practically the same. I cannot spell, I am over critical,
egocentric and vulnerable. I cannot be simple. In my effort to be clear I

become complicated. I know my faults so well that I pay them small heed. They are stronger than I am. They are me.

As I do not live in an age when rustling black silk skirts billow about me, and I do not carry an ebony stick to strike the floor in sharp rebuke, as this is denied me, I rap out a sentence in my note book and feel better. If a grandmother wants to put her foot down, the only safe place to do it these days is in a note book. . . .

My kitchen linoleum is so black and shiny that I waltz while I wait for the kettle to boil. This pleasure is for the old who live alone. The others must vanish into their expected role. . . .

Another day to be filled, to be lived silently, watching the sky and the lights on the wall. No one will come probably. I have no duties except to myself. That is not true. I have a duty to all who care for me—not to be a problem, not to be a burden. I must carry my age lightly for all our sakes, and thank God I still can. Oh that I may to the end. Each day then, must be filled with my first duty, I must be "all right". But is this assurance not the gift we all give to each other daily, hourly?

I wonder if we need be quite so dutiful. With one friend of my own age we cheerfully exchange the worst symptoms, and our black dreads as well. We frequently talk of death, for we are very alert to the experience of the unknown that may be so near and it is only to those of one's own age that one can speak frankly. Talking of one's health, which one wants to do, is generally full of risks. Ill health is unpleasant to most healthy people as it makes them feel helpless, threatened, and it can feel like an unjustified demand for sympathy. Few believe in the pains of another, and if the person in pain has nothing to show, can forget the pain when interested, then where is the reality of it? In one's self, where it ought to be kept I suppose. Disabilities crowd in on the old; real pain is there, and if we have to be falsely cheerful, it is part of our isolation.

Another secret we carry is that though drab outside—wreckage to the eye, mirrors a mortification—inside we flame with a wild life that is almost incommunicable. In silent, hot rebellion we cry silently—"I have lived my life haven't I? What more is expected of me?" Have we got to pretend out of noblesse oblige that age is nothing, in order to encourage the others? This we do with a certain haughtiness, realising now that we have reached the place beyond resignation, a place I had no idea existed until I had arrived here.

It is a place of fierce energy. Perhaps passion would be a better word than energy, for the sad fact is this vivid life cannot be used. If I try to transpose it into action I am soon spent. It has to be accepted as passionate life, perhaps the life I never lived, never guessed I had it in me to live. It feels other and more than that. It feels like the far side of precept and aim. It is just life, the natural intensity of life, and when old we have it for our reward and undoing. It can—at moments—feel as though we had it for our glory. Some of it must go beyond good and bad, for at times— though this comes rarely, unexpectedly—it is a swelling clarity as though all was resolved. It has no content, it seems to expand us, it does not derive from the body, and then it is gone. It may be a degree of consciousness which lies outside activity, and which when young we are too busy to experience. . . .

When a new disability arrives I look about to see if death has come, and I call quietly, "Death, is that you? Are you there?" So far the disability has answered, "Don't be silly, it's me. . . . "

Always, through everything, I try to straighten my spine, or my soul. They both ought to be upright I feel, for pride, for style, for reality's sake, but both tend to bend as under a weight that has been carried a long time. I try to lighten my burden by knowing it, I try to walk lightly, and sometimes I do, for sometimes I feel both light and proud. At other times I am bent, bent. . . .

The woman who has a gift for old age is the woman who delights in comfort. If warmth is known as the blessing it is, if your bed, your bath, your best-liked food and drink are regarded as fresh delights, then you know how to thrive when old. If you get the things you like on the simplest possible terms, serve yourself lightly, efficiently and calmly, all is almost well. If you are truly calm you stand a chance of surviving much, but calmness is intermittent with me. Sensuous pleasure seems necessary to old age as intellectual pleasure palls a little. At times music justifies living, but mere volume of sound can overwhelm, and I find silence exquisite. I have spent my whole life reading, only to find that most of it is lost, so books no longer have their former command. I live by rectitude or reverence, or courtesy, by being ready in case life calls, all lightly peppered with despair. This makes me rest on comfort. I could use the beauty and dignity of a cat but, denied that, I try for her quiet. . . .

In some central part of us mankind must always be trying to understand God. In that poignant core where we call out our questions, and cry for an answer. It is in each of us, even if question and answer are both despair. We are always talking to God even while we argue him out of existence. It is not easy to commune with that great force. Can we do less than speak as creator to creator since that seems the role given us, and in our seeking we honour the honour done us. . . .

I SUPPOSE THIS IS what religion is about, and always has been ever since man began to suffer and to care why he suffered. I've taken a long time to feel it as very truth. The last years may matter most. . . .

I wish I could remember that Blake said, "Any fool can generalize". I generalize constantly. I write my notes as though I spoke for all old people. This is nonsense. Age must be different for each. We may each die from being ourselves. That small part that cannot be shared or shown, that part has an end of its own. . . .

Old people can seldom say "we"; not those who live alone, and even those who live with their families are alone in their experience of age, so the habit of thinking in terms of "we" goes, and they become "I". It takes increasing courage to be "I" as one's frailty increases. There is so little strength left that one wants shelter, one seeks the small and natural, but where to find it?

A garden, a cat, a wood fire, the country, to walk in woods and fields, even to look at them, but these would take strength I have not got, or a man whom also I have not got. So, here in a flat, I must make the round of the day pleasant, getting up, going to bed, meals, letters with my breakfast tray: can I make it total to a quiet heart? I have to be a miracle of quiet to make the flame in my heart burn low, and on some good days I am a miracle of quiet. But I cannot conceive how age and tranquillity came to be synonymous. . . .

But we also find that as we age we are more alive than seems likely, convenient, or even bearable. Too often our problem is the fervour of life within us. My dear fellow octogenarians, how are we to carry so much life, and what are we to do with it?

Let no one say it is "unlived life" with any of the simpler psychological certitudes. No one lives all the life of which he was capable. The unlived life in each of us must be the future of humanity. When truly old, too frail to use the vigour that pulses in us, and weary, sometimes even scornful of what can seem the pointless activity of mankind, we may sink down to some deeper level and find a new supply of life that amazes us. . . .

A long life makes me feel nearer truth, yet it won't go into words, so how can I convey it? I can't, and I want to. I want to tell people approaching and perhaps fearing age that it is a time of discovery. If they say—"Of what?" I can only answer, "We must each find out for ourselves, otherwise it won't be discovery". I want to say—"If at the end of your life you have only yourself, it is much. Look, you will find. . . . "

❧ *Stephen Spender* ❧

Stephen Spender (1909–   ), British poet and critic, also writes plays, novels, and short stories. Educated at University College, Oxford, England, he was part of the Oxford group of the 1930s that sought to influence both poetry and politics. Later in his life he became an editor, a translater, and a visiting professor and lecturer. His poetry is considered by critics to be lyrical, personal, and romantic.

FROM MY DIARY

'She was', my father said (in an aside),
'A great beauty, forty years ago.'
Out of my crude childhood, I stared at
Our tottering hostess, tremulous
In her armchair, pouring tea from silver—
Her grey silk dress, her violet gaze.
I only saw her being seventy,
I could not see the girl my father saw.

Now that I'm older than my father then was
I go with lifelong friends to the same parties
Which we have gone to always.
We seem the same age always
Although the parties sometimes change to funerals
That sometimes used to change to christenings.

Faces we've once loved
Fit into their seven ages as Russian dolls
Into one another. My memory
Penetrates through successive layers
Back to the face which first I saw. So when the last
Exterior image is laid under its lid,
Your face first seen will shine through all.

⋅§ *Elizabeth Coatsworth* §⋅

Elizabeth Coatsworth (1893–1986), born in Buffalo, New York, was first a poet and short story writer and later a prolific writer of children's books. The following excerpt introduces *Personal Geography: Almost an Autobiography*, a compilation from a half-century of journal writing. Published when Coatsworth was eighty-three, the book covers the events and changing insights from her girlhood to old age.

Foreword from

PERSONAL GEOGRAPHY: ALMOST AN AUTOBIOGRAPHY

The bristlecone pine is supposed to be the oldest tree in the world, older than even the sequoia. One measures the age of a tree on a cross-section whose rings show the amount of growth which the tree enjoyed each year. There is a wide circle for good years, and a very narrow one, sometimes almost none at all, marks the years of drought. I know that we show no such physical proofs of our experience, but I think our lives are not unlike those of the trees. Some years are good years and we expand in them; some years are bad ones and the most we can do is to hold our own. But good or bad, like the trees we are still ourselves, growing out from the heartwood of our youth which I believe is a combination of our inheritance and our upbringing. Like the trees, we may be able to correct a bend or knothole which shows in youth; we may cover over the scar of an injury which however will always be there, though it may be hidden from sight.

I like this sense that all my life and experience is contained in me. I am a five-year-old child in Egypt, I am a schoolgirl in a very strict private school on Park Street in Buffalo, I roam the beaches of Lake Erie, barefoot all summer, I explore the winter countryside around Vassar more thoroughly than I do its curriculum, I go to the theatre and art shows in New York and climb California mountains; later I travel in the Far East and around the Mediterranean with a piercing pleasure (and as always the more uncomfortable trips, the more dangerous moments, are the most clearly remembered).

I settle with my mother in an eighteenth-century house in Hingham overlooking Boston Harbor (how I love that house!). By this time travel has jarred me into writing, and writing has become almost as much a part of me as eating or sleeping. Then in my mid-thirties I marry a man both handsome and perceptive, and we have two little girls and buy a Maine farm overlooking hayfields and a lake. Life never stops. The daughters grow up and marry, each has four children. My husband, who is five years older than I, begins the long struggle with old age and for years I fight that inevitably losing battle with him. He dies, and for eight years I have lived the diminished life of a widow, with one daughter living in Alaska and the other in California, but one or both visiting me each summer.

I am an old woman now, fighting my own losing battle with age, but with time to enjoy life along the way, as Henry always did. Naturally I think of death. I don't want to die because even in this narrower radius there are so many people and things still to enjoy. I do not fear death itself I think, but I often do not like its approaches. Only the other day I first formulated for myself the truism: "You cannot conquer death, but perhaps you can conquer the fear of it."

All these things and a thousand more are embodied in me, the good years and the bad, the wide rings of growth and the narrow. One's past is not something we leave behind, but something we incorporate. When I write a story for children I am a child, with perhaps a grownup person's powers of criticism (at least so I hope). When I lunch with a group of young middle-aged people, I feel no difference between us; when I walk in to my neighbor's, watching every step for fear I may trip on something (my sense of balance is irretrievably lost!), I greet her as an equal as she sits in a big chair tatting, with her walker in front of her. Outwardly I am eighty-three years old, but inwardly I am every age, with the emotions and experience of each period. The important thing is that at each age I am myself, just as you are yourself. During much of my life I was anxious to be what someone else wanted me to be. Now I have given up that struggle. I am what I am.

Born in Buffalo, New York, Polly (Delia Margaret Tighe) Francis (1884–1978) studied at the Pratt Institute in Brooklyn, New York, before going to Paris as a fashion illustrator and photographer for *Harper's Bazaar* and *Vogue.* When she and her husband returned to the United States, she continued to work for *Vogue,* and then opened a dress shop in New York City. Between the ages of ninety-one and ninety-four she wrote a series of three articles on old age which were first printed in *The Washington Post,* then reprinted in a dozen other newspapers and journals. Excerpts were broadcast all over the world, and the first article, which follows, was printed in the Congressional Record of April 22, 1975.

THE AUTUMN OF MY LIFE

What a baffling thing old age is! It doesn't bring the peace we were led to expect. I find it hard to drift with the stream; all along the way there are problems which obstruct the smooth flow of life. The area which lies between the "here" and the "hereafter" is a difficult passage to travel. One must make the journey to fully understand it.

The pattern of life today is such that, at a certain point, it seems desirable that we should leave the main stream and be channeled into a small tributary where the flow is at a gentler speed. But even here there are obstacles. While our responsibilities lessen, our limitations and frustrations increase—and certain humiliations can be painful.

Our young folk want to be kind to us, I'm sure. But they don't know what we want and they don't know how we feel. What I crave is withheld, so I go winnowing my way around problems and trying to avoid a head-on crash.

THE YOUNG PEOPLE MAY think that we are unreasoningly demanding. It seems to them that all our needs are met. We are comfortably housed, well fed, protected from hazards, provided with companionship and divertissements. What else do we need?

Our greatest need is not met. It is one that we never outgrow. It is the need to feel cherished by someone—to know that there is a place where we "belong." This is something that no retirement home, nursing home or hospital can provide. These institutions are staffed by dedicated people, but it is not their function to soothe our yearning hearts. The emotional strain would be too heavy.

I've been told that I must not succumb to the facts of my age. But why shouldn't I? I am now in my 91st year and I doubt that my activity, for example, in civic affairs, could restore my spirits to a state of bouncing buoyancy. Lack of physical strength alone keeps me inactive and often silent. I've been called senile. Senility is a convenient peg upon which to hang our nonconformity.

AGE CREEPS UP SO stealthily that it is often with shock that we become aware of its presence. Perhaps that is why so many of us reach old age utterly unprepared to meet its demands. We may be a bit rebellious about accepting it; I want to cry out that the invisible part of me is not old. I still thrill to the beauties of this world—the dew upon the rose at dawn, the glow reflected by the sun on passing cloud when day is done—but unremitting age goes on.

My interest in the goings-on in the world outside my ever-tightening barriers has not been withdrawn. It is not interest that I have lost, but rather the means of getting around and the physical stamina to sustain me as I go.

It is my task now to build a new life. My renunciations are many. The component parts with which I shall build are sometimes unfamiliar and often unappealing. At first a bleak stretch of nothingness seemed to lie before me; I yearned for my comfortable deep furrow dug by my habits of many years.

IN EARLIER TIMES I didn't look beyond the move of the moment. Each move seemed almost fixed and final. But now all feeling of permanency has slipped away. The thought of where I shall go from here lurks in my consciousness. Will it be to a nursing home, or to a hospital or shall I go directly with no stopovers? Whichever it will be, I shall look upon it with no dread.

My new life is taking shape. The barriers of my little world are closing in on me. I am not sad or discontented—just very tired. If I sit alone at twilight, it is because I need solitude and rest. My solace is my memories, left untouched by the devastating hand of time. Tears, too, help—tears of tenderness; tears of grief have dried away. I do not mourn "good old days." I've had them. I've enjoyed them and my memory will preserve them.

The room in which I spend my days and nights is quiet, pleasant and comfortable, with a large window looking out over the treetops toward a distant, jagged horizon. It is not merely an enclosure where my few remaining possessions are stored and where I am safe from the common hazards of living alone; it is the setting of a new kind of life to which I am trying to adjust.

A NEW SET OF faculties seems to be coming into operation. I seem to be awakening to a larger world of wonderment—to catch little glimpses of the immensity and diversity of creation. More than at any other time in my life, I seem to be aware of the beauties of our spinning planet and the sky above. And now I have the time to enjoy them. I feel that old age sharpens our awareness.

I sit by my window and watch a thing of great beauty die with the setting sun. It is gone forever. Time loses its importance. On a bright, clear day, what a challenge to my imagination is the sight of an azure sky with balls of white fluff tumbling and rolling and gathering and dispersing and endlessly forming fantastic patterns.

In the quiet of the night, a siren sounds. A pang of compassion strikes into my heart. I want to rush to the scene of distress, but how utterly useless I've become. I look out at the red lights blinking reassurance to the night travelers streaking through the sky. What emotions these planes carry!

MY WINDOW HAS BECOME a showcase of ever-changing wonderment. The objects in my room take on different aspects with the shifting sun. Like actors on a stage, each thing has its moment in the limelight.

I pick up a much-read book and in it I find new delights. I watch an ant persistently toiling with a tiny bit of something and I realize that a spark of the Great Universal Will keeps it going undespairingly. I look at a cobweb and wonder at the spider's weaving skill and engineering know-how.

The telephone rings. My heart leaps. For a few minutes I listen to a beloved voice. Distance is wiped away. I am no longer on alien ground. I am where I "belong."

W HEN MY COURAGE TURNS limp, I ponder my past. I try to find a yardstick with which to measure the merit of a life. I become so confused that I cannot tell right from wrong. They come so close together and dance so fast from side to side that I am unable to grasp them firmly. And that is where faith comes in. We cannot know; we can only believe.

Old age is not all pain and limitations. It holds its own joys and satisfactions. The time has come when musing replaces activities—when the sleepless hours are filled from the harvest of a well stored mind. Even though our means are scant, we know that our material needs will, somehow, be met. But an impoverished soul is a saddening thing.

One of my joys is the spontaneous kindness of people everywhere—in the home where I live, in the shops, in the street—wherever my faltering step is noticed. It fills me with a warm glow. The quickness of the young boys and girls and the ease and nonchalance with which they offer help give me the feeling that they are trying to minimize my helplessness. I admire them without reservation.

The common expression, "so-and-so is failing," is tossed around too freely. In aging we gain as well as lose. The autumn of human life, like the autumn of nature, can bring richness of beauty. It's a time when our spiritual forces seem to expand. A life of the heart and of the mind takes over while our physical force ebbs away.

A Spirit of Discriminating Wisdom

"Now that the harvest is gathered and you stand in the autumn of your life, your oar is no longer a driving force carrying you over the oceans of your inner and outer worlds, but a spirit of discriminating wisdom, separating moment by moment the wheat of life from the chaff, so that you may know in both wheat and chaff their meaning and their value in the pattern of the universe."
HELEN LUKES
Old Age

"We are all happier in many ways when we are old than when we were young. The young sow wild oats. The old grow sage."
WINSTON CHURCHILL

At twenty, stooping round about,
I thought the world a miserable place,
Truth a trick, faith a doubt,
Little beauty, less grace.

Now at sixty what I see,
Although the world is worse by far,
Stops my heart in ecstasy.
God, the wonders that there are!
ARCHIBALD MACLEISH
With Age Wisdom

❧ *Mark Helprin* ❧

Mark Helprin (1947–   ) first served in the British Merchant
Navy and in the Israeli Infantry and Air Force before turning
toward his serious writing career. He holds degrees from Harvard College and Harvard's Center for Middle Eastern Studies.
The stories in his collection *Ellis Island,* from which this story
is taken, are both humorous and moving.

PALAIS DE JUSTICE

In a lesser chamber of Suffolk
County Courthouse on a day in early August, 1965—the hottest day of the
year—a Boston judge slammed down his heavy gavel, and its pistol-like
report threw the room into disarray. Within a few minutes, everyone had
gone—judge, court reporters, blue-shirted police, and a Portuguese family
dressed as if for a wedding to witness the trial of their son. The door was
shut. Wood and marble remained at attention in dead silence. For quite a
while the room must have been doing whatever rooms do when they are
completely empty. Perhaps air currents were stabilizing, coming to a halt,
or spiders were beginning to crawl about, up high in the woodwork. The
silence was beginning to set when the door opened and the defense attorney
re-entered to retrieve some papers. He went to his seat, sat down, and ran
his hands over the smooth tabletop—no papers. He glanced at the chairs,
and then bent to see under the table—no papers. He touched his nose and
looked perplexed. "I know I left them here," he said to the empty court-
room. "I thought I left them here. Memory must be going, oh well."

But his memory was excellent, as it had always been. He enjoyed pre-
tending that in his early sixties he was losing his faculties, and he delighted
in the puzzlement of where the papers had gone. The first was an opportunity for graceful abstention and serene neutrality, the second a problem

designed to fill a former prosecutor's mind as he made his way out of the courthouse, passing through a great hall arched like a cathedral and mitered by hot white shafts of grainy light.

Years before, when he had had his first trial, one could not see the vault of the roof. It was too high and dark. But then they had put up a string of opaque lighting globes, which clung to the paneled arches like risen balloons and lit the curving ceiling.

One day a clerk had been playing a radio so loudly that it echoed through the building. The Mayor of Boston appeared unexpectedly and stood in the middle of the marble floor, emptiness and air rising hundreds of feet above him. "Turn that radio off!" he screamed, but the clerk could not hear him. Alone on the floor with a silent crowd staring from the perimeter, the Mayor turned angrily and scanned halls and galleries trying to find direction for his rage, but could not tell from where the sound came and so pivoted on the smooth stone and filled the chamber with his voice. "I am your mayor. Turn it off, do you hear me, damn you to hell. I am your mayor!" The radio was silenced and all that could be heard was the echo of the Mayor's voice. The defense attorney had looked up as if to see its last remnants rising through rafters of daylight, and had seen several birds, flushed from hidden nesting places, coursing to and fro near the ceiling, threading through the light rays. No one but the defense attorney saw them or the clerk, a homely, frightened woman who, when the Mayor had long gone, came out and carefully peered over a balcony to see where he had stood. It was then that the defense attorney saw the intricate motif of the roof—past the homely woman, the birds, and the light.

Now he went from chamber to chamber, and hall to hall, progressing through layers of rising temperature until he stood on the street in a daze. It was so hot that people moved as if in a baking desert, their expressions as blank and beaten as a Tuareg's mask and impassive eyes. The stonework radiated heat. A view of Charlestown—mountains and forests of red brick, and gray shark-colored warships drawn up row upon row at the Navy Yard—danced in bright waves of air like a mirage. Across the harbor, planes made languid approaches to whitened runways. They glided so slowly it looked as if they were hesitant to come down. Despite the heat there was little haze, even near the sea. A Plains August had grasped New England, and Boston was quiet.

"Good," thought the defense attorney, "there won't be a single soul on the river. I'll have it all to myself, and it'll be as smooth as glass." He had been a great oarsman. Soon it would be half a century of near-silent speed up and down the Charles in thin light racing shells, always alone. The fewer people on the river, the better. He often saw wonderful sights along the banks, even after the new roads and bridges had been built. Somehow, pieces of the countryside held out and the idea of the place stayed much the same, though in form it was a far cry from the hot meadows, dirt roads, and wooden fences he had gazed upon in his best and fastest years. But just days before, he had seen a mother and her infant son sitting on the weir, looking out at the water and at him as he passed. The child was so beautiful as the woman held up his head and pointed his puzzled stare out over river and fields, that the defense attorney had shaken in his boat—having been filled with love for them. Then there were the ducks, who slept standing with heads tucked under their wings. Over fifty years he had learned to imitate them precisely, and often woke them as he passed, oars dipping quietly and powerfully to speed him by. Invariably, they looked up to search for another duck.

"You shouldn't be going out today, Professor," said Pete, who was in charge of the boathouse. "No one's out. It's too hot."

He was a stocky Dubliner with a dialect strong enough to make plants green. When he carried one end of the narrow craft down the sloping dock to the river he seemed to the defense attorney to resemble the compact engines which push and pull ships in the Panama Canal. Usually the oarsman holding the stern was hardly as graceful or deliberative as Pete, but struggled to avoid getting splinters in his bare feet.

"I haven't seen one boat all of today." Pete looked at him, waiting for him to give up and go home. The defense attorney knew that Pete wanted to call the Department of Athletics and have the boathouse closed at two so he could go to tend his garden. "Really, not one boat. You could get heat stroke you know. I saw it in North Africa during the War—terrible thing, terrible thing. Like putting salt on a leech."

The defense attorney was about to give in, when someone else walked up to the log book and signed so purposefully that Pete changed his strategy, saying to both of them, "If I were you now, I wouldn't stay out too long, not in this weather."

They went as they did each day to get S-40, the best of the old boats. It was the last boat Pat Shea had built for Harvard before he was killed overseas. Though already a full professor in the Law School and over draft age, the defense attorney had volunteered, and did not see his wife or his children for three solid years. When he returned—and those were glorious days when his children were young and suddenly talking, and his wife more beautiful than she had ever been—he went down to the boathouse and there was S-40, gleaming from disuse. Pat Shea was dead in the Pacific, but his boat was as ready as a Thoroughbred in the paddock. For twenty years the defense attorney had rowed loyally in S-40, preferring it to the new boats of unpronounceably named resins—computer designed, from wind tunnels, with riggers lighter than air and self-lubricating ball bearings on the sliding seat, where S-40 had seasoned into a dark blood color, and the defense attorney knew its every whim.

As they carried it from the shadows into blinding light, the defense attorney noticed the other sculler. He could not have been much over twenty, but was so large that he made the two older men feel diminutive. He was lean, muscled, and thick at the neck and shoulders. His face was pitted beneath a dark tan, and his hair long and tied up on his head in an Iroquois topknot. He looked like a Spartan with hair coiled before battle, and was ugly and savage in his stance. Nevertheless, the defense attorney, fond of his students and of his son who had just passed that age, smiled as he passed. He received as recompense a sneer of contempt, and he heard the words "old man" spoken with astonishing hatred.

"Who the hell is that?" asked the defense attorney of Pete as they set S-40 down on the lakelike water.

"I don't know. I never seen him before, and I don't like the looks of him. He brought his own boat, too, one of those new ones. He wants me to help him bring it down. Of course I'll have to. I'll take me time, and you can get a good head start so's you'll be alone up river," said Pete, knowing that informal races were common, and that if two boats pulled up even it nearly always became a contest. He wanted to spare the defense attorney the humiliation of being beaten by the unpleasant young man who had meanwhile disappeared into the darkness of the boathouse.

As S-40 pulled out and made slowly for the Anderson Bridge, the young man, whom the defense attorney had already christened "the barbarian," walked down the ramp, with his boat across his shoulders. Even from 100 feet out the defense attorney heard Pete say, "You didn't have to do that. I would have helped you." No matter, thought the defense attorney, by the time he gets it in the water, places his oars, and fine tunes all his alloy locks and stretchers, I'll be at the Eliot Bridge and in open water with a nice distance between us. He had no desire to race, because he knew that although he could not beat a young athlete in a boat half as light as S-40, he would try his best to do so. On such a hot day, racing was out of the question. In fact, he resolved to let the young man pass should he be good enough to catch up. For it was better to be humiliated and alive than dead at the finish line. He cannot possibly humiliate me anyway, he thought. A young man in a new-style boat will obviously do better than a man three times his age in a wood shell. But, he thought, this boat and I know the river. I have a good lead. I can pace myself as I watch him, and what I do not have in strength I may very well possess in concentration and skill.

And so he started at a good pace, sweeping across glass-faced waters in the large swelling of the stream just north of the Anderson Bridge, gauging his speed expertly from the passage of round turbulent spots where the oars had been, and sensing on the periphery of vision the metered transit of tall ranks of sycamores on the Cambridge side. He was the only man on the river, which was glossy and green with a thick tide of beadlike algae. Always driven to the river by great heat, dogs loped along with the gait of trained horses, splashing up a wave as they ran free in the shallows. S-40 had taut blue canvas decking, and oars of lacquered yellow wood with black and white blades. The riggers were silver-colored, an alloy modification, and the only thing modern about the boat. The defense attorney was lean and tanned, with short white hair. His face was kind and quiet, and though small in stature, he was very strong, and looked impressive in his starched white rowing shorts. The blue decking shone against the green water as in a filtered photograph of a sailing regatta.

It seemed to him that the lonely condition upon the river was a true condition. Though he had had a lot of love in his life, he knew from innumerable losses and separations that one stands alone or not at all. And yet, he had sought the love of women and the friendship of men as if he were a dog rasping through the bushes in search of birds or game. Women were for him so lovely and central to all he found important that their absence, as in the war, was the stiffest sentence he could imagine, and he pictured hell as being completely without them—although from experience he knew that they must have filled a wing or two there to the brim. Often, as he rowed, he slackened to think of the grace and beauty of girls and women he had known or loved. He remembered how sometime in the middle Twenties, when he was courting his wife, he had passed a great bed of water lilies in the wide bay before Watertown. He grasped one for her as he glided by, and put it in the front of the boat. But when he reached the dock the flower had wilted and died. The next day he stopped his light craft and pulled deep down on a long supple stem. Then he tied it to the riggers and rowed back with the lily dangling in the water so that he was able to preserve it, a justly appreciated rare flower. But people did not "court" anymore.

He resumed his pace, even though, without straining, he was as dripping wet as if he had been in a sauna for five minutes. Rounding the bend before the Eliot Bridge, he saw the young man in his new-style boat, making excellent speed toward him. He had intended to go beyond the Eliot, Arsenal Street, and North Beacon bridges to the bay where the lilies still grew, where it was easy to turn (although he could turn in place) and then to come back. All told, it was a course of six miles. It would not pay to go fast over that distance in such killing heat. If they were to race, the finish would have to be the last bridge out. By the time he passed under the Eliot Bridge, with two more bridges to go, the young man had closed to within a few hundred yards.

His resolutions fell away as if they were light November ice easy to break with oars and prow. Almost automatically, he quickened his pace to that of the young man, who, after a furious initial sprint, had been forced to slow somewhat and retrieve his breath. The defense attorney knew that once he had it he would again pour on speed in the excessive way youth allowed, and so the defense attorney husbanded his strength, going as fast as his opponent but with the greatest possible economy. This he achieved by relaxing, saying to himself, "Easy. Easy. The fight is yet to come. Easy now, easy."

Though the young athlete was a hundred yards downriver the defense attorney could see dark lines of sweat in his knotted hair, and could hear heavy breathing. "I'm a fool," he said, "for racing in this heat. It's over 100 degrees. I have nothing to prove. I'll let him pass, and I'll let him sneer. I don't care. My wisdom is far more powerful than his muscular energy." And yet, his limbs automatically kept up the pace, draining him of water, causing salt to burn his eyes. He simply could not stop.

He remembered Cavafy's *Waiting for the Barbarians,* which he—in a clearly Western way—had originally assumed to be a lament. Upon reading it he discovered that the poet shared in the confusion, for it was indeed a lament, that the barbarians were not still on their way. But for the defense attorney this was unthinkable, for he dearly loved the West and had never thought that to constitute itself it required the expectation of a golden horde. And he believed that if one man were to remain strong and upholding, if just one man were not to wilt, then the light he saw and loved could never be destroyed, despite the barbarism of the war, of soulless materialism, of the self-righteous students who thought to remake this intricate and marvelously fashioned world with one blink of an untutored eye. If a man can be said to grit his teeth over a span of years, then the defense attorney had done just this, knowing that it would both pass and come again, as had

the First War, and the Second, in which he had learned the great lessons
of his life, in which he had been broken and battered repeatedly—only to
rise up again.

He did not want to concede the minor victory of a river race on a hot
day in August, not even that, not even such a small thing as that to yet
another wave of ignorance and violence. He started with rage in remembering the sneer. Contempt meant an attack against perceived weakness, and
did not weakness merit compassion? If this barbarian had thought him
weak, he was up against the gates of a city he did not know, a stone-built
city of towers and citadels. The defense attorney increased the rapidity of
his stroke to meet his opponent's ominously growing speed.

The young man was gaining, but by very small increments. Were the
defense attorney to have kept up his pace he would have reached the North
Beacon Street Bridge first, even if only by a few feet. But two things were
wrong. First, such a close margin afforded no recourse in a final sprint.
Because of the unpredictability of the young man's capacities, the defense
attorney was forced to build an early lead, which would as well demoralize
his rival. Second, not even halfway to the finish, he was beginning to go
under. Already breathing extremely hard, he could feel his heart in his chest
as if it were a fist pounding on a door.

He was lucky, because he knew the river so well that he had no need of
turning to see where he was headed. So precise had the fifty years rendered
his navigational sense that he did not even look when he approached bridges,
and shot through the arches at full speed always right in the center. However, the young man had to turn for guidance every minute or so to make
sure he was not straying from a straight course—which would have meant
defeat. That he had to turn was another advantage for the defense attorney,
for the young man not only broke his rhythm and sometimes lost his stroke
or made a weak stroke when doing so, but he was also forced to observe
his adversary still in the lead. If the defense attorney saw the leather thong
in the young man's haircomb begin to dip, and saw the muscles in his back
uplift a bit, making a slightly different shadow, he knew he was about to
turn. This caused the defense attorney to assume an expression of ease and
relaxation, as if he were not even racing, and to make sure that his strokes
were deep, perfect, and classically executed. He had been in many contests,
both ahead and behind.

Though it was a full-blooded race, he realized that he was going no more
than half the sustained speed of which he normally was capable. Like a
cargo of stone, the heat dragged all movement into viscous slow motion.

Time was caught in its own runners, and its elements repeated. Two dogs at the riverside were fighting over a dead carp lapping in the green water. He saw them clash at the neck. Later, when he looked back, he saw the same scene again. Perhaps because of the blood and the heat and the mist in front of his eyes, the salt-stung world seemed to unpiece in complex dissolution. There was a pattern which the darkness and the immediacy of the race made him unable to decipher. Intensified summer colors drifted one into the other without regard to form, and the laziness was shattered only when a bright white gull, sliding down the air, passed before his sight in a heartening straight line.

Though he felt almost ready to die and thought that he might, the defense attorney decided to implement his final strategy. About a mile was left. They were nearing the Arsenal Street Bridge. Here the river's high walls and banks stopped the wind, and the waters were always smooth. With no breeze whatsoever, it was all the hotter. In this quiet stretch races were won or lost. A completely tranquil surface allowed a burst of energy after the slight rest it provided. Usually a racer determined to begin his build-up just at the bridge. Two boats could not clear the northern arch simultaneously. Thus the rear boat had no hope of passing and usually resolved upon commencement of its grand effort after the natural delineation of the bridge. Knowing it could not be passed, the lead boat rested to get strength before the final stretch. But the defense attorney knew that his position was in great danger. A few hundred yards from the bridge, he was only two or three boatlengths ahead. He could see the young man, glistening and red, breathing as if struggling for life. But his deep breathing had not the patina of weakness the defense attorney sensed in his own. He was certain to maintain his lead to the bridge, though, and beyond it for perhaps a quarter of a mile. But he knew that then the superior strength of the younger man would finally put the lighter boat ahead. If it were to be a contest of endurance, steady and torturesome as it had been, he knew he would not win.

But he had an idea. He would try to demoralize the young man. He would begin his sprint even before the Arsenal Street Bridge, with the benefit of the smooth water and the lead-in of the arch. What he did was to mark out in his mind a closer finish which he made his goal—knowing that there he would have to stop, a good half mile before the last bridge. But with luck the shocking lead so far in advance of all expectations would convince the struggling young man to surrender to his own exhaustion. An experienced man would guess the stratagem. A younger man might, and might not. If he did, he would maintain an even pace and eventually pass the defense attorney dead in the water a good distance before the finish line.

A hundred yards before the Arsenal Street Bridge, the defense attorney began his massive strokes. One after another, they were in clear defiance of the heat and his age. He began to increase his lead. When he passed through the dark shadow of the bridge, he was already five boatlengths ahead. He heard the echo of his heart from the cool concrete, for it was a hollow chamber. Back in bright light, clubbed by the sun, he went even faster. The young man had to turn every few seconds to guide himself through the arch. When he did so he lost much time in weak strokes, adjustments to course, and breaking rhythm. But far more important was what he saw ahead. The old man had begun a powerful sprint, as if up to that point he had only been warming up.

Three quarters of a mile before the finish the defense attorney was going full blast. From a distance he looked composed and unruffled, because all his strength was perfectly channeled. Because of this the young man's stroke shattered in panic. The defense attorney beat toward his secret finish, breathing as though he were a woman lost deep in love. The breaths were loud and desperate, abandoned and raw, as if of birth or a struggle not to die. He was ten boatlengths ahead, and nearing his finish.

He had not time to think of what he had endured in his life, of the loss which had battered him, and beaten him, and reduced him at times to nothing but a shadow of a man. He did not think of the men he had seen killed in war, whose screams were loud enough to echo in his dreams decades after. He did not think of the strength it had taken to love when not loved, to raise faltering children in the world, to see his parents and his friends die and fall away. He did not think of things he had seen as the century moved on, nor of how he had risen each time to survive in the palace of the world by a good and just fight, by luck, by means he sometimes did not understand. He simply beat the water with his long oars, and propelled himself ahead. One more stroke, he said, and another, and another. He was almost at his end.

He looked back, and a beautiful sight came to his eyes. The young man was bent over and gliding. His oars no longer moved but only brushed the top of the water. Then he began to work his port oar and turn around, for he had given up. He vanished through the bridge.

The defense attorney was alone on the river, in a thickly wooded green stretch full of bent willows. It was so hot that for a moment he forgot exactly who he was or where he was. He rowed slowly to the last bridge. There he rested in the cool shadow of a great and peaceful arch.

Eminent British philosopher, historian, mathematician, and world statesman, Bertrand Russell (1872–1970) was well known for his outspoken and unconventional views on social and political problems. He wrote books on many different subjects—mathematics, education, philosophy, marriage, ethics, and mysticism among them—and he wrote fiction as well. In 1950 he was awarded the Nobel Prize for Literature. "Reflections on My Eightieth Birthday" was printed in his autobiography, published in 1956. He lived almost twenty years longer, to be ninety-eight years of age.

REFLECTIONS ON
MY EIGHTIETH BIRTHDAY

On reaching the age of eighty it is reasonable to suppose that the bulk of one's work is done, and that what remains to do will be of less importance. The serious part of my life ever since boyhood has been devoted to two different objects which for a long time remained separate and have only in recent years united into a single whole. I wanted, on the one hand, to find out whether anything could be known; and, on the other hand, to do whatever might be possible towards creating a happier world. Up to the age of thirty-eight I gave most of my energies to the first of these tasks. I was troubled by scepticism and unwillingly forced to the conclusion that most of what passes for knowledge is open to reasonable doubt. I wanted certainty in the kind of way in which people want religious faith. I thought that certainty is more likely to be found in mathematics than elsewhere. But I discovered that many mathe-

From *Portraits from Memory*.

matical demonstrations, which my teachers expected me to accept, were full of fallacies, and that, if certainty were indeed discoverable in mathematics, it would be in a new kind of mathematics, with more solid foundations than those that had hitherto been thought secure. But as the work proceeded, I was continually reminded of the fable about the elephant and the tortoise. Having constructed an elephant upon which the mathematical world could rest, I found the elephant tottering, and proceeded to construct a tortoise to keep the elephant from falling. But the tortoise was no more secure than the elephant, and after some twenty years of very arduous toil, I came to the conclusion that there was nothing more that *I* could do in the way of making mathematical knowledge indubitable. Then came the First World War, and my thoughts became concentrated on human misery and folly. Neither misery nor folly seems to me any part of the inevitable lot of man. And I am convinced that intelligence, patience, and eloquence can, sooner or later, lead the human race out of its self-imposed tortures provided it does not exterminate itself meanwhile.

On the basis of this belief, I have had always a certain degree of optimism, although, as I have grown older, the optimism has grown more sober and the happy issue more distant. But I remain completely incapable of agreeing with those who accept fatalistically the view that man is born to trouble. The causes of unhappiness in the past and in the present are not difficult to ascertain. There have been poverty, pestilence, and famine which were due to man's inadequate mastery of nature. There have been wars, oppressions and tortures which have been due to men's hostility to their fellow-men. And there have been morbid miseries fostered by gloomy creeds, which have led men into profound inner discords that made all outward prosperity of no avail. All these are unnecessary. In regard to all of them, means are known by which they can be overcome. In the modern world, if communities are unhappy, it is because they choose to be so. Or, to speak more precisely, because they have ignorances, habits, beliefs, and passions, which are dearer to them than happiness or even life. I find many men in our dangerous age who seem to be in love with misery and death, and who grow angry when hopes are suggested to them. They think that hope is irrational and that, in sitting down to lazy despair, they are merely facing facts. I cannot agree with these men. To preserve hope in our world makes calls upon our intelligence and our energy. In those who despair it is very frequently the energy that is lacking.

The last half of my life has been lived in one of those painful epochs of human history during which the world is getting worse, and past victories which had seemed to be definitive have turned out to be only temporary. When I was young, Victorian optimism was taken for granted. It was thought that freedom and prosperity would spread gradually throughout the world by an orderly process, and it was hoped that cruelty, tyranny, and injustice would continually diminish. Hardly anyone was haunted by the fear of great wars. Hardly anyone thought of the nineteenth century as a brief interlude between past and future barbarism. For those who grew up in that atmosphere, adjustment to the world of the present has been difficult. It has been difficult not only emotionally but intellectually. Ideas that had been thought adequate have proved inadequate. In some directions valuable freedoms have proved very hard to preserve. In other directions, specially as regards relations between nations, freedoms formerly valued have proved potent sources of disaster. New thoughts, new hopes, new freedoms, and new restrictions upon freedom are needed if the world is to emerge from its present perilous state.

I cannot pretend that what I have done in regard to social and political problems has had any great importance. It is comparatively easy to have an immense effect by means of a dogmatic and precise gospel, such as that of Communism. But for my part I cannot believe that what mankind needs is anything either precise or dogmatic. Nor can I believe with any whole-heartedness in any partial doctrine which deals only with some part or aspect of human life. There are those who hold that everything depends upon institutions, and that good institutions will inevitably bring the millennium. And, on the other hand, there are those who believe that what is needed is a change of heart, and that, in comparison, institutions are of little account. I cannot accept either view. Institutions mould character, and character transforms institutions. Reforms in both must march hand in hand. And if individuals are to retain that measure of initiative and flexibility which they ought to have, they must not be all forced into one rigid mould; or, to change the metaphor, all drilled into one army. Diversity is essential in spite of the fact that it precludes universal acceptance of a single gospel. But to preach such a doctrine is difficult especially in arduous times. And perhaps it cannot be effective until some bitter lessons have been learnt by tragic experience.

My work is near its end, and the time has come when I can survey it as a whole. How far have I succeeded, and how far have I failed? From an early age I thought of myself as dedicated to great and arduous tasks. Sixty-one years ago, walking alone in the Tiergarten through melting snow under the coldly glittering March sun, I determined to write two series of books: one abstract, growing gradually more concrete; the other concrete, growing gradually more abstract. They were to be crowned by a synthesis, combining pure theory with a practical social philosophy. Except for the final synthesis, which still eludes me, I have written these books. They have been acclaimed and praised, and the thoughts of many men and women have been affected by them. To this extent I have succeeded.

But as against this must be set two kinds of failure, one outward, one inward.

To begin with the outward failure: the Tiergarten has become a desert; the Brandenburger Tor, through which I entered it on that March morning, has become the boundary of two hostile empires, glaring at each other across an almost invisible barrier, and grimly preparing the ruin of mankind. Communists, Fascists, and Nazis have successively challenged all that I thought good, and in defeating them much of what their opponents have sought to preserve is being lost. Freedom has come to be thought weakness, and tolerance has been compelled to wear the garb of treachery. Old ideals are judged irrelevant, and no doctrine free from harshness commands respect.

The inner failure, though of little moment to the world, has made my mental life a perpetual battle. I set out with a more or less religious belief in a Platonic eternal world, in which mathematics shone with a beauty like that of the last Cantos of the Paradiso. I came to the conclusion that the eternal world is trivial, and that mathematics is only the art of saying the same thing in different words. I set out with a belief that love, free and courageous, could conquer the world without fighting. I ended by supporting a bitter and terrible war. In these respects there was failure.

But beneath all this load of failure I am still conscious of something that I feel to be victory. I may have conceived theoretical truth wrongly, but I was not wrong in thinking that there is such a thing, and that it deserves our allegiance. I may have thought the road to a world of free and happy human beings shorter than it is proving to be, but I was not wrong in thinking that such a world is possible, and that it is worth while to live with a view to bringing it nearer. I have lived in the pursuit of a vision, both personal and social. Personal: to care for what is noble, for what is beautiful, for what is gentle; to allow moments of insight to give wisdom at more mundane times. Social: to see in imagination the society that is to be created, where individuals grow freely, and where hate and greed and envy die because there is nothing to nourish them. These things I believe, and the world, for all its horrors, has left me unshaken.

❧ *Henry Miller* ❧

Henry (Valentine) Miller (1891–1980) was born in New York
City, but went to Paris in the 1930s to begin writing in earnest.
Considered a man ahead of his time, his explicit chronicling of
his own amorous exploits was met with widespread criticism. His
most famous book, *Tropic of Cancer* (1935), was banned in the
United States for many years. As Miller aged, he moved away
from what was considered a pornographic style and in his eighties
lived in seclusion pursuing a life-long interest in watercolor
painting. In this excerpt from an interview with journalist Digby
Diehl, Miller is drawing on his long years of experience to offer
his view of the world.

INTERVIEW WITH
HENRY MILLER

MILLER: I've been characterized as a very bad writer. I mean, one of the
very worst writers. Many critics, especially the British critics, say that I'm
long-winded, monotonous, repetitious, and that I only talk about myself.
In ranting about society, about our way of life, I try to point out a better
way of living. In doing so these critics find me pompous and egotistical. I'm
still ranting and raving, of course. All I have to do is step outside into the
world and see how horrible everything is. There never was a time when
the condition of the world was satisfactory, let alone ideal. We probably
never will have an ideal society. I think, however, that one has to learn to
accept the world as it is. There's no reason why one can't suggest other
kinds of worlds, other ways of living. Learn to be in it, but not of it. But

From *Supertalk* by Digby Diehl.

don't wear yourself out fighting it—which I did in the beginning, as a young man. I really thought I could do something to change the world. I soon found out you can't change the world. The best you can do is learn to live with it. No special group, however high-minded, no one individual can change the world, even if he is called a savior. I think the world is changed by the aggregate of people in it, by how each one lives his life. The great changes come through the things people don't do. Through their inertia. It's the failure to live up to ourselves which creates bad conditions. We always look for some Hitler, some devil to blame. They are not the cause, but the result. There are "the quick and the dead," and most of us are dead.

Q: So what does a man do?

MILLER: There's a big difference between living with a situation and accepting it. You can live in or with a distressing situation and remain detached, mentally and spiritually. Unless, of course, it is too late, as in wars and revolutions. With that attitude one can endure almost anything. With that kind of understanding you enjoy a certain immunity. You may still retain the ability to lead your own life; you won't have the conflicts others go through.

Q: You sound like a man who has found a way to get through life.

MILLER: I get credit for that all the time, but it's not quite true. I'm still searching. I'm not a man who knows all the answers, who's arrived at that serene level where he's skating, if you know what I mean. No. For me it will always be turmoil and chaos and bewilderment. There's another thing you ought to know about me. I never renounce what I've done, even if what I've said was foolish and wrong. That was a part of me then, and it belongs. In other words, the imperfections of a man, his frailties, his faults, are just as important as his virtues. You can't separate them. They're wedded.

Q: You say you're doing nothing now, but I keep hearing about these new projects. It sounds like you're doing a great deal.

MILLER: These new projects are not of my creation. They're thrust on me. There's always a way to get to a man. I would like to be everything—or be, just be. Not do. Being, to me, has become more important than doing. In the early part of my life, doing was important. But now it's being. And that's so much better, because in saying that, you realize that the activity of men is largely humbug, of little import. Men make it seem important to themselves. That's why I revere the sage who doesn't need anything, eats and sleeps very little, has no vices, doesn't need amusements or even companions. He's just himself, and he's content with what he is. His world is a complete, infinite world—to him. That's putting it as best I can. That's what I'm sort of aiming at in my own poor way. But I'm just "a Brooklyn boy," as you know. I was ruined at the start.

Q: How do you spend most of your time now?

MILLER: To tell the truth, I spend most of my time doing what the world would call nothing. I'm busy all the time, it seems, but actually, it's a kind of lazy life I'm leading. And I would like it to be more so. To simply be, that would be my ideal. But I'll never attain it. I haven't the temperament for it. I'm too active inside. I'm involved; I can't help it. I don't like it, either. I would prefer to be unknown.

Q: Really?

MILLER: Yes. Being known doesn't mean a thing to me. A real artist doesn't want fame. All he wants is room enough to move around in and do what he likes. But all the rest—money, fame, success, all these are just as bad as non-recognition and poverty and hunger. It's the obverse of the coin. I do very little writing now. Very little painting either, for that matter. I remember one year I did about two hundred watercolors—on the side, you understand. Usually I paint from fifty to a hundred a year. It's easy for me to do them. Doesn't take me very long. If I have the desire, I can do a watercolor in half an hour or less. After all, I'm eighty-one years old. I've done the major portion of my work. I don't want to repeat myself. I don't want to write a single word that isn't necessary. Now I just want to live and enjoy myself. . . .

Q: Many young people profess allegiance to you, your books, ideas.

MILLER: That's one of the reasons I'm dubious about them. They should not owe allegiance to anyone. They shouldn't be disciples. I want them to be original. I don't give a damn about disciples; no man of any stature wants followers. I want anarchy, real anarchy, but in the highest sense of the word. I want to see and deal with *individuals*.

The whole of society from time immemorial has always worshiped youth. Youth is the great word, isn't it? Now, we all know, who've been through youth, that it's far from being a glorious period in one's life. I don't know how they drummed up all those qualities that are attributed to youth. Youth has to do with spirit, not age. Men of seventy and eighty are often more youthful than the young. Theirs is the real youth. You see what I mean? It's the youth of the mind and spirit, which is everlasting.

Q: Do you really feel younger, spiritually, now that you've reached "four score" years?

MILLER: Absolutely! As you near the end your sense of wonder increases, for one thing. Maybe you get a little more horse sense, too. If you were to ask me on my deathbed—What is your last word?—I'd probably say, "Mystery." Everything understandable becomes more and more mysterious to me. Not more and more familiar, but more and more mysterious. I think the genuine man of science would say the same thing. The more one penetrates the realm of knowledge the more puzzling everything becomes. Knowledge is like cutting into a limitless cake. Cut a chunk, and the cake grows bigger. Cut another, the cake is still bigger. That's why knowledge is so relatively unimportant. No one has real knowledge. All you can aspire to is wisdom.

So what is the most important thing in life? It is Spirit, with a capital S. Without it you are nobody, nothing, or to put it another way—pure shit.

John Neihardt (1881–1973), an epic poet, lived among the Omaha Indians for six years in the early 1900s and later spent time with the Sioux. He wrote often of the lessons and experiences he gained from the Indian customs and culture while pursuing a variety of careers in the Midwest. At various times, he was a teacher, professor of poetry at the University of Nebraska, Literary Editor of the *St. Louis Post Dispatch*, and employee of the U.S. Department of Interior's Bureau of Indian Affairs. His best-known work, *Black Elk Speaks,* was published in 1932. The following excerpt is taken from his autobiography, *All Is But a Beginning.*

from

ALL IS BUT A BEGINNING

The "younger generation" in which I claim honorary membership, regardless of my years, is caught up in the greatest social revolution the world has ever known. Discord and violence are commonplace the world over. Throughout the realm of human values the raucous yawp of anarchy is loud. In wide, densely populated areas of the planet abject misery and chronic terror are ways of life; sordid systematic killing a thriving industry, its success measured by the daily bag of "enemy" dead. It is no wonder that our youngsters would reject the mad world they have inherited. Surely there is more than frivolity and fashion in their hirsute excesses, more than clowning in their irreverence for the Established and the smug.

Do the laughing gods poke cruel fun at us?

But for all the scornful nose-thumbings at the discarded past, the discredited present, and the mistrusted future, a most hopeful sign is to be noted. Among these dissident youngsters there is an upward surge of spiritual longing. Apparently they are seeking a new, direct approach to a viable religion. Even the resort to drugs must be regarded as an attempted shortcut to the desired mystical experience.

As a university lecturer I was intimately and happily associated with young people for some years. They always seemed to be more earnestly questioning than hopeful; less joyous, and older than young people should be.

"What's it all about?" and "What's good about it?" were characteristic and often-recurring questions. They still are, especially now that I have attained this snow-topped summit of my heaped-up ninety years and more. Surely, those young people must think, having come so far and climbed so high, he must have learned some of the vital answers.

But "What's it all about?" Ask God that question. He won't tell; and if He did we would not understand. Anyway, to ask that question is to die a little. No doubt even a tree would wither if it got to thinking what the summers and the winters meant.

But "What's good about it?" That is indeed an important question, and it admits an answer. It has plagued me, too, in my darker moods.

I have a formal garden, hedge-enclosed, where I often go to pray and seek for needed answers. However the faith-inspired religionist or the scientific psychologist may explain the mechanism of prayer, I have found it a rewarding practice; and I suspect that it may be vastly more powerful than we know.

There are times when I enter my garden not to worship but just to *be*—and listen. It is such a time that I now recall. I was thinking lamely of the world's multitudinous woes, including some minor ones of my own, when the shadowy form of a cynical young friend of mine floated across my consciousness. I fancied him pressing the troublesome question upon me: "What's good about this absurd predicament in which we find ourselves? We don't know whence we came; we don't know where we are; we don't know whither we are bound. It is hard to come here, hard to remain, and sometimes very hard to get away."

I listened, and the answer came out of the silence:

"Four things, at least, are good," I found myself replying.

"First: Surely love is good—love given rather than love received. With neither, there is nothing; with either, even sorrow and suffering may become beautiful and dear. All good things come from love, and it is the only thing that is increased by giving it away.

"Second: The satisfaction of the instinct of workmanship is good; for that instinct is the noblest thing in man after love, from which indeed it springs. Just to do your best at any cost, and afterward to experience something of the Seventh Day glory when you look upon your work and see that it is good.

"Third: The exaltation of expanded awareness in moments of spiritual insight is good. This may occur in a flash, glorifying the world; or it may linger for days, when you seem to float above all worldly troubling, and all faces become familiar and dear. This state can be spontaneously generated, but it has often been achieved through fasting and prayer.

"Fourth: Deep sleep is good.

> " 'Not shoaling slumber, but the ocean-deep
>   And dreamless sort,'

as one of my characters in *The Song of Jed Smith* remarks.

> " 'There's something that you touch,
> And what you call it needn't matter much
> If you can reach it. Call it only rest,
> And there is something else you haven't guessed—
> The Everlasting, maybe. You can try
> To live without it, but you have to die
> Back into it a little now and then.
> And maybe praying is a way for men
> To reach it when they cannot sleep a wink
> For trouble.' "

For some time I continued to mull over the implications of the answer. Then I was struck by the realization that both my cynical young friend and I were of necessity concerned with fragmentary conceptions; that each "good" that I had offered involved the loss of the sense of self in some pattern larger than self; that life, as commonly conceived, could be only a fragment of some vaster pattern; and that prayer itself was a striving to be whole.

There is a slogan that I wish to leave with my young friends to be recalled for courage, like a battle cry, in times of great stress. It came to me from an old Sioux friend of mine who was recounting his experience as a youth on Vision Quest.

He had fasted three days and nights upon a lonely hill, praying all the while that Wakon Tonka might send him a vision. But his prayer got lost, far out in the empty night, and it seemed that nothing heard.

Then, on the fourth day, he fell asleep, exhausted, and dreamed a troubled dream that had no glory in it. Any old woman could have dreamed it, nidding and nodding in her tepee. He wakened in despair. And as he stood forlorn upon his hilltop he was thinking: If I have no vision to give me power and guide me, how can I ever be a man? Maybe I shall have to go far off into a strange land and seek an enemy to free me from this shame.

Then, just as he thought this bitter thought, a great cry came from overhead like a fearless warrior hailing his wavering comrade in heat of battle. "Hoka-hey, brother—*Hold fast, hold fast; there is more!*" Looking up, he saw an eagle soaring yonder on a spread of mighty wings—and it was the eagle's voice he heard.

"As I listened," the old man said, "a power ran through me that has never left me, old as I am. Often when it seemed the end had come, I have heard the eagle's cry—*Hold fast, hold fast; there is more. . . .*"

❧ *Dorothy Canfield (Fisher)* ❧

Often associated with fiction about Vermont, author Dorothy
Canfield Fisher (1879–1958) was born in Kansas, educated at
Ohio State and Columbia universities, moved to Vermont after
her marriage, and lived there for the next fifty years. She wrote
novels, short stories, children's literature, memoirs, essays, re-
views, and articles, and for twenty-five years served on the edito-
rial board of the Book-of-the-Month Club. Called "a story teller
of consummate skill," her work reflects her interest in family life
and basic human values.

SEX EDUCATION

It was three times—but at intervals
of many years—that I heard my Aunt Minnie tell about an experience of
her girlhood that had made a never-to-be-forgotten impression on her. The
first time she was in her thirties, still young. But she had then been married
for ten years, so that to my group of friends, all in the early teens, she
seemed quite of another generation.

The day she told us the story, we had been idling on one end of her porch
as we made casual plans for a picnic supper in the woods. Darning stockings
at the other end, she paid no attention to us until one of the girls said, "Let's
take blankets and sleep out there. It'd be fun."

"No," Aunt Minnie broke in sharply, "you mustn't do that."

"Oh, for goodness' sakes, why not!" said one of the younger girls,
rebelliously, "the boys are always doing it. Why can't we, just once?"

Aunt Minnie laid down her sewing. "Come here, girls," she said, "I
want you should hear something that happened to me when I was your
age."

Her voice had a special quality which, perhaps, young people of today would not recognize. But we did. We knew from experience that it was the dark voice grownups used when they were going to say something about sex.

Yet at first what she had to say was like any dull family anecdote; she had been ill when she was fifteen; and afterwards she was run down, thin, with no appetite. Her folks thought a change of air would do her good, and sent her from Vermont out to Ohio—or was it Illinois? I don't remember. Anyway, one of those places where the corn grows high. Her mother's Cousin Ella lived there, keeping house for her son-in-law.

The son-in-law was the minister of the village church. His wife had died some years before, leaving him a young widower with two little girls and a baby boy. He had been a normally personable man then, but the next summer, on the Fourth of July when he was trying to set off some fireworks to amuse his children, an imperfectly manufactured rocket had burst in his face. The explosion had left one side of his face badly scarred. Aunt Minnie made us see it, as she still saw it, in horrid detail: the stiffened, scarlet scar tissue distorting one cheek, the lower lip turned so far out at one corner that the moist red mucous-membrane lining always showed, one lower eyelid hanging loose, and watering.

After the accident, his face had been a long time healing. It was then that his wife's elderly mother had gone to keep house and take care of the children. When he was well enough to be about again, he found his position as pastor of the little church waiting for him. The farmers and village people in his congregation, moved by his misfortune, by his faithful service and by his unblemished character, said they would rather have Mr. Fairchild, even with his scarred face, than any other minister. He was a good preacher, Aunt Minnie told us, "and the way he prayed was kind of exciting. I'd never known a preacher, not to live in the same house with him, before. And when he was in the pulpit, with everybody looking up at him, I felt the way his children did, kind of proud to think we had just eaten breakfast at the same table. I liked to call him 'Cousin Malcolm' before folks. One side of his face was all right, anyhow. You could see from that that he *had* been a good-looking man. In fact, probably one of those ministers that all the women——" Aunt Minnie paused, drew her lips together, and looked at us uncertainly.

Then she went back to the story as it happened—as it happened that first time I heard her tell it. "I thought he was a saint. Everybody out there did. That was all *they* knew. Of course, it made a person sick to look at that awful scar—the drooling corner of his mouth was the worst. He tried to keep that side of his face turned away from folks. But you always knew it was there. That was what kept him from marrying again, so Cousin Ella said. I heard her say lots of times that he knew no woman would touch any man who looked the way he did, not with a ten-foot pole.

"Well, the change of air did do me good. I got my appetite back, and ate a lot and played outdoors a lot with my cousins. They were younger than I (I had my sixteenth birthday there) but I still liked to play games. I got taller and laid on some weight. Cousin Ella used to say I grew as fast as the corn did. Their house stood at the edge of the village. Beyond it was one of those big cornfields they have out West. At the time when I first got there, the stalks were only up to a person's knee. You could see over their tops. But it grew like lightning, and before long, it was the way thick woods are here, way over your head, the stalks growing so close together it was dark under them.

"Cousin Ella told us youngsters that it was lots worse for getting lost in than woods, because there weren't any landmarks in it. One spot in a cornfield looked just like any other. 'You children keep out of it,' she used to tell us almost every day, 'especially you girls. It's no place for a decent girl. You could easy get so far from the house nobody could hear you if you hollered. There are plenty of men in this town that wouldn't like anything better than——' she never said what.

"In spite of what she said, my little cousins and I had figured out that if we went across one corner of the field, it would be a short cut to the village, and sometimes, without letting on to Cousin Ella, we'd go that way. After the corn got really tall, the farmer stopped cultivating, and we soon beat down a path in the loose dirt. The minute you were inside the field it was dark. You felt as if you were miles from anywhere. It sort of scared you. But in no time the path turned and brought you out on the far end of Main Street. Your breath was coming fast, maybe, but that was what made you like to do it.

"One day i missed the turn. Maybe I didn't keep my mind on it. Maybe it had rained and blurred the tramped-down look of the path. I don't know what. All of a sudden, I knew I was lost. And the minute I knew that, I began to run, just as hard as I could run. I couldn't help it, any more than you can help snatching your hand off a hot stove. I didn't know what I was scared of, I didn't even know I *was* running, till my heart was pounding so hard I had to stop.

"The minute I stood still, I could hear Cousin Ella saying, 'There are plenty of men in this town that wouldn't like anything better than——' I didn't know, not really, what she meant. But I knew she meant something horrible. I opened my mouth to scream. But I put both hands over my mouth to keep the scream in. If I made any noise, one of those men would hear me. I thought I heard one just behind me, and whirled around. And then I thought another one had tiptoed up behind me, the other way, and I spun around so fast I almost fell over. I stuffed my hands hard up against my mouth. And then—I couldn't help it—I ran again—but my legs were shaking so I soon had to stop. There I stood, scared to move for fear of rustling the corn and letting the men know where I was. My hair had come down, all over my face. I kept pushing it back and looking around, quick, to make sure one of the men hadn't found out where I was. Then I thought I saw a man coming towards me, and I ran away from him—and fell down, and burst some of the buttons off my dress, and was sick to my stomach—and thought I heard a man close to me and got up and staggered around, knocking into the corn because I couldn't even see where I was going.

"And then, off to one side, I saw Cousin Malcolm. Not a man. The minister. He was standing still, one hand up to his face, thinking. He hadn't heard me.

"I was so *terrible* glad to see him, instead of one of those men, I ran as fast as I could and just flung myself on him, to make myself feel how safe I was."

Aunt minnie had become strangely agitated. Her hands were shaking, her face was crimson. She frightened us. We could not look away from her. As we waited for her to go on, I felt little spasms twitch at the muscles inside my body. "And what do you think that *saint,* that holy minister of the Gospel, did to an innocent child who clung to him for safety? The most terrible look came into his eyes—you girls are too young to know what he looked like. But once you're married, you'll find out. He grabbed hold of me—that dreadful face of his was *right on mine*—and began clawing the clothes off my back."

She stopped for a moment, panting. We were too frightened to speak. She went on, "He had torn my dress right down to the waist before I—then I *did* scream—all I could—and pulled away from him so hard I almost fell down, and ran and all of a sudden I came out of the corn, right in the back yard of the Fairchild house. The children were staring at the corn, and

Cousin Ella ran out of the kitchen door. They had heard me screaming. Cousin Ella shrieked out, 'What is it? What happened? Did a man scare you?' And I said, 'Yes, yes, yes, a man—I ran——!' And then I fainted away. I must have. The next thing I knew I was on the sofa in the living room and Cousin Ella was slapping my face with a wet towel."

She had to wet her lips with her tongue before she could go on. Her face was gray now. "There! that's the kind of thing girls' folks ought to tell them about—so they'll know what men are like."

She finished her story as if she were dismissing us. We wanted to go away, but we were too horrified to stir. Finally one of the youngest girls asked in a low trembling voice, "Aunt Minnie, did you tell on him?"

"No, I was ashamed to," she said briefly. "They sent me home the next day anyhow. Nobody ever said a word to me about it. And I never did either. Till now."

By what gets printed in some of the modern child-psychology books, you would think that girls to whom such a story had been told would never develop normally. Yet, as far as I can remember what happened to the girls in that group, we all grew up about like anybody. Most of us married, some happily, some not so well. We kept house. We learned—more or less—how to live with our husbands, we had children and struggled to bring them up right—we went forward into life, just as if we had never been warned not to.

Perhaps, young as we were that day, we had already had enough experience of life so that we were not quite blank paper for Aunt Minnie's frightening story. Whether we thought of it then or not, we couldn't have failed to see that at this very time, Aunt Minnie had been married for ten years or more, comfortably and well married, too. Against what she tried by that story to brand into our minds stood the cheerful home life in that house, the good-natured, kind, hard-working husband, and the children— the three rough-and-tumble, nice little boys, so adored by their parents, and the sweet girl baby who died, of whom they could never speak without tears. It was such actual contact with adult life that probably kept generation after generation of girls from being scared by tales like Aunt Minnie's into a neurotic horror of living.

Of course, since aunt Minnie was so much older than we, her boys grew up to be adolescents and young men, while our children were still little enough so that our worries over them were nothing more serious than whooping cough and trying to get them to make their own beds. Two of our aunt's three boys followed, without losing their footing, the narrow path which leads across adolescence into normal adult life. But the middle one, Jake, repeatedly fell off into the morass. "Girl trouble," as the succinct family phrase put it. He was one of those boys who have "charm," whatever we mean by that, and was always being snatched at by girls who would be "all wrong" for him to marry. And once, at nineteen, he ran away from home, whether with one of these girls or not we never heard, for through all her ups and downs with this son, Aunt Minnie tried fiercely to protect him from scandal that might cloud his later life.

Her husband had to stay on his job to earn the family living. She was the one who went to find Jake. When it was gossiped around that Jake was in "bad company" his mother drew some money from the family savings-bank account, and silent, white-cheeked, took the train to the city where rumor said he had gone.

Some weeks later he came back with her. With no girl. She had cleared him of that entanglement. As of others, which followed, later. Her troubles seemed over when, at a "suitable" age, he fell in love with a "suitable" girl, married her and took her to live in our shire town, sixteen miles away, where he had a good position. Jake was always bright enough.

Sometimes, idly, people speculated as to what Aunt Minnie had seen that time she went after her runaway son, wondering where her search for him had taken her—very queer places for Aunt Minnie to be in, we imagined. And how could such an ignorant, homekeeping woman ever have known what to say to an errant willful boy to set him straight?

Well, of course, we reflected, watching her later struggles with Jake's erratic ways, she certainly could not have remained ignorant, after seeing over and over what she probably had; after talking with Jake about the things which, a good many times, must have come up with desperate openness between them.

She kept her own counsel. We never knew anything definite about the facts of those experiences of hers. But one day she told a group of us—all then married women—something which gave us a notion about what she had learned from them.

We were hastily making a layette for a not-especially welcome baby in a poor family. In those days, our town had no such thing as a district-nursing service. Aunt Minnie, a vigorous woman of fifty-five, had come in to help. As we sewed, we talked, of course; and because our daughters were near or in their teens, we were comparing notes about the bewildering responsibility of bringing up girls.

After a while, Aunt Minnie remarked, "Well, I hope you teach your girls some *sense*. From what I read, I know you're great on telling them 'the facts,' facts we never heard of when we were girls. Like as not, some facts I don't know, now. But knowing the facts isn't going to do them any more good than *not* knowing the facts ever did, unless they have some sense taught them, too."

"What do you mean, Aunt Minnie?" one of us asked her uncertainly.

She reflected, threading a needle, "Well, I don't know but what the best way to tell you what I mean is to tell you about something that happened to me, forty years ago. I've never said anything about it before. But I've thought about it a good deal. Maybe——"

S HE HAD HARDLY BEGUN when I recognized the story—her visit to her Cousin Ella's Midwestern home, the widower with his scarred face and saintly reputation and, very vividly, her getting lost in the great cornfield. I knew every word she was going to say—to the very end, I thought.

But no, I did not. Not at all.

She broke off, suddenly, to exclaim with impatience, "Wasn't I the big ninny? But not so big a ninny as that old cousin of mine. I could wring her neck for getting me in such a state. Only she didn't know any better, herself. That was the way they brought young people up in those days, scaring them out of their wits about the awfulness of getting lost, but not telling them a thing about how *not* to get lost. Or how to act, if they did.

"If I had had the sense I was born with, I'd have known that running my legs off in a zigzag was the worst thing I could do. I couldn't have been more than a few feet from the path when I noticed I wasn't on it. My tracks in the loose plow dirt must have been perfectly plain. If I'd h' stood still, and collected my wits, I could have looked down to see which way my footsteps went and just walked back over them to the path and gone on about my business.

"Now I ask you, if I'd been told how to do that, wouldn't it have been a lot better protection for me—if protection was what my aunt thought she wanted to give me—than to scare me so at the idea of being lost that

I turned deef-dumb-and-blind when I thought I was?

"And anyhow that patch of corn wasn't as big as she let on. And she knew it wasn't. It was no more than a big field in a farming country. I was a well-grown girl of sixteen, as tall as I am now. If I couldn't have found the path, I could have just walked along one line of cornstalks—*straight*— and I'd have come out somewhere in ten minutes. Fifteen at the most. Maybe not just where I wanted to go. But all right, safe, where decent folks were living."

She paused, as if she had finished. But at the inquiring blankness in our faces, she went on, "Well, now, why isn't teaching girls—and boys, too, for the Lord's sake don't forget they need it as much as the girls—about this man-and-woman business, something like that? If you give them the idea—no matter whether it's *as* you tell them the facts, or as you *don't* tell them the facts, that it is such a terribly scary thing that if they take a step into it, something's likely to happen to them so awful that you're ashamed to tell them what—well, they'll lose their heads and run around like crazy things, first time they take one step away from the path.

"For they'll be trying out the paths, all right. You can't keep them from it. And a good thing too. How else are they going to find out what it's like? Boys' and girls' going together is a path across one corner of growing up. And when they go together, they're likely to get off the path some. Seems to me, it's up to their folks to bring them up so when they do, they don't start screaming and running in circles, but stand tall, right where they are, and get their breath and figure out how to get back.

"And anyhow, you don't tell 'em the truth about sex" (I was astonished to hear her use the actual word, taboo to women of her generation) "if they get the idea from you that it's all there is to living. It's not. If you don't get to where you want to go in it, well, there's a lot of landscape all around it a person can have a good time in.

"D'you know, I believe one thing that gives girls and boys the wrong idea is the way folks *look!* My old cousin's face, I can see her now, it was as red as a rooster's comb when she was telling me about men in that cornfield. I believe now she kind of *liked* to talk about it."

(Oh, Aunt Minnie—and yours! I thought.)

Someone asked, "But how *did* you get out, Aunt Minnie?"

She shook her head, laid down her sewing. "More foolishness. That minister my mother's cousin was keeping house for—her son-in-law—I caught sight of him, down along one of the aisles of cornstalks, looking down at the ground, thinking, the way he often did. And I was so glad to see him I rushed right up to him, and flung my arms around his neck and hugged him. He hadn't heard me coming. He gave a great start, put one arm around me and turned his face full towards me—I suppose for just a second he had forgotten how awful one side of it was. His expression, his eyes—well, you're all married women, you know how he looked, the way any able-bodied man thirty-six or -seven, who'd been married and begotten children, would look—for a minute anyhow, if a full-blooded girl of sixteen, who ought to have known better, flung herself at him without any warning, her hair tumbling down, her dress half unbottoned, and hugged him with all her might.

"I was what they called innocent in those days. That is, I knew just as little about what men are like as my folks could manage I should. But I was old enough to know all right what that look meant. And it gave me a start. But of course the real thing of it was that dreadful scar of his, so close to my face—that wet corner of his mouth, his eye drawn down with the red inside of the lower eyelid showing——

"It turned me so sick, I pulled away with all my might, so fast that I ripped one sleeve nearly loose, and let out a screech like a wildcat. And ran. Did I run? And in a minute, I was through the corn and had come out in the back yard of the house. I hadn't been more than a few feet from it, probably, any of the time. And then I fainted away. Girls were always fainting away; it was the way our corset strings were pulled tight, I suppose, and then—oh, a lot of fuss.

"But anyhow," she finished, picking up her work and going on, setting neat, firm stitches with steady hands, "there's one thing, I never told anybody it was Cousin Malcolm I had met in the cornfield. I told my old cousin that 'a man had scared me.' And nobody said anything more about it to me, not ever. That was the way they did in those days. They thought if they didn't let on about something, maybe it wouldn't have happened. I was sent back to Vermont right away and Cousin Malcolm went on being minister of the church. I've always been," said Aunt Minnie moderately, "kind of proud that I didn't go and ruin a man's life for just one second's slip-up. If you could have called it that. For it would have ruined him. You know how hard as stone people are about other folks' let-downs. If I'd have told, not one person in that town would have had any charity. Not one would have tried to understand. One slip, once, and they'd have pushed him down in the mud. If I had told, I'd have felt pretty bad about it, later—when I came to have more sense. But I declare, I can't see how I came to have the decency, dumb as I was then, to know that it wouldn't be fair."

IT WAS NOT LONG after this talk that Aunt Minnie's elderly husband died, mourned by her, by all of us. She lived alone then. It was peaceful October weather for her, in which she kept a firm roundness of face and figure, as quiet-living country-women often do, on into her late sixties.

But then Jake, the boy who had had girl trouble, had wife trouble. We heard he had taken to running after a young girl, or was it that she was running after him? It was something serious. For his nice wife left him and came back with the children to live with her mother in our town. Poor Aunt Minnie used to go to see her for long talks which made them both cry. And she went to keep house for Jake, for months at a time.

She grew old, during those years. When finally she (or something) managed to get the marriage mended so that Jake's wife relented and went back to live with him, there was no trace left of her pleasant brisk freshness. She was stooped, and slow-footed and shrunken. We, her kins-people, although we would have given our lives for any one of our own children, wondered whether Jake was worth what it had cost his mother to—well, steady him, or reform him. Or perhaps just understand him. Whatever it took.

She came of a long-lived family and was able to go on keeping house for herself well into her eighties. Of course we and the other neighbors stepped in often to make sure she was all right. Mostly, during those brief calls, the talk turned on nothing more vital than her geraniums. But one midwinter afternoon, sitting with her in front of her cozy stove, I chanced to speak in rather hasty blame of someone who had, I thought, acted badly. To my surprise this brought from her the story about the cornfield which she had evidently quite forgotten telling me, twice before.

This time she told it almost dreamily, swaying to and fro in her rocking chair, her eyes fixed on the long slope of snow outside her window. When she came to the encounter with the minister she said, looking away from the distance and back into my eyes, "I know now that I had been, all along, kind of *interested* in him, the way any girl as old as I was would be, in any youngish man living in the same house with her. And a minister, too. They have to have the gift of gab so much more than most men, women get to thinking they are more alive than men who can't talk so well. I *thought* the reason I threw my arms around him was because I had been so scared.

And I certainly had been scared, by my old cousin's horrible talk about the cornfield being full of men waiting to grab girls. But that wasn't all the reason I flung myself at Malcolm Fairchild and hugged him. I know that now. Why in the world shouldn't I have been taught *some* notion of it then? 'Twould do girls good to know that they are just like everybody else—human nature *and* sex, all mixed up together. I didn't have to hug him. I wouldn't have, if he'd been dirty or fat or old, or chewed tobacco."

I stirred in my chair, ready to say, "But it's not so simple as all that to tell girls——" and she hastily answered my unspoken protest. "I know, I know, most of it can't be put into words. There just aren't any words to say something that's so both-ways-at-once all the time as this man-and-woman business. But look here, you know as well as I do that there are lots more ways than in words to teach young folks what you want 'em to know."

The old woman stopped her swaying rocker to peer far back into the past with honest eyes. "What was in my mind back there in the cornfield—partly anyhow—was what had been there all the time I was living in the same house with Cousin Malcolm—that he had long straight legs, and broad shoulders, and lots of curly brown hair, and was nice and flat in front, and that one side of his face was good-looking. But most of all, that he and I were really alone, for the first time, without anybody to see us.

"I suppose if it hadn't been for that dreadful scar, he'd have drawn me up, tight, and—most any man would—kissed me. I know how I must have looked, all red and hot and my hair down and my dress torn open. And, used as he was to big cornfields, he probably never dreamed that the reason I looked that way was because I was scared to be by myself in one. He may have thought—you know what he may have thought.

"Well—if his face had been like anybody's—when he looked at me the way he did, the way a man does look at a woman he wants to have, it would have scared me—some. But I'd have cried, maybe. And probably he'd have kissed me again. You know how such things go. I might have come out of the cornfield halfway engaged to marry him. Why not? I was old enough, as people thought then. That would have been nature. That was probably what he thought of, in that first instant.

"But what did I do? I had one look at his poor, horrible face, and started back as though I'd stepped on a snake. And screamed and ran.

"What do you suppose *he* felt, left there in the corn? He must have been sure that I would tell everybody he had attacked me. He probably thought that when he came out and went back to the village he'd already be in disgrace and put out of the pulpit.

"But the worst must have been to find out, so rough, so plain from the way I acted—as if somebody had hit him with an ax—the way he would look to any woman he might try to get close to. That must have been——" she drew a long breath, "well, pretty hard on him."

After a silence, she murmured pityingly, "Poor man!"

❧ *Anne Morrow Lindbergh* ❧

Anne Morrow Lindbergh (1906–   ) was thrust from a quiet academic life into the glare of publicity when she married transatlantic flying ace Charles Lindbergh in 1929. She temporarily put aside a writing career while she learned to fly, raised five children, and withstood the public notice and sorrow of the kidnap murder of Charles Jr. Returning to her love of literature and poetry, Lindbergh is most noted for her book *Gift of the Sea,* in which she reflects on her life through a comparison of the shells she picks up along the beach. In *The Unicorn and Other Poems,* from which the following poem is taken, she shares her response to love, death, art, and nature. "Bare Tree" appears in a section entitled "Wind of Time."

BARE TREE

Already I have shed the leaves of youth,
Stripped by the wind of time down to the truth
Of winter branches. Linear and alone
I stand, a lens for lives beyond my own,
A frame through which another's fire may glow,
A harp on which another's passion, blow.

The pattern of my boughs, an open chart
Spread on the sky, to others may impart
Its leafless mysteries that once I prized,
Before bare roots and branches equalized;
Tendrils that tap the rain or twigs the sun
Are all the same; shadow and substance one.
Now that my vulnerable leaves are cast aside,
There's nothing left to shield, nothing to hide.

Blow through me, Life, pared down at last to bone,
So fragile and so fearless have I grown!

Robert Coles (1929–   ), psychiatrist and writer, is Professor of Psychiatry and Medical Humanities at Harvard Medical School, and Research Psychiatrist for Harvard University Health Services. Sometimes called "the greatest social conscience of his generation," he is the author of more than thirty-six books for adults and children, and was awarded the Pulitzer Prize for his five-volume study, *Children of Crisis*. "Una Anciana" is representative of his work as commentator on specific segments of American society and interpreter of moral values.

UNA ANCIANA

The man I shall call Domingo García is eighty-three years old. Once, he was measured as exactly six feet tall, but that was half a century ago. He is sure that he has lost an inch or two. Sometimes, when his wife, Dolores, grows impatient with his slouch and tells him to straighten up, he goes her suggestion one better and tilts himself backward. "Now are you happy?" he seems to be asking her, and she smiles indulgently. His wife is also eighty-three. She always defers to her husband. She will not speak until he has his say. As the two of them approach a closed door, she makes a quick motion toward it, opens it, and stands holding it, and sometimes, if he is distracted by a conversation and is slow to move through, one of her hands reaches for his elbow while the other points. "Go now," is the unstated message, "so that I can follow."

They were born within a mile and within two months of one another, in Cordova, New Mexico, in the northcentral part of the state. They are old Americans by virtue not only of age but of ancestry. For many generations, their ancestors have lived in territory that is now part of the United States. Before the Declaration of Independence was written, there were people not far away from Cordova named García and living, as they do, off the land. Domingo and Dolores García are not, however, model citizens of their country. They have never voted, and no doubt the men who framed the Declaration of Independence would not be happy to see the boredom or indifference that these New Mexicans demonstrate when the subject of politics comes up. They don't even make an effort to keep abreast of the news, though they do have a television set in their small adobe house. When Walter Cronkite or John Chancellor appears, neither of the Garcías listens very hard. For that matter, no programs engage their undivided attention, and at first one is inclined to think them partly deaf. But the explanation is taste, not the effects of age. Mrs. García does like to watch some after-noon serials, but without the sound. She takes an interest in how the people dress and what the furniture in the homes looks like. The actors and actresses are company of sorts when Mr. García is outside tending their crops or looking after their horses and cows. Language is not a problem; both Garcías prefer to speak Spanish, but they can make themselves under-stood quite well in English. They have had to, as Mrs. García explains in English and with no effort to conceal her long-standing sense of resignation: "You bend with the wind. And Anglo people are a strong wind. They want their own way; they can be like a tornado, out to pass over everyone as they go somewhere. I don't mean to talk out of turn. There are Anglos who don't fit my words. But we are outsiders in a land that is ours. We are part of an Anglo country, and that will not change. I had to teach the facts of life to my four sons, and, doing so, I learned my own lesson well."

She stops and looks at their pictures, on top of the television set. That is one function of the set, which was given to her and her husband by their oldest son. Like his father, he is named Domingo, but, unlike his father, he attended—though he did not finish—high school, in Española, on good days a ride of twenty minutes or so by car. Now he lives in Los Alamos.

"I am a mother. You will forgive me if I am proud; sometimes I know I have been boastful, and I tell the confessor my sin. Domingo was a smart child. He walked quickly. He talked very well from the start. He did good work in school. We would take a walk, and he would point something out to me; often, I had never noticed it before. Before he'd entered school, he told me he wanted to become a priest. I asked him why. He said because he'd like to know all the secrets of God. It was my fault, of course. He would ask me questions—those endless whys all children ask, I later learned, after I had my second and third and fourth sons—and I would be puzzled, and not know what to answer. So I would say the same thing my

mother used to say to us: 'That is one of God's secrets.' She died when she
was ninety, and well before that my little Domingo had asked her when
she would die. He had spoken out of turn, and I lowered my head in
shame—as I was taught to do when I was a girl, as I brought up my children
to do, as, thank God, my grandchildren now do. But my mother smiled,
and said, 'That is one of God's secrets.' After that, I think, I started to copy
her words with my boy Domingo—though memory becomes moldy after
a while and falls into pieces.

"I am taking you through side streets. I am sorry. Maybe we never know
our own confusion; maybe it takes another to help us see what we have come
to. I wanted to tell you about Domingo's teachers. They were Anglos.
Today, some of our own people teach in the schools, but not many.
Domingo was called brilliant by his teachers. They called me in. They said
he was the only child in his class who was bright and who belonged, really
belonged, in school. They made me listen to their trials. I was young then,
and obedient. I listened. Maybe now I would ask them please to excuse me,
but I have to go home—the bread I have to make, you know, before supper.
But my husband says no, even this very year we would still stay and nod
our heads. Can you dare turn away from your child's teachers, just to satisfy
your own anger? Our Spanish-speaking young people, our college students,
say yes; but they live far away, under different conditions, not these here.

"The teachers never mentioned college to me. They weren't *that* hopeful about Domingo. I don't think they even thought about a person like us
going to college. He just might be worthy of high school, I was told. They
had never before said that about one of our children, I was told. He is an
exceptional boy, I was told. How did it come about, I was asked. Well, of
course, I smiled and said I didn't know. They asked about Domingo's
father: Was he smarter than the others? I said no, none of us are 'smart'—
just trying to get by from day to day, and it's a struggle. That was a bad
time—1930 and the years right after it. Weeks would go by and we would
see no money. (We still see little.) And I had already lost four little
children; the last two were born in good health, but they died of pneumonia—one at age two, one at age three. You can put yourself in my shoes,
I hope. Then, if you will just carry yourself back in time and imagine how
hard it was for us, and how little we knew, you will see that I had no way
of answering those teachers. On the way home, I asked myself, *Is* young
Domingo 'smart'? Is his father 'smart'? I was afraid to ask his father that
evening. He was so tired, so fearful we'd lose even the land under us. He
said he'd die and kill us, the child and me, before we went to a city and

became lost. When I heard him speaking like that, I forgot the teachers and their questions. I served him my bread, and he felt better. Reassured—that is the word."

She stops and serves bread. She pours coffee. It is best black, she says in a matter-of-fact way; the visitor will not be judged for his weak stomach or poor taste. She again apologizes for her failure to tell a brief, pointed, coherent story. Perhaps she should be asked a question or two right now, she says. Her mother was "sunny," was "very sunny," until the end, but she worries about "clouds" over her own thinking. The two Domingos in her life scoff at the idea, though. After the coffee, she wants to go on. She likens herself to a weathered old tree within sight outside the house. It is autumn, and the tree is bare. She likens the coffee to a God-given miracle: suddenly one feels as if spring had come, one is budding and ready to go through another round of things. But she is definitely short of breath, coffee or no coffee, and needs no one to point it out. "Tomorrow, then."

In the morning, Dolores García is usually far stronger, and quicker to speak out, than later in the day. "Every day is like a lifetime," she says, and immediately disavows ownership of the thought. Her husband has said that for years, and, to be honest, she has upon occasion taken issue with him. Some days start out bad, and only in the afternoon does she feel in reasonably good spirits. But she does get up at five every morning, and most often she is at her best when the first light appears. Her visitor arrives at around nine o'clock. By then, he is convinced, she has done enough to feel a little tired and somewhat nostalgic. "Each day for me is a gift. My mother taught us to take nothing for granted. We would complain, or beg, as children do before they fall asleep, and she would remind us that if we were really lucky we would have a gift presented to us in the morning: a whole new day to spend and try to do something with. I suppose we should ask for more than that, but it's too late for me to do so. I prefer to sit here on my chair with my eyes on the mountains. I prefer to think about how the animals are doing; many of them have put themselves to sleep until spring. God has given them senses, and they use them. Things are not so clear for us. So many pushes and pulls, so many voices—I know what Babel means. I go in town shopping, and there is so much argument—everyone has an opinion on something. The only time some people lower their heads these days is on Sunday morning, for an hour, and even then they are turning around and paying attention to others. What is she wearing? How is he doing with his business? Do we any longer care what the Lord wants us to know and do?

"I am sorry. I am like a sheep who disobeys and has to be given a prod. I don't lose my thoughts when they're crossing my mind; it's when they have to come out as words that I find trouble. We should be careful with our thoughts, as we are with our water. When I'm up and making breakfast, I watch for changes in the light. Long before the sun appears, it has forewarned us. Nearer and nearer it comes, but not so gradually that you don't notice. It's like one electric light going on after another. First there is dark. Then the dark lifts ever so little. Still, it might be a full moon and midnight. Then the night is cut up. It becomes a sliver of what it was, and Domingo will sometimes stop for a minute and say, 'Dolores, she is gone, but do not worry. She will be back.' He has memories like mine: his mother lived to be eighty-seven, and all her life she spoke like mine. 'Domingo, be glad,' she would tell him. Why should he be glad? His mother knew: 'God has chosen you for a trial here, so acquit yourself well every day, and never mind about yesterday or tomorrow.' We both forget her words, though. As the sun comes out of hiding and there is no longer any question that the dark will go away, we thank dear God for his generosity, but we think back sometimes. We can't seem to help ourselves. We hold on and try to keep in mind the chores that await us, but we are tempted, and soon we will be slipping. There is a pole in our fire station. Once the men are on it, there is no stopping. We land with a crash, like them, on those sad moments. We feel sorry for ourselves. We wish life had treated us more kindly. I wonder what would happen to us if we did not have a job to do. We might never come back to this year of 1973. We would be the captives of bad memories. But no worry—we are part of this world here. The sun gets stronger and burns our consciences; the animals make themselves known; on a rainy day the noise of the water coming down the side of the house calls to me—why am I not moving, too?"

She actually does move rather quickly—so quickly that she seems almost ashamed when someone takes notice of her quickness, even if silently. When in her seat, she folds her arms, then unfolds them and puts her hands on her lap, her left hand over her right hand. Intermittently, she breaks her position to reach her coffee cup and her bread. "Domingo and I have been having this same breakfast for over fifty years. We are soon to be married fifty-five years, God willing. We were married a month after the Great War ended—it was a week before Christmas, 1918. The priest said he hoped our children would always have enough food and never fight in a war. I haven't had a great variety of food to give my family, but they have not minded. I used to serve the children eggs in the morning, but Domingo and I have stayed with hot bread and coffee. My fingers would die if they didn't have the dough to work over. I will never give up my old oven for a new one. It has been here forty years and is an old friend. I would stop baking bread if she gave out. My sons once offered to buy me an electric range—they called it—and I broke down. It was a terrible thing to do. The boys felt bad. My husband said I should be more considerate. I meant no harm, though. I didn't deliberately say to myself, Dolores García, you have been hurt, so now go and cry. The tears came, and I was helpless before them. Later, my husband said they all agreed I was in the right: the stove has been so good to us, and there is nothing wrong—the bread is as tasty as ever, I believe. It is a sickness, you know—being always dissatisfied with what you have, and eager for a change."

She stops there and looks lovingly around the room. She says she is attached to every piece of furniture. Her husband made it all: a round table, eight chairs, with four more in their bedroom, the beds there, the bureau there. She begins to tell how good Domingo is at carving wood. "That is what I would like to say about Domingo: he plants, builds, and harvests; he tries to keep us alive and comfortable with his hands. We sit on what he has made, eat what he has grown, sleep on what he has put together. We have never had a spring on our bed, but, I have to admit, we bought our mattress. Buying—that is the sickness. I have gone to the city and watched people. They are hungry, but nothing satisfies their hunger. They come to stores like flies to flypaper: they are caught. I often wonder who is better off. The fly dies. The people have to pay to get out of the store, but soon they are back again, the same look in their eyes. I don't ask people to live on farms and make chairs and tables, but when I see them buying things they don't need, or even want—except to make a purchase, to get something—then I say there is a sickness. I talked to the priest about this. He said yes, he knows. But then he shrugged. I knew what he was thinking: the Devil is everywhere, and not until Judgment Day will we be free of him. I watch my son Domingo and his son Domingo. They both have plans: next year, we buy this; the year after, that. Such plans are sad to hear. I try to tell them, but they do not listen. Those are the moments when I feel old—the only time I do. I turn to the priest. He says I am sinning—my pride makes me think I can disagree with the way the whole country works. I reply, 'No, Father, just what I hear my own son and grandson saying.' Hasn't a mother got the right to tell her own flesh and blood that they are becoming slaves—that is it, slaves of habits and desires that have nothing to do with living a good life?"

She sighs, and stops talking. She breaks her bread up into small pieces and eats them one by one. She stirs her coffee with a stick her husband made expressly for the purpose; it is about six inches long, smoothed out and painted green. He jokes with her: one day she will decide to add milk to her coffee, because her stomach will demand it, and she will comply; then she will really need that stick. But she has never used milk. Eventually, she puts the stick down and resumes talking. "I am not a priest. I read the Bible, go to church, make my confession, and know I will soon need to come back to tell more. But a good life is a life that is obedient to God's rules, and a life that is your own, not someone else's. God, and God alone, owns us; it is not right that others own us. There are many kinds of slavery. My children would come home from school and tell me that they were glad they were not colored, because colored people once were slaves. 'Watch out,' I'd say. Their father would agree—you can become a slave without even knowing it. You can be white and have money but not own your soul. I remember years ago I took the children to town; they were young and they wanted to see Santa Claus. He would come once, and only once—and it turned out we had missed him. Next year, I told the boys. They pouted. They besought me. They wanted me to take them somewhere, anywhere, as long as they could catch sight of Santa Claus. I held my ground. They would not stop. I said 'No is no.' They said, 'Please.' Finally, I had to go after them. I talked as if I were giving a sermon in church. Maybe I ought not to have spent so much of their time and mine, but I had to tell them, once and for all, that we have our land, and we feed ourselves and live the best lives we know how to, and we must never feel empty and worthless because of a Santa Claus, or because a salesman has beckoned us and we have said, 'No, I haven't the money.'

"Later, I wondered whether I'd done the right thing. I told my husband that Santa Claus is different. Children love him, and why not try very hard to take them to see him? He thought for a while. When he thinks, he takes up his pipe and uses it more than he usually does. With each puff, I say to myself, There goes one of his thoughts—and I wonder when he'll share them with me. Soon he does, though. It never fails; he puts his pipe down, and then I know I'm to get ready and pay attention. I sit down, and soon I hear. He always starts with, 'My wife, let me tell you what I think.' Soon I know what he thinks, because he's not one to hide behind pretty phrases. As for Santa Claus, Domingo told me what he thought of him: very little. I will never forget his words. He said that Santa Claus has been captured by the storekeepers. He said that they have him locked up, and he will never be free until we stop turning Christmas into a carnival, a time when people become drunk on their greed and take to the stores in order to indulge themselves. Of course, the priest lectures us in the same way. And I know we all can be greedy. I eat too much of my bread—more than I need. I shouldn't. Sometimes I punish myself: the oven is empty for a day or two—once, for a week, after a holiday. That time, Domingo couldn't stand it any longer. 'I am starving,' he told me—even though I made him cereal and eggs instead. But bread for him is life, and I never stopped so long again. I had made a mistake. A nun said to me, 'Punishment for a sin can be a sin.' If you are proud of yourself for doing penance, you are defeated before you start."

She stops to open the window and summon her husband. Maybe *he* should say exactly what he told his boys a long time ago about Santa Claus. But no, it is hopeless—he will not come in until he has finished his work. He is like a clock—so many minutes to do one thing, then another. The cows know the difference between him and anyone else. He is quick. They get fast relief. When one of her sons tries to help, or she does, or a grandchild, it is no good. The animals are restless, make a lot of noise, and Domingo pleads: Leave him his few jobs; then, when he goes, sell the animals. As for Santa Claus, forgotten for a moment, the gist of Domingo's speech is given by his wife: "My children, a saint is in chains, locked up somewhere, while all these stores have their impostors. Will you contribute to a saint's suffering? Santa Claus was meant to bring good news: the Lord's birthday is in the morning, so let us all celebrate by showing each other how much love we feel. Instead, we say, I want, I want, I want. We say, More, more, more. We say, Get this, then the next thing, and then the next. We lose our heads. We lose our souls. And somewhere that saint must be in hiding—maybe in jail, for all we know. If not, he is suffering. I tell you this not to make you feel bad. It is no one's fault. We are all to blame. Only, let us stop. If we stop, others will not, I know. But that will be their sorrow, not ours to share with them."

She is not ready to guarantee every word as his. He is a man of few words, and she readily admits that she tends to carry on. Then, as if to confess what is not a sin, and so is not meant for a priest, yet bothers her, she goes further and admits to talking out loud when no one is around. She is sure her husband doesn't do so, and she envies him his quiet self-assurance, his somewhat impassive temperament. "He is silent not because he has nothing to say. He is silent because he understands the world, and because he knows enough to say to himself, What will words and more words do to make the world any better? I have wished for years that I could be like him, but God makes each of us different. When our son Domingo went to school, they began teaching him English. We had learned English ourselves, enough to speak. But we didn't speak it—only Spanish. When Domingo started learning English, we decided to speak it more and more at home. The same with the other boys. Often, I would rehearse my English by myself. I would learn words and expressions from the priest and from the mayor of the town. He was a cousin, and was always doing business with Anglos. I learned to talk to myself in English—to my husband in Spanish but to myself in English. Once, my husband overheard me, and he thought I was delirious. He asked if I had a fever. I said no, none at all. He said I sounded as if I did. I said I was learning to speak English. He said he could speak English, but not to himself. Then he laughed, and said, 'Dolores, you have spoken Spanish to yourself, too. I have heard you.' Since then, I have been more careful, and I don't believe my husband knows that I still have the habit. I do not talk to teach myself English, though. I talk because my mind fills up with words and then they spill out. Sometimes I talk with someone I imagine nearby. Sometimes I talk to myself. Sometimes it is in Spanish, sometimes in English."

After all the talk of talk, she has nothing more to say. She has to clean the house. She has to start a soup. She always has soup. As one pot begins to empty, she starts another going. It contains bones and vegetables. Soup— that is all it is called. Then she has to sew. There are clothes to mend, clothes to make. Her eyes aren't what they used to be, but with glasses she can see well enough. And, finally, the radio. She prefers the radio to television. She listens to music. She listens to the weather forecast and either nods or scoffs. Her sons hear the forecasts and actually believe what they hear. She knows better. She decides early in the morning what the weather will be like, and only wants to know how good those weathermen are, with their instruments and their reports from God knows what cities far off. She feels sorry for them: they have a lot to learn. She hopes that one day they will go outside and look at the sky rather than take their readings. It is one more bit of foolishness we have to live with now. "Years ago, there were not these weather reports all the time. We would go out and size up the morning. We could tell. We felt the moisture before it turned to rain. If we had any questions, we prayed, and then more often than not we found an answer. I don't believe it was God's either. The priest long ago warned us not to ask Him for favors, and not to expect His answers for the small favors we want. He is up there; we are down here. Once we are born, it is up to us. We pray to show our faith. If we have faith, we can do what is necessary. Not everything was good in the old days: we used to ask God's help all the time and be disappointed. My mother would pray that her bread might come out good. I would pray for rain. I think we have stopped that, Domingo and I."

Now it is time to rest. Several times each day, she and her husband do so. It is up to her to call him, and she does it in such a way that he knows why. In a matter-of-fact way, she speaks his name, and slowly he comes in. It is ten o'clock when they rest first. They lie down for five or ten minutes only, but that does miracles for them. They get up refreshed not only in body but in mind and, evidently, soul. "I pray. I thank God for the time He has given me here, and ask Him to take me when He is ready, and I will tell Him I will have no regrets. I think of all I have seen in this long life—the people, the changes. Even up here, in this small village, the world makes its presence felt. I remember when the skies had no planes in them, houses no wires sticking up trying to catch television programs. I never wanted a refrigerator. I never needed one. But I have one. It is mostly empty. I have one weakness—ice cream. I make it, just as I make butter. I used to make small amounts, and Domingo and I would finish what was there. Now I can make and store up butter and ice cream and give presents of them to my sons and their children. No wonder they bought us the refrigerator! As I lie on our bed and stare at the ceiling, I think how wonderful it is—eighty-three, and still able to make ice cream. We need a long rest afterward, but between the two of us we can do a good job. The man at the store has offered to sell any extra ice cream we have; he says he can get a good price. I laugh. I tell him he's going to turn me into a thief. It would be dishonest to sell food you make in your home for profit at a store. That's the way I feel. My husband gets angry: 'What do you mean, "dishonest"?' he will say. I answer back: My idea of what is dishonest is not his. So we cannot go on about this. It is in my heart where the feeling is, not in my head. 'Oh, you are a woman!' he answers, and he starts laughing. Later, he will tell me that he was picking weeds, or taking care of our flowers, and he thought to himself, She is right, because to make food is part of our life as a family, and to start selling—that is to say that we have nothing that is *ours*. It is what he always comes back to: Better to have less money and feel we own ourselves than more and feel at the mercy of so many strangers."

The two Garcías show a burst of energy after they get up. As they have rested, said their prayers, reminisced, they have also given thought to what they will do next, and so when they are ready they set out decisively. They know that they have limited time, know that soon they will have to interrupt their working rhythm for lunch and another rest afterward. "I am a new person several times a day," she points out, then adds, right away, "But I can suddenly get quite tired." She feels "weakness" and "a loss of breath" come on—her way of describing the effects of a cardiovascular difficulty common to people in their eighties. Yet she sees no doctor—hasn't seen one in decades. "There are no doctors near here. I would have to go to Española. I would if there was a need. I have pains all over. It is arthritis, I know. One can't expect joints to hold up forever. I do not believe in aspirin. I do not believe in medicines. I have to pant like our dog when I move too fast for too long. I have to stop and catch up. It is the lungs and the heart, I know. My son wants me to go get a checkup. My ankles swell at the end of a day, but the next morning they are down again. The body has its seasons. I am in the last one; winter is never without pain and breakdowns. I don't want to spend my last years waiting on myself and worrying about myself. I have already lived over twice as long as our Saviour. How greedy ought one to be for life? God has His purposes. I wake up and feel those aches and I notice how wrinkled my skin is, and I wonder what I'm doing still alive. I believe it is wrong to ask a question like that. One lives; one dies. To ask questions with no good answers to them is to waste time that belongs to others. I am here to care for my husband, to care for this house, to be here when my sons and my grandchildren come. The young have to see what is ahead. They have to know that there is youth and middle age and old age. My grandson Domingo asked me a while ago what it is like to be one hundred. He is ten. I told him to be one hundred is to live ten of his lifetimes. He seemed puzzled, so I knew I had been thoughtless. I put my arms around him. I put my hand beside his and we compared skins. I said it is good to be young and it is good to be old. He didn't need any more explanations. He said that when you're young you have a lot of years before you but when you're old you have your children and your grandchildren and you love them and you're proud of them. I put my arms around him again and hugged him tight, and in a second he was out there with his father and his grandfather looking at the cows."

She doesn't spend much time with the cows, but the chickens are hers to feed and look after. She cleans up their fenced-in enclosure, and delights in their eggs. She and her husband have one hard-boiled egg each for lunch every day. She gives her sons eggs regularly; a nephew and a niece also get some. She feeds the chickens leftovers and, in addition, some of her fresh

bread. She is convinced that they lay better eggs because of her bread. One day, for the sake of a visitor, she borrowed a store-bought egg and compared it with one of hers: each was dropped in hot water for poaching, and hers did indeed stay much more nearly intact and prove to be tastier. "Animals today are turned into machines," she remarked after the experiment. She shook her head. She tried not to be gloomy, but she was worried. "No one my age has the right to demand that the world stand still. So much was wrong in the past that is better now. I didn't want this refrigerator, but it is good to have, now that I'm used to it. My grandchildren have had narrow misses with death, but doctors have saved them. I still mourn the children I lost. Even if I'd been rich back then, I might have lost them. Now there are medicines to kill the bad germs. But to see chickens or cows being kept in one place and stuffed with food that isn't really food—chemicals, Domingo says they are fed—so they will grow fat all of a sudden and have their eggs or become fit for slaughter: that is unnatural. I ask myself, Did God form the beasts of the field and the fowls of the air so that they should be treated this way by man? I asked the priest once, and he scratched his head and said he would have to think about it. The next time I saw him, I looked at him hard and he remembered my question. 'Mrs. García, you don't make it easy for me,' he said. I smiled, and said I didn't want to cause any trouble but I couldn't help thinking about some of these things. He answered, 'I don't know what to say.' Then I decided I'd best not trouble him any more. He once told me that a priest knows only what Christ promised us; He will bring about His promises—that's not for man to know. I thought afterward I ought to confess to him my boldness—the sin of pride. Who am I to decide they have no right to run those chicken farms? But, God forgive me, I still believe it is wrong. I still believe animals ought not to be turned into machines."

She arranges the eggs she brings in very carefully; she takes them out of her basket and puts them in a bowl. Some are brown, some white. She likes to fix them up like flowers, have them give a freckled appearance from afar. As she uses some, she rearranges those left. She handles them not only with care but with affection. Sometimes, as she talks and does her work with the eggs, she will hold a warm one in her hand. "I feel comforted by a fresh egg. It is sad to feel it get colder, but that is life. My granddaughter loves to help me collect eggs. The other day, she asked me if the eggs inside a woman are the same kind as those that come out of a chicken. I was taken aback. I told her I didn't think so. Then I wondered what else to say. My husband said later there isn't anything more to say. I felt I'd failed the little

girl though. I had changed the subject on her before she knew what had happened. A few minutes later, I could tell that her mind was back with the eggs and she wanted to ask me more questions. But I wouldn't let her. I didn't tell her no—at least, not directly. I just kept up my line of chatter. The poor girl, she was overcome by her grandmother's words—and by her own shyness. This time, I didn't go to the priest later and ask him what I should have said. I have never talked to him about such matters. When one is young, they are too personal, and, besides, what is there to ask, and what is there to say? Also, a priest is entitled to respect: he is not living a worldly life, and there is much he doesn't know. I think our new priest is like a youth, even if he is fifty; I mean, he has never tasted of life. That is what a priest is about, of course; his passions go up toward the altar, and then to Heaven. So I sat and thought about how to talk with my grand-daughter the next time. I hope I can do her some justice. Time will tell. One never knows what to say except when the moment is at hand."

She stops abruptly, as if this were one conversation she didn't want to pursue. Anyway, she has been dusting and sweeping the floor as she talked, and now she is finished. Next come the plants, a dozen or so of them; they need to be watered, and moved in or out of the sun. She hovers over them for a minute, doing nothing, simply looking. She dusts them, too. She prunes one. "I've been waiting for a week or so to do this. I thought to myself, That plant won't like it, losing so much. I dread cutting my toenails and fingernails. I am shaky with scissors. But I go after the plants with a surer touch. They are so helpless, yet they are so good to look at. They seem to live forever. Parts die, but new parts grow. I have had them so long—I don't remember the number of years. I know each one's needs, and I try to take care of them at the same time each day. Maybe it is unnecessary nonsense, the amount of attention I give. I know that is what Domingo would say. Only once did he put his belief into words, and then I reminded him that he has his habits, too. No one can keep him from starting in one corner of his garden and working his way to the other, and with such care. I asked him years ago why not change around every once in a while and begin on the farthest side, and go faster. 'I couldn't do it,' he said, and I told him I understood. Habits are not crutches; habits are roads we have paved for ourselves. When we are old, and if we have done a good job, the roads last and make the remaining time useful: we get where we want to go, and without the delays we used to have when we were young. How many plants died on me when I was first learning! How often I forgot to water them, or watered them too much because I wanted to do right! Or I would expose them to the sun and forget that, like us, they need the shade,

too. I was treating them as if they needed a dose of this, a trial of that. But they have been removed from God's forests, from nature, and they need consideration. When we were young, my husband also used to forget chores; he'd be busy doing one thing and he'd overlook another. But slowly we built up our habits, and now I guess we are protected from another kind of forgetfulness. The head tires easily when you are our age, and without the habits of the years you can find yourself at a loss to answer the question: What next?"

She turns to lunch. She stirs the soup. She warms up the bread. She reaches for the eggs. She sets a simple, careful table, a large spoon and a knife for her, her husband, and their guest. Each gets a napkin from a set given her half a century ago by her mother and used on Sundays, holidays, special occasions. She is apologetic. "I fear we often look at these napkins but don't use them. No wonder they survive so well! They remind us to behave ourselves, because it is no ordinary day, and so we eat more carefully and don't have to use them. They are usually in the same condition when I put them away as when I took them out. My grandmother made them, gave them to my mother, and now I have them. My three daughters died as infants; I will give the napkins to my eldest son's wife. I tried to do so when they were married, but she said no. I insisted, and only got more refusals. If she had been my daughter, she would have accepted. But I was not hurt. It takes time to move over from one family and be part of another. She would accept the napkins now, but they would become frightened if I suddenly offered them. 'Is she sick? Does she know something we don't know? How have we neglected her, that she offers us what she loves to put on her own table?' So I will have them until the end, when all possessions obtain new masters."

She has to go outside. It is cold and windy but sunny. There is some fresh milk there in a pail—from cows that, she hastens to add, present no danger of sickness to a visitor who up until that moment has taken for granted the word *pasteurized* that appears on every milk bottle or carton. And she has herself and her husband as proof—a touch of reassurance that she obviously enjoys being able to offer. "My sons' wives sometimes hesitate, too. I can see on their faces what they think. They deny it, but I know: Is it safe to drink milk right from the cow? They are from the city, and they have no way of understanding that many cows are quite healthy and their owners know when they are sick. Anyway, Domingo and I survived without store milk, and we are not young, and not so sick we can't work or eat—or drink milk."

She wraps herself in a sweater she has made and, upon opening the door, quickly turns back for a moment: "Oh, the wind." But she persists, and is gone. When she is back, she resumes where she has left off. "The wind can be a friend or an enemy. A severe wind reminds us of our failures— something we forgot to fasten down. A gentle wind is company. I have to admit I can spend a long time listening to the wind go through trees, watching it sweep across the grass. Domingo will come in and say, 'Oh, Dolores, come out and watch the wind go through the grass.' I hurry out. I often wonder if the ground feels it—like hair being combed and brushed. I walk with our dog, and he gets scents from far off, carried by the wind. I tell him not to be tricked. Better to let things quiet down, then take another scent. He is over ten and should not run long distances. He doesn't know his own limits. But who does, exactly? It takes a lifetime to get used to your body, and by the time you do, then it is almost time to say goodbye and go elsewhere. I often wonder whether the wind carries our souls skyward. It is another of my foolish ideas, and I put it to the priest long ago—not this one but the one who came before him. He was annoyed with me. 'Mrs. García,' he said, 'you have an active imagination.' I apologized. He reminded me that God's ways are not ours. I wanted to tell him that the wind comes mysteriously from above and might be one of many good, strong arms our Lord has. But I knew that to keep quiet was best. He was a very stern priest, and outspoken. He would not have hesitated to talk to me severely and warn me publicly that I would pay for that kind of talk in Hell. Once, he cuffed my husband because Domingo told him he'd heard that much of our weekly collection was being sent to Africa or Asia, to places far off, and meanwhile so many people hereabouts were without work and were going hungry.

"It was in the bad years—in the nineteen-thirties. We were poor, but at least we had our land. Others had nothing. And the priest was fat. He was waited on, and he dined on the best; we were told that by the woman who cooked for him. Mind you, she did not serve him. He had to have someone special to do that. And he paid them a pittance. They had children they were supporting—and, alas, husbands, too. In a good mood, he would promise them an eternity in Heaven. On bad days, he would threaten them with Purgatory and no escape—so, of course, they would leave his kitchen in tears, clutching their rosary beads all the way home. My husband heard of this and was enraged. He said terrible things. I pleaded with him to stop. We were so poor, and the bank threatened to take away our small farm. Some people had thought of marching on the bank. The bank officials heard of the plan and never made a move against us. By then, I had lost four children. I will not repeat what Domingo said about the priest, or the Church. The worse his language, the harder I prayed. I knelt by my bed and prayed one evening after he had carried on a full hour, it seemed; it must really have been a few minutes, I now know, but I thought he would never stop. Then a heavy wind came, later that evening, and I was sure God was approaching us to exact his punishment. And why not, after Domingo's outburst? Domingo was tidying up outside. He had calmed down. I had heard him say a Hail Mary, but I pretended to be lost in my own work. He didn't want me to know that he had taken back the words he had spoken; he is proud. I decided to pray for him, but I was sure something bad would happen. Nothing did, though; the wind came, then left. A week afterward, I told Domingo of my fears. He laughed, and said we are too intelligent, both of us, even without education to be superstitious. I agreed. But a month later he came in one day for lunch and he told me he had to confess something to me. I said, 'Not to me, to the priest.' No, he had very little to tell that priest—only the briefest of admissions once a month. I said nothing. He said that he'd been afraid, too, that evening after he lost his temper. When the wind came, and he was outside, and the horses started whinnying and the dog ran back and forth, he did not know what to do or why the animals were upset, so he had got down on his knees and asked God's forgiveness. He'd even asked Him to take us both, with the house— through a tornado, perhaps. But soon it became very still, and I think both of us must have been holding our breath, without knowing we were doing so together—like so much else we do. I fear that when he goes I will, or when I go he will. But I have no right to such thoughts; it is not up to me or to Domingo but to our Lord and Saviour. We are sinners, though, and we can't help being selfish. There will be no future for either of us alone. I only hope we are not tested by being separated for too long by death."

When her husband comes in, without being called, she says that it is now noon. They go by the sun. They have a clock in their bedroom, but they rarely use it. They forget to wind it, except when their son Domingo is coming and they want to show him that they like his present. "Domingo gave us the clock, and I treasure it," she says. "I look at it and think of him. We have only two sons. It is nice to be reminded of them. I don't mean to sound as if I pitied myself. Our son Domingo works at Los Alamos. He says it is maintenance he does; he looks after all those scientists. They leave their laboratories in a mess, and someone has to pick up after them or everything would stop one day. He gets a good wage, and jobs are few around here, so he is lucky to be there. He could have stayed with us, worked on the land. But all we have is our animals and the crops—no money. I put up many jars for the winter, but jars of food are not enough to attract young people, and I see their view. There are a hundred like Domingo who would like his job. Before they brought in the laboratories at Los Alamos, there was nothing anywhere near here. Domingo would be in Albuquerque, I believe, if it hadn't been for Los Alamos. My younger son is down there. I've never even been to Santa Fe. He drives up here on weekends. His life is different, in the city. I don't ask him much; I wouldn't understand. His wife longs to come back here. He does, too. But how can they? No work. Domingo was interviewed several times for his job. He took a test, I believe. He did well. The teachers who predicted good for him—they were right. It's too bad he didn't finish high school; the war came—the one against Japan and Hitler.

"Then came the next war. My second son, Francisco, went to Korea. He was there for many months. I remember well the Saturday morning that I got news of him. I remember the day he came home. I was sitting in this very chair. I had to mend some of my husband's clothes. I was almost through, and my mind, as it does, was already preparing for the next step in the day—a visit outside to pick some tomatoes. Suddenly, the door opened, with no warning. Who could it be? The front door, hardly ever used, rather than the side one, right here. My boy Domingo—he lived with us then, and worked as a handyman in the school where they had always thought so well of him. He had his suit on. 'Domingo,' I said, 'why the suit?' He did not answer. For a second, I wondered how he had slipped in and put it on without my knowing. We will do anything not to see what is right before us. I believe I might have wondered and wondered about such petty questions, but after Domingo came his father, also with a suit on. I got up and shouted, 'It is not Sunday!' I said it over and over again. 'It is not, it is not!' Then I started crying. They never told me. I never asked. I just knew. My husband asked me if I wanted to change my dress. I said no. I am a plain woman, and my son was a plain man—no pretenses. He did not die in his Sunday clothes. They turned around, and I followed them. We walked down that road, two miles. I saw nothing. I heard nothing. I was alone, even though they were with me, one on each side. Once, I must have looked near collapse. I felt their hands and was surprised to see them standing there. Then I dropped my beads. I picked them up, but I didn't say the Rosary. I just kept holding on to the beads. They had brought the body to the basement of the school building, a United States flag around it. Later, after the funeral, they wanted to give me that flag.

I said no, it could stay at the school. Let children see what war means. That is something they should learn—as much as how to read and write and count."

She has gone beyond her sense of what is correct for her to say. Who is she to talk about wars? They come about through events she has no knowledge of. She has a place in God's scheme of things, and best to stay in it. But something makes her restless, however she tries to put aside her doubts and misgivings. She stands up, walks toward her plants and examines them, one by one. They are all right. She goes back to her chair. Then she is up offering coffee, serving a delicious chocolate marble cake she has made—with the help of a packaged mix, a concession to her daughter-in-law's urging. Once again seated, she interrupts a conversation about "the new road"—the road in front of her house, which now, for the first time, is paved—to put into words what she can't stop thinking about. "There was another time. Two years ago, before that road was fixed up to be so strong it can ignore the weather, I had walked down to talk with my neighbor. She had suffered badly from pneumonia but was on the mend. As I came toward the house, I saw them again. You know, this time I thought my mind had left me. I wiped my eyes, but they wouldn't go away. I called to them, but they didn't answer, so I was sure they were not there. It was late afternoon, a time when shadows begin to appear and one can be fooled anyway. So I wiped my eyes again, and when they remained I looked around, hoping to see them in back of me, too. Then I would know: my eyes, my head—something for a doctor to heal, or a warning from God that it won't be long. Well, soon they were upon me; it was only when I *felt* them that I believed they were there and I was there. I remember thinking that perhaps I'd fallen asleep at my neighbor's, or maybe I'd taken a nap at my own house and now was waking up. In a second, one can have such thoughts. In another second, one can know everything without hearing a word. It was my third son. I said, 'How did it happen?' My husband couldn't talk. I held on to him and wanted him to tell me, but he was speechless. My son Domingo tried to tell me, but he couldn't finish his story. He had used the word *car*, and that was enough for me. Later, they tried to give me the details, and I begged them to stop. Those suits on a day in the middle of the week! There have been days since when I have wanted to burn those suits or tear them to shreds. There have been days when I have lost all faith. I dared not go to confession—I could not let a priest hear what was in my mind. I cringed before God, knowing He hears everything, even what is not spoken but crosses the mind—a rabbit of an idea, suddenly upon you, quickly chased away, but back again in an unsuspecting moment, when all is quiet."

With that, she stops talking and looks out of the window. What ought a visitor to do—sit still and wait or find an excuse to leave immediately? Suddenly, she makes the question rhetorical. She is talking again, a bit more softly and slowly and reflectively, but with no apparent distress. And she seems to want to talk. "The mountains, our mountains—I look at them when I need an anchor. They are here. They never leave us. Birds come, stay awhile, leave. The moon is here, then gone. Even the sun hides from us for days on end. Leaves don't last, or flowers. We have had a number of dogs, and I remember them in my prayers. But those mountains are *here*. They are nearer God than we are. Sometimes I imagine Him up there, on top of one or another mountain, standing over us, getting an idea how we're doing. It is wrong to think like that, I know. But a poor old woman like me can be allowed her foolishness. Who is without a foolish hope? Who doesn't make up dreams to fit his wishes? Sometimes I walk up toward the mountains. I can't go as far now as before. I don't tell my husband I'm going; he would worry that I'd lose my breath completely and no one would be around. But I go slowly, and, as I say, I have to be content with approaching those hills.

"The other day, I walked toward them, and there was a meeting on the side of the road. I stopped and listened. I never went any farther. They were our young, and some people from the city. Chicanos—they spoke of Chicanos. We are Chicanos—nothing else will do, they said. I came home and told my husband. Yes, he said, we are Chicanos. We are so many things, he said. Mexican-American, Mexicano, they'd call my boys at school, those Anglo teachers. I would say nothing. They thought then it was their right to call us what they pleased. Spanish—we are Spanish. Many of us may have some Indian blood, too. But I will tell you: I am a woman and a mother, and Domingo is a man and a father, and both of us belong to this country and no other, and we owe allegiance to the State of New Mexico. Should we give ourselves one name or another, or should we get each day's job done? I can't believe Christ wants us to be Anglo against Chicano, or Chicano against Anglo. But the world is full of bitterness, and when will there be an end to it, *when*, I wondered while I walked home. It is a bad thing to say, but I was glad to come upon that meeting; it took my mind off myself and my memories. I saw that others want to know why there is so much injustice in the world. For a few days after my son was killed in the accident, I wondered again whether God cared. I know He is there,

watching over us, but I would wake up in the night and my forehead would
be wet and I would be shaking. I had dreamed that God had fallen asleep
and so we all were going to suffer: the Devil would win his fight. I thought
of those days, now gone, while I listened to the young people shouting
'Chicano!' They mentioned all the bad, nothing good. Domingo says that
is how it goes when people have been hurt, and I nodded, because I
remembered how I once felt."

One morning, in the midst of a conversation, she scolds herself for
talking too much. She falls silent. She glances up at a picture of Christ at
the Last Supper. Her face loses its tension. She slumps a bit, but not under
the weight of pain, or even age. She feels relaxed. There are a few dishes
to wash. There is a curtain that needs mending. There is not only bread
to make but also pies. Her grandchildren love her pies, and she loves seeing
the pies eaten. "Children eat so fast," she says with a sigh of envy. She
begins talking again. She resumes her activity. She says she has to pick at
her food now. "When one is over eighty, the body needs less," she ob-
serves—but immediately afterward she looks a little shy, a little apprehen-
sive. "I have no business talking like a doctor. Once, the priest told me I
talk like him. I told him, 'I have raised children; it is necessary at times to
give them sermons and hear their confessions.' He smiled. If I had another
life, I would learn to be a nurse. In my day, few of our people could aim
so high—not a woman like me, anyway. It is different today. My sons say
their children will finish high school, and my Domingo in Los Alamos says
his Domingo does so well in school he may go on to a college. I laugh with
my husband—a Domingo García in a college? Maybe the boy will be a
doctor. Who knows? He likes to take care of his dog. He has a gentle side
to him. He is popular with the girls, so I don't think he's headed for the
priesthood. He tells me he'd like to be a scientist, like the men his father
looks after in the laboratories. I worry that he would make those bombs,
though. I wouldn't want that on his conscience. My son told me they do
other things there in the laboratories, not just make bombs. I said, 'Thank
God!'

"Of course, all that is for the future. I do not know if I will be around
to see my grandchildren have children of their own. One cannot take
anything for granted. The priest laughed at Domingo and me last Sunday,
and said, 'You two will outlast me. You will be coming here when you are
both over one hundred.' I said, 'Thank you, Father, but that is a long way
off, to be a hundred, and much can happen.' 'Have faith,' he said, and he
is right. One must."

She pauses for a few seconds, as if to think about her own admonition. Then she is back on her train of thought. "Sometimes, after church, Domingo and I walk through the cemetery. It is a lovely place, small and familiar. We pay our respects to our parents, to our aunts and uncles, to our children. A family is a river; some of it has passed on and more is to come, and nothing is still, because we all move along, day by day, toward our destination. We both feel joy in our hearts when we kneel on the grass before the stones and say a prayer. At the edge of the cemetery, near the gate, is a statue of the Virgin Mary, larger than all the other stones. She is kneeling, and on her shoulder is the Cross. She is carrying it—the burden of her Son's death. She is sad, but she has not given up. We know that she has never lost faith. It is a lesson to keep in mind. We always leave a little sad at the sight of our Lord's mother under such a heavy obligation. But my husband never fails to hold my arm, and each Sunday his words are the same: 'Dolores, the Virgin will be an example to us this week.' It is as if each Sunday he were taking his vows—and me, too, because I say back to him, 'Yes, Domingo, she will be an example to us.' Now, mind you, an hour later one of us, or both of us, will have stumbled. I become cranky. Domingo has a temper. I hush him and he explodes. He is inconsiderate and I sulk. That is the way with two people who have lived together so long: the good and the bad are always there, and they have become part of one life, lived together."

She hears his footsteps coming and quickens her activity a bit. She will not be rushed, but he needs his coffee, and she needs hers. Often, she doesn't so much need coffee as need to drink it because he is drinking it. An outsider may observe how they take coffee: he lifts his up, she follows; he puts his down, and soon hers is also on the table. Always they get through at the same time. This particular morning, Domingo is more expansive and concerned than usual—a foal has just been born. "Well, enough. I must go check on the mother and her infant," he says. Near the door, he turns around to say goodbye. "These days, one never knows when the end will come," he says. "I know our time is soon up. But when I look at that mother horse and her child in the barn, or at my children and their children, I feel lucky to have been permitted for a while to be part of all this life here on earth." His hand is on the door, and he seems a little embarrassed that he has spoken so. But he has to go on. "I am talking like my wife now. After all these years, she sometimes falls into my silences and I carry on as she does. She is not just an old woman, you know. She wears old age like a bunch of fresh-cut flowers. She is old, advanced in years, *vieja,* but in

Spanish we have another word for her—a word that tells you that she has grown with all those years. I think that is something one ought to hope for and pray for and work for all during life: to grow, to become not only older but a bigger person. She is old, all right, *vieja,* but I will dare say this in front of her: she is *una anciana.* With that, I declare my respect and have to hurry back to the barn."

An Intense Eagerness to Live

"I get up before anyone else in my household, not because sleep has deserted me in my advancing years, but because an intense eagerness to live draws me from my bed."
MAURICE GOUDEKET
The Delights of Growing Old

"Awareness is the compensation that age gives us in exchange for mere action. . . . While everything else physical and mental seems to diminish, the appreciation of beauty is on the increase."
BERNARD BERENSON
Sunset and Twilight

"I wish I knew what people mean when they say they find 'emptiness' in this wonderful adventure of living, which seems to me to pile up its glories like an horizon-wide sunset as the light declines. I'm afraid I'm an incorrigible life-lover & life-wonderer & adventurer."

EDITH WHARTON, AGE 74
From *The Letters of Edith Wharton*
R. W. B. Lewis and Nancy Lewis, ed.

French writer Maurice Goudeket (1889–1977) was the husband of the distinguished French novelist and essayist Colette and the author of her biography. He was the "best friend" she speaks of in "The Blue Lantern" (following), her third husband, sixteen years younger. They met in 1925 when he was thirty-six and she was fifty-two, and were married for thirty years. A few years after Colette's death, M. Goudeket was married again to the young widow of an old friend. At the age of seventy-one his first child, a son, was born. The selection that follows is taken from the first chapter of his book of reminiscences about his life, *The Delights of Growing Old*.

from

THE DELIGHTS
OF GROWING OLD

You young people who are frightened at the thought of growing old must learn that there is no happier condition than that of an aged man. Faust was a halfwit who changed his state for yours, and little good it did him. To begin with, let me—I who shall be seventy-five before this book is finished—tell you a secret: it is not really a fact that you grow old at all.

And you, the seventy-five-year-olds, instead of helping to spread the usual mistaken notion based on mere superficial appearances, as you generally do, you ought to look into your hearts: apart from growing purer and more

Translated by Patrick O'Brian.

refined, has the "me" of your first adult years changed in any way? There is shortness of breath, a slowness of movement, a back that will not bend so easily, to be sure, but these are things for our bodies to cope with. The immaterial being that gives our threatened building all its life does not show a single wrinkle, nor will it ever do so.

I know very well that many of you are still disproportionately uneasy about your final exit. One might almost think that death—let's call a spade a spade—has not been at your elbow since you first drew breath. You ought rather to congratulate yourselves on now being safe from the many diseases that only occur in childhood or middle age. A little while ago a friend of mine, a medical man, told me confidentially, "Presently we shall no longer know how to get rid of you people. Pneumonia? Out of the question now; and the same goes for all the infectious diseases. Even your coronary cannot be relied upon. Of course, there's always cancer, but at your age it usually develops so slowly that there is time for you to die of something more agreeable."

For my own part, when the figure 75 happens to force itself upon my attention, my first reaction is astonishment. How can I possibly have got so far? Have I not made some mistake in my reckoning? They tell me I am so absent-minded. What is to be done, where am I to go, and who is going to listen to my complaint? But the next moment I calm down: after all, it is really something of a feat to have lived seventy-five years, in spite of illnesses, germs, accidents, disasters, and wars. And now every fresh day finds me more filled with wonder and better qualified to draw the last drop of delight from it. For up until now I had never known time's inexpressible wealth; and my youth had never entirely yielded itself to happiness. Is it indeed this that they call growing old, this continual surge of memories that comes breaking in on my inner silence, this contained and sober joy, this lighthearted music that bears me up, this wider window on the world, this spreading kindly feeling and this gentleness?

"I have nothing to do today." That is a remark that no longer has any sort of meaning for me. For if it should so chance that I am freed for a while from those everyday duties that by their very monotony give a feeling of emptiness, then so many activities open before me that my only difficulty is choosing between them. With these few free hours of mine in view, thousands of writers have written thousands of books on every conceivable subject, and hosts of artists in every age and country have brought into being a great body of work that the museums have gathered together for my personal benefit. From the earliest recorded time History unrolls, and unrolls for me, its flood of happenings, events so wonderfully wrought up and then resolved that no work of fiction ever reaches such heights of dramatic power and such unexpectedness.

I get up before anyone else in my household, not because sleep has deserted me in my advancing years, but because an intense eagerness to live draws me from my bed. In the same way I drop off every night with a kind of secret satisfaction as I think of the day to come, even if it is likely to be a dark one; for tomorrow is the future and tomorrow contains the whole of that which is possible.

Every morning my breakfast coffee has a fresh taste, and this comes as much from me as it does from the pot. There is the paper too, which will put me in touch with the entire world; and any paper, properly read, has an almost incredible amount of astonishing, moving, ludicrous items in it. Very soon the post will bring me a bill that I had not expected, but it may also bring a touching letter from an unknown correspondent and conceivably—why not indeed?—another from a solicitor telling me that some shatterbrained creature has left me a fortune.

I am surrounded by things, and these things, these objects, constitute my environment. I am surrounded by people, too, people who mean more to me than my own self—I hear them waking up. The morning's routine is made up of renewing my pact of friendship with these things, these beings, and myself.

Eventually I emerge into the street, and of all wonders, the street is the most wonderful. I do not always approach it the same way. Sometimes I adopt what I call my photographic eye, and then it breaks up into snapshots, set portraits, and groups. Sometimes I look rather for color, and the combinations of color. Sometimes it is hearing that takes precedence over the other senses. But always there are faces, a sea of faces, with everything that they conceal and everything that they give away. I set out, walking, walking, and toward me, surrounding me, there comes this passing show, these unresolved destinies that for a fleeting second brush against my own. At the same moment I feel both united to them and entirely separate. I walk on, on and on, faster and more happily; my senses grow sharper, my thoughts soar up and away, and all the time there is the humming of the great swarm of memories feeding upon my past years, and the mere throbbing of my arteries makes my head swim like wine.

My day has only just begun; I have hardly even begun to reckon up my intangible treasure. "We shall have to leave all this behind," groaned the dying Cardinal Mazarin as he dragged himself through the crowded galleries of his collection. Yet he had lived long enough to learn that anything that is capable of being grasped is also capable of slipping between one's fingers like so much sand. Why did he not turn his fading strength toward those possessions that he could own in a truer sense—a last crowning recollection of his happiest hours, a final human contact, a gleam of sunlight . . .

French writer Colette (Sidonie Gabrielle Claudine Colette)
(1873–1954), author of novels, short stories, essays, and plays,
wrote primarily about intimate, private life. Her own life was
rich in varied experiences; in addition to writing, she worked as
a dancer and a mime in music halls; during World War I she
turned her husband's estate into a hospital and worked as an army
nurse; after the war, she became a journalist; she married three
times.

The Blue Lantern was written when Colette was in her
seventies, incapacitated and almost immobilized by arthritis of
the hip following an accident. Although in constant pain, she
determined that she would be a cheerful old person, and resolved
to enjoy life in her lovely red room, lit by a blue shaded lamp,
deep in the heart of Paris.

from

THE BLUE LANTERN

We should not be unreasonably per-
turbed when our precious senses become dulled with age. I say "we", but
I am the text of my own sermon. My chief concern is lest I should mistake
the true nature of a condition which has come upon me gradually. It can
be given a name: it keeps me in a state of vigilance, of uncertainty, ready
to accept whatever may fall to my lot. The prospect gives rise to little that
is reassuring, but I have no choice.

More than once of late, turning my eyes from my book or my blue-tinted

Translated by Roger Senhouse.

writing paper towards the superb quadrangle that I am privileged to view from my window, I have thought 'The children in the Garden are not nearly so noisy this year,' and a moment later found myself finding fault with the door bell, the telephone, and the whole orchestral gamut of the radio for becoming progressively fainter. As for the china lamp—not the blue lantern that burns by day and night, of course, but the pretty one with flowers and arabesques painted on it—I was for ever scolding it unjustly: 'What can this wretched thing have been eating to make it so heavy?' Discoveries, ever more discoveries! Things always explain themselves in the long run. Instead, then, of landing on new islands of discovery, is my course set for the open sea where there is no sound other than that of the lonely heart-beat comparable to the pounding of the surf? Rest assured, nothing is decaying, it is I who am drifting. . . . The open sea, but not the wilderness. The discovery that there is no wilderness! That in itself is enough to sustain me in triumphing over my afflictions.

FOUR YEARS HAVE GONE by since *L'Etoile Vesper* was published; years that sped speedily enough as they must when the mornings are all alike and the evenings are spent in a kind of glass retort, with some unpredictable little incident at the centre, like a kernel. I was honest when I called *L'Etoile Vesper* my last book. I have come to see that it is as difficult to stop writing as it is uncomfortable to go on. Beneath my blue lantern, my life-line grows ever shorter and shorter, my physical torment ever more persistent. Yet how many changes of scene—other than on foot—are still permitted me! Uriage in '46, Geneva and the Beaujolais in '47, Provence, albeit against doctor's orders, in '48. From my seat in a car or a wheel-chair, I proudly compiled a census of the landscapes, streams and shores I have rediscovered. 'After all, I can still visit these.' Visit! Yes, in a manner of speaking and, above all, of experience. During the final infirmity of her life, Anna de Noailles saw more cities, hills and oceans than I, against the backcloth of her perpetually lowered blinds.

I wanted this book to be a journal; but I do not possess the knack of writing a proper journal, that is to say of stringing together, bead by bead, day after day, a rosary whose value and intrinsic lustre are relative to the writer's powers of exact observation, of assessing his own importance and that of his time. The art of selection, of noting things of mark, retaining the unusual while discarding the commonplace, has never been mine, since most of the time I am stimulated and quickened by the ordinary. There I was, vowing never to write anything again after *L'Etoile Vesper,* and now I have covered two hundred pages which are neither memoirs nor journal. Let my reader resign himself to it: this lantern of mine, burning blue day and night between the pair of red curtains, pressed close to the window like one of the butterflies that fall asleep there on a summer morning, throws no light on events significant enough to astonish him.

It is twenty years, or a little more, since Princesse Edmond de Polignac, staunch friend of music and musicians, passed sentence with a glance and a single word on the little four-legged table-desk that used to follow me from Paris to Saint-Tropez and back, taking up its position on the bed at my night's lodging. I set great store by this piece of furniture, originally contrived for me by Luc-Albert Moreau—painter, engraver, and master carpenter—so that I could write other than in a sitting posture, my feet dangling, which has always had an adverse effect on my comfort and my work.

"I have," Princesse de Polignac said to me, "a little English piece which, if enlarged, would be just right for you."

She was not mistaken. Widened, made higher, reinforced, and stripped of most of its English eighteenth-century elegance, it bestrides my divan-bed and indeed, for a quarter of a century, has gladdened both my leisure and my working hours. An adjustable desk has been let into the solid mahogany table and takes the weight of the things I turn to for relaxation from my own writing: telephone, fruit, portable radio, and bulky illustrated volumes. This contraption glides easily from the head of the bed to my feet. Including the all-purpose knife with its scorpion handle, the bunch of fountain-pens and various knick-knacks of no particular use, I have assembled on its back a fair number of good and willing servants.

All round me a litter of papers; but a litter belied by its appearance, with more often than not, to add to the confusion, a boiled chestnut, a half-eaten apple, and for the last month a seed-pod—from some exotic plant, no doubt—the capsules of which retain for a while and then expel, almost with violence, a delicate silvery follicle weighted with a tiny seed and lighter even than thistledown. One by one these feathery tufts break loose, drift up to the warm air beneath my ceiling, float there for some time before descending, and should one of them happen to be caught by the draught from the fire it yields at once, a consenting victim, and flings itself deliberately into the flames, there to perish of its own volition. I do not know the name of the plant which scatters its winged spirits abroad in this fashion, but it has no need of a label to take its place in my dunce's museum.

WHAT HAS BECOME OF those whom I wanted to last for ever, firmly attached to their own lives and mine? How could I ever have conceived that Marguerite Moreno would abandon me? She was kindly treated even by fatigue, and she would laugh me to scorn in my praise of idleness and the forty winks of a siesta. . . . But Marguerite goes and catches cold, and succumbs within a week. But Luc-Albert Moreau, happening to meet a friend, exclaims cheerfully "Hullo, old chap, how pleased I am to see you!" and dies on the spot from heart failure. And before them Léon-Paul Fargue who, on his death bed, grumbled about the blue of his sheets which he had had dyed: "Far too blue . . . won't do at all." And others there are too whom I must give up trying to name, or even count. In my heart of hearts I blame them for dying, calling them careless, imprudent. How could they deprive me of their company, and so abruptly, how could they think of doing such a thing to me! So I have banished from sight and mind the vision of them lying prone and lifeless for ever. Fargue turned suddenly to stone? I'll have none of it. My Fargue is still wearing his dusty walking-shoes, still talking, scratching the head of his black cat, is still ringing me up, still tramping from Lipp to Ménilmontant, and berating his bed for its too maritime blue. . . . Marguerite Moreno's feet still shod with static gold? Certainly not! They live in my memory as they were, wayward, restless, vulnerable and never tired.

My juniors in the prime of life sometimes look sternly at me; they feel anxious. They gather the recalcitrant fold of a shawl across my shoulder with a "You're not feeling a draught?" No, I am not feeling chilly, I am not feeling *that particular* draught you have in mind. My thoughts are too out of joint for me to feel it. I have so many reasons for avoiding what you tactfully call "the dangerous draught". Chief among them is pain, pain ever young and active, instigator of astonishment, of anger, imposing its rhythm on me, provoking me to defy it; the pain that enjoys an occasional respite but does not want my life to end: happily I have pain. Oh, I know perfectly well that by using the adverb "happily" I sound affected, like someone putting on the brave smile of an invalid! Very few invalids do remain entirely natural, but I would not like it thought that I am making my infirmity an occasion for sinful pride, that I require respect and special consideration, or that it fosters an inferiority complex, that root cause of acerbity. I am not referring to those who pretend to be sufferers, who are of no interest and are in any case a small minority, nor am I alluding to a category of sufferers who are far from reluctant when surprised or discovered in the very act of suffering. My doctor-brother summed up in a few words the pleasure enjoyed by such as these. "It is," he said, "a kind of ecstasy. It's akin to scratching the hollow of your ear with a match-stalk. Aphrodisiacal, almost."

A prominent politician, who was lame, once confided something to me which I had no difficulty in understanding, though at the time I was myself in excellent health. This man of politics liked to elevate my mind to the realm of general ideas, at least he made a good try. I struggled to follow his line of thought, but not for very long. I believe he would have found me mediocre all in all had he not so enjoyed one of my books, *Break of Day*, and had he not wished to expand (I would have said 'restrict') the scope of my life by the help of some great idea that should serve me as, in a sense, religion, high purpose (his phrase), inspiration. Out of malice and to get my own back, I asked him one day whether he could conceive of what a life laid waste by a single idea would be like, and I was astonished by his unhesitating reply: "Perfectly well, since all my life long, every day and almost at every hour, I have remembered that I was lame."

Up to the time of his untimely death he endured with great fortitude one accident and operation after another, and his legacy to us was a considerable corpus of learned works entirely devoted, as had been his life, to political matters—all, that is, save one, a story of some length, in its way a masterpiece, a single story whose hero was a cripple.

So, as luck will have it, I am fated to suffer pain, which I reconcile with a gambler's spirit, my ultra-feminine gambler's spirit, my instinct for the game of life, if you prefer it; the Last Cat, towards the end of her life, gave every indication by the movement of a paw, by the smile on her face, that a trailing piece of string was still for her a plaything, food for feline thought and illusion. Those who surround me will never let me want for pieces of string. . . .

Rare are the days on which I receive no presents. Let us understand each other; I mean, almost exclusively, presents from those who know me well, and know how to cater for what I call my insatiable appetite. Today I have received the first chestnuts, small, hard, and dark brown, finished off with a broad, light birth-mark and three stiff little hairs at the tip, showing that they have only just reached maturity. They come from a wood quite close to Paris, some seven or eight kilometres away, which I can see from here:

a steep, wooded slope, sparsely planted with ill-tended oak and fir and chestnut. A mere slit in the road beckons the passer-by, uninvitingly, to come upon a wooden chalet, set on brick-work that is losing all its mortar. What can this *dacha* be doing there? Hush! We must respect the cerebral repose of two overworked doctors—"my doctors" I call them—who cut themselves off from the world on Sundays. On one occasion I was able to follow them into their retreat, where they gave proof of a blissful resemblance to all children who ever hid in a wood, lit a camp fire, ate off a paper plate, drank from the same bottle, and they listened to the silence perforated only by the whistle of a train and the twitter of a tomtit. Having tracked them to their lair but once, I know that squirrels frolic high above them and that one blazing hot day they covered the escape of a large grass snake. Their view consists of unpeopled tracts of the Ile-de-France and the surrounding countryside, both scoured by railway lines, both speckled with small villas, but serene and all the more expansive for the sky above them.

It is but seldom that I can accompany these two ambitious women, who dream of putting behind them consulting room and laboratory for a few hours. Their several skills long since outdistanced what the untutored mind can grasp, yet they gaze in wonder at the mimetic spider simulating a pink pearl among the pink heather flowers, at the rotund puff-ball, that unspotted egg laid when the nights are freshening. They know what it is I long to see and bring it back to me: a hatful of ripening chestnuts and edible mushrooms, to appease my greed, and for my pleasure a variety of wild flowers, the matted head of the rose-gall, together with three unripe chestnuts, tight-packed in a single husk. The husk is beginning to split and through the cleavage can be seen the gleam of the three light mahogany fruits. By a trick of my peculiarly tenacious memory, I can close my hand over the ligneous twig-tip that held suspended this lovely green sea-urchin and then all I have to do is to clamber up as far as the solid wall of leaves to reach the neighbouring pines. Further on it is all sand, birch trees, heather and bramble-bushes laden with berries. Just let me go there, I shall not lose myself. Shut the door of my bedroom. I need nobody to guide me on my walk. All that I needed were these three chestnuts, packed tight in a single half-split-open husk. Au revoir, au revoir, I may be a little late for dinner.

Mary Ward Brown (1917–   ) lives in Browns, Alabama.
The deep South, both the Old South and the New South, are an
integral part of her stories which reflect the changing relationships and interdependences of her black and white characters.
Her themes of loss and hope, however, are universal. Many of
the protagonists are old people. Her stories have been selected for
The Best American Short Stories of 1983 and 1984, and her
collection, *Tongues of Flame,* from which "The Amaryllis" was
taken, won the Pen-Faulkner Award in 1987.

THE AMARYLLIS

It came to be the first thing he
thought of each morning. What did it do overnight?

He would get up and go straight to the parlor for a quick look. More
fascinated each day, he would hurry through breakfast, then take his second
cup of coffee back to sit and study the newest development.

The amaryllis was now two feet tall, its first lilylike bloom the diameter
of a salad plate and a twin bloom rapidly opening to the same glowing red.
There was also a slightly lower second stalk with three heavy buds still to
come.

The whole thing was so beautiful it had come to dominate the entire
house. It was not only alive but dramatically alive. It had presence, almost
like a person, and he was conscious of it off and on all day. More and more,
however, it seemed to be asking something of him, he wasn't sure what.

Today, Thursday, with the bloom at its peak and the bud half open, he
got the message. He couldn't have something that special in the house and
not share it. But with whom? The question had flawed every good thing
that happened since Margaret died.

Margaret would have loved the amaryllis, but all the other appreciators he could think of were either busy working, far away, or dead.

Their son, Angus, was as worthy as Margaret, in his way, but he was both busy and far away. Still, the thought of Angus with the flower was irresistible. At seven-fifteen he dialed the house. Mary Ann answered.

"Oh, Judge Manderville?" She was surprised, also anxious.

"Nothing is wrong," he assured her. He never called in the morning except in an emergency. "I wanted to invite you all down for the weekend. I have something to show you."

"*This* weekend?" Silence. "Angus has already gone, Judge Manderville. He has surgery this morning. But I know we can't come. We're all involved, the children too. What do you have to show?"

"Remember the amaryllis bulb you gave me? It's blooming and it's unbelievable."

She laughed. "I know. It's a hybrid from California. Did I tell you?"

"Yes. But you didn't prepare me for anything like this. Maybe I couldn't have been prepared. It's the most beautiful thing I ever saw."

"I'm glad you like it, Judge Manderville. Angus will be too. I'm really sorry we can't come. It'll be a while, two or three weeks, before we can get away, I expect. You know how things are here."

He knew. He could see Mary Ann dressed for a nonstop day, about to chauffeur his grandchildren to school, her time all planned straight through to dinner.

"Well, thanks, Mary Ann." He knew she had to go. "Sorry you can't make it. Love to everyone. Good-bye."

Going back for his coffee, now cold, he entered the parlor with a sense of apology, and left at once without looking at the flower. He hadn't really expected that they could come, so why was he disappointed?

His son had become almost inaccessible, he thought, as he washed up the dishes. He knew Angus was there but he no longer saw him except on holidays, parts of vacations, and when he was pressured into going for annual physicals. Angus belonged to his patients first and his immediate family second. The Judge no longer thought of himself as immediate.

Which was not really fair. Angus didn't like the distance between them. Sometimes he called as late as ten, apologized, and talked on. One night the Judge was awakened at ten-thirty to hear Angus saying, "I just called to say I miss you, Dad. Go on back to sleep." Angus' voice had sounded bone-tired and lonely, and the old father-sonship had flamed up to bring the Judge instantly awake and available. They had talked for an hour.

There was no doubt that Angus loved him. To Mary Ann he thought he must be something of an obligation, regularly and necessarily on the list but never quite convenient, certainly never a first choice. He felt she was fond of him and would visit him with reasonable regularity in the nursing home. She would see that he had a nurse, but she herself would not sit and hold his hand if the last days drew out.

His two grandchildren were beloved, close strangers. And the fact remained. He was quite alone in the world.

Hanging up the dish towel, he went to finish dressing. He could invite McGowin over to see the amaryllis. McGowin would look and never really see it. Then he would stay all day and talk about the past. "Listen, James, do you remember . . ." he would say, and launch into some long-ago episode. The Judge hadn't mentioned the amaryllis to McGowin.

In his study he tried to get down to work, as he liked to call the self-appointed task of going through the letters, papers, scrapbooks, diaries, and financial records collected in the house since the time of his parents.

"What do you do with yourself these days, Judge Manderville?" people asked him in the grocery store or on the street.

"Right now I'm cleaning out the attic," he would say, and smile.

After all those years on the bench, years of power and some prestige as circuit judge, it embarrassed him a little to say what he was busy with now, going through his and Margaret's letters and papers, trying to separate the wheat from the chaff.

On the desk before him now were several small memorandum books to be filed away or discarded. Margaret had been a reader who looked up words she didn't know, then wrote word and meaning in a small notebook. It was a habit like brushing her hair, to which he had paid no real attention.

Opening the first notebook, he saw she'd written *deciduous, synecdoche,* and *ankh,* with meanings. Then she wrote *ubi sunt,* but gave no meaning. Why not? he wondered. What did it mean? Out of context, he had no idea.

Near at hand, the phone rang. In the large, empty house the telephone was his link with the outside world, with the living. He always picked up expectantly on the first or second ring.

"Good morning, James," said McGowin.

"Hello, Mack."

"What you doing?"

"Working. How about you?"

"Not working." McGowin chuckled. "It's my birthday."

"How about that! How many?"

"You don't know? I'm eight months ahead of you. Don't you remember I got to go to school a year before you did? But you skipped the fourth grade and caught up in the fifth."

"Congratulations, Mack. Happy birthday. Are your children coming down or anything?"

"No. But they called, and I got presents from everybody. Shirts, ties, pajamas. You know."

The Judge hesitated briefly. "What're you doing this afternoon?"

"Nothing. Why?"

"What about my coming over around four?"

"Fine! Sure, James. That'll be great. I'll brew us some Sanka."

"How do you feel on your birthday?"

"I feel like hell. I know I'm on the shelf for good and I can't get used to it. Can you?"

"No, I can't either."

"We retired too soon. We should have hung on longer. But I had that little stroke. And you wanted to take care of Margaret."

"Yes. I don't regret it."

"Well. Like Satchel Paige said, 'Don't never look back. Something might be gainin' on you.' " They both laughed. "I'll let you get back to work, James. See you later."

"Have a good day, Mack."

Feeling selfish and justified at the same time, he put the receiver back on the hook. If he'd asked McGowin over, it would have started something that would go on for the life of the amaryllis. For McGowin it would be merely an excuse for companionship.

Protecting himself, however, did nothing for the plant. Sitting up there in absolute silence, it projected pressure through the walls.

He stared out the study window, trying again to come up with appreciators. All still busy, far away, dead. He sighed and gave up.

For McGowin's birthday, he decided to call the bakery and get a cake to take over. A cake with candles to go with their decaffeinated coffee.

He didn't look at the amaryllis again until after supper, when he went up and turned on all the lights in the front of the house. He turned on crystal chandeliers, table lamps, all. In his mind's eye he could see the house as it looked from the street, an 1850 colonial cottage in its original setting of trees and boxwoods, all lit up as though guests were expected.

He took a seat on the sofa, in front of which the plant stood on a low table from which he and Margaret used to serve demitasses or port after dinner. They had never cared much for society, but entertained when they had to and enjoyed having friends for dinner until her heart problems stopped even that.

In the handsome room, in artificial light, the amaryllis seemed to have taken on glamour, like a beautiful girl all dressed up for the evening. All dressed up and no place to go, he thought.

The strange thing was, he'd never "felt" anything for a plant before. On the contrary, he'd dismissed them all as more or less inanimate like potatoes and turnips, not animate in the way of cats and birds. He had bought dozens of hospital chrysanthemums, often delivering them himself in their foil wrapping and big bows, but they had seemed more artificial than real.

The amaryllis was different, entirely. He liked just being with it. Because of its size, he supposed, it seemed to have individuality, and then he had watched it grow daily, with his naked eye. Looking at the blooms, he thought of words like *pure* and *noble,* and old lines of poetry like "Euclid alone has looked on *Beauty bare.*

In return, the plant seemed neither friendly nor unfriendly. It was simply there in all its glory, however fleeting. It was the fleetingness, he thought, that put on the pressure.

He took off his glasses, dropped them in his shirt pocket, and rubbed a hand across both eyes. Then he turned off the lights, one by one.

Next morning the second bloom was wide open, as breathtaking as the first. Red was not his favorite color, but this red was both muted and vibrant, the color of a winter sunrise, or a robin's breast. The two blooms exuded a kind of concentrated freshness like early morning in the woods, a baby's skin, or eyes just waking from sleep. Pure, unblemished by anything yet to come.

He dressed before breakfast and, while drinking coffee, wrote a note to the postman. "Eddie: Can you spare a minute to look at something in the house? Just ring the bell. Thank you. J.M." He was making a list of names when Pot arrived.

Pot came on Fridays. Years ago he had come every day of the week, including Sunday, and Margaret had taught him to clean, cook, and serve to a fine point. She had wanted him called Potiphar, a fitting name she thought, but it seemed affected no matter who said it, so they soon settled for his nickname. Pot didn't need to work now. His children were successful and had bought him a house. He drew his pennies. But he still came one day a week out of their mutual dependence, the Judge supposed.

He and Pot had been through all kinds of ups and downs together, on both sides, including the loss of their wives. They had even gone through civil rights together, with him on the bench and Pot's people in the streets. There was a time when Pot had said, "I got to stay out awhile, Judge. But you understand it ain't between me and you."

Today he met Pot at the back door. "Hurry up, I've got something to show you!"

"Morning, Judge. What you got?" Tall and lean to the bone, Pot looked the part of a king's officer, superannuated perhaps. He stood up to his years with a blend of dignity and submission. Age was becoming to him.

"Let's go to the parlor," the Judge said. At the door, he stepped aside for Pot to go first.

"It done bloomed," Pot said, smiling. "I never saw nothing like that before."

"Neither did I."

"Makes you feel like you ought to go down on your knees, don't it, Judge?"

"It does."

Pot sighed. "Well, I got to get on to the house." Bowing unconsciously, like an Anglican to the cross, he backed out of the room.

"I'm inviting some people in to see the flower," the Judge said as they went to the back hall. "Not many, maybe a dozen."

"You want to serve something?" Pot opened the closet door and got out the vacuum cleaner. He put on an attachment as carefully and precisely as if it were a saxophone.

"Coffee, maybe, if anyone wants it. But Mr. McGowin will be here for lunch, I expect."

"I'll take care of it."

A surge of love for Pot rose up in the Judge's chest, remained like a cramp as he put Eddie's note in the mailbox. How could he have overlooked Pot as an appreciator? Pot had looked at the flower with what it deserved, reverence.

He squared his shoulders and hurried to the phone with his list. If the elect couldn't come, he would get them from the highways and hedges. He put on his glasses and began to dial numbers, beginning with his nearest neighbor whom he never saw, separated as they were by three wooded acres.

He said approximately the same thing to each. "This is James Manderville. I have something here that you might like to see. It's a hybrid amaryllis in bloom, really beautiful. I hope you'll drop in if you can." Any time would be convenient, he said. He'd be at home all day.

And then he called McGowin. When it got down to bedrock, McGowin was all he had. McGowin said he'd be right over.

The rest of the day was a happening. McGowin arrived first, in a tweed coat and tie, his face red from chronically elevated pressure for which he took pills when he didn't forget them. He chose to sit on a chair opposite the amaryllis and stayed there all morning, a kind of noncirculating co-host.

When a lady entered the room, McGowin rose at once, a cross between southern gentleman and perpetual fraternity boy drilled in manners, and stood stalwartly until she sat down or left. He was fluent with anecdotes, flattery, and occasional wit, an old party man back in action.

The Buick dealer and his wife, neighbors, came around ten, the Buick dealer being his own boss, and able to take off at his pleasure. It was obvious that they were glad to be there, and to say later they had been. They did not come to see the amaryllis.

"I've seen them before, Judge," he said of the plant. "They come in other colors, too. Pink. White. Some are even variegated, but yours is beautiful.

"How old is this house, Judge? Did you inherit the antiques or collect them yourself? They're worth a fortune now. Look at those mirrors!"

His wife asked, "What kind of table is that, Judge Manderville, with the mirror below?"

It was called a "petticoat table," he explained, and why. He answered all questions and showed them the whole house. Then Pot served coffee. Their faces glowed with deference and interest. They had been here before, they told him as they left, but had never had a personal tour and they loved it. As they said, they had already seen an amaryllis.

As she started down the steps, the Buick dealer's wife looked him tentatively in the eye. "If you ever need anything, here all alone, you call us, Judge Manderville," she said. "Day or night."

"I may have to do that," he said. "And I won't forget. Thank you."

"I see your light at night through the trees, and I think of you often," she said. "Your wife was lovely."

Suddenly, to his great surprise, his eyes filled with tears and so, he saw, did hers.

The flower-shop owner, in the midst of making floral arrangements for a funeral, had to squeeze in her visit just before lunch. She wore a knit pantsuit, another squeeze, the Judge thought; she might as well have been stark naked. He caught a glimpse of McGowin's eyes. Poor old devil. He'd been a real ladies' man in his day and still got occasional calls from widows. But he no longer rose to the bait. After his wife died and the little divorcée turned him down, he seemed satisfied with, even somehow proud of, his bachelorhood.

The flower-shop owner was all business, however. "Do you know how much the bulbs cost, Judge? I'd like to get a few for the shop if they're not too expensive."

He said he'd get the address from Mary Ann and she could write the nursery. She sat long enough to drink a quick cup of coffee and smoke a cigarette.

"People pick the worst times to die," she said. "They wait until I have a wedding or a big party, like now. Then they all try to go at once. And you know the old superstition, that if there's one there's got to be three? It never fails. I've seen it happen so often it scares me."

"Well, don't look at James and me," said McGowin. "We've got other plans."

At noon Pot called them in for T-bone steaks, baked potatoes, and a fine tossed salad. The Judge and Pot always ate well on Fridays, but the Judge usually did the cooking while Pot worked on the house.

"This is better than my birthday, James," McGowin said, looking around the table set with Spode and good silver.

They ate hungrily, saying little. McGowin cut his steak cleanly to the bone on both sides, eating fat and all, plus large chunks of French bread and butter.

"Bring out the rest of that cake, Pot," McGowin directed when they'd finished. "And light up the candles!"

"You brought your cake over, Mack?"

"Sure I did. I'm still celebrating, or holding my own wake, I don't know which."

With one quarter missing but with the candles lit, their small flames bowing over backward as he walked, Pot brought in the cake on a round silver tray. Ceremoniously he set it in front of McGowin and placed a cake knife beside it.

Catching the spirit, the Judge said, "Get out a bottle of cream sherry, Pot. Put it in a decanter."

Pot was smiling. Wearing the white coat he kept in the pantry for special occasions, he soon came back with a decanter of wine and two Waterford sherry glasses on a tray.

"Hot damn!" said McGowin. "Long live the big petunia—or whatever the hell its name is."

Since he drew laughter, McGowin was inspired to go on. "What do you think that thing is, Pot, male or female? It looks like a stud petunia to me, but it could be a liberated female. They outdo us every which way now, you know."

Eddie the postman rang the doorbell as if on cue. Pot went to let him in while the Judge and McGowin took their second glass of wine to the parlor.

Eddie was a fine appreciator. Standing straight as for the national anthem, he made a ringing statement. "That is the most beautiful thing I ever saw in my life, Judge Manderville. That is really something. I wish my wife could see it."

"Bring her over, Eddie," said the Judge. "Bring her, by all means."

"Just call before you come, Eddie," said McGowin. "So James will have his shoes on."

"His shoes, Mr. McGowin? Ha Ha. You're still a card!" Eddie came a few steps nearer McGowin, leaned down and said in a whisper intended for the Judge to hear, "I've known the Judge for years, you know. He's a real gentleman. A gentleman if I ever knew one."

"Scholar, too, Eddie." McGowin winked. "Don't forget that."

"Oh, yes, sir. A scholar, too. You should see the books and papers I bring him."

Eddie said he had no time for coffee or wine, though a glass of wine would certainly be nice. People had to have their mail on time or they got upset. All down the street they were waiting for him right now, he told them.

There were no more visitors until late afternoon. McGowin's body, struggling with too much food and alcohol, both forbidden, dragged down his spirit like a stone. He first began to nod, then put his head back on the chair and slept soundly, snoring from time to time. The Judge went back to his notebooks in the study. He too felt drowsy, but down the hall he heard the vacuum cleaner going. If Pot could work, so could he.

Ubi sunt was not in the dictionary they usually used. So that was it. Margaret had been reading in bed, probably, and hadn't felt like getting up for a word. In the unabridged dictionary, which badly needed dusting, he found it at once: "adj. (L. 'where are (they)?') Relating to a type of verse which has as principal theme the transitory nature of life and beauty."

Suddenly Margaret's wordbooks became intimate, as if they were journals, in a way. Someone else would have to throw them out, he decided, not he.

He took out his handkerchief and dusted off the dictionary, then shook the handkerchief and put it back in his pocket. At his desk he pushed the wordbooks aside and sat staring out at the winter afternoon. The light of the desk lamp seemed to focus on his hands, quietly folded.

Soon after the hall clock struck four, McGowin appeared in the doorway, rumpled and dazed. "Any coffee left, James?"

"Yes. Let's have some."

They went to the kitchen, where a percolator of fresh coffee was set on "warm." At the kitchen table they drank a cup together, black, and in silence.

"Thanks, pal," said McGowin, draining his cup. "I got to be going."

"You'll miss the others."

"Can't help it, James. I'm through for the day. Has Pot gone?"

"No, but he should have finished by now. Would you give him a ride?"

"That's what I had in mind. Round him up."

McGowin drove a twelve-year-old Mercedes, but he drove it less and less, having been warned by the police about driving across yellow lines, turning into wrong lanes and onto one-way streets.

As he and Pot drove off, their faces said the party was over and they were tired. Their faces also said they'd been to many parties, that they were always over, and everyone went home.

The legal contingent arrived together after five, though not in full force. To be strictly ethical the Judge had kept his distance from other lawyers while in office. When he retired he might as well have died, he sometimes thought. Now only the district attorney and two young lawyers, with their wives, showed up. There was also the small daughter of one of the couples.

When the Judge asked the child's age, she grinned and held up four tender fingers.

The lawyers wanted drinks, not coffee, and the Judge was glad to have good Christmas scotch and expensive birthday bourbon to bring out. A happy hour was soon under way.

Both the lawyers and their wives, however, took the amaryllis in stride. Sitting around it in the parlor, one wife quickly abstracted an article she had read.

"There's a whole new thing about plants now," she told them. "They're supposed to thrive on tender loving care. They like to have music played in the room, like to be talked to. It seems to be a proven thing. They want love and affection like everybody else. You should talk to it, Judge Manderville."

A lawyer, not her husband, interrupted. "But I also read where that talking-to business is explained. People breathe out carbon dioxide and plants breathe it in. So it's not a matter of TLC, but chemistry."

The amaryllis was dismissed. "Have you kept up with the house-trailer controversy, Judge?"

Opinions flew at him from the lawyers while their wives sat drinking, smoking, listening. The little girl sat on the floor beside her mother's chair, holding on to what appeared to be a French shopping bag filled with toys. She didn't take out the toys, however, but stared at the amaryllis. From time to time she changed her attention to a person or object in the room, but always brought it back to the flower.

The Judge noticed. After a while, he got up and moved to a chair beside the child.

"What do you think of my flower?" he whispered.

"I love it," she whispered back through a wide, tongue-cluttered smile, then ducked her head, blonde hair falling around her cheeks. From her hidden mouth she said something he couldn't hear.

"What, dear?" he asked.

Conversation had stopped and everyone was looking at the child.

She raised her head only enough to meet his eyes with her own. "I want to touch it," she said.

"Well, I think *it* would like that too." He led her to the flower and lifted her up.

"Easy now," cautioned the mother.

With one finger she reached out, gingerly touched a red petal as though it were hot, and laughed delightedly.

When the Judge put her down she didn't move. "I want to kiss it!" she cried.

Everyone laughed except the mother, who said, "We're going too far now."

But the Judge lifted her up again. "Kiss it easy, then," he said.

Wrinkling her nose to avoid the long, yellow-padded stamens, she pressed one cheek lightly against a bloom. Her lips missed altogether.

Her mother stepped up to lead her away.

"No!" The child stood stubbornly, close to tears. "I want it. I want to take it to my home!"

"Oh, Lord, here we go." The mother gripped the child's arm with authority. "Time to leave, Judge Manderville. It's been delightful. Come to see us soon. Promise me you will!"

On the porch, as his visitors walked away, the Judge heard the phone ring. It was Angus saying Mary Ann had told him he'd called, that they would try to come in two weeks and spend one night. The Judge could tell Angus was pleased to hear about his flower show, about guests having been in the house.

He made a quick check to see that all the doors were locked, then gathered up empty cups and glasses, overflowing ashtrays. He took them all to the kitchen but left them unwashed, unemptied. Like McGowin and Pot, he was tired. Too tired even to eat, he decided.

As he undressed, however, he thought of the amaryllis alone in the parlor. In bedroom slippers, he went back and turned on a light. The flower stood as beautiful as ever. Carefully, he picked up the pot and carried it back to his bedroom, where he set it on a table in front of a window. From there he could see it first thing in the morning.

He slept soundly all night but woke up vaguely depressed. In front of the window, backed by candid morning light, the amaryllis's blooms were like heavy translucent bells. Their hue, lightest at the edges, grew deeper and darker in each secret throat. In the sunlight, the living veins were apparent as never before.

But were the blooms quite as fresh, really as perfect, as yesterday?

On the second stalk, all three buds were opening at once. Their promise, however, was not as exciting as the first. The composition of the whole plant—pot, blooms, stalks— was no longer as good, for one thing. The center of interest was being lowered and to the wrong place. He couldn't analyze the difference. He only knew that any change, or beginning of change, was already for the worse.

Each day the amaryllis continued to do something new but in a downhill direction. The first blooms passed their prime and began to age in the same way that people did, the Judge thought. There was the same pitiful wither- ing around the edges, subtle drooping and shriveling, gradual letting go of form. The shrunken petals finally turned the color of purple veins in old legs and hung down like deflated parachutes.

The lower set of blooms was smaller than the first and seemed replicas, not originals. Petty princes, not majesty.

The Judge was vaguely ashamed that he lost interest in the plant toward the last. When all the blooms had died, he was told to stop watering the bulb and put it away in a dark place, or even outside in the ground.

When he cleaned and straightened the house for his children's visit, he put the pot in the back-porch pantry. Tall green leaves had grown up around the stalks, and they flopped over awkwardly, hanging off the pantry shelf by the side of empty fruit jars, obsolete ice-cube trays, discarded dishes, and cooking vessels with missing tops.

He was told to leave the pot in the pantry and forget it until next year, when he could bring it out, start watering, and the amaryllis would grow and bloom again. It seemed incredible, but all the gardeners and flower people assured him it was true.

Born in Austin, Minnesota, Richard Eberhart (1904–   ) had
a variety of jobs including floor walker, tramp steamer deck boy
and private tutor to the son of the King of Siam before serving
in the European front during World War II. After the war, he
became one of the United States' leading lyrical poets, his themes
exploring the thoughts, actions and mortality of the human race.
As he ages, he writes increasingly about growing old. In 1987,
he served as U.S. Poet Laureate.

HARDY PERENNIAL

In youth we dream of death,
In age we dream of life.

    I could not have cared less for life
    When young, employing savage pursuit
    Into the glories of the unknown,
    Fascinated by death's kingdom.

    The paradox was my brimming blood.
    My bright, my brimming blood, my force
    And power like a bridge to the future,
    Could not contain itself in white flesh.

In youth we dream of death,
In age we dream of life.

    Now that death's savagery appears,
    Each day nipping at my generation,

The hard facts of the world negate
Symbols of the mind striving otherwhere.

I would give love to every being alive,
Penetrating the secrets of the living,
Discovering subleties and profundities in
Any slightest gesture, or delicate glance.

✥ *Bernard Berenson* ❧

Bernard Berenson (1865–1959), distinguished scholar, art historian, expert on the Italian Renaissance, and humanist, was born in Lithuania, came to the United States at the age of ten, and graduated from Harvard University in 1887. He lived much of his life in Europe, and at his death gave his villa, I Tatti, near Florence, Italy, with its lovely gardens, paintings, and library, to Harvard to be used as a center for humanist studies. His diary, kept throughout the last eleven years of his life, from ages eighty-three to ninety-four, testifies to his continuing appreciation of beauty and his zest for living in his old age.

from

SUNSET AND TWILIGHT: DIARIES OF 1947–1958

1947—IN BB'S 82ND YEAR

February 24th, I Tatti   Three Italian friends to lunch. Talk almost entirely of who was married to whom and what descendants and in same objective tone of who was the mistress and lover of whom. Then who, married or not, left whom or was deserted by whom. And all enjoyed it, including myself, who did not know most of the people discussed. Why did we enjoy it? Only because chatter we must, and such talk is the next-to-anthropoid unsemantic use of what in our case have become organs of speech.

After such talk the easiest and zestfullest is about medicines. With what heat we praise those that have helped us.

June 17th, I Tatti   After tea, a drive to the very top of Monte Senario. I took a few steps and enjoyed the air, and gazed around, at hills and knolls and upland meadows where I used to tramp on foot, leaving no hummock unexplored. Distance scarcely existed, mile on mile, up hill and down dale. Now the grasshopper is a burthen, and it is hard to believe that I was not so very long ago so muscularly alert, so resistant to fatigue. I do not let regret get the better of me. There is a certain sweetness in being what one is now—not reduced but contracted—so appreciative, so enjoying, so grateful for what has been, and for what is now. It means something to be able to rise above aches and pains, and inertias, and to glory in the world as displayed to one's experienced senses and ordered mind.

1947—IN BB'S 83RD YEAR

October 8th, I Tatti   Why at my advanced age do I let myself get agitated, driven, fussy; still eager to write and worse still to publish, still wanting to enjoy *Freude am Ursache sein?* And I can be so happy when, away from home, I wander carefree, sight-seeing and enjoying the beauties of art and nature for which seventy years of experience (trial and error) have so well prepared me. I should give the example of disinterested attainment beyond the itch for transitive activities. I should let myself be dominated by my strong feeling that in some mystical way enjoyment like mine benefits society more than anything that could be achieved by further publications.

1949—IN BB 84TH YEAR

January 1st, I Tatti   What do I want this year? To live for Nicky's sake, and to write. To finish the supplementary essays on which I am engaged and to start writing the book on Man and His Society as Works of Art. I think of this in my waking hours at night, and when alone in daytime. Happy thoughts come in shoals, but shall I be able to marshal them into a book? Of course I shall enjoy my friends, enjoy gulping information, enjoy nature, enjoy works of art. These, however, like poetry, are no longer a craving. I now am my own artist and see in nature what no painter can reproduce. If only I don't get too invalid, keep my head and a certain capacity for work!

1950—IN BB'S 85TH YEAR

February 13th, I Tatti   Woke up feeling well. Insides quiet, warm, and cosy. No disturbing gasses under the ribs. Muscles distended. No tingling in the feet, no hardness in calves of legs. Throat clear, neither rasping nor smoky. Mouth not sour, gums not aching. Head not heavy or muzzy. In short, a harmony of all functions in tranquillity, and a feeling as if pleasant glow were caressingly warming the whole system, and as if an ichor of the gods were flowing through the veins. For a moment I felt a physiological happiness which I may have had thousands of times in childhood, and youth, but then seldom if ever with the awareness and enjoyment that I have now. And awareness is the compensation that age gives us in exchange for mere action.

1950—IN BB's 86TH YEAR

August 5th, Vallombrosa   While everything else physical and mental seems to diminish, the appreciation of beauty is on the increase. Landscape, animals, men, women, and children, and all man-made things, fascinate, delight, and evoke my critical sense more and ever more. Yesterday toward sunset stopped at Vallombrosa. Enraptured over the light on the brownish façade of the monastery, with the detail of capitals, columns, inside and outside church, with the incline leading from the main door to the paved courtyard. And looking through grand entrance on the right at the tunnelled road leading down to Tosi, I saw a picture that reminded me of Velasquez's Villa Medici sketches, but ever so much finer. And the young women in many-coloured garments—how lovely, how paintable, at the distance from which I saw them. And then driving down toward Reggello, the fairy light over the already darkened "badlands" of the Val d'Arno, and the distances!

1953—IN BB's 89TH YEAR

June 26th, Rome   My eighty-eighth birthday—shall I have another? I want another and another, although every year, every month even, my body gets more unfit for habitation as a dwelling, and rebellious as slave of my mind. There is so much I still want to and could write, so much in nature and art and people I still could enjoy.

The gains of the past year are that I have revised my *Lorenzo Lotto* of sixty years ago, and sent it to the press. *Rumour and Reflection* is the only book that cost me no effort, has had considerable success, and the fully illustrated edition of my *Italian Painters,* a great one, for that kind of book.

The loss is in elasticity of body and mind. My blood pressure a couple of months ago rose alarmingly. Limbs stiff, hands tingling, heats, memory of names gone, and for faces greatly diminished. Tire quickly and more and more time wasted resting with eyes closed, harder of hearing, drowsy.

1954—in BB's 90th Year

December 31st, I Tatti   1954—a year in which Old Age has increasingly got hold of me, making me timid about going downstairs, increasing every natural deficiency, restricting more and more the time I can walk, or talk, or work. On the other hand, I have never enjoyed work more than now. Indeed, it is almost the "only carnal pleasure" left me. In spite of everything, I have done this year most of the catalogue of Venetian paintings, finished and even put through the press the new edition of the *Lotto,* written a monthly article for the *Corriere,* and kept up a continuous correspondence with women chiefly. A new woman has swum into my ken and although we met for an hour or two only, we have been writing every few days. I wonder how this friendship would stand the test of being together.

1956—in BB's 92nd Year

August 13th, Vallombrosa   I could live comfortably the rest of my days, despite all the troubles flesh so aged is heir to, if I gave up work that required serious effort, people who do not stimulate or amuse, travel, the reading of newspapers. I literally suffer bodily when I read what is going on in the world. Perhaps easier for distant observers than actors to see and understand what the actors themselves are doing, and what the consequences will be. But I still want to learn, I still want to understand, and I still want to write. How shall I get rid of these lusts? Physical incompetence only will emancipate me from their slavery, but what kind of freedom will it be? The antechamber of the End. But how I still enjoy sunlight, nature, and stormy skies, and sunsets, and trees and flowers, and animals including well-shaped humans, and reading, and conversing!

1957—in BB's 92nd Year

May 12th, I Tatti   With the eyes I live and enjoy more than ever before. The road sweeps in living curves before me, and helps me on like a rolling platform. Distance fascinating beyond possibility of art. Near at hand everything alive for me. Middle distances with their paths and tracks call up poignantly the hazardous climbs I used to make, and that now with *Wehmut* I can enjoy only with my eyes. But as I look far and near, I recall the friends I have had as companions on my strolls. Their number would be great if I attempted to enumerate them, and their individuality and qualities of nearly every possible nature. Loves, bedfellows, of all European nationalities, companions of an hour whom I never saw again, or intimates of a lifetime, loyal or enemy-friends, exploiting me, journalists, writers of every kind, politicians—in short, members of nearly every profession. None survive, except much younger, forty years younger, than myself. Not only gone my near contemporaries, but forgotten like the leaves of the Man tree that they were.

1957—IN BB's 93RD YEAR

December 20th, I Tatti   I ought to consult an aurist, a urologist, an eye specialist, an up-to-date dentist, etc.—in fact spend most of my time and money in an effort to prolong life. Why? Living at my age with all my disabilities is anything but a picnic. So why cling to it? Partly out of mere animal instinct. Partly out of curiosity about tomorrow and day after tomorrow. Partly because I am not resigned to giving up, and still am eager to achieve, if only as inspirer. Most of all, for Nicky's sake. I am still the spool, the reel around which all the threads of I Tatti are wound.

Author Josephine Jacobsen (1908–   ) was born in Canada but was educated by private tutors in Baltimore, Maryland, where she still lives. She was poetry consultant at the Library of Congress from 1971 to 1973 and remains a consultant in American Letters. Her stories have appeared in *The Best American Short Stories,* in the *O. Henry Prize Stories,* and in *Fifty Years of the American Short Story.* Her stories are often open-ended and unresolved, leaving, as she says, "a ragged edge," true to life itself.

JACK FROST

Mrs. Travis was drinking a sturdy cup of tea. She sat in the wicker rocker on her back porch, in a circle of sun, after picking Mrs. James her flowers. Exhausted, she felt a little tired, and she rested with satisfaction. Mrs. James's motley bouquet sat by her knee, in one of the flower tins.

Mrs. Travis wore a blue cotton dress with a man's suitcoat over it, and around that a tie, knotted for a belt. Her legs were bare, but her small feet had on them a pair of child's galoshes, the sort that have spring buckles. Since several springs were missing, she wore the galoshes open, and sometimes they impeded her.

Half of her back porch, the left-hand side, was clear, and held her wicker rocker with its patches of sprung stiff strands; but the other half was more fruitful, a great pile of possessions which she needed, or had needed, or in certain possible circumstances might come to need: a tin foot-tub containing rope, twine, and a nest of tin containers from the insides of flower baskets; a hatchet; a galosh for the right foot; garden tools; a rubber mat; a beekeeper's helmet for the black-fly season. Near by, a short length of hose; chunks of wood. The eye flagged before the count.

There was a small winding path, like the witch's in a fairy tale, between cosmos so tall they brushed the shoulders. To its right almost immediately, vegetables grew: the feathery tops of carrots, dusty beetgreens, a few handsome mottled zucchini, the long runners of beans. Last year there had still been tomatoes, but the staking-up and coaxing had become too much; she said to herself instead that such finicking had come to bore her. To the left of the cosmos, below a small slope of scratchy lawn, was the garden proper—on this mellow September afternoon a fine chaos of unchosen color, the Mexican shades of zinnias, the paper-cutout heads of dahlias, a few grownover roses, more cosmos, the final spikes of some fine gladioli, phlox running heavily back to magenta, and closer to the cooling ground, the pink and purple of asters. There were even a few pansies, wildly persisting in a tangle of grass and weeds.

Until a few years ago her younger brother Henry had driven over two hundred miles, up from Connecticut, to help her plant both gardens, but Henry had died at eighty-two. Mrs. Travis herself did not actually know how old she was. She believed herself to be ninety-three; but having several years ago gone suddenly to check the fact of the matter in the faint gray handwriting of her foxed Bible, a cup of strong tea in her hand, she had sloshed the tea as she peered, and then on the pulled, run surface, she could no longer read the final digit. 3? 7? 1883? Just possibly, 1887? For a moment she felt youth pressing on her; if it were, if it possibly were 1887, several years had lifted themselves off. There they were, still to come with all the variety of their days. Turn those to hours, those to minutes, and it was a gigantic fresh extension. But she thought the figure was a 3. It was the last time she looked in the back of the Bible.

Tacked onto the porch wall was a large calendar; each day past was circled in red. Only three such showed; she would circle September 4th when she closed the door for the night.

Now before she could swallow the last of her tea, here came Mrs. James's yellow sweater, borne on a bicycle along the dirt road outside the hedge. Dismounted, Mrs. James wheeled the bicycle up the path and leaned it against the porch post. She was sweaty with effort over the baked ridges of the road, and, half a century younger than her hostess, she radiated summer-visitor energy and cheer.

"Oh Mrs. Travis!" she cried. "You've got them all ready! Aren't they lovely!" She was disappointed, since she had hoped to choose the picking; but she and her summer friends regarded Mrs. Travis's activity as much like that of Dr. Johnson's dog walking on its hind legs.

Mrs. Travis looked with satisfaction at the jumble of phlox, gladioli, dahlias, and zinnias which, with all the slow, slow bending and straightening, had cost her an hour.

"Oh, it's so *warm*," said Mrs. James with pleasure, sitting down on the step at Mrs. Travis's feet.

Mrs. Travis had so few occasions to speak that it always seemed to take her a minute to call up her voice, which arrived faint with distance. "Yes," she said, almost inaudibly. "It's a very good day."

"Oh look!" said Mrs. James, pleased. "Look how well the rose begonia's doing!" She had given it to Mrs. Travis early in the summer, it was one of her own bulbs from California, and she could see its full gorgeousness now, blooming erratically beside the path, hanging its huge rosy bloom by the gap-toothed rake and a tiny pile of debris, twigs, dead grass, a few leaves.

Mrs. Travis did not answer, but Mrs. James saw it was because she was looking at the begonia's gross beauty with a powerful smugness. They sat companionably for a moment. Mrs. James seemed to Mrs. Travis like one of the finches, or yellow-headed sparrows, which frequented her for the warmest weeks. Exactly as she thought so, Mrs. James said, suddenly sad, "Do you know the birds are all going, *already?*"

"No, not all," said Mrs. Travis soothingly. "The chickadees won't go." But Mrs. Travis did not really care; it was the flowers she created out of nothing.

"I hate to see them go so soon," said Mrs. James, stubbornly sad.

"But you'll be going too," said Mrs. Travis, faintly and comfortingly. Mrs. James, lifting her chin, looked at Mrs. Travis. "Are you going to stay here all winter, *again?*" she asked.

Mrs. Travis looked at her with stupefaction. Then she said, "Yes." She was afraid Mrs. James was going to repeat what she had said for the past two autumns, about Mrs. Travis moving into the village for the winter; here she was, no phone, no close neighbors; nothing but snow, and ice, and wind, and the grocery boy with his little bag, and the mailman's Pontiac passing without stopping. But Mrs. James said only, "Look, here comes Father O'Rourke."

There was the clap of a car door, and Father O'Rourke appeared between the cosmos, surprisingly wearing his dog collar, his black coat slung over his white shoulder. Mrs. James stood up, pleased that Mrs. Travis had a visitor. "I've got to get these flowers back," she said. Now came the embarrassing moment. "How—er, they're so lovely; what . . . ?"

"That's three dollars for the pailful," said Mrs. Travis with satisfaction. Mrs. James, whose grandmother, as a little girl, had known Mrs. Travis in Boston, continued to feel, no matter what she paid, that the flowers had come as a gift from Mrs. Travis's conservatory. She laid three dollars inconspicuously on the table by the oil lamp, and Mrs. Travis watched her and Father O'Rourke saying hello, and good-bye for the winter, to each other in the hot slanting sun.

As Mrs. James wheeled her bicycle away, Father O'Rourke replaced her on the step. He did not offer to shake hands, having noticed that such gestures seemed to distract Mrs. Travis, as some sort of clumsy recollected maneuver. He had just come from making the final plans for the Watkins wedding, and, fresh from all that youth and detail, he looked at Mrs. Travis, whose pale small blue eyes looked back at him, kindly, but from a long distance. The purpose of Father O'Rourke's visit embarrassed him; he was afraid of Mrs. Travis's iron will.

"What a lot of flowers you've still got," began Father O'Rourke, obliquely.

Mrs. Travis looked out over the ragged rainbow on the slope. The sun, at its western angle, was still a good bit above the smaller of the big dark mountains behind which it would go. "Oh yes," she said, "they'll be here for a long time. A couple of weeks, probably." He saw that she meant just that.

"Well," he said, "you know, Mrs. Travis, after five years here, I've found we just don't know. Things may go on almost to October; and then, again, a night in late August will do it."

Mrs. Travis did not reply to this, and Father O'Rourke plunged. "I saw Mrs. Metcalfe at the post office this morning," he said, looking placatingly at Mrs. Travis's profile. "Did you know that she's finished making that big sitting-room off her south porch into that little apartment she's going to rent out?"

Mrs. Travis, who had had enough of this for one day, indeed for one lifetime, turned her head and looked him straight in his hazel eye.

"I'm not going anywhere," she said, surprisingly loudly, adding, from some past constraint, "Father O'Rourke."

A final sense of the futility of his effort struck him silent. They sat quietly for a few seconds. What on earth am I trying to do? he thought suddenly. Why *should* she move? Well, so many reasons; he wondered if they were all worthless. He knew that before he was born, Mrs. Travis had enlisted in the army of eccentric hermits, isolates, writing their own terms into some curious treaty. But she was so much older than anyone else that the details became more and more obscure; also, more romanticized. There was even doubt as to a dim and distant husband. A fallen or faithless lover appeared, along with factual but tinted tales of early privilege. But the Miss Havisham motif he tended to discount; it was so widely beloved.

All he knew for certain was that, with Mrs. Travis, he was in the presence of an authenticity of elimination which caused him a curiously mingled horror and envy. At times he thought that her attention, fiercely concentrated, brought out, like a brilliant detail from an immense canvas, a quality of some nonverbal and passionate comprehension. At other times he saw a tremendously old woman, all nuances of the world, her past, and the earth's present, ignored or forgotten; brittle and single, everything rejected but her own tiny circle of motion.

With a fairly complex mind, Father O'Rourke combined a rather simple set of hopes, not many of which were realized. One of these was to enter Mrs. Travis's detail, as some sort of connection with a comfort, or even a lack of finality. The bond between them, actually, was a belief in the physical, a conviction of the open-ended mystery of matter. But since Mrs. Travis had never been a Catholic, that particular avenue wasn't open to him. Her passion was in this scraggy garden, but he distinguished that it was coldly unsentimental, unlike that of most lady gardeners he knew. He was not sure just how Mrs. Travis did feel about her flowers. He considered that, in homily and metaphor, the garden thing—Eden to Gethsemane—had been overdone; nevertheless, in connection with Mrs. Travis, he always thought of it. He had, on a previous visit last month, brought up some flower passages from the Bible; but the only interest she had shown was by a question as to which type of lily the lilies of the field had been. She had at least five kinds, lifting their slick and sappy stalks above confusion. But when he had said they were most like anemones, she had lost interest, having forgotten, after fifty years in the New Hampshire mountains, what anemones looked like.

"I have to go back to the Watkinses again tomorrow," said Father O'Rourke. He knew he should have been back at the rectory half an hour ago. Here he sat, mesmerized somehow by the invisible movement of the sun across the step, by the almost total stillness. It was cooling rapidly, too. He picked up his coat and hunched his arms into it. "Can I bring you anything, then?"

"No," she said. She was sorry to see him go. She turned her head to look fully at him. "Do you want any flowers?" she asked.

He hesitated, thinking of Mrs. Metcalfe's pious arrangement, three pink gladioli in a thin-stemmed glass on each side of the altar. "Well," he said, "how about some zinnias for my desk? I'll pick them tomorrow," he added hastily, as he saw her eyes cloud, rallying for action. On the step he lingered, smiling at her. Oppressed. "Well," he said idiotically, "don't let Jack Frost get your flowers."

She watched him attentively down the path. Just as his starter churned, the sun left the porch and, looking up to the mountain, Mrs. Travis saw that it had gone for the day.

She went in at once, forgetting her rake, lying in the garden, her empty teacup and the three dollars on the table, but carrying a short chunk of wood under each arm. She took at least one each time she went into the house. She never turned on the furnace before October, but there was a small chunk stove in the corner, by the lamp table, and it warmed the room in a matter of minutes. She decided to have supper right now. She had a chop; and there was still some lettuce. She had picked a fine head this morning, it was right in the collander, earth still clinging to its bottom.

By eight o'clock it had got very cold, outside. But the room was warm. Mrs. Travis went to sleep in her chair. Sleep often took her now with a ferocious touch, so that everything just disappeared, and when she woke up, she found that hours had passed. On a warm night in July she had slept in her chair all night long, waking up, disoriented, to a watery dawn.

Now she not only slept, she dreamed. An unpleasant dream, something extremely unusual. She was in a dark huge city lit by thin lamps, and she was afraid. She was afraid of a person, who might be coming toward her, or coming up behind her. And yet, more than a person—though she knew it was a man in a cap. She must get into a house before he found her. Or before he found someone else. A strange-looking girl went by her, hurrying, very pale, with a big artificial rose in her hair. She turned suddenly into an opening on the dreamer's right; it was the darkest of alleys and the dreamer hurried faster than ever. Ahead of her, in the fog, she could see the dimly lit sign of an inn, but as she hurried faster, a terrible scream, high and short, came out of the alley. It woke Mrs. Travis, her hands locked hard on the arms of the chair.

She sat quite still, looking around the familiar room. Then memory handed her one of the clear messages that now so seldom arrived. The Lodger. That was just it. She had suddenly, after all these years, had a dream about Jack the Ripper, as she had had several times when she first read of his foggy city streets a very long time ago. But why this dream should have escaped from the past to molest her, she could not think.

The little fire in the stove was out, but the stove itself still ticked and settled with heat. The wall clock said two minutes to eight. Stiff from sleep, Mrs. Travis reached over and turned the dial of the small discolored radio under the table lamp, and immediately a loud masculine voice said, ". . . front, all the way from the Great Lakes, throughout northern New England, and into Canada. Frost warnings have been issued for the mountain areas of Vermont and New Hampshire. Tomorrow the unseasonable cold will continue, for a chilly Labor Day; but by Wednesday . . ." Appalled, Mrs. Travis switched off the evil messenger.

Frost. It was not that it was so strange; it was so sudden. She could still feel the heat of the sun, on the porch, on her hands and her ankles. Two weeks, she had thought.

As she sat, staring for a moment straight ahead, a brand-new fury started up, deep inside her. Two weeks. It was an eternity of summer. The long nights, the brutal chill, the endless hardness of the earth, they were reasonable enough, in their time. In their time. But this was her time, and they were about to invade it. She began to tremble with anger. She thought of her seeds, and how dry and hard they had been; of her deathlike bulbs, slipping old skin, with everything locked inside them, and she, her body, had turned them into that summer of color and softness and good smells that was out there in the dark garden.

She turned her head, right, and left, looking for an exit for her rage. Then suddenly she sat forward in her chair. An idea had come to her with great force and clarity. It grew in the room, like an enormous plant covered with buds. Mrs. Travis knew exactly what she was going to do. Her intention was not protective, but defiant; her sense was of battle, punitive battle.

She stood up carefully, and went and got the flashlight from the shelf over the woodbox. She went to the porch door and opened it, and then closed it hastily behind her, protecting the room's warmth. There was no sound or light in any direction, but there was a diffused brightness behind the mountain's darker bulk. She tipped over the pail that had held Mrs. James's flowers, so that the leafy water poured down the sloping porch. Then she began fitting the tin flower-holders into it. She could not get them all in, and she took her pail into the house and came back for the last three. She arranged the pail and the tins on the kitchen floor, and then she attached a short length of hose to the cold-water spigot, dropped the other end in the pail, and turned on the water. She filled the big tins the same way, and then lifted the small ones into the sink, removing the hose, and filled them. Turning with satisfaction to look through the doorway at the clock, she was disconcerted to see that it said five minutes after nine. She stared at it, skeptical but uncertain. It could *stop;* but surely it couldn't skip *ahead.* Perhaps she had mistaken the earlier time. She began to move more rapidly; though she was so excited, all her faculties had come so strongly into one intention, that it seemed to her that she was already moving at a furious pace.

She went over to the kitchen door and took off its hook a felt hat and an ancient overcoat of Henry's. She put the hat on her head, got carefully into the overcoat and stuffed her flashlight into the pocket. She took down from the top of the refrigerator a cracked papier-mâché tray Mrs. James had sent her several Christmases ago; its design of old coins had almost disappeared. At an open drawer she hesitated over a pair of shears. Lately she had found them hard to open and close, and after standing there for half a minute, she took a thick-handled knife instead. She went to look at the empty sitting room and then moved back through the kitchen faster than seemed possible.

Out on the porch, a square of light came through the window, and looking up, she could make out a cloud over the mountain, its edges stained with brightness.

She lit her flashlight, and went cautiously down the step and along the path, carrying her tray under her arm. Faces of cosmos, purple and pink, loomed at her as she went, but even in her tremendous excitement, she knew she couldn't bring in everything, and she went on, the tops of her galoshes making a little flapping noise in the silence. She turned carefully down the slight slope, and here were the zinnias, towered over by the branchy dahlias. She laid her tray on the ground.

But now, breathing more rapidly, she saw that she was in trouble. To cut with her knife, she had to hold the flower's stem, and she had to hold her flashlight to see it, and she had two hands. Fiercely she looked about for an idea; and at just that moment, a clear thin light streamed over the edge of the cloud and lit her. The moon was full. She might have known; that was when a black frost always came.

Mrs. Travis made an inarticulate sound of fierce pleasure and dropped the flashlight into the tray. Then she began to cut the flowers, working as fast as she could, giving little pants of satisfaction as the shapes heaped themselves up below her. Inch by inch she moved along the ragged rows, pushing, with a galoshed toe, the tray along the ground before her. She cut all the gladioli, even the ones which were still mostly flaccid green tips; she cut all the dahlias, even the buds, and every zinnia. She felt light and warm, and drunk with resistant power. Finally the tray was so full that blooms began to tip over and fall into the cold grass.

Very cautiously indeed she got the tray up, but she could not hold it level and manipulate the flashlight. It made no difference. The moon, enormous and fully round, had laid light all over the garden; the house's shadow was black, as though a pale sun were shining.

Teetering a little to hold the tray level, Mrs. Travis went up the path, carefully up the step. She set the tray on the table, knocking over her dirty teacup and saucer, and each broke cleanly in two pieces. She stepped over them, opened the door on warmth, and went back for her load.

First she filled the pail; then every tin. There was a handful of zinnias left, and a pile of phlox. Threatened, Mrs. Travis looked about the kitchen, but saw nothing helpful. She could feel her cheeks burning in the room's summer, and with a little noise of triumph, she went through the door to the bedroom and came back with the big china chamberpot. It had a fine network of fractured veins, and on it was a burst of painted magenta foliage. When she had filled it under the tap it was too heavy to lift down, so she stuffed in the flowers and left it there. A small chartreuse-colored spider began to run up and down the sink's edge.

Then, just as she was turning to look at all she had done, like a cry from an alley, like a blow between the shoulders, to her mind's eye came the rose begonia. She could positively see in the air before her its ruffled heavy head, the coral flush of its crowded petals; from its side sprang the bud, color splitting the sheath. The bulb had thrust it up, and there it was, out there.

Though she felt as though she were drunk, she also felt shrewd. Think of the low ones you can't stoop to tonight, she thought, the nasturtiums, the pansies, the bachelor's buttons, the ragged robins. But it made no difference. She knew that unless she took the rose begonia, she had lost everything. She looked at the clock; it was half past ten. She could be back in ten minutes; and she decided that then she would sit right down by the stove and sleep there, deliberately, and not move into the cold bed and take off bit by bit so many clothes.

There were four sticks of wood by the stove, and under the lid the embers were bright. She put in three sticks; then she went empty handed to the porch. It was very cold and absolutely still. The moon was even brighter; it was almost halfway up the sky. She found a terra-cotta flowerpot on the porch corner, and she rooted in the footbath until she found her trowel. Then she went, as fast as she could go, down the path to the halfway point, where she came upon the rose begonia, paled by the chill of the light. As she bent over, her head roared; so she kneeled, and drove the blunt trowel-edge into the earth.

When the roots came up in a great ball of earth she pressed them into the pot, stuffing more clods of fibrous earth around them. Then she started to get up. But with the pot in one hand and the trowel in the other, it was impossible.

She dropped the trowel. She did not even think that she could get it tomorrow. Suddenly she was cold to her very teeth. She thought just of the room, the hot, colored, waiting room. Holding the pot in her left hand, pushing with her right, she got herself upright; but it made her dizzy, and as she lurched a little to the side the rake's teeth brought her down in a heavy fall. The flower shot from her hand and disappeared into the shadows and a bright strong pain blasted her. It was her ankle; and she lay with her face close to the cold dirt, feeling the waves of pain hit her.

Mrs. Travis raised her head, to see how far away the porch was. It was perhaps ten or eleven yards. Another country. Things seemed dimmer, too, and wrenching her head sideways and up, she saw that the huge moon had shrunk; it sat high and small, right at the top of the sky.

Mrs. Travis lowered her head gently and began to crawl, pushing with her hands and the knee of her good leg. She went along, inch by inch, foot by foot; she had no fear, since there was an absolute shield between one second and the next.

The porch was so shadowed now that she nearly missed it, the step struck her advancing hand. It took her three tries, but she got up over it, and went on, inch by inch, toward the door. A sliver of china bit her hand. Bright light came through the keyhole. She reached up and easily turned the doorknob, then like a crab she was across the sill.

She could not, she found, turn; but she pushed out with her left foot, and miraculously the door clicked shut just behind her. She felt no pain at all, but there was something forming under her ribs.

In the room's heat, the foilage of the marigolds gave out a spicy smell, stronger than the fragrance of the phlox. A dozen shapes and colors blazed before her eyes, and a great tearing breath came up inside her like an explosion. Mrs. Travis lifted her head, and the whole wave of summer, advancing obedient and glorious, in a crest of color and warmth and fragrance broke right over her.

❧ *Mona Van Duyn* ❧

Mona Van Duyn (1921–   ) is an editor as well as a poet. For many years she edited, with her husband, *Perspective: A Quarterly of Literature.* Born in Iowa, she was educated at the University of North Iowa and the University of Iowa, and now lives in St. Louis, Missouri. She has been awarded the Bollingen Prize for her poetry.

LETTERS FROM A FATHER

I

Ulcerated tooth keeps me awake, there is
such pain, would have to go to the hospital to have
it pulled or would bleed to death from the blood thinners,
but can't leave Mother, she falls and forgets her salve
and her tranquilizers, her ankles swell so and her bowels
are so bad, she almost had a stoppage and sometimes
what she passes is green as grass. There are big holes
in my thigh where my leg brace buckles the size of dimes.
My head pounds from the high pressure. It is awful
not to be able to get out, and I fell in the bathroom
and the girl could hardly get me up at all.
Sure thought my back was broken, it will be next time.
Prostate is bad and heart has given out,
feel bloated after supper. Have made my peace
because am just plain done for and have no doubt
that the Lord will come any day with my release.
You say you enjoy your feeder, I don't see why
you want to spend good money on grain for birds
and you say you have a hundred sparrows, I'd buy
poison and get rid of their diseases and turds.

II

We enjoyed your visit, it was nice of you to bring
the feeder but a terrible waste of your money
for that big bag of feed since we won't be living
more than a few weeks longer. We can see
them good from where we sit, big ones and little ones
but you know when I farmed I used to like to hunt
and we had many a good meal from pigeons
and quail and pheasant but these birds won't
be good for nothing and are dirty to have so near
the house. Mother likes the redbirds though.
My bad knee is so sore and I can't hardly hear
and Mother says she is hoarse from yelling but I know
it's too late for a hearing aid. I belch up all the time
and have a sour mouth and of course with my heart
it's no use to go to a doctor. Mother is the same.
Has a scab she thinks is going to turn to a wart.

III

The birds are eating and fighting, Ha! Ha! All shapes
and colors and sizes coming out of our woods
but we don't know what they are. Your Mother hopes
you can send us a kind of book that tells about birds.
There is one the folks called snowbirds, they eat on the ground,
we had the girl sprinkle extra there, but say,
they eat something awful. I sent the girl to town
to buy some more feed, she had to go anyway.

IV

Almost called you on the telephone
but it costs so much to call thought better write.
Say, the funniest thing is happening, one
day we had so many birds and they fight
and get excited at their feed you know
and it's really something to watch and two or three
flew right at us and crashed into our window

and bang, poor little things knocked themselves silly.
They come to after while on the ground and flew away.
And they been doing that. We felt awful
and didn't know what to do but the other day
a lady from our Church drove out to call
and a little bird knocked itself out while she sat
and she brought it in her hands right into the house,
it looked like dead. It had a kind of hat
of feathers sticking up on its head, kind of rose
or pinky color, don't know what it was,
and I petted it and it come to life right there
in her hands and she took it out and it flew. She says
they think the window is the sky on a fair
day, she feeds birds too but hasn't got
so many. She says to hang strips of aluminum foil
in the window so we'll do that. She raved about
our birds. P.S. The book just come in the mail.

v

Say, that book is sure good, I study
in it every day and enjoy our birds.
Some of them I can't identify
for sure, I guess they're females, the Latin words
I just skip over. Bet you'd never guess
the sparrows I've got here, House Sparrows you wrote,
but I have Fox Sparrows, Song Sparrows, Vesper Sparrows,
Pine Woods and Tree and Chipping and White Throat
and White Crowned Sparrows. I have six Cardinals,
three pairs, they come at early morning and night,
the males at the feeder and on the ground the females.
Juncos, maybe 25, they fight
for the ground, that's what they used to call snowbirds. I miss
the Bluebirds since the weather warmed. Their breast
is the color of a good ripe muskmelon. Tufted Titmouse
is sort of blue with a little tiny crest.
And I have Flicker and Red-Bellied and Red-
Headed Woodpeckers, you would die laughing
to see Red-Bellied, he hangs on with his head

flat on the board, his tail braced up under,
wing out. And Dickcissel and Ruby Crowned Ringlet
and Nuthatch stands on his head and Veery on top
the color of a bird dog and Hermit Thrush with spot
on breast, Blue Jay so funny, he will hop
right on the backs of the other birds to get the grain.
We bought some sunflower seeds just for him.
And Purple Finch I bet you never seen,
color of a watermelon, sits on the rim
of the feeder with his streaky wife, and the squirrels,
you know, they are cute too, they sit tall
and eat with their little hands, they eat bucketfuls.
I pulled my own tooth, it didn't bleed at all.

VI

It's sure a surprise how well Mother is doing,
she forgets her laxative but bowels move fine.
Now that windows are open she says our birds sing
all day. The girl took a Book of Knowledge on loan
from the library and I am reading up
on the habits of birds, did you know some males have three
wives, some migrate some don't. I am going to keep
feeding all spring, maybe summer, you can see
they expect it. Will need thistle seed for Goldfinch and Pine
Siskin next winter. Some folks are going to come see us
from Church, some bird watchers, pretty soon.
They have birds in town but nothing to equal this.

So the world woos its children back for an evening kiss.

Charles Baxter (1947–   ), author of a novel, poetry, and short
stories, lives in Michigan and teaches at Wayne State University
in Detroit. He has been awarded a Guggenheim grant and his
stories have appeared in the *Best American Short Stories* and the
Pushcart Prize anthologies. The story "Fenstad's Mother" was
inspired by and dedicated to the memory of Baxter's aunt, Helen
Baxter.

FENSTAD'S MOTHER

On Sunday morning after Commu-
nion Fenstad drove across town to visit his mother. Behind the wheel, he
exhaled with his hand flat in front of his mouth to determine if the wine
on his breath could be detected. He didn't think so. Fenstad's mother was
a lifelong social progressive who was amused by her son's churchgoing, and,
wine or no wine, she could guess where he had been. She had spent her life
in the company of rebels and deviationists, and she recognized all their
styles.

Passing a frozen pond in the city park, Fenstad slowed down to watch
the skaters, many of whom he knew by name and skating style. From a
distance they were dots of color ready for flight, frictionless. To express
grief on skates seemed almost impossible, and Fenstad liked that. He parked
his car on a residential block and took out his skates from the back seat,
where he kept them all winter. With his fingertips he touched the wooden
blade guards, thinking of the time. He checked his watch; he had fifteen
minutes.

Out on the ice, still wearing his churchy Sunday-morning suit, tie, and
overcoat, but now circling the outside edge of the pond with his bare hands
in his overcoat pockets, Fenstad admired the overcast sky and luxuriated

in the brittle cold. He was active and alert in winter but felt sleepy through-out the summer. He passed a little girl in a pink jacket, pushing a tiny chair over the ice. He waved to his friend Ann, an off-duty cop, practicing her twirls. He waved to other friends. Without exception they waved back. As usual, he was impressed by the way skates improved human character.

Twenty minutes later, in the doorway of her apartment, his mother said, "Your cheeks are red." She glanced down at his trousers, damp with melted snow. "You've been skating." She kissed him on the cheek and turned to walk into her living room. "Skating after church? Isn't that some sort of error?"

"It's just happiness," Fenstad said. Quickly he checked her apartment for any signs of memory loss or depression. He found none and immediately felt relief. The apartment smelled of soap and Lysol, the signs of an old woman who wouldn't tolerate nonsense. Out on her coffee table, as usual, were the letters she was writing to her congressman and to political dictators around the globe. Fenstad's mother pleaded for enlightened behavior and berated the dictators for their bad political habits.

She grasped the arm of the sofa and let herself down slowly. Only then did she smile. "How's your soul, Harry?" she asked. "What's the news?"

He smiled back and smoothed his hair. Martin Luther King's eyes locked into his from the framed picture on the wall opposite him. In the picture King was shaking hands with Fenstad's mother, the two of them sur-rounded by smiling faces. "My soul's okay, Ma," he said. "It's a hard project. I'm always working on it." He reached down for a chocolate-chunk cookie from a box on top of the television. "Who brought you these?"

"Your daughter Sharon. She came to see me on Friday." Fenstad's mother tilted her head at him. "You *want* to be a good person, but she's the real article. Goodness comes to her without any effort at all. She says you have a new girlfriend. A pharmacist this time. Susan, is it?" Fenstad nodded. "Harry, why does your generation always have to find the right person? Why can't you learn to live with the wrong person? Sooner or later everyone's wrong. Love isn't the most important thing, Harry, far from it. Why can't you see that? I still don't comprehend why you couldn't live with Eleanor." Eleanor was Fenstad's ex-wife. They had been divorced for a decade, but Fenstad's mother hoped for a reconciliation.

"Come on, Ma," Fenstad said. "Over and done with, gone and gone." He took another cookie.

"You live with somebody so that you're living with *somebody,* and then you go out and do the work of the world. I don't understand all this pickiness about lovers. In a pinch anybody'll do, Harry, believe me."

On the side table was a picture of her late husband, Fenstad's mild, middle-of-the-road father. Fenstad glanced at the picture and let the silence hang between them before asking, "How are you, Ma?"

"I'm all right." She leaned back in the sofa, whose springs made a strange, almost human groan. "I want to get out. I spend too much time in this place in January. You should expand my horizons. Take me somewhere."

"Come to my composition class," Fenstad said. "I'll pick you up at dinnertime on Tuesday. Eat early."

"They'll notice me," she said, squinting. "I'm too old."

"I'll introduce you," her son said. "You'll fit right in."

FENSTAD WROTE BROCHURES IN the publicity department of a computer company during the day, and taught an extension English-composition class at the downtown campus of the state university two nights a week. He didn't need the money: he taught the class because he liked teaching strangers and because he enjoyed the sense of hope that classrooms held for him. This hopefulness and didacticism he had picked up from his mother.

On Tuesday night she was standing at the door of the retirement apartment building, dressed in a dark blue overcoat—her best. Her stylishness was belied slightly by a pair of old fuzzy red earmuffs. Inside the car Fenstad noticed that she had put on perfume, unusual for her. Leaning back, she gazed out contentedly at the nighttime lights.

"Who's in this group of students?" she asked. "Working-class people, I hope. Those are the ones you should be teaching. Anything else is just a career."

"Oh, they work, all right." He looked at his mother and saw, as they passed under a streetlight, a combination of sadness and delicacy in her face. Her usual mask of tough optimism seemed to be deserting her. He braked at a red light and said, "I have a hairdresser and a garage mechanic and a housewife, a Mrs. Nelson, and three guys who're sanitation workers. Plenty of others. One guy you'll really like is a young black man with glasses who sits in the back row and reads *Workers' Vanguard* and Bakunin during class. He's brilliant. I don't know why he didn't test out of this class. His name's York Follette, and he's—"

"I want to meet him," she said quickly. She scowled at the moonlit snow. "A man with ideas. People like that have gone out of my life." She looked over at her son. "What I hate about being my age is how *nice* everyone tries to be. I was never nice, but now everybody is pelting me with sugar cubes." She opened her window an inch and let the cold air blow over her, ruffling her stiff gray hair.

When they arrived at the school, snow had started to fall, and at the other end of the parking lot a police car's flashing light beamed long crimson rays through the dense flakes. Fenstad's mother walked deliberately toward the door, shaking her head mistrustfully at the building and the police. Approaching the steps, she took her son's hand. "I liked the columns on the old buildings," she said, "the old university buildings, I mean. I liked Greek Revival better than this Modernist-bunker stuff." Inside, she blinked in the light at the smooth, waxed linoleum floors and cement-block walls. She held up her hand to shade her eyes. Fenstad took her elbow to guide her over the snow melting in puddles in the entryway. "I never asked you what you're teaching tonight."

"Logic," Fenstad said.

"Ah." She smiled and nodded. "Dialectics!"

"Not quite. Just logic."

She shrugged. She was looking at the clumps of students standing in the glare of the hallway, drinking coffee from paper cups and smoking cigarettes in the general conversational din. She wasn't used to such noise: she stopped in the middle of the corridor underneath a wall clock and stared happily in no particular direction. With her eyes shut she breathed in the close air, smelling of wet overcoats and smoke, and Fenstad remembered how much his mother had always liked smoke-filled rooms, where ideas fought each other, and where some of those ideas died.

"Come on," he said, taking her hand again. Inside Fenstad's classroom six people sat in the angular postures of pre-boredom. York Follette was already in the back row, his copy of *Workers' Vanguard* shielding his face. Fenstad's mother headed straight for him and sat down in the desk next to his. Fenstad saw them shake hands, and in two minutes they were talking in low, rushed murmurs. He saw York Follette laugh quietly and nod. What was it that blacks saw and appreciated in his mother? They had always liked her—written to her, called her, checked up on her—and Fenstad wondered if they recognized something in his mother that he himself had never been able to see.

At 7:35 most of the students had arrived and were talking to each other vigorously, as if they didn't want Fenstad to start and thought they could delay him. He stared at them, and when they wouldn't quiet down, he made himself rigid and said, "Good evening. We have a guest tonight." Immediately the class grew silent. He held his arm out straight, indicating with a flick of his hand the old woman in the back row. "My mother," he said. "Clara Fenstad." For the first time all semester his students appeared to be paying attention: they turned around collectively and looked at Fenstad's mother, who smiled and waved. A few of the students began to applaud; others joined in. The applause was quiet but apparently genuine. Fenstad's mother brought herself slowly to her feet and made a suggestion of a bow. Two of the students sitting in front of her turned around and began to talk to her. At the front of the class Fenstad started his lecture on logic, but his mother wouldn't quiet down. This was a class for adults. They were free to do as they liked.

Lowering his head and facing the blackboard, Fenstad reviewed problems in logic, following point by point the outline set down by the textbook: *post hoc* fallacies, false authorities, begging the question, circular reasoning, *ad hominem* arguments, all the rest. Explaining these problems, his back turned, he heard sighs of boredom, boldly expressed. Occasionally he glanced at the back of the room. His mother was watching him carefully, and her face was expressing all the complexity of dismay. Dismay radiated from her. Her disappointment wasn't personal, because his mother didn't think that people as individuals were at fault for what they did. As usual, her disappointed hope was located in history and in the way people agreed with already existing histories.

She was angry with him for collaborating with grammar. She would call it unconsciously installed authority. Then she would find other names for it.

"All right," he said loudly, trying to make eye contact with someone in the room besides his mother, "let's try some examples. Can anyone tell me what, if anything, is wrong with the following sentence? 'I, like most people, have a unique problem.'"

The three sanitation workers, in the third row, began to laugh. Fenstad caught himself glowering and singled out the middle one.

"Yes, it is funny, isn't it?"

The man in the middle smirked and looked at the floor. "I was just thinking of my unique problem."

"Right," Fenstad said. "But what's wrong with saying, 'I, like most people, have a unique problem'?"

"Solving it?" This was Mrs. Nelson, who sat by the window so that she could gaze at the tree outside, lit by a streetlight. All through class she looked at the tree as if it were a lover.

"Solving what?"

"Solving the problem you have. What is the problem?"

"That's actually not what I'm getting at," Fenstad said. "Although it's a good *related* point. I'm asking what might be wrong logically with that sentence."

"It depends," Harold Ronson said. He worked in a service station and sometimes came to class wearing his work shirt with his name tag, HAROLD, stitched into it. "It depends on what your problem is. You haven't told us your problem."

"No," Fenstad said, "my problem is *not* the problem." He thought of Alice in Wonderland and felt, physically, as if he himself were getting small. "Let's try this again. What might be wrong with saying that most people have a unique problem?"

"You shouldn't be so critical," Timothy Melville said. "You should look on the bright side, if possible."

"What?"

"He's right," Mrs. Nelson said. "Most people have unique problems, but many people do their best to help themselves, such as taking night classes or working at meditation."

"No doubt that's true," Fenstad said. "But why can't most people have a unique problem?"

"Oh, I disagree," Mrs. Nelson said, still looking at her tree. Fenstad glanced at it and saw that it was crested with snow. It *was* beautiful. No wonder she looked at it. "I believe that most people do have unique problems. They just shouldn't talk about them all the time."

"Can anyone," Fenstad asked, looking at the back wall and hoping to see something there that was not wall, "can anyone give me an example of a unique problem?"

"Divorce," Barb Kjellerud said. She sat near the door and knitted during class. She answered questions without looking up. "Divorce is unique."

"No, it isn't!" Fenstad said, failing in the crucial moment to control his voice. He and his mother exchanged glances. In his mother's face for a split second was the history of her compassionate, ambivalent attention to him. "Divorce is not unique." He waited to calm himself. "It's everywhere. Now try again. Give me a unique problem."

Silence. "This is a trick question," Arlene Hubbly said. "I'm sure it's a trick question."

"Not necessarily. Does anyone know what *unique* means?"

"One of a kind," York Follette said, gazing at Fenstad with dry amusement. Sometimes he took pity on Fenstad and helped him out of jams. Fenstad's mother smiled and nodded.

"Right," Fenstad crowed, racing toward the blackboard as if he were about to write something. "So let's try again. Give me a unique problem."

"You give *us* a unique problem," one of the sanitation workers said. Fenstad didn't know whether he'd been given a statement or a command. He decided to treat it as a command.

"All right," he said. He stopped and looked down at his shoes. Maybe it *was* a trick question. He thought for ten seconds. Problem after problem presented itself to him. He thought of poverty, of the assaults on the earth, of the awful complexities of love. "I can't think of one," Fenstad said. His hands went into his pockets.

"That's because problems aren't personal," Fenstad's mother said from the back of the room. "They're collective." She waited while several students in the class sat up and nodded. "And people must work together on their solutions." She talked for another two minutes, taking the subject out of logic and putting it neatly in politics, where she knew it belonged.

THE SNOW HAD STOPPED by the time the class was over. Fenstad took his mother's arm and escorted her to the car. After letting her down on the passenger side and starting the engine, he began to clear the front windshield. He didn't have a scraper and had forgotten his gloves, so he was using his bare hands. When he brushed the snow away on his mother's side, she looked out at him, surprised, a terribly aged Sleeping Beauty awakened against her will.

Once the car had warmed up, she was in a gruff mood and repositioned herself under the seat belt while making quiet but aggressive remarks. The sight of the new snow didn't seem to calm her. "Logic," she said at last. "That wasn't logic. Those are just rhetorical tactics. It's filler and drudgery."

"I don't want to discuss it now."

"All right. I'm sorry. Let's talk about something more pleasant."

They rode together in silence. Then she began to shake her head. "Don't take me home," she said. "I want to have a spot of tea somewhere before I go back. A nice place where they serve tea, all right?"

He parked outside an all-night restaurant with huge front plate-glass windows; it was called Country Bob's. He held his mother's elbow from the car to the door. At the door, looking back to make sure that he had turned off his headlights, he saw his tracks and his mother's in the snow. His were separate footprints, but hers formed two long lines.

Inside, at the table, she sipped her tea and gazed at her son for a long time. "Thanks for the adventure, Harry. I do appreciate it. What're you doing in class next week? Oh, I remember. How-to papers. That should be interesting."

"Want to come?"

"Very much. I'll keep quiet next time, if you want me to."

Fenstad shook his head. "It's okay. It's fun having you along. You can say whatever you want. The students loved you. I knew you'd be a sensation, and you were. They'd probably rather have you teaching the class than me."

He noticed that his mother was watching something going on behind him, and Fenstad turned around in the booth so that he could see what it was. At first all he saw was a woman, a young woman with long hair wet from snow and hanging in clumps, talking in the aisle to two young men, both of whom were nodding at her. Then she moved on to the next table. She spoke softly. Fenstad couldn't hear her words, but he saw the solitary customer to whom she was speaking shake his head once, keeping his eyes down. Then the woman saw Fenstad and his mother. In a moment she was standing in front of them.

She wore two green plaid flannel shirts and a thin torn jacket. Like Fenstad, she wore no gloves. Her jeans were patched, and she gave off a strong smell, something like hay, Fenstad thought, mixed with tar and sweat. He looked down at her feet and saw that she was wearing penny loafers with no socks. Coins, old pennies, were in both shoes; the leather was wet and cracked. He looked in the woman's face. Under a hat that seemed to collapse on either side of her head, the woman's face was thin and chalk-white except for the fatigue lines under her eyes. The eyes themselves were bright blue, beautiful, and crazy. To Fenstad, she looked desperate, percolating slightly with insanity, and he was about to say so to his mother when the woman bent down toward him and said, "Mister, can you spare any money?"

Involuntarily, Fenstad looked toward the kitchen, hoping that the manager would spot this person and take her away. When he looked back again, his mother was taking her blue coat off, wriggling in the booth to free her arms from the sleeves. Stopping and starting again, she appeared to be stuck inside the coat; then she lifted herself up, trying to stand, and with a quick, quiet groan slipped the coat off. She reached down and folded the coat over and held it toward the woman. "Here," she said. "Here's my coat. Take it before my son stops me."

"Mother, you can't." Fenstad reached forward to grab the coat, but his mother pulled it away from him.

When Fenstad looked back at the woman, her mouth was open, showing several gray teeth. Her hands were outstretched, and he understood, after a moment, that this was a posture of refusal, a gesture saying no, and that the woman wasn't used to it and did it awkwardly. Fenstad's mother was standing and trying to push the coat toward the woman, not toward her hands but lower, at waist level, and she was saying, "Here, here, here, here." The sound, like a human birdcall, frightened Fenstad, and he stood up quickly, reached for his wallet, and removed the first two bills he could find, two twenties. He grabbed the woman's chapped, ungloved left hand.

"Take these," he said, putting the two bills in her icy palm, "for the love of God, and please go."

He was close to her face. Tonight he would pray for her. For a moment the woman's expression was vacant. His mother was still pushing the coat at her, and the woman was unsteadily bracing herself. The woman's mouth was open, and her stagnant-water breath washed over him. "I know you," she said. "You're my little baby cousin."

"Go away, please," Fenstad said. He pushed at her. She turned, clutching his money. He reached around to put his hands on his mother's shoulders. "Ma," he said, "she's gone now. Mother, sit down. I gave her money for a coat." His mother fell down on her side of the booth, and her blue coat rolled over on the bench beside her, showing the label and the shiny inner lining. When he looked up, the woman who had been begging had disappeared, though he could still smell her odor, an essence of wretchedness.

"Excuse me, Harry," his mother said. "I have to go to the bathroom."

She rose and walked toward the front of the restaurant, turned a corner, and was out of sight. Fenstad sat and tried to collect himself. When the waiter came, a boy with an earring and red hair in a flattop, Fenstad just shook his head and said, "More tea." He realized that his mother hadn't taken off her earmuffs, and the image of his mother in the ladies' room with her earmuffs on gave him a fit of uneasiness. After getting up from the booth and following the path that his mother had taken, he stood outside the ladies' room door and, when no one came in or out, he knocked. He waited for a decent interval. Still hearing no answer, he opened the door.

His mother was standing with her arms down on either side of the first sink. She was holding herself there, her eyes following the hot water as it poured from the tap around the bright porcelain sink down into the drain, and she looked furious. Fenstad touched her and she snapped toward him.

"Your logic!" she said.

He opened the door for her and helped her back to the booth. The second cup of tea had been served, and Fenstad's mother sipped it in silence. They did not converse. When she had finished, she said, "All right. I do feel better now. Let's go."

At the curb in front of her apartment building he leaned forward and kissed her on the cheek. "Pick me up next Tuesday," she said. "I want to go back to that class." He nodded. He watched as she made her way past the security guard at the front desk; then he put his car into drive and started home.

That night he skated in the dark for an hour with his friend Susan, the pharmacist. She was an excellent skater: they had met on the ice. She kept late hours and, like Fenstad, enjoyed skating at night. She listened attentively to his story about his mother and the woman in the restaurant. To his great relief she recommended no course of action. She listened. She didn't believe in giving advice, even when asked.

THE FOLLOWING TUESDAY, FENSTAD'S mother was again in the back row next to York Follette. One of the fluorescent lights overhead was flickering, which gave the room, Fenstad thought, a sinister quality, like a debtors' prison or a refuge for the homeless. He'd been thinking about such people for the entire week. For seven days now he had caught whiffs of the woman's breath in the air, and one morning, Friday, he thought he caught a touch of the rotten-celery smell on his own breath, after a particularly difficult sales meeting.

Tonight was how-to night. The students were expected to stand at the front of the class and read their papers, instructing their peers and answering questions if necessary. Starting off, and reading her paper in a frightened monotone, Mrs. Nelson told the class how to bake a cheese soufflé. Arlene Hubbly's paper was about mushroom hunting. Fenstad was put off by the introduction. "The advantage to mushrooms," Arlene Hubbly read, "is that they are delicious. The disadvantage to mushrooms is that they can make you sick, even die." But then she explained how to recognize the common shaggymane by its cylindrical cap and dark tufts; she drew a model on the board. She warned the class against the *Clitocybe illudens,* the

Jack-o'-Lantern. "Never eat a mushroom like this one or *any* mushroom that glows in the dark. Take heed!" she said, fixing her gaze on the class. Fenstad saw his mother taking rapid notes. Harold Ronson, the mechanic, reading his own prose painfully and slowly, told the class how to get rust spots out of their automobiles. Again Fenstad noticed his mother taking notes. York Follette told the class about the proper procedures for laying down attic insulation and how to know when enough was enough, so that a homeowner wouldn't be robbed blind, as he put it, by the salesmen, in whose ranks he had once counted himself.

Barb Kjellerud had brought along a cassette player, and told the class that her hobby was ballroom dancing; she would instruct them in the basic waltz. She pushed the play button on the tape machine, and *Tales from the Vienna Woods* came booming out. To the accompaniment of the music she read her paper, illustrating, as she went, how the steps were to be performed. She danced alone in front of them, doing so with flair. Her blond hair swayed as she danced, Fenstad noticed. She looked a bit like a contestant in a beauty contest who had too much personality to win. She explained to the men the necessity of leading. Someone had to lead, she said, and tradition had given this responsibility to the male. Fenstad heard his mother snicker.

When Barb Kjellerud asked for volunteers, Fenstad's mother raised her hand. She said she knew how to waltz and would help out. At the front of the class she made a counterclockwise motion with her hand, and for the next minute, sitting at the back of the room, Fenstad watched his mother and one of the sanitation workers waltzing under the flickering fluorescent lights.

"WHAT A WONDERFUL CLASS," Fenstad's mother said on the way home. "I hope you're paying attention to what they tell you."

Fenstad nodded. "Tea?" he asked.

She shook her head. "Where're you going after you drop me off?"

"Skating," he said. "I usually go skating. I have a date."

"With the pharmacist? In the dark?"

"We both like it, Ma." As he drove, he made an all-purpose gesture. "The moon and the stars," he said simply.

When he left her off, he felt unsettled. He considered, as a point of courtesy, staying with her a few minutes, but by the time he had this idea he was already away from the building and was headed down the street.

He and Susan were out on the ice together, skating in large circles, when Susan pointed to a solitary figure sitting on a park bench near the lake's edge. The sky had cleared; the moon gave everything a cold, fine-edged clarity. When Fenstad followed the line of Susan's finger, he saw at once that the figure on the bench was his mother. He realized it simply because of the way she sat there, drawn into herself, attentive even in the winter dark. He skated through the uncleared snow over the ice until he was standing close enough to speak to her. "Mother," he said, "what are you doing here?"

She was bundled up, a thick woolen cap drawn over her head, and two scarves covering much of her face. He could see little other than the two lenses of her glasses facing him in the dark. "I wanted to see you two," she told him. "I thought you'd look happy, and you did. I like to watch happiness. I always have."

"How can you see us? We're so far away."

"That's how I saw you."

This made no sense to him, so he asked, "How'd you get here?"

"I took a cab. That part was easy."

"Aren't you freezing?"

"I don't know. I don't know if I'm freezing or not."

He and Susan took her back to her apartment as soon as they could get their boots on. In the car Mrs. Fenstad insisted on asking Susan what kind of safety procedures were used to ensure that drugs weren't smuggled out of pharmacies and sold illegally, but she didn't appear to listen to the answer, and by the time they reached her building, she seemed to be falling asleep. They helped her up to her apartment. Susan thought that they should give her a warm bath before putting her into bed, and, together, they did. She did not protest. She didn't even seem to notice them as they guided her in and out of the bathtub.

Fenstad feared that his mother would catch some lung infection, and it turned out to be bronchitis, which kept her in her apartment for the first three weeks of February, until her cough went down. Fenstad came by every other day to see how she was, and one Tuesday, after work, he went up to her floor and heard piano music: an old recording, which sounded much played, of the brightest and fastest jazz piano he had ever heard—music of superhuman brilliance. He swung open the door to her apartment and saw York Follette sitting near his mother's bed. On the bedside table was a small tape player, from which the music poured into the room.

Fenstad's mother was leaning back against the pillow, smiling, her eyes closed.

Follette turned toward Fenstad. He had been talking softly. He motioned toward the tape machine and said, "Art Tatum. It's a cut called 'Battery Bounce.' Your mother's never heard it."

"Jazz, Harry," Fenstad's mother said, her eyes still closed, not needing to see her son. "York is explaining to me about Art Tatum and jazz. Next week he's going to try something more progressive on me." Now his mother opened her eyes. "Have you ever heard such music before, Harry?"

They were both looking at him. "No," he said, "I never heard anything like it."

"This is my unique problem, Harry." Fenstad's mother coughed and then waited to recover her breath. "I never heard enough jazz." She smiled. "What glimpses!" she said at last.

After she recovered, he often found her listening to the tape machine that York Follette had given her. She liked to hear the Oscar Peterson Trio as the sun set and the lights of evening came on. She now often mentioned glimpses. Back at home, every night, Fenstad spoke about his mother in his prayers of remembrance and thanksgiving, even though he knew she would disapprove.

❧ F O U R ❧

To Make a
Contribution

"When you cease to make a contribution, you begin to die. I think it is a necessity to be doing something which you feel is helpful in order to grow old gracefully and contentedly."
    ELEANOR ROOSEVELT
    Letter to Mr. Horne, February 19, 1960

"The mere fact that you keep doing is self-creating. . . . One needs to try to continue doing those things you find interesting, satisfying, self-fulfilling."
    JESSICA TANDY AND
    HUME CRONYN
    I'm Too Busy to Talk Now, an interview by
    Connie Goldman (NPR series)

"There is only one solution if old age is not to be an absurd parody of our former life, and that is to go on pursuing ends that give our existence a meaning—devotion to individuals, to groups or to causes, social, political, and to intellectual or creative work. . . . One's life has value so long as one attributes value to the life of others, by means of friendship, indignation, compassion."
    SIMONE DE BEAUVOIR
    Coming of Age

✺ Jessica Tandy and Hume Cronyn ✺

In 1985, Connie Goldman, an independent radio producer, interviewer and reporter, spoke with Jessica Tandy (1909–   ) and Hume Cronyn (1911–   ) as part of a public radio series entitled "I'm Too Busy to Talk Now: Conversations with American Artists Over 70," from which this excerpt was taken. Through interviews with thirteen well-known older artists, Goldman addressed the evolution of creativity in later life. Cronyn and Tandy, considered by many to be the first couple of the American theater, have been married for more than forty years.

INTERVIEW WITH JESSICA TANDY AND HUME CRONYN

CONNIE GOLDMAN: America's most well-known theater couple are in their mid-seventies now. Separately and together, they have a long list of theater and film credits which have brought them awards, recognition, and international acclaim. Jessica Tandy is well remembered for her role as Blanche DuBois in *A Streetcar Named Desire.* And Hume Cronyn's roles have ranged from *The Caine Mutiny Court-Martial* to *Death of a Salesman.* Together, they're best known for *The Four-Poster, Foxfire,* and *The Gin Game.* You'd think after fifty years of a busy career they'd be ready to slow up. But as one journalist put it, "for the Cronyns, their best race is the one they haven't run yet." Although their initial response to my request for an

From *I'm Too Busy to Talk Now: Conversations with American Artists Over 70* (NPR series).

interview was ironically, "Well, we're really too busy to talk now," we eventually found some moments to discuss their creative process, their motivation and energy, and the changes that have come with the passing of the years. . . .

JESSICA TANDY: If anyone had said to me when I started, by the time you are seventy-four, seventy-five, or whatever I am now, this will be your position in life, I would have thought, Wow, how wonderful. I never even thought I'd live to seventy-five. And be active. Because in those days a woman of seventy was thought to be remarkable if she could feed herself, almost. There were exceptions obviously, but people did age more quickly. I think we are able to keep active longer and I think it's the activity that is creative, if we have to use that word. I think the mere fact that you keep doing is self-creating as it were. It's just flexing your muscles, that's what it is. I'm happiest, I love to have good times between work, when I'm vegetating and absorbing the world and so forth, but I love to go back to work.

GOLDMAN: Creativity in your life, or creating new things, or looking for new things, or doing new things, is the thing that in a sense, keeps you young, sustains and renews.

HUME CRONYN: Absolutely. I think it does.

GOLDMAN: Now let's talk about how. Now let's look back. Remember the first question I asked you, to look at the whole change in your creative process from when you were young and now.

CRONYN: It hasn't changed. It really hasn't changed. I haven't got the energies I used to have, I don't bring the same enthusiasm to certain elements of my work, acting, for instance, that I did when I was in my twenties or even my thirties. I mean then, any job that came along I took. I now am very choosy. I only do what I want to do or, on occasion, do things for the money it produces because I enjoy spending money and the fun it gives in life. It allows me to travel, it allows me to live comfortably. I don't think I ever stopped to dwell on that when I was in my twenties and thirties. I just took the job, and the next job and the next job. I don't think I had a philosophy about it. . . .

TANDY: You're being busy because you want to be busy. If you are busy just for the sake of being busy, that's very unproductive. Oh, life is full of that. There is an awful lot of work that is just the same thing over and over again, and you have to find ways to make it more interesting. I mean even if it's somebody who does not have a profession, shall we say, but the oldest one, which is to keep a home going, and make it interesting and see that everyone is well fed and has a pleasant house to come into. That's a very productive job. A very creative job, and if it's done in the spirit of "it's a bore" it will be unproductive. I think one has to look forward to what's coming next using the knowledge of what's gone before, if you can. Of course we all repeat our mistakes over and over again, and you recognize that, you say "damn it, I've done it again." But, the wisdom, if that's what it is, or experience that one has gained, it's in there and you call on it and use it. . . .

GOLDMAN: The challenge for all of us is to find our own creativity. A commodity that's an attribute of every human being, not just the great, the gifted or the young. Yet, in a world that often implies that old is over the hill, it's difficult to remember that age can bring an enriched sense of self and new satisfactions.

CRONYN: There's something about our society, I think, which contributes to a point in one's life where you face deadly inertia. And it has to do with the pension fund, with social security, with reaching certain benchmarks of age. Sixty, sixty-five, seventy, whatever. This is the moment when, quote, "I retire." Then what. It's the unusual individual and the admirable individual who can continue to involve themselves in a way which allows them to continue to grow and stimulates what reserve of energies they've got at that benchmark age. Jessie said it earlier. It all boils down to a matter of personal choice. I don't think one dwells on it until possibly you hit a very unhappy moment in your life when you find yourself in a state of suspended animation. This job's done, that's finished, my children have gone, and perhaps one of the worst things, I'm secure. Yes. And then what? The blood doesn't stop flowing through the veins, the creative juices, whatever they are, and please don't ask me to analyze them, are still flowing and they demand being put to some sort of use. One needs to try to continue doing those things that you find interesting, satisfying, self-fulfilling. And for some it can be a garden, a very real one, it can be, I guess, knitting, it can be, to some degree, reading, if your eyes are good enough. But we're fortunate, we are among the very, very fortunate. We found ourselves doing something for which we had a passion and the passion has never abated. What has abated is the energy to continue it on the kind of schedule that we were capable of. I mean . . . when I first started acting, if I had a matinee, when the matinee was over, I could go out and go to the movies, come back for the evening performance, go out, sit with my friends and drink, find a pretty girl, go dancing, get up in the morning and take some exercise, go look at pictures in a museum, go read a book, but, no more. If I have a matinee, I come home and go to sleep, then I go back and give a performance. And when that performance is over, I come home and go to sleep. I've also become much more aware that creative process, lovely and dreadful phrase, just won't function at all unless I take some degree of rest in between. . . .

GOLDMAN: Wisdom and confidence often come with age. Certainly the experience of experience is worth something.

TANDY: I think that the only way to keep fresh in one's skills is never to be sure that you know how to do it because you can branch out and do things differently, learn new ways of doing things. If you are set in your ways and know just how to do it and repeat it, it will become stale and not only stale to one's audience but boring to one's self so that each new project has to be attacked as though this were the first effort. Now of course one has skills that are built into you and that one can draw on, but I think it's unwise to rely on them.

CRONYN: When you were explaining to us the nature of the question all I could think of was probably Sam Beckett's most famous line which was "I can't go on, I can't go on, I'll go on." I think that's partly what drives you, and also an awareness which I don't think either of us dwell on but which terrifies us, and that is, we're terrified that if we stop we'll fall down.

TANDY: I don't know if this is as pertinent but I was just thinking right now that when I really really began, I was quite sure of how to do every-thing. I really knew. The older I get the less I am sure of how to do anything. But actually I know more. I know it's there to be drawn on. But I'm much less sure that I know how to go about anything. I really don't. There now.

CRONYN: I don't share Jessie's becoming modesty. I think we are artists and I think we've been among the most fortunate. We've led long, rich, artistically fulfilling lives. We're skilled in our craft, which is creative. I refuse to be modest about that. We can contribute to the same extent, I think, as the writer or the director. I have been both writer and director as well as actor, so I know something about those three processes. The fellow who hammers out a pretty piece of brass gives you an original form as an artist. That old lady down in Appalachia putting together a basket of wood splints is an artist, we are artists in our own modest way.

TANDY: I've lost my train of thought, I'm afraid.

CRONYN: It's probably my smoking.

TANDY: No. No. *(laughter).*

CRONYN: That's all right. It happens to me all the time. Where were we, Connie?

GOLDMAN: Well you know, people often jest about just this thing, about what happens to your mind, with age.

TANDY: I'll tell you what I was thinking back to was that this is an accepted myth, that it is general, that people fall apart and don't do anything. I don't think that is altogether true. I think it is absolutely up to the individual. It isn't any good blaming it on society, that says you're over the hill. I mean, if you feel over the hill, you are over the hill, so I don't think one can blame people out there, each one himself must do what they have a passion to do.

GOLDMAN: In the not too distant future there will be millions more who will say something similar. By the year 2000, 35 million Americans will be over the age of sixty-five.

CRONYN: I'd like to bet that within the next decade or the next twenty years you will find more and more and more of the senior citizens continuing to lead an active professional life. Perhaps on a volunteer basis. Perhaps on a continuing professional basis with a paid job and regular hours. That doesn't really matter, which you opt for, but surely it's obvious, even simplistic, to say that if you don't continue to exercise, the muscles atrophy.

And I'm not just speaking of muscles. I'm speaking of what goes on between the ears and your general enthusiasm for life. It's lovely and absolutely essential to rest at times, but if you say from now on I rest and that's my main activity, atrophy. I'm going to digress one minute and tell you a little story about I. F. Stone. He retired about the age of seventy-two, or something like that, from journalism, in which he'd had a very distinguished career. Somebody was interviewing him just as you are interviewing us and said to him, "But Mr. Stone, beyond this, what do you have to look forward to." And he said, "I hope to die young, as late as possible." I mean, isn't that a marvelous philosophy. And I think it applies to us. I wish I'd said it, instead of Mr. Stone. . . . Jessie, how old were the children when they started to walk?

TANDY: About a year.

CRONYN: Well, all right. I couldn't walk till I was a year old, I'm coming to the end of that cycle now. It's inevitable, it's inevitable, you don't brood about it, you just hope that this inevitable process of disintegration you'll fight off as long as you can. And the sum total of all that we're saying is, keep swinging. It's a lot easier to do when you are enthusiastic about what you're doing. And for those people who go through that terrible six months, a year, two years, three years of loss and when they find that they are not simply alone, but horribly lonely, the strength of character it takes and the effort of will to find an involvement in life, that will keep them going and give them something to think of outside of themselves and the tooth ache, the back ache, the bum eyesight, whatever it may be, is not easy, but it's essential, I think. Absolutely essential. I haven't faced that yet. It scares me. I haven't faced it because I haven't had to face it. I can still write, I can still act, I can still swim, I can still do this, that, the other, and I, along with all the broodiness and complaint and bitchiness, I still am able to enjoy an enormous amount of what I do. Lucky, fortunate, blessed. I suddenly think of melding two quotations. One I've already used very early in our talk, from Beckett, "I can't go on, I can't go on, I'll go on." And add to that Shakespeare, "With mirth and laughter, let old wrinkles come." I think I've misquoted it.

TANDY: No, that's right, "with mirth and laughter, let old wrinkles come."

Elwyn Brooks White (1899–1985) was a poet, essayist, and the author of three popular and well-loved children's books: *Stuart Little, Charlotte's Web,* and *The Trumpet of the Swan.* He was closely associated with *The New Yorker* magazine, published over nineteen books, received numerous awards for his work, and, in 1977, was elected to the American Academy of Arts and Letters.

E. B. White edited and wrote the Introduction for his wife's book, *Onward and Upward in the Garden.* Katharine White was an editor at *The New Yorker* for thirty-four years from its founding in 1925. She was also a gardener.

from

INTRODUCTION: ONWARD AND UPWARD IN THE GARDEN BY KATHARINE S. WHITE

In its issue of March 1, 1958, under the heading BOOKS, *The New Yorker* ran a critical article on garden catalogues. It was signed Katharine S. White, its subhead was "Onward and Upward in the Garden," and it was the first of what was to become a series of fourteen garden pieces extending over a period of twelve years.

To readers of the magazine, this first piece came as a surprise—I think a pleasant one. It was innovative in that its author, without warning or apology, plunged boldly into reviewing the books of seedsmen and nurserymen as though she were reviewing the latest novel. To the best of my knowledge, nobody had ever done this before in a magazine of general circulation. If *The New Yorker*'s readers were surprised, imagine the condition of the seedsmen and nurserymen themselves! It must have been a dream come true for them to wake up and discover that their precious catalogues and their purple prose were being examined by a critical mind in the pages of a well-regarded publication. . . .

I did not know at the time, and still don't know, what moved Katharine to write that first garden piece. Ever since I'd known her, she had been surrounded by seed catalogues in the wintertime, by seedlings pushing up in flats in spring, and she had always arranged bouquets for our house or apartment, whether the blooms came out of her own garden in Maine or out of a florist's shop in town. But no writing of all this had occurred. In 1958, her job as an editor was coming to a close and this provided her with more time to look about, more time to think about the gardens of her life. I suspect, though, that the thing that started her off was her discovery that the catalogue makers—the men and women of her dreams—were, in fact, writers. Expression was the need of their souls. To an editor of Katharine's stature, a writer is a special being, as fascinating as a bright beetle. Well, here in the garden catalogues, she stumbled on a whole new flock of creative people, handy substitutes for the O'Haras, the Nabokovs, the Staffords of her professional life. I imagine this was what did it—she couldn't stay out of the act any longer. She began reading Will Tillotson, Cecil Houdyshel, Amos Pettingill, Roy Hennessey ("Oregon's angry man"), H. M. Russell (the day-lily man of Texas), and many others. She was out of the *New Yorker* office but back among writers again, and in a field that had endless allure for her—the green world of growing things. "Reading this literature," she wrote, "is unlike any other reading experience. Too much goes on at once. I read for news, for driblets of knowledge, for aesthetic pleasure, and at the same time I am planning the future, and so I read in dream."

"Onward and Upward," a phrase swiped from the Unitarian creed, had often appeared in *The New Yorker* as a heading in other contexts. It was Katharine's invention, however, and it proved a happy choice of title for her adventure in garden writing. After two years of giving the catalogues an annual going-over and assessing the prose style and idiosyncrasies of the writers, she set to work, onward and upward, exploring other aspects of the garden world: the history of gardens, the literature of gardens, the arranging of flowers, the herbalists, the trends and developments. She was blessed with a curious mind and she ranged widely. She continuously revealed her own prejudices, her likes and dislikes, her crochets. Katharine was a traditionalist, not only in the garden, but everywhere else. She preferred the simple to the ornate, the plain to the fancy, the relaxed to the formal, the single to the double, the medium-size to the giant. She detested abbreviations: snaps, mums, glads, dels. She did not care for flowers that, to her eye, were gross or pretentious or stiff. (She seldom grew dahlias or gladiolas on our place.) She loved old clay pots, despised new plastic ones—the "hideous green, lavender, or gray plastic pot, often striated with pink." She knew where she stood, and she was not a woman who looked with indulgence on a pot striated with pink. . . .

How she loved shopping in catalogues! Hour after hour she studied, sifted, pondered, rejected, sorted—in the delirium of future blooming and fruiting. Harris was her dream catalogue, it was always within reach. No longer able to sit at a desk or at a typewriter, she had abandoned her cozy study at the front of the house and taken up a place at one end of the living-room sofa, propped with pillows. This became the control center of the house. The sofa served as desk as well as seat and it soon became buried under a mountain of catalogues, books, letters, files, memoranda, Kleenex, ash trays, and miscellany. The extraordinary accumulation, which would have driven me crazy, never seemed to annoy her or slow her up. I built her a coffee table, to catch the overflow from the sofa. The table was soon groaning under its own load. Yet she usually knew where something was, however deeply it was buried.

Although she spent a lot of time in dreamy admiration of the seductive pictures in catalogues—the Impossible Tomato, the Ultimate Rose—she was actually a hardheaded planner and organizer. She did little of the physical work of gardening herself; in youth she lacked the time, in age she lacked the strength. Henry Allen, our caretaker and himself an ardent gardener, was her strong right arm. But she masterminded everything. She got her seed orders in early, sometimes directing the campaign from her bed in a hospital, and we always ended up with a vegetable garden that loaded our freezer and nourished our bodies, and with flower borders that filled the eye and the spirit. She shopped among the seedsmen lavishly but cannily.

She also added them to her already long list of personal friends. Soon she knew intimately a great many of the people behind the catalogues, and when she sent in a seed order or a plant order it was usually accompanied by a long chatty letter in which she gave a quick rundown of the doings on our own place and then sought news of the trials, illnesses, and problems of the recipient. The garden people were quick to respond. "Dear Mrs. White," one letter began. "I am very happy to hear from you again, but so sorry you now feel old and ill. . . . I fractured my shoulder a couple of years ago, and somewhere along the way I lost my sense of equilibrium." And so the letters went, back and forth. I got the impression that my wife was in close touch with about half of the professional gardeners in America and worried about all of them. . . .

For Katharine, a room without a flowering plant was an empty shell. After she became so weakened by failing health that she required constant nursing, I equipped her bedroom with a hospital bed, a hospital table that spanned the bed, an oxygen kit, and a wonderful green device called a Bird Respirator. The patient gazed quizzically at this orderly and aseptic scene and immediately countered by calling for a Bird of Paradise plant in a tub. It was duly brought in and was about the size of a Shetland pony. Soon it was producing its bizarre parrot-like blossoms. It was a lecherous old thing, always grabbing at the nurses as they went by. We finally arranged matters so the Bird Respirator, when not in use, could sit lurking behind the Bird of Paradise, out of sight. It all worked out very nicely. The room was acceptable again.

WHEN MISS GERTRUDE JEKYLL, the famous English woman who opened up a whole new vista of gardening for Victorian England, prepared herself to work in her gardens, she pulled on a pair of Army boots and tied on an apron fitted with great pockets for her tools. Unlike Miss Jekyll, my wife had no garden clothes and never dressed for gardening. . . .

The only moment in the year when she actually got herself up for gardening was on the day in fall that she had selected, in advance, for the laying out of the spring bulb garden—a crucial operation, carefully charted and full of witchcraft. The morning often turned out to be raw and overcast, with a searching wind off the water—an easterly that finds its way quickly to your bones. The bad weather did not deter Katharine: the hour had struck, the strategy of spring must be worked out according to plan. This particular bulb garden, with its many varieties of tulips, daffodils, narcissi, hyacinths, and other spring blooms, was a sort of double-duty affair. It must provide a bright mass of color in May, and it must also serve as a source of supply—flowers could be stolen from it for the building of experimental centerpieces. . . .

As the years went by and age overtook her, there was something comical yet touching in her bedraggled appearance on this awesome occasion—the small, hunched-over figure, her studied absorption in the implausible notion that there would be yet another spring, oblivious to the ending of her own days, which she knew perfectly well was near at hand, sitting there with her detailed chart under those dark skies in the dying October, calmly plotting the resurrection.

Isaac Bashevis Singer (1904–   ), considered the foremost living writer of Yiddish literature, came from his native Poland to the United States in 1935. He still lives in New York City and writes in Yiddish for a Yiddish newspaper, *The Jewish Daily Forward.* He is the author of short stories, novels, memoirs, and children's books, and was awarded the Nobel Prize for Literature in 1978. "The Hotel" is representative of his many stories that are concerned with aging men and women and their particular interests and problems.

THE HOTEL

When Israel Danziger retired to Miami Beach it seemed to him as if he were retiring to the other world. At the age of fifty-six he had been compelled to abandon everything he had known: the factory in New York, his houses, the office, his children, his relatives, and his friends. Hilda, his wife, bought a house with a garden on the banks of Indian Creek. It had comfortable rooms on the ground floor, a patio, a swimming pool, palms, flower beds, a gazebo, and special chairs designed to put little strain on the heart. The creek stank a bit, but there was a cool breeze from the ocean just across the street.

The water was green and glassy, like a stage decoration at the opera, with white ships skimming over its surface. Seagulls squeaked shrilly above and swooped down to catch fish. On the white sands lay half-naked women. Israel Danziger did not need binoculars to view them; he could see them behind his sunglasses. He could even hear their gabble and laughter.

He had no worries of being forgotten. They would all come down from

Translated by the author.

New York in the winter to visit him—his sons, his daughters, and their in-laws. Hilda was already concerned about not having enough bedrooms and linen, and also that Israel might have too much excitement with all the visitors from the city. His doctor had prescribed complete rest.

It was September now, and Miami Beach was deserted. The hotels closed their doors, posting signs that they would reopen in December or January. In the cafeterias downtown, which only yesterday had swarmed with people, chairs were piled atop bare tables, the lights extinguished, and business at a standstill. The sun blazed, but the newspapers were full of warnings of a hurricane from some far-off island, admonishing their readers to prepare candles, water, and storm windows, although it was far from certain whether the hurricane would touch Miami. It might bypass Florida entirely and push out into the Atlantic.

The newspapers were bulky and boring. The same news items which stirred the senses in New York seemed dull and meaningless here. The radio programs were vacuous and television was idiotic. Even books by well-known writers seemed flat.

Israel still had an appetite, but Hilda carefully doled out his rations. Everything he liked was forbidden—full of cholesterol—butter, eggs, milk, coffee with cream, a piece of fat meat. Instead she filled him up with cottage cheese, salads, mangoes, and orange juice, and even this was measured out to him by the ounce lest, heaven forbid, he might swallow a few extra calories.

Israel Danziger lay on a deck chair, clad only in swimming trunks and beach sandals. A fig tree cast its shadow over him; yet he still covered his bald pate with a straw cap. Without clothes, Israel Danziger wasn't Israel Danziger at all; he was just a little man, a bundle of skin and bones, with a single tuft of hair on his chest, protruding ribs, knobby knees, and arms like sticks. Despite all the suntan lotion he had smeared on himself, his skin was covered with red blotches. Too much sun had inflamed his eyes.

He got up and immersed himself in the swimming pool, splashed around for a few minutes, and then climbed out again. He couldn't swim; all he did was dip himself, as if in a *mikvah*. Some weeks ago he had actually begun to read a book, but he couldn't finish it. Every day he read the Yiddish newspaper from beginning to end, including the advertisements.

He carried with him a pad and pencil, and from time to time he would estimate how much he was worth. He added up the profits from his apartment houses in New York and the dividends earned by his stocks and bonds. And each time the result was the same. Even if he was to live to be a hundred, Israel Danziger would still have more than enough, and there'd even be plenty for his heirs. Yet he could never really believe it. How and when did he amass such a fortune? And what would he do during all the years he still was destined to live: sit in the deck chair and gaze up at the sky?

Israel Danziger wanted to smoke, but the doctor allowed him only two cigars a day, and even that might be harmful. To dull his appetite for tobacco and for food, Israel chewed unsweetened gum. He bent down, plucked a blade of grass, and studied it. Then his eyes wandered to an orange tree nearby. He wondered what he would have thought if someone in Parciewe, his hometown in Poland, had told him that one day he would own a house in America, with citrus and coconut trees on the shores of the Atlantic Ocean in a land of eternal summer. Now he had all this, but what was it worth?

Suddenly israel danziger tensed. He thought he heard the telephone ringing inside. A long-distance call from New York, perhaps? He got up to answer it, and realized it was just a cricket which made a noise like a bell. No one ever called him here. Who would call him? When a man liquidates his business, he's like a corpse.

Israel Danziger looked around again. The sky was pale blue, without even a cloud-puff. A single bird flew high above him. Where was it flying? The women who earlier had lain in the sand were now in the ocean. Although the sea was as smooth as a lake, they jumped up and down as if there were waves. They were fat, ugly, and broad-shouldered. There was about them a selfishness that sickens the souls of men. And for such parasites men worked, weakened their hearts, and died before their times?

Israel had also driven himself beyond his strength. The doctors had warned him. Israel spat on the ground. Hilda was supposed to be a faithful wife, but just let him close his eyes and she'd have another husband within a year, and this time she'd pick a taller man . . .

But what was he to do? Build a synagogue where no one comes to pray? Have a Torah inscribed that nobody would read? Give away money to a kibbutz and help the atheists live in free love? You couldn't even give money to charity these days. For whatever purpose you gave, the money was eaten up by secretaries, fund-raisers, and politicians. By the time it was supposed to reach the needy, there was nothing left.

In the same notebook that Israel Danziger used to total up his income lay several letters which he had received only that morning. One from a yeshiva in Brooklyn, another from a Yiddish poet who was preparing to publish his work, a third from a home for the aged which wanted to build a new wing. The letters all sang the same refrain—send us a check. But what good would come of a few additional students at the yeshiva in Williamsburg? Who needed the poet's new verse? And why build a new wing? So that the president could arrange a banquet and take the cream off the milk? Perhaps the president was a builder himself, or else he had a son-in-law who was an architect. I know that bunch, Israel Danziger grumbled to himself. They can't bluff me.

Israel danziger couldn't remain seated any longer. He was engulfed by an emptiness as painful as any heart attack. The force that keeps men alive was draining from him and he knew without a doubt that he was only one step away from death, from madness. He had to do something immediately. He ran inside to his bedroom, flung open the doors of his closet, put on pants, a pair of socks, a shirt, a pair of shoes, then took up his cane and went out. His car was waiting in the garage, but he didn't want to drive a car and speed without purpose over the highway. Hilda was out shopping for groceries; the house would be empty, but no one stole things here. And what did it matter if someone did try to break in? Besides, Joe the gardener was out tending the lawns, sprinkling water from a hose onto the bluish grass that had been brought here in sheets and now was spread over the sand like a carpet. Even the grass here has no roots, Israel Danziger thought. He envied Joe. At least that black man was doing something. He had a family somewhere near Miami.

What Israel Danziger was living through now was not mere boredom; it was panic. He had to act or perish. Maybe go to his broker and see how his stocks were getting along? But he'd already been there that morning for an hour. If he should take to going there twice a day, he would become a nuisance. Besides, it was now twenty minutes to three. By the time he got there, they'd be closed.

The bus station was just across the street, and a bus was pulling up. Israel Danziger ran across the road, and this very act was like a drop of medicine. He climbed on the bus and threw in the coin. He'd go to Paprov's cafeteria. There he'd buy the afternoon paper, an exact duplicate of the morning paper, drink a cup of coffee, eat a piece of cake, smoke a cigar, and, who knows, perhaps he would meet someone he knew.

The bus was half empty. The passengers all sat on the shaded side and fanned themselves, some with fans, others with folded newspapers, and still others with the flaps of pocketbooks. Only one passenger sat on the side where the sun burned, a man who was beyond caring about heat. He looked unkempt, unshaven, and dirty. Must be a drunk, Israel Danziger thought, and for the first time he understood drunkenness. He'd take a shot of whiskey, too, if he were allowed. Anything is better than this hollowness.

A passenger got off and Israel Danziger took his seat. A hot wind blew in through the open window. It tasted of the ocean, of half-melted asphalt and gasoline. Israel Danziger sat quietly. But suddenly perspiration broke out over all his body and his fresh shirt was soaked in a second. He grew more cheerful. He had reached the point where even a bus ride was an adventure.

On Lincoln Road were stores, shop windows, restaurants, banks. Newsboys were hawking papers. It was a little like a real city, almost like New York. Beneath one of the storefront awnings, Israel Danziger saw a poster advertising a big sale. The entire stock was to be sold. To Israel Danziger, Lincoln Road seemed like an oasis in the wilderness. He found himself worrying about the owners of the stores. How long would they hold out if they never saw a customer? He felt impelled to buy something, anything, to help business. It's a good deed, he told himself, better than giving to shnorrers.

The bus stopped, and Israel Danziger got off and entered the cafeteria. The revolving door, the air-conditioned chill, the bright lights burning in the middle of the day, the hubbub of customers, the clatter of dishes, the long steam tables laden with food and drink, the cashier ringing the cash register, the smell of tobacco—all this revived the spirit of Israel Danziger. He shook off his melancholy, his hypochondria and thoughts of death. With his right hand he grabbed a tray; his left hand he stuck into his rear pocket, where he had some bills and small change. He remembered his doctor's warnings, but a greater power—a power which makes the final decision—told him to go ahead. He bought a chopped-herring sandwich, a tall glass of iced coffee, and a piece of cheese cake. He lit a long cigar. He was Israel Danziger again, a living person, a businessman.

At another table, across from Israel Danziger, sat a little man, no taller than Danziger but stocky, broad-shouldered, with a large head and a fat neck. He wore an expensive Panama hat (at least fifty dollars, Danziger figured), and a pink, short-sleeved shirt. On one of his fingers, plump as a sausage, a diamond glittered. He was puffing a cigar and leafing through a Yiddish newspaper, breaking off pieces from an egg pretzel. He removed his hat, and his bald head shone round and smooth. There was something childlike about his roundness, his fatness, and his puckered lips. He was not smoking his cigar; he was only sucking at it, and Israel Danziger wondered who he was. Certainly he was not a native. Perhaps a New Yorker? But what was he doing here in September, unless he suffered from hay fever? And, since he was reading a Yiddish paper, Israel Danziger knew he was one of the family. He wanted to get to know the man. For a while he hesitated; it wasn't like him to approach strangers. But here in Miami you can die of boredom if you're too reserved. He got up from his chair, took the plate with the cheese cake and the coffee, and moved over to the other man's table.

"Anything new in the paper?"

The man removed the cigar from his mouth. "What should be new? Nothing. Not a thing."

"In the old days there were writers, today scribblers," said Israel Danziger, just to say something.

"It's five cents wasted."

"Well, what else can you do in Miami? It helps kill time."

"What are you doing here in this heat?"

"And what are you doing here?"

"It's my heart . . . I'm sitting around here six months already. The doctor exiled me here . . . I had to retire . . . "

"So—then we're brothers!" Israel Danziger exclaimed. "I have a heart, too, a bad heart that gives me trouble. I got rid of everything in New York, and my good wife bought me a house with fig trees, like in Palestine in the old days. I sit around and go crazy."

"Where is the house?"

Danziger told him.

"I pass it every day. I think I even saw you there once. What did you do before?"

Danziger told him.

"I myself have been in real estate for over thirty-five years," the other man said.

THE TWO MEN FELL into a conversation. The little man in the Panama hat said his name was Morris Sapirstone. He had an apartment on Euclid Avenue. Israel Danziger got up and bought two cups of coffee and two more egg pretzels. Then he offered him one of his cigars, and Sapirstone gave him one of his brand. After fifteen minutes they were talking as if they had known each other for years.

They had moved in the same circles in New York; both came from Poland. Sapirstone took out a wallet of alligator leather and showed Israel Danziger photographs of his wife, two daughters, two sons-in-law—one a doctor, one a lawyer—and several grandchildren. One granddaughter looked like a copy of Sapirstone. The woman was fat, like a Sabbath stew pot. Compared to her, his Hilda was a beauty. Danziger wondered how a man could live with such an ugly woman. On the other hand, he reflected, with one of her kind, you wouldn't be as lonesome as he was with Hilda. A woman like that would always have a swarm of chattering biddies around her.

Israel Danziger had never been pious, but since his heart attack and his retirement to Miami Beach he had begun to think in religious terms. Now he beheld the finger of God in his coming together with Morris Sapirstone.

"Do you play chess?" he asked.

"Chess, no. But I do play pinochle."

"Is there anybody to play with?"

"I find them."

"You're a smart man. I can't find anybody. I sit around all day long and don't see a soul."

"Why did you settle so far uptown?"

In the course of their talk Morris Sapirstone mentioned that there was a hotel for sale. It was almost a new hotel, all the way uptown. The owners had gone bankrupt, and the bank was ready to sell it for a song. All you needed was a quarter of a million in cash. Israel Danziger was far from ready for a business proposition, but he listened eagerly. Talk of money, credit, banks, and mortgages cheered him up. It was proof, somehow, that the world had not yet come to an end. Israel Danziger knew nothing at all about hotels, but he picked up bits of information from Morris Sapirstone's story. The owners of the hotel had failed because they had sought a fancy clientele and made their rates too high. The rich people had stopped coming to Miami Beach. You had to attract the middle class. One good winter season and your investment would be covered. A new element was coming to Miami—the Latin Americans who chose Florida during their summers to "cool off." Israel Danziger groped in his shirt pocket for a pencil stub. While Morris went on talking, Israel wrote figures in the margin of his newspaper with great speed. At the same time, he plied Sapirstone with questions. How many rooms in the hotel? How much can one room bring in? What about taxes? Mortgages? Personnel costs? For Israel, it was no more than a pastime, a reminder that once he, too, had been in business. He scratched his left temple with the point of the pencil.

"And what do you do if you have a bad season?"

"You have to see to it that it's good."

"How?"

"You have to advertise properly. Even in the Yiddish newspapers."

"Do you have a hall for conventions?"

AN HOUR HAD PASSED and Israel Danziger did not know where it had gone. He clenched his cigar between his lips and turned it busily around in his mouth. New strength welled up inside him. His heart, which in recent months had alternately fluttered and hesitated, now worked as if he were a healthy man. Morris Sapirstone took a small box from his coat pocket, picked out a pill, and swallowed it with a drink of water.

"You had an attack, eh?"

"Two."

"For whom do I need a hotel? For my wife's second husband?"

Morris Sapirstone did not answer.

"How can I get to look at the hotel?" Israel Danziger asked after a while.

"Come with me."

"Do you have a car here?"

"The red Cadillac across the street."

"Ah, a nice Cadillac you got."

The two men left the cafeteria. Israel Danziger noticed that Sapirstone was using a cane. Water in his legs, he thought. An invalid and he's hunting for hotels . . . Sapirstone settled behind the steering wheel and started the engine. He gave a whack to the car behind him, but he didn't even turn around. Soon he was racing along. One hand expertly grasped the steering wheel; with the other, he worked a cigarette lighter. With a cigar clamped in his teeth, he mumbled on.

"There's no charge for looking."

"No."

"If my wife hears about this, she'll give me plenty of trouble. Before you know it, she'll tell the doctor and then they'll both eat me up alive."

"They told you to rest, eh?"

"And if they told me? One must rest *here,* in the head. But my mind doesn't rest. I lie awake at night and think about all kinds of nothings. And when you're up you get hungry. My wife went to a locksmith to find out whether she can put a lock on the refrigerator . . . All these diets make you more sick than well. How did people live in the old days? In my time there were no diets. My grandfather, he should rest in peace, used to eat up a whole plateful of onions and chicken fat as an appetizer. Then he got busy on the soup with drops of fat floating on top. Next he had a fat piece of meat. And he finished up with a shmaltz cake. Where was cholesterol then? My grandfather lived to be eighty-seven, and he died because he fell on the ice one winter. Let me tell you: someday they'll find out that cholesterol is healthy. They'll be taking cholesterol tablets just as they take vitamin pills today."

"I wish you were right."

"A man is like a Hanukkah dreidel. It gets a turn, and then it spins on by itself until it drops."

"On a smooth table, it'll spin longer."

"There aren't any smooth tables."

The car stopped. "Well, that's the hotel."

Israel Danziger took one look and saw everything in a moment. If it was true that you only had to lay down a quarter of a million, the hotel was a fantastic bargain. Everything was new. It must have cost a fortune to build. Of course it was located a little too far uptown, but the center was moving uptown now. Once, the Gentiles ran away from the Jews. Now the Jews were running away from the Jews. Across the street there was already a kosher meat market. Israel Danziger rubbed his forehead. He would have to put in a hundred and twenty-five thousand dollars as his share. He could borrow that much from the bank, giving his stocks as security. He might even be able to scrape together the cash without a loan. But should he really get involved in such headaches? It would be suicide, sheer suicide. What would Hilda say? And Dr. Cohen? They'd all be at me—Hilda, the boys, the girls, their husbands. That in itself could lead to a second attack . . .

Israel Danziger closed his eyes and for a while remained enveloped in his own darkness. Like a fortune-teller, he tried to project himself into the future and foresee what fate had in store for him. His mind became blank, dark, overcome with the numbness of sleep. He even heard himself snore. All his affairs, his entire life, hung in the balance this second. He was waiting for a command from within, a voice from his own depths . . . Better to die than to go on living like this, he mumbled finally.

"What's the matter, Mr. Danziger, did you fall asleep?" he heard Sapir-stone ask.

"Eh? No."

"So come in. Let's take a look at what's going on in here."

And the two little men climbed the steps to the fourteen-story hotel.

Anna Mary Robertson Moses (1860–1961), best known as "Grandma Moses," was born on a farm in New York State. She started painting in her old age, when she was in her seventies, and her fingers had become too stiff to stitch embroidery. Her primitive oil paintings of scenes from rural life soon were exhibited internationally. When she was one hundred years old, in 1960, she illustrated an edition of *The Night Before Christmas* that was published a year after she died, in 1962. The following excerpts are from her autobiography.

from

MY LIFE'S HISTORY

What a strange thing is memory, and hope; one looks backward, the other forward. The one is of today, the other is the Tomorrow. Memory is history recorded in our brain, memory is a painter, it paints pictures of the past and of the day. . . .

As for myself, I started to paint in my old age, one might say, though I had painted a few pictures before. My sister Celestia came down one day and saw my worsted pictures and said: "I think you could paint better and faster than you could do worsted pictures." So I did, and painted for pleasure, to keep busy and to pass the time away, but I thought of it no more than of doing fancy work.

When I had quite a few paintings on hand, someone suggested that I send them down to the old Thomas' drug store in Hoosick Falls, so I tried that. I also exhibited a few at the Cambridge Fair with some canned fruits and raspberry jam. I won a prize for my fruit and jam, but no pictures.

And then, one day, a Mr. Louis J. Caldor of New York City, an engineer and art collector, passing through the town of Hoosick Falls, saw and bought my paintings. He wanted to know who had painted them, and they told him it was an old woman that was living down on the Cambridge Road by the name of Anna Mary Moses. So when I came home that night, Dorothy said: "If you had been here, you could have sold all your paintings, there was a man here looking for them, and he will be back in the morning to see them. I told him how many you had." She thought I had about ten, something like that.

Well, I didn't sleep much that night, I tried to think where I had any paintings and what they were, I knew I didn't have many, they were mostly worsted, but I thought, towards morning, of a painting I had started on after house cleaning days, when I found an old canvas and frame, and I thought I had painted a picture on it of Virginia. It was quite large, and I thought if I could find frames in the morning I could cut that right in two and make two pictures, which I did, and by so doing I had the ten pictures for him when he came. I did it so it wouldn't get Dorothy in the dog house. But he didn't discover the one I had cut in two for about a year, then he wanted to know what made me cut my best picture in two. I told him, it's just Scotch thrift.

He wanted me to paint more, he came back several times, he bought the pictures and paid for them. He took them down to New York to show in the galleries, three of these found their way into a Museum of Modern Art exhibition. Then in October of 1940 I had the first exhibit of my paintings placed at the Galerie St. Etienne, 46 West 57th Street. When my exhibition opened large numbers of elderly people came having heard my story. . . .

When I paint, I study and study the outside lots of times. Often I get at loss to know just what shade of green, and there are a hundred trees that have each three or four shades of green in them. I look at a tree and I see the limbs, and then the next part of the tree is a dark, dark black green, then I have got to make a little lighter green, and so on. And then on the outside, it'll either be a yellow green, or whitish green, that's the way the trees are shaded. And the snow—they tell me that I should shade it more or use more blue, but I have looked at the snow and looked at the snow, and I can see no blue, sometimes there is a little shadow, like the shadow of a tree, but that would be grey, instead of blue, as I see it. I love pink, and the pink skies are beautiful. Even as a child, the redder I got my skies with my father's old paint, the prettier they were.

THE FIRST RADIO I ever saw was a crystal set made by hand and given to Dorothy and Hugh for a Christmas present in 1920. The first time I had the experience of being on the radio myself was several years ago while I was in New York. There I met Bessie Beattie who asked me to go on the air at one of her broadcasts. I didn't think too much of this idea, but was glad to help her, so I accepted. The second time it was on the program "We the People," in April 1946. They had gone to a lot of trouble, sending two men from New York City. Carl Schutzman, an engineer, who came with a portable transmitting apparatus, was very patient listening for the switch-over to Eagle Bridge. Then there were four men from the Troy Telephone Company, to make connections between Grandma Moses and New York City.

I presume there were some nervous moments for those men who had gone to all that trouble and expense, for fear all would not go right. We found that we had but three minutes time allowed for the talk. Now who can say much in three minutes? So we had to boil it down to the three minutes.

The interview was with Mr. Gene Hurley, he was very nice and patient with me. We went over the program several times, I am a dumb Dora when it comes to such work, it is out of my line of business, but I enjoyed it, and I hope all the others did too. First I was asked, what kind of pictures I liked best, so I said, "I like pretty things the best, what's the use of painting a picture if it isn't something nice? So I think real hard till I think of something real pretty, and then I paint it. I like to paint old timey things, historical landmarks of long ago, bridges, mills and hostelries, those old time homes, there are a few left, and they are going fast. I do them all from memory, most of them are day dreams, as it were. . . . " Then he asked me, how it feels to be famous, and what I think of those millions of Christmas cards, made from my pictures. "Oh, I don't think about fame much, I keep my mind on what I am going to paint next, I have got a lot of catching up to do! And as to the Christmas cards, I can't think of much to say about them. My granddaughter out in Arizona jokes a lot about them, she says I am a witch, except I ride around the country on a paint brush, instead of a broom."

When all was over we had refreshments, then they all departed for their homes. Leaving the house so lonesome. . . .

If I didn't start painting, I would have raised chickens. I could still do it now. I would never sit back in a rocking chair, waiting for someone to help me. I have often said, before I would call for help from outsiders, I would rent a room in the city some place and give pancake suppers, just pancake and syrup, and they could have water, like a little breakfast. I never dreamed that the pictures would bring in so much, and as for all that publicity, and as for the fame which came to Grandma so late, that I am too old to care for now. Sometimes it makes me think of a dream that my father once told at the breakfast table one morning many years ago. He said, "I had a dream about you last night, Anna Mary." "Was it good or bad, Pa?" And he said, "That depends on the future, dreams cast their shadows before us." He dreamed, I was in a large hall and there were many people there, they were clapping their hands and shouting and he wondered what it was all about. "And looking I saw you, Anna Mary, coming my way, walking on the shoulders of men; you came right on stepping from one shoulder to another, waving to me." Of late years I have often thought of that dream, since all the publicity about me, and of my mother saying to father, "Now, Russell, Anna Mary would look nice walking on men's shoulders!" She saw the folly of that dream. Or did that dream cast its shadows before? I often wonder, now that I am getting such kind well-wishing letters from almost every country on the globe. . . .

Even now I am not old, I never think of it, yet I am a grandmother to eleven children, I also have seventeen great-grandchildren, that's aplenty!

⋆§ *Theodore Roethke* ⋆•

Theodore Roethke (1908–1963) was born in Michigan and educated at the University of Michigan and at Harvard. He taught
literature at Lafayette, Penn State, Bennington, and the University of Washington at Seattle. Among his many honors and
awards was the Pulitzer Prize in 1953 and the Bollingen Prize
in 1958. The poem "Old Florist" harkens back to his early years
growing up in Michigan where his family owned and operated
greenhouses and nurseries.

OLD FLORIST

That hump of a man bunching chrysanthemums
Or pinching-back asters, or planting azaleas,
Tamping and stamping dirt into pots,—
How he could flick and pick
Rotten leaves or yellowy petals,
Or scoop out a weed close to flourishing roots,
Or make the dust buzz with a light spray,
Or drown a bug in one spit of tobacco juice,
Or fan life into wilted sweet-peas with his hat,
Or stand all night watering roses, his feet blue in rubber boots.

§•

British writer Doris Lessing (1919–   ) was born in Persia, moved to Southern Rhodesia as a child, and now lives in London. She has written novels, short stories, plays, science fiction, and poetry. In her work, she is most interested in confronting the social, political, and cultural problems of the modern world. Under the pseudonym of Jane Somers she has written two novels concerned with old age.

WOMB WARD

Eight beds in a large room, four on either side and too close to each other. This was a shabby Victorian hospital in west London, and probably the room had not been designed as a ward. But it was decent, with pink flowery curtains at the windows, and on runners to separate the beds for moments needing privacy. Because the room was tidied for visiting time the long decorous swathes of pink were tied back. A lot of people sat about on chairs or on the beds. Mothers and sisters, brothers and cousins, friends and children had been coming and going since two in the afternoon. Not the husbands: they would be in later. But there was one husband who sat close to the head of a bed where a pretty woman of about forty-five lay turned toward him. She gazed into his face while he held both her hands, one in each of his. They were large hands, and he was a big man, wearing good clothes, tweedy gray jacket and a white shirt that dazzled, like those in the advertisements. But he had taken off his tie, which hung on his chair back, and this gave him an informal look. The intensity of his concern for his wife and her imploring gaze at him isolated them as if a curtain had gone up on them in their own home. Certainly neither was aware of the visitors who came and went.

He had brought her in at midday and had been sitting with her ever since, before formal visiting hours began.

This was a ward for gynecological problems, or, as the women joked, a womb ward. The seven other women had had or would have operations or other treatment. No one was seriously ill, and more joking went on than in any other kind of ward, yet low spirits were never far away, and the nurses who were always in and out kept an eye open for a woman weeping, or one silent for too long.

At six o'clock the suppers were brought in and most visitors went home. No one had an appetite, but the husband coaxed his wife to eat, while she protested she did not want to. She cried a little but stopped when he soothed her like a father, and she sat obediently with a bowl of custard in her hand while he fed her with a spoon from it, sometimes putting down the spoon to blot her eyes with a large old-fashioned very white handkerchief, for she could not keep back the tears for long. She wept like a child, with little gulps and snuffles and heaves of her chest, always watching him with her wide, wet blue eyes. Blue eyes meant to be happy, for crying did not suit her.

The other women watched this scene. Sometimes their gazes met, commenting on it. Then husbands came in after work, and for an hour or so the room contained couples in close practical talk about children and domestic matters. Four husbands had come. One old woman sat alone, turning the pages of a magazine and watching the others over it. Another, Miss Cook, had never been married. She, too, watched what went on, while she knitted. The third who had no man beside her read a book and listened to her Walkman. She was "the horsy one." (Whether she was horsy or not no one knew; she was presumed to be, being upper class.)

Then it was time for the men to leave, and they went: kisses, waves, see you tomorrow. The woman who had come that day clung to her husband and wept. "Oh don't go, don't go, Tom, please don't go." He held her and stroked her back, her shoulders, her soft gray nicely waved hair, now in pitiable disorder. He repeated, "I must go, dear. Please stop crying. Mildred, you must pull yourself together—please, dear." But she saw no reason to stop. She lifted her face to show a mask of tragedy, and then she laid it against her husband's shoulder again and cried even harder.

"Mildred, Mildred, please stop. The doctor told us he didn't think it would be anything much. He told us that, didn't he? I said to him that we had to know the worst, but he said there wasn't any worst. You'd be out in a week, he said. . . . " He went on talking like this in a soothing, firm voice, and stroked her, and made concerned noises, and she burst out in worse sobs and clung and then shook her head to say she wasn't crying about her medical treatment but for reasons he knew about yet willfully chose to ignore.

So noisy were her tears that a nurse came in and stood staring, but did not know what to do. The husband, Tom, looked gravely at the nurse. This was not a helpless look, far from it; rather, he was saying, There's no more I can do and now it's your job.

"Mildred, I am going now." And he disengaged himself, pulling down her arms, which instantly flew up again around his neck. He finally got free, laid her back on her pillows, stood up, and said generally (not apologetically, for this was not a man who would easily see a need for apologies, but giving an explanation they were entitled to have), "You see, my wife and I have never been separated, not even for one night, not since we were married, not for twenty-five years." Hearing this, his wife nodded frantically while the tears rained down all over her pretty pink jacket. Then, seeing him stand upright there, refusing to bend down to her again, she turned her gaze away from him and stared at the wall.

"I'm going now, dear," said Tom, and went out, giving the nurse a look that silently commanded her to take over.

"Well, now, Mrs. Grant," said the nurse in the cheerful voice of her discipline. She was a girl of about twenty, and she looked tired, and the last thing she needed was an old woman (as she would see it) complaining and carrying on. "You're disturbing all the others; you mustn't be selfish," she attempted, hopefully.

The appeal had no effect, as the ironical faces of the other women showed they had expected. But Mildred Grant was crying less noisily now. "Would you like a nice cup of tea?" No reply. Only gasps and little sniffs. The nurse looked at the others, who were all so much older than she was, hesitated, went out.

Nine o'clock. Soon they would be expected to sleep. In came a trolley with milky drinks of a sleep-inducing kind. Some of the women were brushing their hair, or putting in rollers, or rubbing cream methodically into their necks and faces. There was a feeling of lull, of marking time: the day shift had gone home and the night staff were coming on.

The old woman—the really old woman, whom the nurses called Granny—remarked brightly, "My husband died twenty years ago. I've lived by myself for twenty years. We were happy, we were. But I've been alone since he died."

The crying stopped. One or two of the women sent congratulatory smiles and grimaces to the speaker, but then there was a fresh outburst from the abandoned wife.

A sigh from the old woman, a shrug. "Some people don't know their luck," she said.

"No, they don't," said the woman opposite her, Miss Cook. "I've never had a husband at all. Every time I thought I had one nice and hooked, he wriggled away!" She laughed loudly, as she had often done at this brave joke, and glanced quickly at the others to make sure she had made her effect. They were laughing. Miss Cook was a comic. Probably it was this very joke that had set her off on her career of being one, decades ago. She was a large, formidable, red-faced woman of about seventy.

Soon they were all washed, brushed, tidy, and in bed. The night nurse, another fresh young woman, came to look them over. She had heard from the nurses going off duty about the difficult patient, and now she gave the sobbing Mildred Grant a long, dubious inspection and said, "Good night, ladies, good night." She hesitated, seemed as if she might try admonitions or advice, but went out, switching off the light.

IT WAS NOT DARK in the room. The tall yellow lamps that illuminated the hospital car park shone in here. There was a pattern of light and dark on the walls, and the pink of the curtains showed, a subdued but dauntless note.

Seven women lay tense in their beds, listening to Mildred Grant.

Her bed was near the door. In the two beds close to hers were matrons in the full energies of middle age, who commanded children, daughters-in-law, sons-in-law, husbands, relatives of all kinds, and these were always dropping in with flowers and fruit in what seemed to the others like a continuing family party. Mrs. Joan Lee and Mrs. Rosemary Stamford demanded the movable telephone several times a day to organize dentists' and doctors' appointments, to remind their families of this or that, or to ring up butchers' or greengrocers' shops to order food the happy-go-lucky ones at home were bound to forget. They might be in the hospital with womb problems, but in spirit they had hardly been here at all. Now they were forced to be here, to listen. The fourth bed on that side held the joker, Miss Cook. Opposite her was the very old woman, the widow. Beside her, "the horsy one," a handsome young woman with the high, clear, commanding voice of her class, who was neither chummy nor standoffish, defended a stubborn privacy with books and her Walkman. Atavistic dislikes had caused the others to agree (when she was out of the room) that her abortion on the National Health was selfish: she should have gone to a private hospital, for, with those clothes and her general style, she could certainly afford to. Next to her, a recently married young woman who had miscarried lay limp in her bed, like a drowned girl, pale and sad but brave. Next to her and opposite Mildred Grant was a dancer, no longer young, and so now she had to teach others how to dance. She had fallen and as a result suffered internal hurt. She was depressed but putting a good face on it. "Laugh, and the world laughs with you!" she often cried, full of vivacity. This was her motto, and, too, "It's a great life if you don't weaken!"

The women were shifting about in their beds. Their eyes shone in the lights from the car park. An hour passed. The night nurse heard the sound of weeping from outside, and came in. She stood by the bed and said, "Mrs. Grant, what are you doing? My patients have to get some sleep. And you should, too. You're going to have an examination in the morning. There's nothing to be afraid of, but you should be rested."

The sobbing continued.

"Well, I don't know," said the nurse. "If she doesn't stop in a few minutes, ring the bell." And she went out.

Mildred Grant was now crying more softly. It was a dreary automatic sobbing, and by now it was badly on their nerves. In every one of them dwelled the unappeased child with her rights and her claims, and they were being forced to remember her, and how much it had cost each of them to subdue her. The pale girl who had miscarried was weeping. Silently, but they saw the tears glisten on her cheeks. The gallant dancer lay curled in a fetal position, her thumb in her mouth. "The horsy one"—she in fact loathed horses—had slipped the Walkman's earpieces back on, but she was watching, and probably unable to stop herself listening through whatever sounds she had chosen to shut out the noise of weeping. The women were all aware of each other, watched each other, afraid that one of them would really crack and even begin screaming.

Mrs. Rosemary Stamford, a tough matron, the last person you'd think would give way, said in a peevish end-of-her-tether voice, "They should move her into another ward. It's not fair. I'm going to talk to them."

But before she could move, Miss Cook was getting out of her bed. She was not only large and unwieldy but full of rheumatism, and it took time. Then, slowly, she put on a flowered dressing gown, padded because she said her room was cold and she couldn't afford what was needed to keep it heated, and bent to pull on her slippers. Was she going out to appeal to the nurses? Taking herself to the toilet? At any rate, watching her took their minds off Mildred Grant.

It was to Mildred Grant she was going. She settled herself in the chair that had been occupied for all those hours by the husband, and laid a firm hand on Mildred's shoulder.

"Now, then, love," she said, or commanded. "I want you to listen to me. Are you listening? We are all in the same boat here. We've got our little troubles, we have, all of us. I had to have a hysteriaectomy"—so she pronounced it, as a joke, for while she was a real old-style working-class woman, unlike the others here except for the widow, she knew quite well how the word should be said. "The way I see it, it's not fair. What's my womb ever done for me, in the way of children at least? . . . " Here she raised her face so the others could see that she was closing her left eye in a large and pronounced wink. Always good for a laugh, that's me, said this wink. Now she said loudly, to be heard over the sobbing, "Look, dear, if you've had someone to say good night to every night of your life, then it's more than most people have. Can't you see it like that?"

Mildred went on crying.

They could all see Miss Cook's face in the light from the window. It looked strained and tired, the jolly clown notwithstanding.

She laid her arm around the weeping woman's shoulders and gently shook her. "Now, my dear," she said, "don't cry like that, you really mustn't. . . . "

But Mildred had turned and flung her arms around Miss Cook's neck. "Oh," she wept, "I'm sorry, but I can't help it. I've never had to sleep by myself, not ever. I've always had Tom. . . . "

Miss Cook put her arms right around Mildred, cradling and rocking the poor bereft little girl. Her face was, as they say, a study. She seemed to be struggling with herself. When at last she spoke, her voice was rough, even angry. "What a lucky girl you are, aren't you? Always had Tom, 'ave you? And I'm sure a lot of us wish we could say the same." Then she checked her anger and began again in a soothing monotonous tone: "Poor little thing, poor little girl, what a shame, is that what it is, then, oh dear, poor thing. . . . "

The other women were remembering that Miss Cook had not had children, had never been married, and lived alone, and apart from her cat had no one to touch, stroke, hold. And here she was, her arms filled with Mildred Grant, and probably this was the first time in years she had had her arms around another person, man or woman.

What must it feel like, being reminded of this other world where people hugged and held and kissed and lay close at night, and woke in the dark out of a dream to feel arms around them, or were able to reach out and say, "Hold me, I've been dreaming"?

But her voice was going on, kindly, impersonal, firm. "Poor little thing. Poor little girl. What a shame, but never mind, you'll have your Tom back soon, won't you. . . . "

This went on for a good quarter of an hour. The sobbing stopped. Miss Cook laid down the exhausted woman, letting her limbs and head flop gently into a comfortable position, as one does with a child.

When she stood up and looked down at the sleeping woman, Miss Cook's face was, if possible, even more of a study than it had been. She went to her bed, removed her flowery gown and her slippers, and lay carefully down.

It was necessary for someone to say something. It was she, Miss Cook, who had to say it. "Well," she remarked, "you live and learn, don't you?"

Soon they were all in their own worlds, fast asleep, or nearly.

❧ *Albert Schweitzer* ❧

Best known for his work as a missionary physician in the African jungle, Albert Schweitzer (1875–1965) was also a widely published philosopher and theologian and a concert organist. In his later years, Schweitzer turned his energy toward still another urgent task, the prevention of a nuclear holocaust. The letter to President Kennedy is taken from *Albert Schweitzer's Mission, Healing and Peace* by Norman Cousins.

LETTER TO PRESIDENT JOHN KENNEDY

Stamp:

PERSONAL THE WHITE HOUSE
APR 30 9:52 AM '62
RECEIVED

Dr. Albert Schweitzer
Lambaréné, April 20, 1962

Dear President Kennedy,

Would you have the great kindness to forgive me, old as I am, for taking the courage to write to you about the tests, which the United States, together with England, want to carry out when Russia does not accede to your request that an international inspection on their territory takes care that no tests will take place.

I take the courage to write to you about this as someone who has occupied himself for a long time with the problem of atomic weapons and with the problem of peace.

From *Albert Schweitzer's Mission* by Norman Cousins.

I believe that I may assure you that, with the newest scientific inventions, each test carried out by the Soviets can be detected at a distance by highly developed instruments, which your country possesses and which protect the United States.

I also take the courage, as an absolutely neutral person, to admit that I am not quite convinced that the claim that one state can oblige the other to tolerate an international control commission on its territory is juridically motivated. This right can only exist after the states agree on disarmament. Then a new situation will have been established, which will put an end to the cold war and which will give each state the right to know, through international inspection on each other's territory, that each country meets its obligations to disarm according to the agreement. The same international control will see to it that no test can be carried out.

An urgent necessity for the world is that the atomic powers agree as soon as possible on disarmament under effective international control. The possibility of such disarmament negotiations should not be made questionable by unnecessary appeals for international verification of the discontinuance of testing.

Only when the states agree not to carry out tests any more can promising negotiations about disarmament and peace take place. Also, when this cannot be achieved, the world is in a hopeless and very dangerous state.

I take the courage to draw your attention also to something that concerns you personally. The terrible discovery has been made, as you surely know, that the children of parents who were exposed to radioactive radiation, even a slight one, are normal in the first and the second generations, but from the third and the fourth generations on horrible deformities occur. The children born then are in danger of having deformed feet, hands, and organs, of being blind or of having deformed brains.

These sad happenings are caused by the great sensitiveness of the cells of the reproductive organs to small doses of radioactive radiation. The effect of this radiation is hereditary *and increasing.* From the third and fourth generations on the children are no longer normal but deformed. People do not like to talk about these facts and prefer not to give any importance to them. But nobody can declare it non-existent.

It is possible that the tests carried out in these times give less fallout than those made before. But this smaller amount of fallout will still cause men and women of our generation to receive radiation through radioactive milk, radioactive vegetables, radioactive water, or in any other way. The smallest doses of radiation on the so sensitive cells of the reproductive organs are sufficient to cause the future misery in the third and fourth generations.

It depends on you, dear President, if this horrible misery of future human beings will be realized, when new atomic tests will be carried out. You are, by the position which you have in the present world, the personality who will be burdened with this responsibility.

Please, do consider, if you will take this responsibility by insisting on not absolutely necessary conditions for the cessation of atomic tests or if this terrible responsibility will move you to let the time come in which tests belong to the past and in which promising negotiations about disarmament and peace are at last possible.

It was not easy for me to draw your attention to the great responsibility you hold to protect future generations. Please, forgive me; I could not do otherwise, not only for the sake of humanity, but also out of consideration for you personally.

Yours devotedly,
Albert Schweitzer

(George) Bernard Shaw (1856–1950), celebrated Irish play-wright and critic, is best known for his lengthy plays of ideas like *Major Barbara* and *Man and Superman,* and for his resplendent wit, displayed often in his penetrating critiques. Lesser known is Shaw's penchant for letter writing. The letters excerpted here are from the last of four volumes of collected letters that contain over 2,500 letters, and cover the last twenty-four years of his life, from age seventy to ninety-four. Shaw never stopped working and commenting on the world of the theatre and the world at large, and was still writing plays in his ninety-fourth year.

from

COLLECTED LETTERS: 1926–1950

To EDYTH GOODALL

10 Adelphi Terrace WC2[A/I]   3rd March 1926
[Edyth Goodall (1882–1929) played Kitty Warren in the new production opening that night. Gladys Cooper (1888–1971), a musical comedy actress who later became a celebrated star in drawingroom comedy, had recently appeared in Frederick Lonsdale's *The Last of Mrs. Cheyney.*]

My dear Edyth

What a horrid audience! My heart bled for you. Why didn't you put out your tongue at them? However, tonight it will be quite different. The people will be there because they want to be there and have paid to be there.

Edited by Dan H. Laurence.

You must let yourself rip accordingly. Last night was only cup-and-saucer comedy. Tonight you can give them the rough stuff, as broad, vulgar, and vigorous as you can make it. Never mind if you drop a line or two: nobody will know except the author; and HE don't matter. Play strongly at Crofts in your bits of temper in the first act; for if you make it too light you will not get in on top of Praed and Vivie, who have been leading up to you in a fairly energetic scene. Exaggerate the contrasts: don't smooth them out: too much trade finish takes the life out of my lines.

What you missed was the climaxes on "I despise such women &c.", "What's a woman worth without self-respect," which should come out with overwhelming conviction. They are the keynotes of the part: character, self-respect, resistance to temptation &c. Unless these come out triumphantly, and Mrs Warren is morally wiping the floor with Vivie, Mrs Warren appears a mere snivelling apologist for her career instead of a victorious vindicator of it. You can do this if you get hold of the idea, and put all your *joyous* force into it (not, O God! your pathos); and if you don't, I'll kill you.

And for your life dont forget to turn the tears off after "I meant to see you oftener." The only moment when I was really terrified last night was when you turned on your fortissimo with your throat full of tears, and, of course, your voice went. You must not go on trusting to the emotion of the moment, and being taken by surprise by my quick changes every time. There is time to make the effect, but not to wallow in it—do you hear, Edyth, to wallow in it?—the next change is on you before you can say knife; so you must get it all mechanically, knowing everything and feeling nothing. If you try to play those two acts on your feelings you will be in an asylum in a fortnight: it's utterly impossible.

What business has an actress with feelings?

Tonight I will stimulate you from my box with shouts of Attaboy! or whatever it is that modern producers say. I want fifty thousand million times as much energy on and after "Oh, *I'll* sit down." If you play that scene quietly I'll get Gladys Cooper to do it. Dont do what ANYBODY can do: do what only Edyth Goodall can do. What are you afraid of?

Why dont [you] say a prayer before you enter? God will not desert you then.

If you dont make an *enormous* success tonight I will throw thunderbolts and reduce you to a little heap of ashes in the middle of the stage. This time you will have a house worth playing to. The ball is at your toe. Kick it hard, Edyth, *hard;* and live happily ever after.

GBS

[A postcard, written just after the performance on 3rd March, proclaimed: "Hooray, Edyth! GBS."]

To BEATRICE WEBB

Ayot St. Lawrence. Welwyn[H/14]   17th February 1941
[Throughout the war years, from 1939 to 1945, Shaw found an outlet for his articles and letters to the editor in the pages of *Forward,* a Glasgow socialist weekly edited by Emrys Hughes. The "last three" articles dealt with De Valera and the problem of the Irish ports in wartime. In the early months of 1941 Shaw prepared a *R.A.D.A. Graduates' Keepsake & Counsellor* for students of the Royal Academy of Dramatic Art, for which he provided an unsigned introduction and edited the "messages of advice" he had obtained from actors, managers, and friends of the theatre. Copies were printed by R.&R. Clark at Shaw's expense.

H.G. Wells had organized the Sankey Committee for a new Declaration of Human Rights of Man. A "trial statement" was published in *The Times* on 23rd October 1940; in the same year Penguin issued as a "Special" volume (No. 50) Wells's *The Rights of Man, or What Are We Fighting For?* Shaw's list "of things rulers must understand" developed into *Everybody's Political What's What?* Richard Albert Wilson's *The Birth of Language: Its Place in World Evolution and Its Structure in Relation to Space and Time* was first published in 1937. Shaw was so enthusiastic about it that he provided a cogent preface for a paperback edition in 1941, issued as *The Miraculous Birth of Language.*

Anderson war shelters were built of corrugated steel, half above and half below ground. Shaw's shelter was his glass-enclosed hut, built on a pivot to allow for maximum sunlight, in which he worked at the bottom of his garden. It was originally constructed as a retreat for Charlotte.]

My dear Beatrice

Charlotte has had another very bad bout of lumbago and has been in bed for many weeks. She cannot write, as her back will not stand the writing posture; but she can now come downstairs for meals and will soon, I hope, be able to get about out of doors. Neither of us has been in London since the blitzing began. Blanche lives with us, and is a great comfort.

Up to the middle of November we had a searchlight here, and were consequently under fire. After a grand bombardment in which we had 8

H.E. [High Explosive] bombs in the village (one in the next garden) and incendiaries *ad lib,* the searchlight was taken away; we ceased to be a military objective; and we now see and hear the raids on London 30 miles off; but nothing has since come near enough to keep us awake. I have bought a stirrup pump, two longhandled spades, and a load of sand; and I am ordering a ladder (all quite useless with no one to handle them except a rheumatic gardener of 75 and an ancient author of 85) so as to get incendiaries out of the gutters when they roll off the roof into them. I therefore cannot be reproached for not taking precautions. I am thinking of buying one of the new portable indoor shelters for our dauntless Irish parlormaid [Margaret Cashin] who sleeps just under the tiles regardless of bombs.

I am very occasionally moved to write something about the war. I do not send it to The New Statesman because I do not want to embarass Kingsley Martin: one editor is enough for one paper. I send the stuff to Forward, which is very glad to have it, and to Hearst, who pays me £100 for an article, though he can have them for nothing. I enclose the last three. Send them back to me at your convenience. I have written nothing for the stage since Charles, and will perhaps not write for it again. I have been kept busy all the winter with three jobs. 1. Revising a biography of me by Hesketh Pearson, which will contain some hitherto unpublished matter that has been set free by the deaths of Mrs Besant and Mrs Patrick Campbell. This took me rather longer than writing the book myself. 2. Writing for the Royal Academy of Dramatic Art a booklet full of advice for beginners on the stage to be presented to our students when they finish their course and get their diploma. When I proposed this to the Council they naturally said "Write it yourself." It was a funny job; but I felt it had to be done. 3. Something in our line. The Wells Bill of Rights left me out of all patience with abstractions on which Stalin and Lord Halifax are perfectly agreed. Also I am convinced that what is the matter with everybody is ignorance, and every day read something about our own time which occurred without my ever hearing a word of it. But there is no remedy for it. No statesman can ever know the facts of the moment at which he must act: he will not learn them for at least 20 years, and then only some of them. He must guess by instinct and knowledge of human nature and history. The wisdom of the people is a myth. Democracy should secure them a means of ventilating their grievances and give them a choice of *qualified* rulers every four or five years. Anything more means the sort of government we have, or worse.

The problem to be solved is the qualification. I cannot solve it, nor can anyone else; but somebody must begin with a minimum list of things rulers must understand, no matter what their conclusions may be. I am drafting such a list, leaving those who can to amend it. If I ever finish this beginning I will send it to you and Sidney before I publish it.

This has just been interrupted by another job. Professor Wilson at the University of Sascatchewan in the city of Saskatoon (of which I had never heard) sent me a book called The Birth of Language, which was so up to date and emancipated from the damnable post-Darwinian Materialism cum Determinism, that I immediately urged Dent to publish a cheap edition, and offered to write a preface. This preface has taken me a goodish while; but I have just finished the first draft of it, and will have a copy made for the Passfield criticism.

I work at this job until lunch in my shelter in the garden (not an Anderson one), sleep for an hour or so after lunch and then go out carrying a chopper and a saw and do amateur woodman's jobs or cut up firewood until the black-out, when I come indoors again and write letters until dinner. I am very old and ought to be dead. My failing memory plays me the most terrifying tricks. I am losing weight so fast that I shall presently have totally disappeared. I look when stripped like a native in a famine picture, an imperfectly concealed skeleton. I am still 6 feet high; but I weigh only 9 stone, my old weight having been between 10 stone 8 lbs and 11 stone.

I could tell you lots of other senilities, and what is much more interesting some new young growths; but this is enough for one letter.

I cannot write as I used to or invent stories; but I can still gossip quite smartly, and am less discursive and excessive than I was in my prime.

Your account of Sidney is very encouraging.

Obituary: William Maxwell's wife and Stephen Sanders: no doubt you know of these already.

Both our loves to both of you.

GBS

To The Editor,
Strand Magazine

Ayot St Lawrence, Welwyn[C/5]   2nd May 1945
[John Burdon Sanderson Haldane (1892–1964), author of *New Paths in Genetics* (1941), was professor of biometry at London University. A Marxist philosopher, he later emigrated to India and took citizenship there. Dr Maurice Ernest (1872–

1955), a homœopath, was the author of *The Longer Life: A Critical Survey of Many Claims to Abnormal Longevity . . .* (1938).]

Thanks for the invitation; but I cannot write an article on How to Live Long, because I don't know.

I have just done it: that is all; but how or why I can tell you no more than a cabbage can tell you how or why it grew.

Get some popular biologist who has studied a thousand cases to do it. J.B.S. Haldane would suit. But why not Dr Maurice Ernest, author of The Longer Life . . . on *Why has Shaw Lived 30 Years Longer than Shakespear?*

That would drag me in all right.

G. Bernard Shaw

To Sidney Webb

Ayot St Lawrence. Welwyn[H/14]   26th October 1945

[Shaw's review of Margaret Cole's *Beatrice Webb,* under the caption "The History of a Happy Marriage," appeared in the *Times Literary Supplement* on 20th October. H.G. Wells died on 13th August 1946; Shaw's generous notice, "The Man I Knew," appeared in the *New Statesman* on 17th August. Wells, belying Shaw's description of him as a man without malice, pre-wrote an acidulous obituary of Shaw, which appeared in the British and American press in November 1950.]

My dear Sidney

When they asked me to do the Cole book I rather shrank, feeling that I knew too much to do justice in a couple of thousand words. But as I also felt that I could not trust Beatrice to anyone else I took it on to secure the human touch[.]

I had hardly finished it when Kingsley Martin wrote to say that H.G. Wells is dying, and would I write an obituary for the Statesman, to be kept in cold storage until he passed out. It also is a delicate job; but I have done it. . . .

I am very groggy on my legs, and without a stick, or even with one, stagger like a drunk and incapable, and cannot go far. Otherwise I can still keep up appearances and write a bit, though I make all sorts of mistakes and blunders, as you may see by my typing; and I forget names so desperately—even Napoleon and Shakespear have become uncertain—that when I write history I have to do it with an encyclopedia at my elbow.

Curiously though, I have developed a talent for business, and am arranging my affairs with a bossy competence that surprises me. They all treat me as a Great Man now: even De Valera passed an Act to legalize my method of municipalizing my Irish estate. I have sold out some of my gilt edged stocks and bought ten-year annuities in separate Canadian offices. I am throwing superfluous money about to some extent; so if you want any let me know.

The war and the atomic bomb have produced a situation which is far beyond the political capacity not only of our new rulers but of mankind. I seriously think that unless the term of the human prime of life can be extended to 300 years, and political careers begin instead of ending at our age, which is biologically possible, we shall be superse[ded] by some super-Fabian species capable of behaving decently.

I hope you are properly looked after at home. I have been lucky enough to secure a first class housekeeper (Mrs Laden, Scotch) to succeed the Higgses retired.

My last remaining tooth is to be extracted tomorrow.

                                                                    GBS

This bachelor life with nobody to consult but myself—eat when I like, go to bed when I like, work when I like, order the house and garden as I fancy, and be solitary (or social) all to myself—suits me very well; it actually develops me at 90!

Set against this all the things I should never have done if I had not had to consider Charlotte. Quite a new experience for both of us.

To Roy Limbert

[H.t/3]   12th July 1949
[Rehearsals had begun for the Malvern Festival production of *Buoyant Billions,* directed by Esmé Percy, who brought several of the performers to Ayot to obtain Shaw's directorial advice at first hand. Frances Day (1908–84), a brisk blonde former showgirl from East Orange, New Jersey, had appeared since 1925 in British cabaret, variety, farce, and films. When signed for Malvern she was starring in the London revue *Latin Quarter;* "She" (Clementina) was her first serious rôle in the theatre. After six scheduled performances at Malvern the production was transferred, with original cast intact, to London, where it survived for only forty performances. "He" (Junius) was played by Denholm Elliott (b. 1922), the Native by Kenneth Mackintosh.]

Dear Roy

I have met Esme Percy, Frances Day, the Native, and the He at the Winstens, and gone over the Panama scene with them.

There are two things you have to procure, regardless of expense. One is a fancy dress of great beauty and strangeness for F.D. Theodora [Winsten] will design it.

The other is a saxophone record of some well-known air, played by a first rate artist, not as a comic squeak as the jazz bands have it, but properly played and enchanting enough to hold the audience and the two men enjoying it until the snakes and gaters start. The Londonderry air or any other familiar tune of which there is a good record obtainable will do; but it must be a very pleasant classical record, not a jazz.

You must get the chairs from Parkes, and let Esme and Theodora select them. These three points are of vital importance. They may make all the difference between a flop and a success; and a flop will cost you the London option.

F.D. is all right if she is properly handled: a born actress. But she has no conception of her part as yet; and her notion of playing the sax herself and wearing slacks and so forth is out of the question. HE has good looks and the necessary charm; but he has been trained to gabble his words so as to get over all that dull stuff as fast as possible, and must be coached to make the most of them, and never to hurry, as the play is on the short side, and if gabbled will not only bore the audience to tears but be over too soon.

The NATIVE knows his job, and will do it well. F.D's travelling dress and her Orinthia dress had better be designed by Theodora. I cannot sufficiently impress on you the importance of this dress designing. It is a stroke of pure luck that the foolish girl has peroxided her hair white, and produced a bizarre effect that will fit into her two parts; but she will soon find it necessary to shave her head clean and let her hair grow naturally again, wearing wigs until this happens.

Percy was all wrong about the stage business; but I think I convinced him of this and got him on to the right lines. He thought he should keep the players moving and changing sides. My players should never move except to get on or off the stage. Essentially my plays are church services: the spoken word is everything and what people call action nothing.

This is enough for you [to] take in one dose.

G.B.S.

To Ada Tyrrell

[H/1]   8th June 1950

[Maud Clarke was Mrs Tyrrell's last surviving sister. Ada Tyrrell, a year older than Shaw, lived to be a centenarian. Shaw's final will was signed on 12th June, witnessed by Harold O. White (1909–80), master printer of the Leagrave Press, Luton, and his wife Marjorie.]

My dear Addie

Maud was wise to die; for old age is bearable only when there is nothing else wrong with one's body.

As you say, I am lucky in having no relatives to plague me; but I have on my hands a mass of business from which I cannot, like most men, retire; for when I leave it to an agent I have to undo it and do it right myself. If you build a house, you know where it is, and can live in it, or let it and live on its rent. But when I write a book or a play, which is my way of building a house, that book or play is my property in every civilized country in the world except Russia. I cannot live in it, but must let it over and over again, not for years but for weeks, and not only bargain about it every time but protect it against pirates everywhere.

Just now I am recovering very slowly from an abominable attack of lumbago, and laboring at my very complicated last will and testament in daily dread of dying before I have executed it. Such are the worries of an old author.

I have to keep 20 printed postcards to deal with my correspondence: the enclosed specimens will amuse you.

You and I will soon be the oldest inhabitants of the globe. It is perhaps as well that we cannot meet; for even if I could walk farther than my garden, and that only with a stick, and long distance motoring is beyond my powers, I had rather be remembered by you as Sonny than as the ghastly old skeleton of a celebrity I now am.

Enough! This letter is only a grumble. I write it because I am always glad to hear from you, and must play up when your welcome postmark appears on the breakfast table.

                                                      G. Bernard Shaw

To St John Ervine

[H/3]   19th July 1950

[For an example of Shaw's borrowing from *The Importance of Being Earnest*, compare Jack Worthing's reaction to Miss Prism's presumed motherhood with that of Jack Tanner to Violet Robinson's condition in *Man and Superman*.]

My dear St John

Do not let yourself be trapped into the silly cliché that The Importance is Wilde's best play. It's a mechanical cat's cradle farce without a single touch of human nature in it. It is Gilbert and Sullivan minus Sullivan.

The other plays—except, of course, the boyish [Duchess of] Padua—have the conventional woman-with-a-past plot of their day; and the feeling of which they are full is a bit romantic: but the characters are all human, and their conversation the most delightfully brilliant in the annals of the English stage, knocking Congreve and Sheridan into a cocked hat.

Remember that nothing is more ridiculous than artists' opinions of one another. I have a collection of these verdicts (knowing the parties); and they are absurd beyond belief. I was present at all the Wilde first nights, and enjoyed them intensely, except The Importance, which amused me by its stage tricks (I borrowed the best of them) but left me unmoved and even a bit bored and quite a lot disappointed.

A week from now I shall be 94. Yet the day before yesterday I began a new play: a very little one. I cannot write big plays now. I could if my old big ones had left me anything to say; but they havnt: my bolt is shot.

This is all I have to say just now.

Love to Leonora.

GBS

The Art of Loving

"Literature has neglected the old and their emotions. The novelists never told us that in life, as in other matters, the young are just beginners and that the art of loving matures with age and experience."

ISAAC BASHEVIS SINGER
Author's Note, *Old Love*

"From Grandparents children learn to understand something about the reality of the world not only before they were born but also before their parents were born. . . . Experience of the past gives them means of imaging the future."

MARGARET MEAD
Family

What thou lovest well remains,
the rest is dross
What thou lov'st well shall not be reft from thee
What thou lov'st well is thy true heritage
EZRA POUND
Canto LXXXI

William Carlos Williams

William Carlos Williams (1883–1963) was both a pediatrician and a writer. He studied medicine at the University of Pennsylvania and the University of Leipzig, and practiced in his hometown of Rutherford, New Jersey. His clients were primarily poor immigrants from nearby industrial areas. He wrote poetry, essays, plays, four volumes of short stories, four novels, an autobiography, and a memoir of his mother. In 1963 he won the Pulitzer Prize for his poem "Pictures from Brueghal." The poem "The Ivy Crown" was written to Flossie, his wife for fifty-one years.

THE IVY CROWN

The whole process is a lie,
    unless,
        crowned by excess,
it break forcefully,
    one way or another,
        from its confinement—
or find a deeper well.
    Anthony and Cleopatra
        were right;
they have shown
    the way. I love you
        or I do not live
at all.

Daffodil time
    is past. This is
        summer, summer!

the heart says,
       and not even the full of it.
          No doubts
are permitted—
       though they will come
       and may
before our time
       overwhelm us.
          We are only mortal
but being mortal
       can defy our fate.
          We may
by an outside chance
       even win! We do not
          look to see
jonquils and violets
       come again
          but there are,
still,
       the roses!

Romance has no part in it.
       The business of love is
          cruelty *which,*
by our wills,
       we transform
          to live together.
It has its seasons,
       for and against,
          whatever the heart
fumbles in the dark
       to assert
          toward the end of May.
Just as the nature of briars
       is to tear flesh,
          I have proceeded
through them.
       Keep
          the briars out,

they say.
　　　　You cannot live
　　　　　　and keep free of
briars.

Children pick flowers.
　　　　Let them.
　　　　　　Though having them
in hand
　　　　they have no further use for them
　　　　　　but leave them crumpled
at the curb's edge.

At our age the imagination
　　　　across the sorry facts
　　　　　　lifts us
to make roses
　　　　stand before thorns.
　　　　　　Sure
love is cruel
　　　　and selfish
　　　　　　and totally obtuse—
at least, blinded by the light,
　　　　young love is.
　　　　　　But we are older,
I to love
　　　　and you to be loved,
　　　　　　we have,
no matter how,
　　　　by our wills survived
　　　　　　to keep
the jeweled prize
　　　　always
　　　　　　at our finger tips.
We will it so
　　　　and so it is
　　　　　　past all accident.

❧ *Richard Bausch* ☙

Richard Bausch (1945–   ) is a contemporary fiction writer who often includes older characters in his stories of family, fear, and love. Bausch has earned a reputation as a storyteller whose short stories and novels portray a moving yet unsentimental vision of human struggle. The story included here won an O. Henry Award. Bausch lives and teaches in northern Virginia.

WHAT FEELS LIKE
THE WORLD

Very early in the morning, too early, he hears her trying to jump rope out on the sidewalk below his bedroom window. He wakes to the sound of her shoes on the concrete, her breathless counting as she jumps—never more than three times in succession—and fails again to find the right rhythm, the proper spring in her legs to achieve the thing, to be a girl jumping rope. He gets up and moves to the window and, parting the curtain only slightly, peers out at her. For some reason he feels he must be stealthy, must not let her see him gazing at her from this window. He thinks of the heartless way children tease the imperfect among them, and then he closes the curtain.

She is his only granddaughter, the unfortunate inheritor of his big-boned genes, his tendency toward bulk, and she is on a self-induced program of exercise and dieting, to lose weight. This is in preparation for the last meeting of the PTA, during which children from the fifth and sixth grades will put on a gymnastics demonstration. There will be a vaulting horse and a mini-trampoline, and everyone is to participate. She wants to be able to do at least as well as the other children in her class, and so she has been trying exercises to improve her coordination and lose the weight that keeps her rooted to the ground. For the past two weeks she has been eating only one meal a day, usually lunch, since that's the meal she eats at school, and swallowing cans of juice at other mealtimes. He's afraid of anorexia but trusts her calm determination to get ready for the event. There seems no desperation, none of the classic symptoms of the disease. Indeed, this project she's set for herself seems quite sane: to lose ten pounds, and to be able to get over the vaulting horse—in fact, she hopes that she'll be able to do a handstand on it and, curling her head and shoulders, flip over to stand upright on the other side. This, she has told him, is the outside hope. And in two weeks of very grown-up discipline and single-minded effort, that hope has mostly disappeared; she's still the only child in the fifth grade who has not even been able to propel herself over the horse, and this is the day of the event. She will have one last chance to practice at school today, and so she's up this early, out on the lawn, straining, pushing herself.

He dresses quickly and heads downstairs. The ritual in the mornings is simplified by the fact that neither of them is eating breakfast. He makes the orange juice, puts vitamins on a saucer for them both. When he glances out the living-room window, he sees that she is now doing somersaults in the dewy grass. She does three of them while he watches, and he isn't stealthy this time but stands in the window with what he hopes is an approving, unworried look on his face. After each somersault she pulls her sweat shirt down, takes a deep breath, and begins again, the arms coming down slowly, the head ducking slowly under; it's as if she falls on her back, sits up, and then stands up. Her cheeks are ruddy with effort. The moistness of the grass is on the sweat suit, and in the ends of her hair. It will rain this morning—there's thunder beyond the trees at the end of the street. He taps on the window, gestures, smiling, for her to come in. She waves at him, indicates that she wants him to watch her, so he watches her. He applauds when she's finished—three hard, slow tumbles. She claps her hands together as if to remove dust from them and comes trotting to the door. As she moves by him, he tells her she's asking for a bad cold, letting herself get wet so early in the morning. It's his place to nag. Her glance at him acknowledges this.

"I can't get the rest of me to follow my head," she says about the somersaults.

They go into the kitchen, and she sits down, pops a vitamin into her mouth, and takes a swallow of the orange juice. "I guess I'm not going to make it over that vaulting horse after all," she says suddenly.

"Sure you will."

"I don't care." She seems to pout. This is the first sign of true discouragement she's shown.

He's been waiting for it. "Brenda—honey, sometimes people aren't good at these things. I mean, I was never any good at it."

"I bet you were," she says. "I bet you're just saying that to make me feel better."

"No," he says, "really."

He's been keeping to the diet with her, though there have been times during the day when he's cheated. He no longer has a job, and the days are long; he's hungry all the time. He pretends to her that he's still going on to work in the mornings after he walks her to school, because he wants to keep her sense of the daily balance of things, of a predictable and orderly routine, intact. He believes this is the best way to deal with grief—simply to go on with things, to keep them as much as possible as they have always been. Being out of work doesn't worry him, really: he has enough money in savings to last awhile. At sixty-one, he's almost eligible for Social Security, and he gets monthly checks from the girl's father, who lives with another woman, and other children, in Oregon. The father has been very good about keeping up the payments, though he never visits or calls. Probably he thinks the money buys him the privilege of remaining aloof, now that Brenda's mother is gone. Brenda's mother used to say he was the type of man who learned early that there was nothing of substance anywhere in his soul, and spent the rest of his life trying to hide this fact from himself. No one was more upright, she would say, no one more honorable, and God help you if you ever had to live with him. Brenda's father was the subject of bitter sarcasm and scorn. And yet, perhaps not so surprisingly, Brenda's mother would call him in those months just after the divorce, when Brenda was still only a toddler, and she would try to get the baby to say things to him over the phone. And she would sit there with Brenda on her lap and cry after she had hung up.

"I had a doughnut yesterday at school," Brenda says now.

"That's lunch. You're supposed to eat lunch."

"I had spaghetti, too. And three pieces of garlic bread. And pie. And a big salad."

"What's one doughnut?"

"Well, and I didn't eat anything the rest of the day."

"I know," her grandfather says. "See?"

They sit quiet for a little while. Sometimes they're shy with each other—more so lately. They're used to the absence of her mother by now—it's been almost a year—but they still find themselves missing a beat now and then, like a heart with a valve almost closed. She swallows the last of her juice and then gets up and moves to the living room, to stand gazing out at the yard. Big drops have begun to fall. It's a storm, with rising wind and, now, very loud thunder. Lightning branches across the sky, and the trees in the yard disappear in sheets of rain. He has come to her side, and he pretends an interest in the details of the weather, remarking on the heaviness of the rain, the strength of the wind. "Some storm," he says finally. "I'm glad we're not out in it." He wishes he could tell what she's thinking, where the pain is; he wishes he could be certain of the harmlessness of his every word. "Honey," he ventures, "we could play hooky today. If you want to."

"Don't you think I can do it?" she says.

"I know you can."

She stares at him a moment and then looks away, out at the storm.

"It's terrible out there, isn't it?" he says. "Look at that lightning."

"You don't think I can do it," she says.

"No. I know you can. Really."

"Well, I probably can't."

"Even if you can't. Lots of people—lots of people never do anything like that."

"I'm the only one who can't that *I* know."

"Well, there's lots of people. The whole thing is silly, Brenda. A year from now it won't mean anything at all—you'll see."

She says nothing.

"Is there some pressure at school to do it?"

"No." Her tone is simple, matter-of-fact, and she looks directly at him.

"You're sure."

She's sure. And of course, he realizes, there *is* pressure; there's the pressure of being one among other children, and being the only one among them who can't do a thing.

"Honey," he says lamely, "it's not that important."

When she looks at him this time, he sees something scarily unchildlike in her expression, some perplexity that she seems to pull down into herself. "It is too important," she says.

HE DRIVES HER TO school. The rain is still being blown along the street and above the low roofs of the houses. By the time they arrive, no more than five minutes from the house, it has begun to let up.

"If it's completely stopped after school," she says, "can we walk home?"

"Of course," he says. "Why wouldn't we?"

She gives him a quick wet kiss on the cheek. "Bye, Pops."

He knows she doesn't like it when he waits for her to get inside, and still he hesitates. There's always the apprehension that he'll look away or drive off just as she thinks of something she needs from him, or that she'll wave to him and he won't see her. So he sits here with the car engine idling, and she walks quickly up the sidewalk and into the building. In the few seconds before the door swings shut, she turns and gives him a wave, and he waves back. The door is closed now. Slowly he lets the car glide forward, still watching the door. Then he's down the driveway, and he heads back to the house.

IT'S HARD TO DECIDE what to do with his time. Mostly he stays in the house, watches television, reads the newspapers. There are household tasks, but he can't do anything she might notice, since he's supposed to be at work during these hours. Sometimes, just to please himself, he drives over to the bank and visits with his old co-workers, though there doesn't seem to be much to talk about anymore and he senses that he makes them all uneasy. Today he lies down on the sofa in the living room and rests awhile. At the windows the sun begins to show, and he thinks of driving into town, perhaps stopping somewhere to eat a light breakfast. He accuses himself with the thought and then gets up and turns on the television. There isn't anything of interest to watch, but he watches anyway. The sun is bright now out on the lawn, and the wind is the same, gusting and shaking the window frames. On television he sees feasts of incredible sumptuousness, almost nauseating in the impossible brightness and succulence of the food: advertisements from cheese companies, dairy associations, the makers of cookies and pizza, the sellers of seafood and steaks. He's angry with himself for wanting to cheat on the diet. He thinks of Brenda at school, thinks of crowds of children, and it comes to him more painfully than ever that he can't protect her. Not any more than he could ever protect her mother.

He goes outside and walks up the drying sidewalk to the end of the block. The sun has already dried most of the morning's rain, and the wind is warm. In the sky are great stormy Matterhorns of cumulus and wide patches of the deepest blue. It's a beautiful day, and he decides to walk over to the school. Nothing in him voices this decision; he simply begins to walk. He knows without having to think about it that he can't allow her to see him, yet he feels compelled to take the risk that she might; he feels a helpless wish to watch over her, and, beyond this, he entertains the vague notion that by seeing her in her world he might be better able to be what she needs in his.

So he walks the four blocks to the school and stands just beyond the playground, in a group of shading maples that whisper and sigh in the wind. The playground is empty. A bell rings somewhere in the building, but no one comes out. It's not even eleven o'clock in the morning. He's too late for morning recess and too early for the afternoon one. He feels as though she watches him make his way back down the street.

HIS NEIGHBOR, MRS. EBERHARD, comes over for lunch. It's a thing they planned, and he's forgotten about it. She knocks on the door, and when he opens it she smiles and says, "I knew you'd forget." She's on a diet too, and is carrying what they'll eat: two apples, some celery and carrots. It's all in a clear plastic bag, and she holds it toward him in the palms of her hands as though it were piping hot from an oven. Jane Eberhard is relatively new in the neighborhood. When Brenda's mother died, Jane offered to cook meals and regulate things, and for a while she was like another member of the family. She's moved into their lives now, and sometimes they all forget the circumstances under which the friendship began. She's a solid, large-hipped woman of fifty-eight, with clear, young blue eyes and gray hair. The thing she's good at is sympathy; there's something oddly unspecific about it, as if it were a beam she simply radiates.

"You look so worried," she says now, "I think you should be proud of her."

They're sitting in the living room, with the plastic bag on the coffee table before them. She's eating a stick of celery.

"I've never seen a child that age put such demands on herself," she says.

"I don't know what it's going to do to her if she doesn't make it over the damn thing," he says.

"It'll disappoint her. But she'll get over it."

"I don't guess you can make it tonight."

"Can't," she says. "Really. I promised my mother I'd take her to the ocean this weekend. I have to go pick her up tonight."

"I walked over to the school a little while ago."

"Are you sure you're not putting more into this than she is?"

"She was up at dawn this morning, Jane. Didn't you see her?"

Mrs. Eberhard nods. "I saw her."

"Well?" he says.

She pats his wrist. "I'm sure it won't matter a month from now."

"No," he says, "that's not true. I mean, I wish I could believe you. But I've never seen a kid work so hard."

"Maybe she'll make it."

"Yes," he says. "Maybe."

Mrs. Eberhard sits considering for a moment, tapping the stick of celery against her lower lip. "You think it's tied to the accident in some way, don't you?"

"I don't know," he says, standing, moving across the room. "I can't get through somehow. It's been all this time and I still don't know. She keeps it all to herself—all of it. All I can do is try to be there when she wants me to be there. I don't know—I don't even know what to say to her."

"You're doing all you can do, then."

"Her mother and I . . ." he begins. "She—we never got along that well."

"You can't worry about that now."

Mrs. Eberhard's advice is always the kind of practical good advice that's impossible to follow.

He comes back to the sofa and tries to eat one of the apples, but his appetite is gone. This seems ironic to him. "I'm not hungry now," he says.

"Sometimes worry is the best thing for a diet."

"I've always worried. It never did me any good, but I worried."

"I'll tell you," Mrs. Eberhard says. "It's a terrific misfortune to have to be raised by a human being."

He doesn't feel like listening to this sort of thing, so he asks her about her husband, who is with the government in some capacity that requires him to be both secretive and mobile. He's always off to one country or another, and this week he's in India. It's strange to think of someone traveling as much as he does without getting hurt or killed. Mrs. Eberhard says she's so used to his being gone all the time that next year, when he retires, it'll take a while to get used to having him underfoot. In fact, he's not a very likable man; there's something murky and unpleasant about him. The one time Mrs. Eberhard brought him to visit, he sat in the living room and seemed to regard everyone with detached curiosity, as if they were all specimens on a dish under a lens. Brenda's grandfather had invited some old friends over from the bank—everyone was being careful not to let on that he wasn't still going there every day. It was an awkward two hours, and Mrs. Eberhard's husband sat with his hands folded over his rounded belly, his eyebrows arched. When he spoke, his voice was cultivated and quiet, full of self-satisfaction and haughtiness. They had been speaking in low tones about how Jane Eberhard had moved in to take over after the accident, and Mrs. Eberhard's husband cleared his throat, held his fist gingerly to his mouth, pursed his lips, and began a soft-spoken, lecture-like monologue about his belief that there's no such thing as an accident. His considered opinion was that there are subconscious explanations for everything. Apparently, he thought he was entertaining everyone. He sat with one leg crossed over the other and held forth in his calm, magisterial voice, explaining how everything can be reduced to a matter of conscious or subconscious will. Finally his wife asked him to let it alone, please, drop the subject.

"For example," he went on, "there are many collisions on the highway in which no one appears to have applied brakes before impact, as if something in the victims had decided on death. And of course there are the well-known cases of people stopped on railroad tracks, with plenty of time to get off, who simply do not move. Perhaps it isn't being frozen by the perception of one's fate but a matter of decision making, of will. The victim decides on his fate."

"I think we've had enough, now," Jane Eberhard said.

The inappropriateness of what he had said seemed to dawn on him then. He shifted in his seat and grew very quiet, and when the evening was over he took Brenda's grandfather by the elbow and apologized. But even in the apology there seemed to be a species of condescension, as if he were really only sorry for the harsh truth of what he had wrongly deemed it necessary to say. When everyone was gone, Brenda said, "I don't like that man."

"Is it because of what he said about accidents?" her grandfather asked. She shook her head. "I just don't like him."

"It's not true, what he said, honey. An accident is an accident."

She said, "I know." But she would not return his gaze.

"Your mother wasn't very happy here, but she didn't want to leave us. Not even—you know, without . . . without knowing it or anything."

"He wears perfume," she said, still not looking at him.

"It's cologne. Yes, he does—too much of it."

"It smells," she said.

IN THE AFTERNOON HE walks over to the school. The sidewalks are crowded with children, and they all seem to recognize him. They carry their books and papers and their hair is windblown and they run and wrestle with each other in the yards. The sun's high and very hot, and most of the clouds have broken apart and scattered. There's still a fairly steady wind, but it's gentler now, and there's no coolness in it.

Brenda is standing at the first crossing street down the hill from the school. She's surrounded by other children yet seems separate from them somehow. She sees him and smiles. He waits on his side of the intersection for her to cross, and when she reaches him he's careful not to show any obvious affection, knowing it embarrasses her.

"How was your day?" he begins.

"Mr. Clayton tried to make me quit today."

He waits.

"I didn't get over," she says. "I didn't even get close."

"What did Mr. Clayton say?"

"Oh—you know. That it's not important. That kind of stuff."

"Well," he says gently, "*is* it so important?"

"I don't know." She kicks at something in the grass along the edge of the sidewalk—a piece of a pencil someone else had discarded. She bends, picks it up, examines it, and then drops it. This is exactly the kind of slow, daydreaming behavior that used to make him angry and impatient with her mother. They walk on. She's concentrating on the sidewalk before them, and they walk almost in step.

"I'm sure I could never do a thing like going over a vaulting horse when I was in school," he says.

"Did they have that when you were in school?"

He smiles. "It was hard getting everything into the caves. But sure, we had that sort of thing. We were an advanced tribe. We had fire, too."

"Okay," she's saying, "okay, okay."

"Actually, with me, it was pull-ups. We all had to do pull-ups. And I just couldn't do them. I don't think I ever accomplished a single one in my life."

"I can't do pull-ups," she says.

"They're hard to do."

"Everybody in the fifth and sixth grades can get over the vaulting horse," she says.

How much she reminds him of her mother. There's a certain mobility in her face, a certain willingness to assert herself in the smallest gesture of the eyes and mouth. She has her mother's green eyes, and now he tells her this. He's decided to try this. He's standing, quite shy, in her doorway, feeling like an intruder. She's sitting on the floor, one leg outstretched, the other bent at the knee. She tries to touch her forehead to the knee of the outstretched leg, straining, and he looks away.

"You know?" he says. "They're just the same color—just that shade of green."

"What was my grandmother like?" she asks, still straining.

"She was a lot like your mother."

"I'm never going to get married."

"Of course you will. Well, I mean—if you want to, you will."

"How come you didn't ever get married again?"

"Oh," he says, "I had a daughter to raise, you know."

She changes position, tries to touch her forehead to the other knee.

"I'll tell you, that mother of yours was enough to keep me busy. I mean, I called her double trouble, you know, because I always said she was double the trouble a son would have been. That was a regular joke around here."

"Mom was skinny and pretty."

He says nothing.

"Am I double trouble?"

"No," he says.

"Is that really why you never got married again?"

"Well, no one would have me, either."

"Mom said you liked it."

"Liked what?"

"Being a widow."

"Yes, well," he says.

"Did you?"

"All these questions," he says.

"Do you think about Grandmom a lot?"

"Yes," he says. "That's—you know, we remember our loved ones."

She stands and tries to touch her toes without bending her legs. "Sometimes I dream that Mom's yelling at you and you're yelling back."

"Oh, well," he says, hearing himself say it, feeling himself back down from something. "That's—that's just a dream. You know, it's nothing to think about at all. People who love each other don't agree sometimes—it's—it's nothing. And I'll bet these exercises are going to do the trick."

"I'm very smart, aren't I?"

He feels sick, very deep down. "You're the smartest little girl I ever saw."

"You don't have to come tonight if you don't want to," she says. "You can drop me off if you want, and come get me when it's over."

"Why would I do that?"

She mutters. "*I* would."

"Then why don't we skip it?"

"Lot of good *that* would do," she says.

FOR DINNER THEY DRINK apple juice, and he gets her to eat two slices of dry toast. The apple juice is for energy. She drinks it slowly and then goes into her room to lie down, to conserve her strength. She uses the word *conserve,* and he tells her he's so proud of her vocabulary. She thanks him. While she rests, he does a few household chores, trying really just to keep busy. The week's newspapers have been piling up on the coffee table in the living room, the carpets need to be vacuumed, and the whole house needs dusting. None of it takes long enough; none of it quite distracts him. For a while he sits in the living room with a newspaper in his lap and pretends to be reading it. She's restless too. She comes back through to the kitchen, drinks another glass of apple juice, and then joins him in the living room, turns the television on. The news is full of traffic deaths, and she turns to one of the local stations that shows reruns of old situation comedies. They both watch *M*A*S*H* without really taking it in. She bites the cuticles of her nails, and her gaze wanders around the room. It comes to him that he could speak to her now, could make his way through to her grief—and yet he knows that he will do no such thing; he can't even bring himself to speak at all. There are regions of his own sorrow that he simply lacks the strength to explore, and so he sits there watching her restlessness, and at last it's time to go over to the school. Jane Eberhard makes a surprise visit, bearing a handsome good-luck card she's fashioned herself. She kisses Brenda, behaves exactly as if Brenda were going off to some dangerous, faraway place. She stands in the street and waves at them as they pull away, and Brenda leans out the window to shout goodbye. A moment later, sitting back and staring out at the dusky light, she says she feels a surge of energy, and he tells her she's way ahead of all the others in her class, knowing words like *conserve* and *surge.*

"I've always known them," she says.

It's beginning to rain again. Clouds have been rolling in from the east, and the wind shakes the trees. Lightning flickers on the other side of the clouds. Everything seems threatening, relentless. He slows down. There are many cars parked along both sides of the street. "Quite a turnout," he manages.

"Don't worry," she tells him brightly. "I still feel my surge of energy."

It begins to rain as they get out of the car, and he holds his sport coat like a cape to shield her from it. By the time they get to the open front doors, it's raining very hard. People are crowding into the cafeteria, which has been transformed into an arena for the event—chairs set up on four sides of the room as though for a wrestling match. In the center, at the end of the long, bright-red mat, are the vaulting horse and the mini-trampoline. The physical-education teacher, Mr. Clayton, stands at the entrance. He's tall, thin, scraggly-looking, a boy really, no older than twenty-five.

"There's Mr. Clayton," Brenda says.

"I see him."

"Hello, Mr. Clayton."

Mr. Clayton is quite distracted, and he nods quickly, leans toward Brenda, and points to a doorway across the hall. "Go on ahead," he says. Then he nods at her grandfather.

"This is it," Brenda says.

Her grandfather squeezes her shoulder, means to find the best thing to tell her, but in the next confusing minute he's lost her; she's gone among the others and he's being swept along with the crowd entering the cafeteria. He makes his way along the walls behind the chairs, where a few other people have already gathered and are standing. At the other end of the room a man is speaking from a lectern about old business, new officers for the fall. Brenda's grandfather recognizes some of the people in the crowd. A woman looks at him and nods, a familiar face he can't quite place. She turns to look at the speaker. She's holding a baby, and the baby's staring at him over her shoulder. A moment later, she steps back to stand beside him, hefting the baby higher and patting its bottom.

"What a crowd," she says.

He nods.

"It's not usually this crowded."

Again, he nods.

The baby protests, and he touches the miniature fingers of one hand—just a baby, he thinks, and everything still to go through.

"How is—um . . . Brenda?" she says.

"Oh," he says, "fine." And he remembers that she was Brenda's kindergarden teacher. She's heavier than she was then, and her hair is darker. She has a baby now.

"I don't remember all my students," she says, shifting the baby to the other shoulder. "I've been home now for eighteen months, and I'll tell you, it's being at the PTA meeting that makes me see how much I *don't* miss teaching."

He smiles at her and nods again. He's beginning to feel awkward. The man is still speaking from the lectern, a meeting is going on, and this woman's voice is carrying beyond them, though she says everything out of the side of her mouth.

"I remember the way you used to walk Brenda to school every morning. Do you still walk her to school?"

"Yes."

"That's so nice."

He pretends an interest in what the speaker is saying.

"I always thought it was so nice to see how you two got along toge-ther—I mean these days it's really rare for the kids even to know who their grandparents *are,* much less have one to walk them to school in the morn-ing. I always thought it was really something." She seems to watch the lectern for a moment, and then speaks to him again, this time in a near whisper. "I hope you won't take this the wrong way or anything, but I just wanted to say how sorry I was about your daughter. I saw it in the paper when Brenda's mother. . . . Well. You know, I just wanted to tell you how sorry. When I saw it in the paper, I thought of Brenda, and how you used to walk her to school. I lost my sister in an automobile accident, so I know how you feel—it's a terrible thing. Terrible. An awful thing to have happen. I mean it's much too sudden and final and everything. I'm afraid now every time I get into a car." She pauses, pats the baby's back, then takes something off its ear. "Anyway, I just wanted to say how sorry I was."

"You're very kind," he says.

"It seems so senseless," she murmurs. "There's something so senseless about it when it happens. My sister went through a stop sign. She just didn't see it, I guess. But it wasn't a busy road or anything. If she'd come along one second later or sooner nothing would've happened. So senseless. Two people driving two different cars coming along on two roads on a sunny afternoon and they come together like that. I mean—what're the chances, really?"

He doesn't say anything.

"How's Brenda handling it?"

"She's strong," he says.

"I would've said that," the woman tells him. "Sometimes I think the children take these things better than the adults do. I remember when she first came to my class. She told everyone in the first minute that she'd come from Oregon. That she was living with her grandfather, and her mother was divorced."

"She was a baby when the divorce—when she moved here from Oregon."

This seems to surprise the woman. "Really," she says, low. "I got the impression it was recent for her. I mean, you know, that she had just come from it all. It was all very vivid for her, I remember that."

"She was a baby," he says. It's almost as if he were insisting on it. He's heard this in his voice, and he wonders if she has, too.

"Well," she says, "I always had a special place for Brenda. I always thought she was very special. A very special little girl."

The PTA meeting is over, and Mr. Clayton is now standing at the far door with the first of his charges. They're all lining up outside the door, and Mr. Clayton walks to the microphone to announce the program. The demonstration will commence with the mini-trampoline and the vaulting horse: a performance by the fifth- and sixth-graders. There will also be a break-dancing demonstration by the fourth-grade class.

"Here we go," the woman says. "My nephew's afraid of the mini-tramp."

"They shouldn't make them do these things," Brenda's grandfather says, with a passion that surprises him. He draws in a breath. "It's too hard," he says, loudly. He can't believe himself. "They shouldn't have to go through a thing like this."

"I don't know," she says vaguely, turning from him a little. He has drawn attention to himself. Others in the crowd are regarding him now—one, a man with a sparse red beard and wild red hair, looking at him with something he takes for agreement.

"It's too much," he says, still louder. "Too much to put on a child. There's just so much a child can take."

Someone asks gently for quiet.

The first child is running down the long mat to the mini-trampoline; it's a girl, and she times her jump perfectly, soars over the horse. One by one, other children follow. Mr. Clayton and another man stand on either side of the horse and help those who go over on their hands. Two or three go over without any assistance at all, with remarkable effortlessness and grace.

"Well," Brenda's kindergarden teacher says, "there's my nephew."

The boy hits the mini-tramp and does a perfect forward flip in the air over the horse, landing upright and then rolling forward in a somersault.

"Yea, Jack!" she cheers. "No sweat! Yea, Jackie boy!"

The boy trots to the other end of the room and stands with the others; the crowd is applauding. The last of the sixth-graders goes over the horse, and Mr. Clayton says into the microphone that the fifth-graders are next. It's Brenda who's next. She stands in the doorway, her cheeks flushed, her legs looking too heavy in the tights. She's rocking back and forth on the balls of her feet, getting ready. It grows quiet. Her arms swing slightly, back and forth, and now, just for a moment, she's looking at the crowd, her face hiding whatever she's feeling. It's as if she were merely curious as to who is out there, but he knows she's looking for him, searching the crowd for her grandfather, who stands on his toes, unseen against the far wall, stands there thinking his heart might break, lifting his hand to wave.

Raymond Carver (1939–1988) is perhaps best known as a short story writer. His collections of stories have been recommended for the National Book Award and the National Book Critics Circle Award. He was twice given grants by the National Endowment for the Arts, won a Guggenheim Fellowship in 1979, and in 1983 received the Mildred and Harold Strauss Living Award. The poem "Happiness in Cornwall" comes from a late collection, *Where Water Comes Together with Other Water.* He was born in Oregon and lived in Washington State and Syracuse, New York, before his death.

HAPPINESS IN CORNWALL

His wife died, and he grew old
between the graveyard and his
front door. Walked with a gait.
Shoulders bent. He let his clothes
go, and his long hair turned white.
His children found him somebody.
A big middle-aged woman with
heavy shoes who knew how to
mop, wax, dust, shop, and carry in
firewood. Who could live
in a room at the back of the house.
Prepare meals. And slowly,
slowly bring the old man around
to listening to her read poetry
in the evenings in front of
the fire. Tennyson, Browning,

Shakespeare, Drinkwater. Men
whose names take up space
on the page. She was the butler,
cook, housekeeper. And after
a time, oh, no one knows or cares
when, they began to dress up
on Sundays and stroll through town.
She with her arm through his.
Smiling. He proud and happy
and with his hand on hers.
No one denied them
or tried to diminish this
in any way. Happiness is
a rare thing! Evenings he
listened to poetry, poetry, poetry
in front of the fire.
Couldn't get enough of that life.

Helen Norris (1916–   ) of Alabama is the author of three novels and numerous short stories. She has been awarded the 1983 Andrew Lytle Fiction Award and several of her stories have been chosen for the O. Henry Prize story anthologies.

THE CLOVEN TREE

She was slipping her fingers along the keys, flexing them lightly at the end of each run.

"Please listen to me," he was saying to her.

"I *am* listening," Abby said.

"Why can't you stop?"

"I'm practicing. You've come at a terrible time, Max dear. I have to practice every day." She was doing trills. She found she could still accomplish them, but not with the ease that she would like. "When you've reached the age of seventy-one and you've scarcely played for fifty years, you have to work at it every day." But then, as he did not offer to leave or let her be, she lifted her hands and patted his arm and turned to him with a smile and a sigh.

He sat on the bench with her, solid and square. Even his glasses were heavily chocolate-rimmed and square, too small for his ample, florid face, like dollhouse windows she would find herself looking through for Max. He was never there. If only the windows were large enough, she might have seen on the opposite wall the code of laws Max had posted for her. She had given up thinking to catch him home. He had secrets he didn't want her to share. Or else he had none and kept her at bay lest she find him dull. Max, as the world would have it, was dull. But he was her son. Their embers glowed whenever they met, and she warmed herself at the little blaze.

"I've brought you a tree," he said to her.

"A tree?"

"It's Christmas, Mama. That time again."

"It isn't yet, but that's nice of you."

"I want you to come and have a look. I have one like it for Daddy too."

"Not now, Max, dear. I'm practicing." She glanced at his face. "Later, dear."

She knew from his tone there was something unpleasant he wished her to see, so she wasn't in such a hurry about it. But after he gave up and went away, she wandered into the living room and saw it in front of the fireplace. She supposed it was meant to shock her into mending her ways. It merely struck her as quite bizarre. He had split a pine tree down the center and given her half, embellished with tinsel and colored balls. The raw, severed edge was displayed to the room, displayed to her. The spangled tree appeared struck and sundered by lightning. For this particular ruinous bolt she felt herself most surely condemned by the never visible code of laws that Max had posted for her within. His heart might have stirred with clemency, but codes for a parent know little of grace. Her eyes sought the very tip of the tree and, sure enough, the dove of peace had one leg and a wing, like something waiting its turn to be grilled. Poor Max, she thought. Why can't he get married, have a life of his own and a wife who would keep him from such excesses?

She would leave the tree standing just as it was so he couldn't rejoice that she minded it there. Max was all of fifty-two and had long since left the family nest. He managed a furniture store with ease. Without him the Chamber of Commerce would fold. And yet he behaved like an eight-year-old because his father had moved away and was living now at the end of the block.

She left the room, went into the kitchen, made some tea, and sat at the kitchen table to drink it. Through the flowered curtains above the sink she could see the oak tree shedding its leaves, and she whispered a line—from a poem, was it? "Now is the winter of our discontent . . ." Dave would know who had said it, of course. He remembered poems.

One day in the early afternoon he had come to her as she sat with her music. She had felt him behind her before she turned. "I've been thinking," he said. "If it's right for you, there's the Widow Wilson's hut in back where I can be out of your way with my stuff. It's getting a little crowded here. And I have to say the music gets in the way of things."

A pause fell like a single note. "I can always stop."

"You mustn't think of it," he said at once. His voice was warm. "I can spread out there. If it's all right."

"Of course," she said, "if it's all right with her. I thought she rents it."

"I'm paying her rent."

She had felt a little shock at that, to hear that arrangements were already made. Silently she stroked the keys. "Does this have to do with the bottle I broke?"

"Of course it doesn't. How could you ask?"

She heard him moving his boxes out. He was making several trips of it. His maps were coming down from the walls. She could hear them slither across the floor. She did not want to watch him go. She sat with her music and softly played. Finally he stood behind her again. She had always known when he was near. As if it had been in motion before, the air around her would settle a bit and then grow dense, as it does before one feels a touch. "I want you to know you can call anytime you feel uneasy. Call me anytime, day or night."

The final word struck into her heart. She had thought they were talking about the days!

"And anything else that comes up," he said. "Anything at all . . . I've given them all my billing address." She felt he had rehearsed the tone to take the chill from the words for her.

She found that her fingers were rooted in keys. Their roots grew down and into the earth. She could not turn to say goodbye.

When he was gone and the house was still she went in and lay across the bed. It belonged to her now, the whole of it . . . She lay there trying to make sense of it.

They had a room at the back of the house where he used to make all those useful things—tables, benches, toys for the children when they were young. One end of it had held his desk and all the accounting machines for his work. When he had retired he sold the machines, but the tools for working with wood remained. One day beside the planes and saws there began to appear the models of boats and shelves with books about sailing the seas. And maps on the walls of places that seemed to be far away. "What is this?" she asked.

"It's the road not taken."

"That's a poem," she said.

Then on the desk there appeared a bottle with a boat inside. "Did you make that yourself?"

"I bought it," he said.

She would pass the door and see him gazing at the ship inside. It was full of sails. Like flowers, she thought. Sometimes when she had looked in on him he seemed to be inside the bottle. Inside the ship inside the glass. She wanted to shatter the glass to free him. To free herself from having to watch him looking in.

One day she was cleaning the room for him. It had to be done when he was away. She had dusted the bottle and picked it up. She was putting it back when the boat within seemed to surge ahead. The bottle leapt from her hand and crashed. As she recalled, there had been an instant, which memory stretched to infinity, when she might, just might, have caught it up before it struck and splintered its hull on the rock of the desk and lay in the shards of its crystal shell. She was perfectly sure it had slipped from her of its own free will, but might she have saved it even so? She would never be sure, she told herself. And Dave had looked at the ruins in silence. She had placed the remains in a box for him. "I'm sorry," she said to him over and over. "I'll get you another one. Tell me where."

"Forget it," he said. "I don't need another."

She had gone to the kitchen then to think, and it came to her that she understood: Their families had summered for years at the lake. And she and Dave . . . how young they had been! There were sunlit days that flickered still in her mind like flame, and evenings sweet with heron voices that skimmed the water to haunt the wood. And her mother making her music for them, the children she loved, or for the lake. Lady of the Lake her mother was called. Their life was a story she wove for them out of the music she made at dusk. And the end was that they would fall in love. Like fish they seemed to dart below and lurk in shadows and flash in sun, and the story sank to their young ears muffled with rippling water and cries of birds. And Abby knew they would rise one day when the story was done and claim its end . . .

Yet first Dave had loved the water and boats. He told her he wanted a life at sea, but when you are young you want everything. He had a sea dream in his eyes that were bluer than any part of the lake, and he talked of boats till her mind was numb, while her fingers pressed the long dark braid that had drunk the lake and then unwove it to dry in the sun. He was planning a trip with his friend to an island. Next, they would sail down the coast of Brazil and down, down. They would round the Cape, to be gone a year. He made it so real she could see in her mind the roll of the waves and hear them break on the lonely shore. She could feel the spray. She could hear the gulls.

And then one day they had walked in the wood. She remembered it well and how he had kicked the trunk of a birch when he said to her with tears in his eyes, "You got yourself in the way of my life. I want to go on this boat trip, see, then around the world. Around the world." He was raising his voice. "I told you I wanted it all my life. You knew I did. You know the mess you make of my life."

"Go! Go!" She began to cry. "I want you to go. Who's stopping you?"

"You're so little. You're nothing at all. I could break you in two with one hand," he said. "I always hated girls who cry. So why can't I go? You tell me that!"

She started to run but he caught and held her. She struggled with him. "You think I want you to stay?" she sobbed. "You're crazy to think that. Crazy," she said. And through her tears she could see the lake. The clouds and birches were drowned in it. Her mother's music was drowned in it.

"I can tell all the time what you want me to do. I can wake up at night and know how you want me to stay here with you. I can tell it now."

He would not free her. She twisted to face him. "You want me to tell you what I can tell? I can tell it's you wanting to stay with me and wanting to hold me to blame for that."

He was crying too.

". . . Just hold you," he said.

And they cried together and then got married, and never mentioned the sea again. Even now it was never mentioned with them, but the maps had appeared and the shelves of sailing books had grown, and he had stared into the bottled ship. She knew without his having to say that now, at the age of seventy and four months and seven days, he dreamt of sailing around the world.

So that's how it is, she had thought to herself. You push things down and after a lifetime out they come. You give things up but you want them still. She had sat and looked out and into the thinning winter light and into the trees that were shedding leaves as they were today. She had felt herself grown old with the year, and wise as well.

The sea was a thousand miles away and still he dreamt of it day and night. She didn't exactly feel like singing but she could come to terms with it. She searched her mind for what should be done . . . If she could feel an answering pull, a long regret to match his own, it would be like climbing and sharing a rope and feeling from time to time the tug that kept you safe . . . that let you dream as much as you liked but kept you from slipping into space. That kept him from sailing around the world.

She had been very good with the music. It had broken her gifted mother's heart when Abby had married instead of going on and on to become the performer she herself had been. Whenever her mother recalled the stage her eyes were dark and bottomless pools. The excitement, the lights, the trains that were hurtling through the night, and the long call of the engine ahead, like a trumpet calling her into fame. She was rocked to sleep inside her berth, the womb from which she would wake into music and light, applause. However soundly now she slept, slept in the grave these twenty years, she would smile to dream that at seventy-one Abby was back at her scales again.

She would let him have his boats and books, a little of what he'd lost for her. And she would have what she'd lost for him. She had the blind man in to tune the old piano that stood in the hall. Together they moved it into the light. ("You could have waited for me," Max said.) It took the man three days to tune it. The moths had eaten most of the felts. And the cost was more than she liked to think, but the boats and books were hardly cheap.

And so they had finished the winter between them and then the spring and a summer and fall, each at separate ends of the rope. At times his saw would shatter her notes. But her music would lap at the ship he carved and give it a sea to sail upon. She hummed a lot. The opening bars of a Bach she was learning. Or a Schubert theme; he was easy to hum. It began to seem quite a natural thing, this life they lived, this rounding back when the children were past. This reaching back to take a direction each might have taken. The things regretted could be done after all. Not to perfection—no time for that—but certainly with pleasure. Certainly with that, and a sense of having sacrificed nothing, of having had both worlds. She rejoiced that it must be the same for Dave. He had seemed content.

So why had he moved to the end of the block? She was worn with the effort to understand. At last she saw, or she thought she saw, that he couldn't just leave her all at once without anything that came between. She supposed the hut was a step to the sea, a halfway house. He had simply moved from her to the pier and then from the pier he would board his ship. The Widow's hut was the pier for him . . .

The Widow Wilson was new to the block. Abby had welcomed her with a call. She had been inside the Widow's house but never inside the hut behind. They had always called her the Widow Wilson since she had come two years ago. She had been widowed twice or thrice, or so it was said by those who knew. She had lived for years on the Florida Keys, but she was a drifter she often said. She was tall with hair the color of jet, a woman neither young nor old, preserved in her bracing self-regard with just a tang of slow ferment. Her yard in back was longer than theirs. They could easily see what she was about. They always spoke of her with a smile or with a tone that contained a smile: The Widow Wilson is beating her rug. The one with the storks? That's the one . . . The Widow Wilson is planting a bush. What kind of a bush? It has no leaves. No leaves at all? No leaves at all. A kind of litany it became whenever the Widow came up with them. She was anchored here for a while, she said, because of the grandson she called Jimbo, who was seventeen. And while he remained and she remained she studied the tongues of various nations that had won her favor. She was currently into Spanish and French. She studied them on alternate days. But on the Sabbath she rested, she said, and let it all sink sweetly in. She touched her breast. "I have it here." The Widow Wilson had ceased to be a cause for smiles. She was the ferryman on the bank that rowed Dave across to the other side.

For Abby the winter had settled in. She had settled into her own widowed state, a haunted state. Sometimes she was sure he was in the house, back in the room where his boats had been. Perhaps he had come for something he'd left. Or perhaps he had come home to stay. She seemed to hear the tap of his hammer nailing his maps against the wall . . . Sometimes while she played she would feel him behind her, listening, waiting for her to turn. And when she did he was never there. Sometimes at night he slept beside her. When she awoke his place was bare. Rarely she saw him out for a walk. From a distance he waved to her. None of it seemed real at all. There was about it an air of play, a kind of biding of their time as if to see what would happen next. By day her mind was thick with memories that jostled and murmured like birds that were bedding down in the trees. She played her music till weariness seized her and then she slept the dreamless night.

The children were bent on sackcloth and ashes. They dropped in now to rend their garments and look their shock at the state of things, Amy from a distant suburb, Max from his quarters near the store. From the first she would not discuss it with them. She understood it little more than they.

And here was Max with his silly tree intended to chide her once again. Or simply to be his primal scream.

She roamed the house with her cup of tea and could not avoid a glimpse of the tree. She wandered into the dining room and laid her cup beside the piano. She sat before it and stared into the slate-gray sky. The wind was tossing leaves from the trees. A squirrel's nest rocked in the swaying boughs. With her eyes shut she ran her fingers over the keys. They glided into the Raindrop Prelude. She saw Dave cling to the wheel of his ship, coughing his lungs up into the wind, the rain beating against his face. Everything went to his chest, of course. It seemed to her that he wanted to die, catch pneumonia and die at sea. Or split his ship on a treacherous reef. She could see it sundered like the tree . . .

But the worst of it wouldn't come to pass. He would simply get sick and come back home and sit around with a lump in his throat and a fever that came and went for months.

She finished the piece and dropped her hands. I think he will never go, she said.

It had been a month since he'd left the house. A month and almost seven days. The basket she kept beside the door was spilling over with mail for him. She was spilling over with need for him, with need to know he was wintering well. She had promised herself she would wait for him to come to her. But she told herself she was seventy-one and had no time to wait for him.

She put on her cape and wound a scarf around her hair. With his basket of mail she picked her way down the alley in back. Wind from the north was rushing at her. Clouds were boiling, fleeing south. Leaves were circling her like birds. The little brown hut stood back of the Widow Wilson's house, some ten or twelve feet to the rear of it, nesting among the leaves like a hen. The Widow professed to love it even more than she did her house. She was fond of calling it her adjunct, when she wasn't calling it her papoose. It was linked to the big house, also brown, by an arched umbilical cord of a walk. Between the two ran a drainage ditch and over its culvert the little walkway rose and fell. She called it her Japanese humpbacked bridge. It was bordered by lattice-work laced with vines, which rattled now in the frenzied wind. The Widow named them wisteria woven with muscadine, a union which had its charm for her. The blossoms of early summer, she said, passed on their purple to the grapes of fall. Her favorite color was purple, she said. Mauve, lilac, whatever, she said. "The color of love, I always say."

The drainage ditch, which the Widow Wilson called her brook, had not succumbed to the winter freeze. Abby heard its patter off to the left as she mounted the steps of the hut and knocked. Clutching her basket, muffled in cape, she felt like an aging Red Riding Hood. She all but turned and walked away.

Without delay Dave opened the door. He was looking well, she noted at once. Young, young, she thought with pride and then with sorrow. His stolid body could pass for younger. His skin was fresh. His hair that was once as yellow as sand, like a shore of the sea that was more to him now than all the land, had gone to white like a bone in the sun, but live it was and crisp and full. His eyes were still the color of sea, as filled with the dream as they had been fifty years ago.

He smiled as if he were shy of her, the way he had been when they told their names beside the lake so long ago. They had got their fishing lines in a tangle . . . And so their lines had always been. She held out the basket of mail in silence. He took it in some embarrassment. "I should have come for it," he said. But she saw that it would be hard for him to come and then to leave again. "You shouldn't be out in weather like this."

She was turning away, but he said, "Please stay."

After a moment she entered enough to let him lock outside the cold. It was very strange to be standing there like an alien child in an alien place. At least it was warm. A fire burned away on the hearth and made things shine all over the room. She saw at once that here was a brighter place to be than what he'd left. But small, small, too small for him. And full of the Widow Wilson's past. Her years, it seemed, on the Florida Keys. Her conch shells lined the mantel shelf. Her cowrie shells were strung in a festive loop by the door. And a glistening creature, mouth agape, looking very fresh from the sea and nailed as it were in a writhing leap, was mounted against the opposite wall.

But she did not care about the room. She searched his face, as if whatever had changed his heart must have changed his face. But it was the same face, solid with bone, the cheekbones wide, the skin of it tanned and faintly freckled, with lines about his eyes and brow, but the rest of it taut for his seventy years. She closed her eyes. For his face had become a forever face, one that the hands of her mind had known. One that her eyes didn't need to see and wanted somehow to keep that way.

He took her cape and gently unwound the scarf from her head. She held her breath when she felt his touch. Only his hands were wintered and old. The blow of a hammer had mangled one. With one the saw had bitten a bone, the one that was lashed with a purple scar. The lash of a whip it had seemed to her. She had loved his hands for the pain in them.

She was conscious that she, a year older than he, looked older still. Her hair, though yet with a measure of brown, had begun to thin. Each day she arranged it to hide the fact. More and more was her face a stranger. When she combed her hair before the glass, she had mastered a trick of creasing her eyes to let in only the face of her youth. Sometimes the face was her mother's face in the pictures made in the days of fame.

Her coming seemed to have humbled him. He tried to conceal it with throwing logs upon the fire and standing before it to watch them catch. She sat at one end of the sofa that faced it. The room was like a cove of the sea with its shimmer of light on stagnant water, with its mammoth shells each side of the hearth and the smaller ones lining the mantel above. Shapes of driftwood were here and there. She caught the faintest smell of brine. A ship's black anchor was fixed to the ceiling above the table where his maps were laid. A cord wove through a length of chain that swooped from wall and looped through anchor to shackle the hanging lamp above. A table of driftwood covered with glass was standing quite within her reach, and on it rested a bottled ship, larger than the one before.

She said to him in her warmest tone, "I'm glad you got another ship."

He half turned. "Vera gave it to me."

"Vera, is it?"

"She asked me to call her that," he said.

In the corner stood Max's tree, the other half of the one that stood before her hearth. It was lodged among the firewood. Its tinsel rippled with firelight. The cloven dove was smudged with ash. She could not take her eyes from it.

He turned to her. "I'm sorry you had to bother," he said, as if she were all of a stranger to him.

"I don't mind," she said, as if she were.

"I've given them all a change of address. You shouldn't be out in weather like this."

"I don't mind," she said.

They fell into silence.

A boy with a stocking cap pulled low came in with an armful of wood for the box. It was Jimbo, Abby saw at once. He had been around since his mother had gone in search of a job in the Windy City, as the Widow Wilson liked to call it. He was thin as a bean. He felled the tree when he dropped the wood. Then he propped it up among the logs. It fell again with a shower of tinsel. He tried once more while they watched in silence.

"Hello, Jimbo," Abby said.

"Hello," he growled through his clenched teeth. He pulled his stocking cap down to his chin and went straight out.

"Have I offended him?" Abby asked.

Dave gave a laugh. He seemed relieved by the brief intrusion. "No, he got in a fight and his jaw got broke. It's wired shut."

"I see," she said. "So how does he eat?"

"He sucks in soup and chocolate malts."

"I see," she said. "It must be awkward. Audible too."

"It is," he said.

She dropped her eyes to the bottled boat.

"Sometimes she invites me to dinner," he offered. "He inhales in the kitchen."

"I see," she said. She asked him after a silent moment, "Is there anything that you need from the house?" He seemed to consider and shook his head. "Then you're all right here? You have a kitchen." She supposed it was there behind the screen that was studded with pink and orange shells. She could hear the purr of refrigeration. "Are you eating well? Are you getting your fiber?"

He seemed to be touched, amused but troubled. "I'm fine," he said. "What about yourself?" He glanced at her and then away. "There's a phone, you know . . . You must call if you need anything at all."

The door from the passage flew open again. The Widow Wilson walked in upon them with a cake on a tray and a generous bottle. She bristled with hospitality. "Jimbo said you were here, lucky for me. I can't miss the chance for some *bonhomie*. My word for today. Today is French." She clattered in on her tall sandals and laid the tray down with the bottled boat. "You know that I'm studying Spanish and French. I refuse to hold one above the other, so I study them on alternate days. All languages are precious to me. When Jimbo is gone, which may be soon, I plan to travel again, you know, and I like to penetrate the culture. The culture is always dear to me." She was wearing green slacks, a white middy blouse, and a double loop necklace of small fat shells. Her face was long, as white and glistening as a pearl, with questioning brows. Her hair was copious and black. It swept from one ear, swirled up and back, then down to the other in a shining curl.

On her tray there were glasses, plates, and forks. She gave a shriek. "I forgot the knife." She dashed at once to the shell-studded screen and slipped behind it to reappear wigwagging a knife. "Don't worry, Dave. I'll wash it, I promise."

She smiled at Abby. "I'm much at home in my little papoose." She sliced them fruitcake and poured them sherry. "If ever I build again, you know, which well may be, it well may be, I shall want nothing more than this little adjunct. Nothing to anchor me down again." She flourished her fork and dipped to her cake.

"This is good," said Abby, her lips in a smile.

"I bake it each year wherever I am. Every year on the Florida Keys—I lived on more than one, you know. All the Keys are precious to me— though there my neighbors found it strange."

The fire settled. The room shimmered and settled too.

The Widow gave a mysterious smile at a ribbon of tinsel beside her shoe. She lifted it gently by its end and tossed it gaily into the ash. "You may wonder why they found it strange. I think you would have to have known the Keys. Really, you would have to have known the sea." She glanced at Dave from under her brows. "It calls for something tart and sweet. And full of the wind. Key lime pie." She raised her eyes to the shells on the mantel. "Or a guava mousse." She was reverent. She raised her glass and then her voice. *"Votre santé,"* she toasted them. *"C'est la vie, mes amis."*

Her eyes were dreaming into the flame. Dave swirled his sherry, his eyes on the fire, his face remote. And quietly Abby's astonishment grew that he was here in this clutter of shells, this bother of woman and firewood, with no more room for his books and maps than he'd had before. With no more peace . . . His models of ships were not about. Perhaps he had packed them all away. She studied his face. He wasn't there.

The Widow Wilson put down her glass and fluttered her hand. "I miss the Keys. I loved their warmth. And Christmas is such a time for warmth. Families gathered about the hearth . . ." Her smile took in the severed tree.

Abby felt her joy in the severed tree.

When she left, it had begun to snow. The wind had died. The Widow's brook drank chips of snow. Back at her house she plunged into the Moonlight Sonata. Yes, she thought, he will surely go. I felt it there . . . She gave it up to her fingers at last. Yet even the music was not enough to say to herself what the hut had held.

Soon at the bank a great deal of money was in her account. When she learned of it her heart despaired.

The days passed. They were full of snow. She tried to retreat again into her youth. A sleighride once back into the hills. And the snow-muffled voices, her breath like milk, and her fingers so numb that it seemed she would never make music again. The scenes were touched with a fresh delight, but something would whirl them into the future, or whirl the future into them. The snow would be mixed with her honeymoon in a mountain resort. The snow-muffled voices would shift to the voices of Dave and Amy calling to her in the frosty air. Or Dave was building a fire for them, for her and Max, while they watched the snow melt off the wood and the flames hiss and all but sleep and wake again.

The snow outside her window now was falling on all the snows she'd known.

There had been so little between her life in her mother's life and her life in Dave's. So little life that had been her own. When she tried to slip into her own, she was in her mother's past instead. She played the music her mother had played. She was rushing through night to the next concert hall, the long piano gleaming with light, the long moment while her fingers hovered, then struck the keys.

At night the lake was in her dreams. The white-limbed birches that circled the shore drew back like dancers to form a sea and the quiet waters foamed and raged. She would wake and will them calm again and will the sea to become the lake and will herself beside the lake unweaving her long dark braid for the sun, and Dave would be telling her of the sea. Sleeping and waking, she lived the sea.

She was glad when Amy dropped by.

"You came for shopping? How are my grandsons? Are they home from school?"

Amy stood in the hall. "They came last night." She walked past Abby to the living room and sat on the sofa to face the tree. She studied it briefly. "Max sent for me."

Abby followed her in and sat in the rocker to face her daughter. Nothing about the woman before her resembled the wistful girl she had been. Today she was wearing a sweater topped with a gray jumper. Summer and winter she wore a jumper. Her boys were grown and off at school, but still she had the look of a woman called from the kitchen, putting her apron by as she came, with not much time to give to you before she had to go back again. She had as little time for herself. Her hair was abandoned to graying, slightly untidy curls. Her shoes were scuffed. Her clothes were mussed. But those who found the look of her somewhat disarrayed were unprepared for the double-entry cast of her mind, the ledgered spirit of charity that organized holiday meals for the homeless and benefits for the children's home. The eyes were as sharply blue as her father's but older and shrewd as they took your measure. They rested upon her mother now. "Max sent for me," she said again.

Abby managed a smile. "I've set to music what he has to say. In E flat minor. I'll play it for us and then we can talk about Tim and Cal."

But Amy rose and circled the sofa and sat in the rocker made of wicker. It crackled like flame. "Mama, it's hard to give you a lecture."

"It's hard to take one," Abby said.

But her daughter was staring down a tunnel with the tree at the end of it, Abby could see. "I know Max has spoken. I'll put it my way . . . There are times in a marriage . . . there are times in my own when I've wanted to call the whole thing off, just go my way. This is hard to say. I'm fond of Nick, but there hasn't been all that much for years. He doesn't feed me. Oh, I don't mean food, for god's sake no, I don't mean groceries. I mean he doesn't nourish me." She tore her eyes away from the tree.

Abby had listened with the pillows of the chair lumped into her back. "Are you telling me that you're leaving Nick?"

Amy ran her fingers through her graying curls and set the chair into a crackle. "I'm certainly not! I'm telling you just the opposite of that. I'm telling you I've stuck it out and will stick it out. Because I have children. As you have children."

"My children are grown and on their own. I've finished with them except to love them. And that I do. I want them to have a happy life. And if they don't it makes me sad."

In the silence that followed she felt how Amy searched her mind for the file marked Mother and tossed it aside. "And that is all you have to say?"

"I'm afraid it is, but I'm glad you came. So how is Tim and how is Cal?"

Amy stood with a protest from the chair. Her jaw was set. "Well, Mama, if that's the way it is, well, we won't be able to make it for Christmas. It would be too painful for all of us."

"Not for me . . . You must do what you think is best for yourself. If you've made up your mind, you can take home a box of the gifts I've wrapped."

Amy waited where she stood and took the box without a word. At the door she turned. "Get rid of that tree. It's obscene, Mama. Have you any idea what you've done to Max?"

Abby searched her daughter's face for a hint of the charity others enjoyed. "Drop in on your father before you leave."

Through the window she watched her daughter go. She watched cars pass in a flutter of snow. She watched their tracks fill up with snow. She was heavy with empty days to come, as if with child.

She decided not to think about Christmas, not to give it another thought. When the Widow Wilson learned from Dave that the children would not be coming this year, it would be like her to have him over the humpbacked bridge and give him a cozy holiday meal, with Jimbo sucking it up in the kitchen. She would end perhaps with a Key lime pie, tart and sweet and full of the wind, to give them just a taste of the sea. And then she would load a plate for Abby, bear it, mincing, through the snow, and knocking sweetly she would say, *"Bonjour, ami"* or *"Buenos días,"* whatever her lesson for the day.

Abby threw her tree into the trash. She played her music for the rest of the day.

The mail kept piling up for Dave, papers and books that she thought could wait. But then came letters from a Capt. Trent, a series of them. So she took them down on a misting day, and there was Dave with an eager look when he saw the lot. He was actually getting a deeper tan and a weathered skin and a distant look in his sea-blue eyes. Or so it seemed to her he was. The Widow Wilson called from within, "Come in, *amigo, por favor."*

"Come in," said Dave and apologized for the trouble she took. "I've given this man my new address. I don't understand. I've given it."

She stepped inside, but just to say that Max would come for the Christmas meal. His silence told her the fact was hers. He had sailed away from Christmas Day. A kind of mist enveloped them now, as if it had followed her through the door. It dimmed the face he turned to her. It muted the words she tried to speak.

The Widow Wilson presided here. She had slipped into the vacancy. Free of the mist, she was sharp and clear. She stood with towels looped over her arm, regally stood like a consort queen supplying order and lively care and a leavening for the soggy day. A tray of food was before the hearth. She laid her burden of linens down to glide to the couch against the wall, and with a practiced sleight of hand she stripped the sheets from under the spread and wound them into a snowy muff through which she plunged her braceleted arm. She was wearing slacks and a middy blouse with an anchor appliquéd to the breast. And in the lobe of either ear was a small white coral gull in flight.

A fire was burning in the grate. The shells in the screen seemed to purr with light. And the ocean creature nailed to the wall writhed in the shadows that flickered there.

"Are you ready for Christmas?" the Widow asked. The firelight danced in her lacquered hair. "I can't help thinking," she mused aloud, "how it would be, a Christmas at sea. Can't you just see the spray at the porthole looking for all the world like snow? Does it snow at sea? I wonder, now. Of course it didn't off the Keys." She turned to Abby. "I lived for years on the Florida Keys. I have the sea in my heart and bones." With a hand that protruded from the muff she waved at the anchor fixed to the ceiling and dipped to the anchor fixed to her breast. "The anchor isn't my thing at all. Whenever I've had to drop my own, as I've had for a while to do it for Jimbo, it's always been against my wish. *A bon voyage* is the life for me."

Dave was silent, into his letters. A gleam of tinsel came from the tree. It was lying prone in the box of wood. "I'll just be on my way," said Abby. She passed the table spilling over with maps, continents of a shifting green with seas between that were fathoms deep, so deep-down blue they took her breath. The deeper the blue, the deeper the sea.

"If you must," said the Widow, smiling. *"Hasta la vista,* my words for the day." She waved goodbye from the snowy muff.

The house was dusk after all the pulsing light of the hut. Abby played her music and could not stop. When the hours passed into an early night, she played in the dark and went to bed without her supper. She lay and waited for sleep to come. The wind had risen. She heard it back in the trees again, stripping the last of their summer away, blowing her summer away as well. Her years with Dave were blowing away. The fine young years and the later ones that were crisp and warm as apples ripening in the sun. These final days, most precious to her, that might have glowed with a golden light . . . the Widow Wilson was gifted with them. This was the hardest thing to bear.

In the chill of the night she blew on the coal of her dying dream to make their division a noble thing. A fork in the river of their lives when each would wander a different field, when the current of each would channel its course, till they came together somewhere beyond to pool their memories of various banks and flow the richer into the sea. But the Widow Wilson diminished it. She reduced it all to the sly glance, to the middy blouse with the anchor attached and stripping the sheets before their eyes.

She did not walk to the hut again. She would let him drift away from her like a ship that has gently slipped its moorings. She let the mail for him pile up. After a while it would cease to come.

But Christmas came, and with it Max on the stroke of twelve. With a show of bluster he stood in the hallway rubbing his hands. The green plaid scarf embraced his ears that were rimmed with pink. He unwound the scarf from about his neck. He made an elaborate gesture of it, not meeting her eyes, not saying a word but making sounds to support the cold, making the weather seem worse than it was. He shrugged his coat into her waiting arms.

"Do you want your present now?" he asked. "It's in the car." He seemed embarrassed and ill at ease, anxious to put the day to rest.

She scanned his face. "Let's wait," she said. She wanted to say, Let's wait forever. When one was young it was hard to wait, but later on, the occasion seemed to require much. She led him straight to the dining room.

He circled and straddled the piano bench. "I don't mind saying I find you hard to select for now." She smiled at him. He gazed at her sadly. "I made a mess of it," he confessed. "I ended up with a thing from the store. It's fairly big. And nothing you want. That's why I left it in the trunk."

"Don't worry about it." She brought him a little wine in a glass. "We'll have some wine and then we'll eat. I've made you something you've always liked. Macaroni with tons of cheese. And maybe next week we'll give our gifts."

He looked relieved. She patted his hand. "We're fine, Max. We're really fine. I think I'll turn up the heat a bit. Sometimes I like it to get too hot, then run outside to be glad it's cold."

He sipped his wine and relaxed for her. He watched her dot the table with silver and plates of food. Then he ate with absorption. He was down in the food, the way she was sometimes down in her music. Down so far it was hard to return. He was helping himself to far too much. And when he had surfaced, cornering the crumbs of her apple pie, he raised his eyes. "I thought he might come. Did you ask him to?"

She waited a bit. "I told him you would be coming today."

"Amy might at least have showed . . . You haven't eaten a thing, you know." He pushed his plate away at last. "I'm glad I never got married," he said. "If this is what . . ." He could not finish. Through the dollhouse windows she saw his tears.

She rose and took him in her arms. "It will be all right. You'll see, my dear."

"I could move in and look after you."

"Of course not, Max, I'll be fine. You'll see."

He drew away and took off his glasses to wipe his eyes. He blew his nose. There were lines in his face she had never seen until this day. He circled the room. He rattled the change in his pocket a while. "Did you get him a gift?"

"I did," she said.

"What is it?" he asked.

She hesitated and then she smiled. "It's a wonderful sweater to wear at sea."

"And that's all? You used to get him a dozen things."

She gave a little rueful laugh. "You think a dozen would bring him back? The one I got is costly, Max. And it will stand for all the rest . . . I wanted to bless the waves for him."

He was looking at her with astonishment.

"The way the bishops used to do. Before the ships went out to sea."

"You want him to go?"

She waited and turned her face away. "If he can go, he may come back before it's too late." She scarcely knew what she meant by it. "And if he can't, he may just move from us farther away. To the coast next time, to be near the boats. I want him to have the courage to go."

Max ducked his head and prowled the room. "I think it's really that woman," he said. "He's lusting after that damn fool woman."

"Really, Max . . ."

"Well, have you seen her make up to him? The outfits she wears? Ready and waiting to climb aboard. Doesn't his being there get to you?" He struck the table with his fist. "That kid around with the wired jaw!"

She did not answer him at once. "It should be a sad but beautiful thing. A worthy thing, with dignity. She doesn't seem to belong in this . . ."

"This plot?" he said. "This mad sea tale? Maybe she's right at home in it. I'll bet she sings him a chantey at night and plies him with grog before the fire."

She ignored his excess. She dropped to her chair. "I'm afraid I haven't coped with her well."

He stared at her. "You'd do far better to cope with him. I find him even more absurd. An old man taking off to sea."

"Not that," she said. "It's a dream of his for all his life. We cannot call his life absurd."

"Then why is he down there? Tell me that."

She waited. She wanted to do her best. "I think it's a place on the way to the sea. A place he will find it easy to leave. A place that's too absurd to mourn . . . A halfway house while he waits for spring."

"I made him show me the tub he's chartered, a picture of it. And a snap of the pilot, beard and all, a murderer's face. He'll rob him and throw him overboard."

"Part of him doesn't want to go . . ." She turned away. "I pray he will. Once I stood in the way of his dream, and now I must help him get on with it."

Max blew his nose and fogged his glasses. He polished them with the hem of his shirt. "I don't understand either one of you."

"Where is it written you must?" she asked.

Then he was gone to work off his meal. To bowl, he said, if an alley was open. She left the table just as it was. She went to her music, searching the notes, becoming the sea. She blessed the waves, and blessed herself.

Now at last she would go to the hut. But a weariness came over her, like a wave from the music, a wave she had made. She wandered into the living room and lay on the sofa to rest a bit. At once she slept and began to dream.

In her dream she had already reached the hut. When Dave let her in, his face was strange. His lips were smiling, his eyes blue ice. The fire had died. She was very cold. She heard herself: "I came to say we are married still. And that if you take this woman to bed it is very wrong . . ." She became aware that the Widow Wilson was behind the screen. She could not finish and turned away. She saw the gleam of the tree in the box. "Would you care if I should do the same?" She turned to see him smiling at her. "Whatever gives you pleasure," he said. She could scarcely breathe for the weight of sorrow.

She woke up weeping. She was very cold. She lay quite still, rejecting the dream with all her soul. An unworthy dream. Unworthy of her, unworthy of him. Though perhaps not so of the woman who lurked behind the screen. She got up at last and slipped her cape about her shoulders and tied the scarf about her head. By the clock it was three in the afternoon. She got his gift from the bedroom where it had been for weeks.

She picked up her music, an armful of it, and went out the back. The wind was sour with stale smoke and cold ash. She tasted it in her mouth at once. My life, she thought, has gone to smoke. The fire of it has gone to smoke. No shape to it, all drift and gray. The boxwoods that bordered her walk were trembling, as if they knew and feared the worst. Dead leaves like pigeons were refuged in them. Roses gone to tangle and stem were bobbing beside the wooden fence. Above the Widow Wilson's house birds were blown about like kites. From one of the houses a carol came.

When he opened the door and saw her gift his eyes were stricken, almost angry, then resigned. "I knew it would come to this," he said. "I looked for yours but it didn't work."

"I know," she said. "I understand." She laid her music on the seat of a chair—she couldn't think why she had brought it along—and held out the box she had for him. "This is really something for going away."

He did not want to take it from her. He stifled a cough. The winter had gone to his chest at last. "You shouldn't be out in the wind," he said. When his chest was bad he would always speak as if it were hers.

"I'm not anymore. So open it."

At last he let it be given to him. She took off her scarf and then her cape. "May I sit for a moment?"

"Please," he said. A smudge of ink was on his face. His table was littered with charts and maps spilling their seas upon the floor. The deeper the blue, the deeper the sea . . . The fire had almost died in the grate, as in her dream. The room was cool. She could not avoid a glance at the screen where her dream had placed the Widow Wilson.

She was filled with a need to talk with him. Simple words about simple things. "Have you eaten?" she asked.

"I wasn't hungry." He coughed once more. She knew that tonight she would lie awake and his cough would be borne to her on the wind. She would hear it later far out at sea.

He laid her box on the mantel where it nudged the shells. He began to pace before the hearth. He seemed to her like a man who is trapped, not one who is free to find his dream.

Trapped in his dream, it came to her. But perhaps he chafed at the long delay. He waited for spring. He felt time running out for him. As it is, she thought. Dear God, it is. She was in his body pacing with him, feeling how time ran out for him and for herself and for them both. She was feeling how empty her bed had been. How empty his had been as well. He was sleeping now on the narrow couch against the wall. And this was only a step away from one narrower still that rocked at sea. And this was only a step away from one narrower still . . . She stopped herself.

He coughed again. She knew the sweet and bitter smell of the syrup he never wanted to take but waited for her to measure and bring. Fear for him gathered and struck at her with a violence that left her trembling. The day had suddenly been too long. She hungered for night to let her sleep. She calmed herself enough to speak. "Please open the box," she said to him. She prayed that the Widow would leave them in peace, grant them a little space to be.

He tore off the wrapping to get her gifting over and done. He lifted the cover and saw the sweater. He did not take it out of the box. He only continued to look at it.

"It's something to wear at sea," she said. "It comes from Ireland. They're made on the Aran Islands there. The wool isn't washed, so the oil keeps out the spray and rain . . ."

He would not lift his eyes to her.

"It smells a little like sheep, I'm afraid."

After a while he spoke as if he were seeing the words. "The way it's knit . . . Each family had a different way. When a man is lost and a piece of this is washed ashore . . . they will know who it is gone down, they say."

She looked away from him in pain. "I forget how many books you read. I didn't know . . . If that is so, it's a good thing."

They could not speak. After a moment she said again, "It's a good thing." For the moment they seemed to cling in mourning. Fragile as glass their spirits were. If the Widow Wilson should enter now, they would break and shatter before her eyes.

He laid her gift beside the hearth. The vein in his temple sprang to life. The embers burnished his wounded hands. He straightened and stared at the anchor that hung above his maps. "You must understand that all these years I have been asleep. My life has been a sleep, a dream. A fine dream with the children and you . . . yet still a dream. If I don't go now, I shall die in my sleep . . . But when the ship is under me, when I feel it move, I shall wake and live."

She told herself, No, the ship is a dream. Like a child in the womb he made it sound. He seemed to have memorized the words and saved them up for her to hear. Said them until they became a poem and after that they were true for him. Poems had always been true for him, turning his dreams into things to touch. She said at last, "And all this time you slept in my arms."

He did not reply.

"Shall I sleep, then, while you're awake?"

"No," he said firmly, "you have your music."

"My music is dreaming" was all she could say. A truer thing she had never said. The music had sung her mother awake. But Abby had left it back, back in her dreaming youth, when Dave had waked her out of the dream. And now it was all that was left for her. She was seeing the sheaf of it on the chair. "I want you to go to sea," she said. "You're young and strong as you ever were. I want you to go as far as you can. The world is round and will bring you back." Bring you home, she wanted to say.

He seemed to be lost in the fireshine. She gave him up to the sea at last, knowing he wasn't as she had said, either young or strong enough to go, knowing that if he came back at all he would be weary and old and sick, wind haunted and wave spent. And she would be left with a pillar of salt to care for till the day he died or she died, whichever it was. But still she wanted him to go. All her will was gathered up and loosed like winds upon his ship.

The fire roused and shimmered over the cowrie shells. She rose and walked to the box in the corner. She lifted the severed slice of pine and laid it gently across the embers. The tinsel shone; the drying needles caught and flamed. "We want the same," she said to him. "You'll be at sea and I'll be here but closer to you than I am today. For nothing will keep my mind from you, my dreams from you . . . my heart from you."

She lifted the music from the chair. "You call this mine but it isn't mine. This is the house I live in now, but it isn't mine." She laid it among the flaming boughs. "The music makes me dream," she said. "I want to be awake with you."

The pages curled, the notes danced, the sap rose with the fervor of spring, the tree sang.

She seemed to have taken his words from him or thrust them down too far to reach. Then he turned and with a thrust of his hand he swept the bottled ship from the table and laid it down in the midst of the song. The flames curled about the glass. It shuddered a moment like water and burst. For a time the ship was afloat in it, in molten glass and running sap. Till the sails flamed.

Her voice shook. "How can we think we have time enough left to play games?" she asked. "Games are for children with plenty of time . . . I cannot bear it to be a game."

"It isn't a game. It was never a game."

"It will be a game unless you go. You must go to make it a part of our life. The way our life was going to be. It will have a strange and sorrowful end, but meant to be."

He backed to the sofa and sat to watch. The ship was in flames, but he had not told her what it meant. She stood there looking down at him, and she seemed to catch the glint of his tears. "Tell me not to go," he said.

"Nobody gives me the right," she said.

"I give you the right."

But she shook her head.

"All the years with me gives you the right."

She could not speak.

He smiled at the fire and went on smiling. It seemed to her he would smile forever. He had been so far away at sea. The voyage home was long for him. She could hear the wind in the eaves of the hut. Down through the chimney it puffed the fire into a rage till it roared like the sea, then gentled it. He dropped his head to the pillow behind. "There's an old ship . . . has lost its rudder."

"Not old." She could only whisper it. "A fine brave ship. Not old to me."

The wind was whispering in the pine. "Then what?" he said. "Give me a name. An old boxcar . . . has got derailed."

The fire was burning into her face and down her throat and into her breast. She would not reach out a hand to him lest, seeing it, he turn and flee. She spoke in the low, remembering voice with which she had given her past away to Max and Amy when they were small. The voice of her mother giving her daughter the vanished world that glowed in the dark. "Whatever happened to trains?" she said. "When I was a girl . . . when I was a girl there was nothing sadder than trains at night, away in the distance yearning away. I always wanted to comfort them . . . Give them whatever they cried to have."

"Help them back on the rails again."

Not for the world would she turn to him. The past was all that was safe for her. She was gone back and boarding the train. She was her mother rushing through night to the long piano shining like silk, no, shining like flame in the lights of the stage . . . And then she was Abby rushing out of her mother, hurtling into her own sweet life.

He said, "You were being your mother again. I can always tell it whenever you are . . . And now you're back in yourself again. Now you're the Abby I married," he said.

"You will always hold me to blame for that."

She waited for him.

". . . Just hold you," he said.

They were starting again beside the lake. He drew her down and into his arms. They smelled to her of the burning pine. The tree, steeped in its wine, sang . . .

The Widow Wilson stood in the doorway bearing a tray. It contained two glasses and a carafe. A sprig of holly was pinned to her collar; her bell-bottomed trousers were banded with red. Her amazed eye caught the blackened ship among the boughs. It caught the embrace.

"This room is occupied," said Abby. "*Occupé, occupado,* whatever," she said.

In the Widow Wilson's astonished eye a dream died. She shut them away. She shut them in.

Honor and achievement came to Robert Penn Warren (1905–1989) not only in his youth but also when he was an old man. At the age of eighty-one, in 1986, he was appointed America's first Poet Laureate, and his best poetry, critics agree, was written during the last twenty years of his life. Born in Kentucky, educated at Vanderbilt University, he won a Rhodes Scholarship to study at Oxford before starting to teach. He won three Pulitzer Prizes, and is the only person to have won the prize for both fiction and poetry. He had a very successful career as a professor of English, teaching at Lousiana State, the University of Minnesota, and, for thirty years, at Yale. The poem "At the Dinner Party" was written in his old age, between 1980 and 1984.

AFTER THE
DINNER PARTY

You two sit at the table late, each, now and then,
Twirling a near-empty wine glass to watch the last red
Liquid climb up the crystalline spin to the last moment when
Centrifugality fails: with nothing now said.

What is left to say when the last logs sag and wink?
The dark outside is streaked with the casual snowflake
Of winter's demise, all guests long gone home, and you think
Of others who never again can come to partake

Of food, wine, laughter, and philosophy—
Though tonight one guest has quoted a killing phrase we owe

To a lost one whose grin, in eternal atrophy,
Now in dark celebrates some last unworded jest none can know.

Now a chair scrapes, sudden, on tiles, and one of you
Moves soundless, as in hypnotic certainty,
The length of table. Stands there a moment or two,
Then sits, reaches out a hand, open and empty.

How long it seems till a hand finds that hand there laid,
While ash, still glowing, crumbles, and silence is such
That the crumbling of ash is audible. Now naught's left unsaid
Of the old heart-concerns, the last, tonight, which

Had been of the absent children, whose bright gaze
Over-arches the future's horizon, in the mist of your prayers.
The last log is black, while ash beneath displays
No last glow. You snuff candles. Soon the old stairs

Will creak with your grave and synchronized tread as each mounts
To a briefness of light, then true weight of darkness, and then
That heart-dimness in which neither joy nor sorrow counts.
Even so, one hand gropes out for another, again.

In the 1970s, Barbara Myerhoff (1936–1985), a noted an-
thopologist, received a grant to study the process of aging. She
decided that, as a Jew, it would be more relevant for her to study
a group of elderly Jewish people at a nearby Community Center
than to investigate another foreign or ethnic culture. *Number
Our Days* relates the many hours she spent with a small group
of old people, most of whom had migrated from the ghettos of
Eastern Europe and the garment centers of New York and
Chicago to the beaches of Southern California. In this excerpt,
she is telling them of her relationship with her own grandmother.

NUMBER OUR DAYS

Sofie Mann, born in the Ukraine,
had raised me. As a child, I remember thinking that she had always been
old. She liked being old, liked her "drapes" as she called her wrinkles, liked
being stout and thought her long hair made her look dignified. . . .

Sofie seemed to have been born a grandmother. The photographs of her,
beginning in her girlhood, show the same calm, ready dignity, the unconscious patience that never left her. Always the long gray and black braids
were twisted into a bun held by enormous hairpins. She seemed to have been
corseted even as a young woman. The photographs do not reveal her
capacity for pranks and foolishness. Very little is really known about her.
Her maiden name is not known, and even her birthday is lost, as it was
celebrated on the nearest Jewish holiday, the traditions of the race absorbing
her individual history. In all the photographs she wore black dresses and
ropes of fake pearls. But I remember her in cheap cotton starched dresses,
and over those an apron—uniform, armor, and vessel, banks for ponds of
soft, vast flesh that I peeked at when she struggled into her flannel night-

gown each night. It made me sad to see her big yielding body marked by the tracks and notches of her whalebone corset stays. The aprons were as soft as the dresses were stiff.

Sofie had the capacity of transforming the world for those she loved. Her great gift was her ability to stand between the outside and the inner domain of home and children, protecting them against real and imagined dangers. She had a way of seizing small adversities and making them into adventures. This in particular she did through her penchant for storytelling. Entertainment, instruction, consolation, and distraction were provided in these stories for all who needed them.

As a child, I was a notoriously bad eater, and Sofie took this on as a personal challenge. We spent hours and months, sitting in the breakfast nook in the kitchen of the house on Taylor Road in Cleveland, spread before us the special morsels that she prepared to tempt me. We looked out the windows together, past our yard to the houses on the hill. For each bite I took, she gave us entry into one of the houses, and told a different story each day, about the people who lived inside.

These accounts informed my entire life, more than any teacher or book or country I later encountered. Sofie Mann, without her maiden name, without her own birthday, without education, undifferentiated from the stream of her people, Sofie knew and taught me that everyone had some story, every house held a life that could be penetrated and known, if one took the trouble. Stories told to oneself or others could transform the world. Waiting for others to tell their stories, even helping them do so, meant no one could be regarded as completely dull, no place people lived in was without some hope of redemption, achieved by paying attention. Boredom was completely banished by this approach, a simple essential lesson that decades later was to be the most basic message I tried to convey to my own students. None of this did Sofie say. She simply lived as she always had. The stories carried her through the monotony of her work, the pain of perpetual fatigue, through loneliness, eventually through blindness and crippling. And all this prepared the way for my work at the Center. Even now, when I walk along the street, my own, or one in a foreign country, or on the boardwalk near the ocean, I look deeply into the rooms, the faces, greedily and gratefully entering, owning what I behold.

What Sofie knew so did some of the Center people. Perhaps her storytelling was part of shtetl kitchen life. Perhaps that is why her maiden name was lost, why no one even called her Sofie—she was "Ma," or "bobbe," or to my grandfather, "Mrs. Mann." Years later, Shmuel told me about his practice as a child—the practice Sofie had shown me as a child—of making a peephole in a window covered by frost. One winter day, I cried because I could not see outside and thought that meant no stories could be told. Sofie laughed and warmed a penny in her palm, then pressing it against the pane, she made a small, round opening. This framing suddenly transformed the view; the street, now focused and contained, became a magic scene. The houses on the hill rose and twirled about, animated by our gaze, dancing on chicken legs like the home of Baba Yaga, the Russian witch.

The best stories came on the days when I had a cold and was allowed to stay home from school. Then Sofie and I were alone all day, in the big, cold house on Taylor Road (coal was too expensive to heat a whole house just for two). Then she would tuck me into the big bed in the front room where at night three grown-ups slept. And from the closet floor she would bring stacks of old magazines, and from the drawer one of Grandpa's huge hankies. The chicken soup was put on in the kitchen below. She lugged her huge sewing machine into the room. The stories pulsed out steadily, accompanied by the *pocketa pocketa* of the pedal, her feet riding up and down on invisible currents throughout the afternoon. Outside the snow settled evenly and in time the soup delivered up its primal odors. The world was ample, timeless, and complete.

Many years later, Sofie and I shared a room again. Now it was my room, time and fortune having divested her of home and husband. She was a perpetual visitor in her grown children's households. I liked having her sleep next to me, though my mother thought an adolescent girl should have a room to herself. Sofie, toothless, shorn of braids, status, property, and independence, tossed and grunted on her bed like a beached porpoise. Sometimes she would awaken and we would begin whispering in the darkness, gathering in all our past, telling the stories again, forestalling everything that waited outside the room. When her eyes and legs were gone, in extreme old age, the stories were with her still, lasting as long as she needed them.

✥ *Archibald MacLeish* ✥

Archibald MacLeish (1892–1982) attended both Yale and Harvard Schools of Law, but practised law only three years before going to Paris to write. Returning to the United States in 1930, MacLeish became a well-known stateman and poet. His poetry scrutinized American actions and beliefs and often traced the course of human lives. In his later years, MacLeish's work began to hint of his reflections on mortality and immortality.

THE WILD OLD WICKED MAN

Too old for love and still to love!—
Yeats's predicament and mine—all men's:
the aging Adam who must strut and shove
and caper his obscene pretense . . .

And yet, within the dry thorn grove,
singer to singer in the dusk, there cries
(Listen! Ah, listen, the wood dove!)
something conclusion never satisfies;

and still when day ends and the wind goes down
and not a tree stirs, not a leaf,
some passion in the sea beats on
and on . . .
                    (Oh, listen, the sea reef!)

Too old for love and still to long . . .
for what? For one more flattering proof
the flesh lives and the beast is strong?—
once more upon the pulse that hammering hoof?

Or is there something the persistent dove,
the ceaseless surges and the old man's lust
all know and cannot say? Is love

what nothing concludes, nothing must—
pure certainty?

And does the passionate man
most nearly know it when no passion can?
Is this the old man's triumph, to pursue
impossibility—and take it too?

ॐ

Carolyn Osborn (1934–   ) was born in Tennessee, but
moved to Texas at age twelve and has lived and worked primarily in Austin. Her stories usually narrate the patterns and lives
of city people. In her collection of short stories *Fields of Memory,* from which this one is taken, Osborn is exploring the ways
that memory affects people's lives.

Man Dancing

A tie. Anyone could buy a tie. First
he had to find a cab, though. He rifled through the directory. Cabinets,
Cable Splicing . . . Cabs—See Taxicabs, Cafes—See Restaurants. He
would never understand the mind behind the yellow pages. There it was,
a two and a bunch of ones. A child could remember it. A seventy-year-old
man could forget it.

Mr. Isaac called the cab to come pick him up at nine. He would go to
one of the men's stores on Guadalupe Street across from the university.
They catered mostly to students; however, the older shops he'd used in
years past were downtown, further away, a more expensive trip to make.
Bending down, he scratched the top of Homer's head. Kate had named him.
She'd named everything including both children—Theo, the oldest, after
him, but they called him Ted. And Kenneth, the youngest, after her uncle.
He could see her standing in the kitchen doorway saying, "Theo, let's give
our children family names. I like that tradition." Wearing a loose pink
dress, her cheeks rosy in its reflected light, she wavered a moment more in
his memory then was gone.

The cabbie honked just as he was knotting his old tie; he had no chance
to inspect his clothes. Not until he was inside the store did Mr. Isaac catch
a glimpse of himself in a mirror. The oil spots from the salad he'd spilled

yesterday at Rose Davis's house gleamed wetly on the front of his trousers. Black as they were, they still showed stains. Black as a crow he looked and dingy! Umph! Shaking his head in disgust, he turned to a round table where ties were laid in an overlapping kaleidoscopic design and considered the wild flowered prints, silk stripes, polka dots. He'd not seen such a profusion of color and pattern since 1923 in London when he'd gone with Kate to Liberty's, where a clerk unrolled bolt after bolt for her to examine. He saw them again tumbling down the counter, the bolts thudding softly, richly until the bare surface was covered with shining rivers of silk. And he could afford just enough for one dress.

1923. Thirty-six then, an associate professor in the history department. His first grant, their only year abroad, all of it spent in England and most of that time he'd hidden in dimly lit libraries. Ah, no use to denigrate it now. He had loved those hours he gave to searching out British views of the American Revolution. When he came home, he wrote a book that other American historians had to read until yet another writer furnished a newer view, something he'd expected. Historians seldom had the last word. Who were they reading now in 1967? Somehow it didn't matter much. When he'd retired from teaching, he'd also retired from keeping up with the latest books in his field. There were a great number of others he'd been promising himself he'd read—Dr. Johnson's letters, Southwestern history, travelers' tales, and every once in a while, a glossy new novel, though he liked rereading the Victorian ones better.

This shop looked like something straight out of Dickens's novels. Everywhere he looked there was nineteenth-century golden oak and brass. Must be the fashion now, to make the new look old. Where was the clerk? Didn't they wait on people anymore?

"Can I help you, sir?"

Though he kept his gaze on the ties, he said, "I would like to see some suits. Summer suits."

"What size, sir?"

Mr. Isaac coughed discreetly and let his eyes run over what seemed to be almost a hundred suits catalogued behind size numbers. Then he looked at the clerk. The young man was wearing a veritable flower garden on his tie and a shirt marked with thin green stripes. He lifted his eyes and confessed, "I'm not sure. I haven't bought a suit in some time." Not since Kate's funeral, and he'd planned to be dressed in it when he died. Since yesterday though, since meeting Rose Davis again—she must have thought him a melancholy sight—he'd decided he needed some more clothes. Vanity? Yes. But when so much else was stripped away from a man—when vigor was gone, when so many of his friends were dead, when wrinkles clustered, why not indulge his vanity? He'd never done so. As a history professor he'd dressed like all the other birds in the flock, and except for an occasional red tie around Christmas time, they were a colorless bunch.

"You'd take a thirty-eight, I'd say." The clerk slid his hand between the racks, pushing away all the other sizes as if they were offensive to him.

Mr. Isaac bought three suits: a dark blue, a light gray, and a blue and white striped seersucker, he thought. Dacron and cotton, said the clerk, who was full of information about exotic blends. He also bought five shirts to go with his new suits. All of them mixtures of something or other. He was particular about the collars. "I like them soft, not floppy though." The clerk displayed them against the suit coats, slapping each folded shirt down authoritatively. One was blue. Mr. Isaac accepted it. He selected five ties, stripes and small paisley prints. "No blooms. I draw the line at flowers. You're young enough for them, but I'm not, decidedly not."

He paid his bill with a check, adamantly refusing to start a charge account. Since Kate's death he'd spent money only on groceries, household bills, occasional cabs, insurance, taxes, his yearly medical examinations, and a few things for his grandchildren. He had plenty of cash. Now he wondered at his carefulness. For years, especially when the boys were growing up, thrift was a necessity. Later it was a habit. Until today, frugality was one of the ways of accepting loneliness—he'd gone on as before, looked after himself, and asked nothing from anyone. Perhaps his self-sufficiency, a characteristic he might have admired too much, had added to his isolation.

He felt at least ten years younger when he left the store carrying a bulging sack. His only regret was he couldn't have the suits until the tailor was finished with trouser alterations on Wednesday. When he got outside in the sun he glanced up at the clock on the university's tower. It was almost noon. He started to a taxi stand on the corner. A screech from a transistor radio assaulted his ears, a primitive wail from an electric guitar. Would his grandchildren, growing up with such sounds, ever have to learn how to waltz? Could he teach them to? He stepped under the projecting awning of a women's shoe store with a window displaying rainbow-colored shoes. What color were Rose's shoes Sunday? He hadn't noticed then. He would notice next time. Waiting at the taxi stand he traced a diminutive waltz step on the pavement, an old man fidgeting, someone might have thought. Light-headed, hungry, and precariously joyful, he knew he was dancing on a street corner at high noon.

THE DOG NOSED AT the sacks, then ran under the bed and stayed. He was too deaf to hear paper crackling. Perhaps he smelled the clothes, smelled something new and fled. Everything else in the house was old. Mr. Isaac coaxed him out, fixed himself some lunch, and deviating from his usual schedule for the second time that day, went to his study to write to his sons.

Dear Ted,

I received your letter dated March 17, and am delighted to know your research is going well. As for the teaching, though it is, no doubt, a strain to lecture in another language, you are to be congratulated for attempting to do so. The year in Mexico City will also be good for the children. They have probably learned a lot of Spanish by now.

My situation here remains much the same except an old friend Rose Davis has moved back here from France. You may not remember her. She has a son Phillip about your age. He lives in Dallas, and his daughter is living with Rose until May when she graduates from college.

Mr. Isaac stopped. Entangled in generations. Well, out with it!

When Melrose, the granddaughter, leaves, I am going to live with Mrs. Davis. We are both old and both live in big, empty houses. Hers is emptier than mine because she brought no furniture back from France. I will take a few pieces from here. If you and Margaret want any of this furniture, let me know, and I will have it shipped to Tulsa. It can be stored till you return. I will make the same offer to Kenneth and Sally.

As I do not want to worry with renters, I will sell the house.

Let me hear from you as soon as time allows. My best to Margaret and the children.

Love,
Father

He read it through, carefully tore the letter into neat squares, and began again, this time neglecting the amenities:

Dear Ted,

This is to let you know I'm selling the house and moving to an apartment in June. Write to me if you want any of the furniture, and I will have it shipped to Tulsa and stored there until your return. This place is far too large for one person. I'm weary of rattling around in it and tired of taking care of the yard.

My love to you, Margaret, and the children.

Father

He could be devious if he pleased, and after all, it was none of Ted's business who he lived with. Sociologist though he was, Ted was only forty-three; he would understand his moving in with Rose as an old man's folly. And Margaret might let her children call her by her first name, yet she was a wife.

He sent approximately the same letter to Kenneth and Sally in Palo Alto. Somehow it was easier to write Ted first; probably it was because he was the farthest away, the one least likely to interfere. He did not anticipate any repercussions. Both sons were university professors. Though both had their summers free, neither liked hauling their families back to Austin to simmer there in hundred-degree heat. He'd gone to Tulsa to spend last Thanksgiving with Margaret and Ted and to Palo Alto for a surreal Christmas with Kenneth's family. When his mind was ready to accept Santa Clauses in bathing suits and the scent of roses in bloom, he'd arrived to find instead dark gray rain blowing across dark green hills and the acrid sour smell of soggy eucalyptus trees. He sat in front of a fire most of the time telling his two grandsons all he knew about cowboys and Indians. The damp wind and the boys' war whoops drove him back to Texas. Perhaps he would return for a visit in the summer. He certainly had a traveling wardrobe now, not that he could actually see himself hand-washing his clothes. The drip-dry idea was ridiculous. The sound of anything dripping, faucet or suit, would keep him awake all night.

THE WEEK PASSED UNEVENTFULLY as usual. Then he began to wonder if Rose's invitation was serious. Suppose she often said such things capriciously?

She'd asked him. He remembered the laughter in her voice when she said, "Why not stay with me? I'll put a sign on the wall saying OLD FOLKS' HOME, and we'll sit here and be cranky together."

He demurred. He told her she ought to decide if she really wanted an old man around.

"I don't want a gigolo, and I don't want just another old lady. That might be worse than any old man. I like my sex, but I prefer to live with the opposite one. We ought to get some young people too, have a *ménage à trois* or *à quatre.*"

He sat there all locked up, knowing what he wanted and too scared to say so. It was easy to write to his sons, easy to decide what to do, almost impossible to voice his decision. His existence had narrowed so—the house, the grocery, his part-time job at the museum on Saturdays. It had been a great deal wider when he was twenty-five and Rose was eighteen, when he was her professor. Now she seemed to be his teacher. Her world was less cramped, less hedged about with custom. Even her house was larger.

By Wednesday, unable to stand his own silence anymore, he called Rose.

"If I'm still welcome, I'll move to your house when Melrose leaves."

"Of course you're welcome. I need someone here, Theo."

"I would like to share expenses, and you must charge me rent, too. That's only fair."

"Why should you pay rent? The house is already paid for. You'll be staying in what would only be an empty room otherwise."

"Rose, I insist. It's a matter of pride."

"All right. But it's not like you were moving to an institution."

It took him ten minutes to calm her. Still, that was easier than the conversation he had with Kenneth Thursday night.

"Dad, what's this about moving to an apartment all of a sudden? I thought you hated apartments."

"Yes . . . well." Though he could lie on paper, it was much more difficult on the phone.

"Well, why are you moving to one?"

"For all the reasons I told you and Ted." They had been conferring. He could almost hear the sound of Ted's voice coming through the wires from Mexico City to Palo Alto. "Did you get a strange letter from Dad about selling the house?" That's what he would have said.

"Dad, are you feeling all right?"

"Except for creeping senility, I'm fine." Kenneth was inclined to pry.

"I've always liked that house." He was inclined to hold onto things, too. Kate wanted to get rid of his rock collection when he went to college. None of them were identified or labeled. They were just rocks that Kenneth happened to like the looks of. He had insisted on putting them in boxes in the attic. They were still up there with his electric train, his old yearbooks, and all the letters he'd received from girls. Did Kenneth want him to remain as custodian? Was every old person required to run a private Smithsonian containing the relics of his children's past?

"I'll ship anything you want, but you'll have to take care of the charges." Mr. Isaac had a welcome vision of movers heaving out boxes of rocks.

"No, Dad. I may want something, yes. I only meant I liked the house."

"I'm tired of it. I intend to move."

"Have you picked out an apartment? Can we help you? Sally says she'll be glad to come to Austin and—"

"I appreciate the offer, Kenneth, but Sally has enough to do. I can find an apartment. I'm looking for one now, and I can move. I'm not feeble. I'm just a little slow." He laughed. He was almost beginning to enjoy himself.

"Well, we thought being uprooted might—"

"I'm not being uprooted. I'm transplanting myself, and in the same town I've lived in for most of my life." What he really needed to say to his son finally came to him. "Don't worry, Kenneth. Even old people need a change. I'm just providing myself with one."

Mr. Isaac put the receiver down, heard a gratifying final click, and said to the night, "Whoosh!" Whirling slowly around, he stopped the swivel chair, stood up, and moved across the carpet to the light switch while humming "Tea for Two" unconsciously. Then he heard himself, and for the second time that night he laughed aloud.

SATURDAY MR. ISAAC WORE his new gray suit to the museum. Ever since Kate's death it had been the one place he was needed. He liked going to the Ney even though all he had to do was hand out pamphlets to a few visitors, make sure they signed the book, and answer the phone. Tim, the Negro caretaker, did all the real work, and no matter what he was doing, he wore a starched white jacket. Mr. Isaac never asked him why. He guessed the jacket made Tim feel less like a janitor, or maybe it was an old-fashioned museum uniform. Tim never mentioned it, so he didn't either. They talked of other things. Some days when the quiet was too heavy for both of them they shouted through the vast rooms to each other. Tim's rich baritone and his own reedy voice swirled up and down stairs, in and out doors. Though they had worked together for only two years, Tim knew more about Mr. Isaac than some of his best friends did. Sometimes Mr. Isaac suspected that the reverse was also true.

There was Ricardo waiting for him on the front portico. The boy followed him inside as soon as he opened the door. Mr. Isaac showed no surprise. Last Saturday Ricardo had happened into the Elisabet Ney by accident when playing in the surrounding park. Once he came in, he seemed fascinated by the work—plaster casts of various European and Texas dignitaries mostly. Shabby-looking lot on the whole, laughable to eyes accustomed to Epstein and Moore; still, a nineteenth-century sculptress couldn't be denied in a state as young as Texas. Ney deserved some notice. The museum had been her home; it had become her monument. Working there every Saturday, Mr. Isaac saw that she suffered more from neglect than from derision. Few people were interested in what she'd done. They had forgotten or never learned she'd turned the mighty into stone.

Ricardo looked up at him. "My father, he says I should come with him, but I don't this morning."

"Where was your father going?" Mr. Isaac turned on the lights in the north studio.

"He goes to cut grass for people. I help him some."

"Your father does yardwork?"

The boy tensed his hands into fists and hit them together. "You got a yard?"

"I've got a friend, a lady, who needs help with her garden. There are fountains and all sorts of flowers."

"Are fish in the fountains?"

"I doubt it."

"Goldfishes eat mosquitoes."

"Do they?" How many things he didn't know still, how much Ricardo already knew—Spanish as well as English, his way all over town on a bicycle, how to rid pools of mosquitoes.

"Every fountain must have goldfishes. Next Saturday I bring my father and the fishes. Okay?"

"All right." Mr. Isaac gave him Rose's address. "I can't be there, as I have to come to the museum, but you will like Mrs. Davis."

"I like the flowers. I don't like the grass."

"Well, you can't have all flowers." Mr. Isaac turned to go upstairs and check on the latest abominations that had arrived for the art show—the directors' most recent attempt to bring people to the museum. He was stopped by a shout from Tim in the back. Mr. Isaac couldn't hear exactly what he was saying, but it was a complaint of some kind. When he was working—dusting statues, sweeping, painting, watering the lawn—he would seldom allow Mr. Isaac to help him. "No," he'd say, "I'm hired to

do this. Besides, I'm a lot younger than you." Then he'd laugh because he
was sixty-five. But he did like an audience for his troubles.

He stood with his hands on his hips before a large crate. "Look here. I
got this thing to undo, and it says 'Glass, Fragile' all over it—Say, you got
a new suit." Tim laid his hammer on top of the box and came over to him.
"That's sure a good-looking suit."

Mr. Isaac thanked him. Foolish how a little praise from Tim made him
feel so good. One new suit or three didn't make him a new person, yet praise
from a kind-hearted man gave him an almost childish pleasure.

"And a new tie too!"

Tim grinned, then began prying nails out of one side of the crate. Ricardo
stepped around him to the opposite side.

"You hold it steady now, and we'll find out what's in here."

Mr. Isaac left to turn on the lights in the west studio. Overcast as it was
that morning, the figures all took on a ghostly appearance, especially Lady
Macbeth wringing her hands in mid-air. She and Prometheus were the only
literary characters Ney had attempted. Miss Ney had frozen her in the "All
the perfumes of Arabia will not sweeten this little hand" scene. It wasn't
a bad idea to try, but under bright light her permanent anguish seemed
overwrought. Friedrich Wöhler, prominently displayed on the mantel-
piece, gazed indifferently toward the tortured lady. The green streak running down one side of his lean nose only served to increase his hauteur. A
German chemist, he had been one of Ney's best-known works. How he had
discovered her, or exactly how the Munich Polytechnic Institute had chosen her to sculpt his head, or how the cast had arrived in Texas, Mr. Isaac
didn't know. He marveled at the ability of anyone to discover anyone else.
The tenuous strands connecting one person to another, how insubstantial
they were, yet how tough and elastic. He had known Rose's parents, had
her briefly for a student, admired her beauty and her spirit, supposed she
was gone forever, and found her again.

"Mr. Isaac, come see what we got!" Ricardo was calling. "It's a box, a
glass box with a pink man dancing. You got to come see."

He didn't think he wanted to, but Ricardo kept insisting, so he went out
to them.

Tim was laughing. "I don't know. I don't know why he—"

Ricardo jumped up and down as excited as if it was a gift he'd just
opened.

A square glass box firmly attached to an iron stand and on two sides
pictures of a Negro man—pink. At right angles on the other two sides the

man was reflected in bright green. Mr. Isaac didn't know what to think. He'd never confronted anything like it.

"Whoo-ee!" Tim shook with laughter. "That fellow's colorblind all right." He was sitting on part of the crate, his head thrown back.

"I like the colors," Ricardo said.

"So do I, boy."

Mr. Isaac stopped frowning over the box and looked at them, the Negro man in his white jacket, white on black, the Mexican child, his yellow tee shirt against his light brown skin, himself, a gray on white. Then he looked again at the pink and green Negro dancing. It didn't matter. Their color didn't. He had never believed it would matter in the end, someday after all the suffering was over, when the wars were fought, the marches finished. Sometime . . . years after he was gone, a man's color would no longer determine his life, but this artist broke the barriers now, broke them laughing.

"He managed to get it here just in time. They will judge the pictures this afternoon."

"Do you think he'll win?" Tim asked.

Mr. Isaac agreed that "Man Dancing" should win. He and Ricardo stayed past closing hours that afternoon waiting for the jury to decide. They promised to call Tim, though he said his phone was "on vacation," which meant he hadn't been able to pay his bill. The phone went on vacation often.

"You can call next door. Those people will get hold of me."

Mr. Isaac started to offer to pay Tim's bill then checked himself. He'd offered before, and Tim said he'd rather owe Bell Telephone than anyone else he knew.

The jury arrived at five and spent an hour and forty-five minutes making up their minds. There were three judges; a young man who was head of the art department of a nearby Catholic college, a woman painter of some distinction who lived in Austin, and a museum director from San Antonio. Mr. Isaac would have liked to have heard every word they said. The temptation to eavesdrop was so great he confined himself to Miss Ney's old kitchen in the basement, where he made himself a cup of tea. As soon as it was ready, he escaped into the adjoining dining room. Perhaps it was cheerful when a fire was burning. Now it was simply cold and empty. Stone walls with tiny barred windows at ground level might have made Miss Ney feel safe. He felt imprisoned and was glad Ricardo kept running down from his post at the bottom of the stairwell to repeat muddled phrases and impressions.

"Somebody, the San Antonio man, I think, says, 'Not much!' The lady she likes the picture of the old tire. The other man walks around and around."

Mr. Isaac sighed. He was as impatient as Ricardo. They met the jury at the bottom of the stairs. "Man Dancing" won first. The depressing picture of a flat tire was second, and a still life of some lemons was chosen third.

They dialed Tim's neighbor, who went to get him. When he came to the phone he spoke first to Ricardo, who reported, "He says he don't believe us. I told him 'Man Dancing' won, and he says, 'How could a pink nigger win?' "

"Ricardo's right, Tim," Mr. Isaac shouted, then took the receiver. "He's right." Tim was saying something to his neighbor.

"He thinks I'm crazy, Mr. I. He don't understand about that picture. I been trying to tell him—"

"It did win."

"How much does it cost? I wish I could remember. I never saw a picture I wanted to buy in my life, but I sure would like to buy that one."

"Three hundred and fifty dollars, I think."

"Humph! That's more than I owe Bell Telephone."

"Perhaps the museum will buy it. Sometimes galleries keep permanent collections of pictures just as we have Miss Ney's things."

"Well, it's her place. I don't see no pink black man getting in there for good." Tim's voice was mournful.

"You can never tell what they'll decide to do here next."

"That's true, Mr. I."

Before he left Mr. Isaac put an envelope containing a check for $350 and a note saying he wished to remain anonymous in the Voluntary Contributions box by the door. On front of the envelope he wrote: "For the Museum's Purchase of 'Man Dancing.' " He did it for himself as much as for Tim. It was peculiarly satisfying to be an anonymous benefactor. It would have been more practical to give Tim the money. He wouldn't have taken it as a gift, and if he had, his conscience and his wife wouldn't have allowed him to spend it on a picture. Three hundred and fifty dollars would have gone to the telephone company, to doctors, to department stores. He and Tim needed the picture more than any of those people needed their money. It was the first modern thing that either one of them had liked. He debated about telling Rose and decided against it. Better to remain completely anonymous, to have a private joy, much more rewarding than a private sorrow.

He would see her that evening. "My Fair Lady" was showing at one of the theaters near the university and within easy walking distance of her house. It was her idea, the first time she'd been to a movie since returning to the states. He couldn't remember the last time he'd been. He used to take Kate to musicals. She liked them. He didn't particularly because most of them seemed vapid. Since "My Fair Lady" was based on one of Shaw's plays it should contain enough of the original vitriol to be amusing.

He found he'd worried needlessly about amusing Rose. As a returned expatriate she found novelties everywhere. After years of walking about Paris, she could not make up her mind if she missed the surge of traffic or not.

"It's so calm," was her first reaction. Then, "Maybe it's too calm. I miss the feeling of achievement after crossing a street."

They cut through a small park near her house, and she wondered at the lack of chairs. Twilight drew in around them.

"It doesn't last long here. I'd forgotten. In Paris the spring and summer evenings are much longer. There's no gabble of conversation in the streets, only me complaining like the French do when they're in another country. Oh, I have become hard to please!"

Walking down Guadalupe she could not help but notice that houses had been replaced by cheap restaurants and small businesses. A giant figure of a man in a red shirt and blue trousers, his feet planted wide apart, glared at them from the roof of an open-walled shed. A sign stuck in the asphalt read, "Car Wash." The man, twice as large as the building he straddled, had a square-jawed smile more forbidding than beckoning.

"Even if I had a car I'd never drive it in there!" She tilted her head back and stared up. "He makes me feel like a pigmy! Isn't that the most terrible smile."

"Yes, but you should see some of the other figures around town. There's a monstrous termite that revolves twenty feet above the corner of Enfield and Lamar, and on Congress there's a grotesque steer, also turning. Every time I go past it I hope a small boy with a B-B gun will use it for a target." Ricardo might do it. No, it wasn't a thing to suggest to a child, destruction of property. English common law had made respect for private property a virtue, and Adam Smith had justified free enterprise by defining it. No point in taking up a B-B gun against all of that. He sighed quietly. Rose heard him anyway.

"Why, Theo, what's the matter?"

"I was plotting the overthrow of the government."

"What's the first thing you'd do?"

"Oh, I don't know. I was thinking I'd send out bands of young boys to shoot holes in things . . . a sort of old grouch's program."

"I don't know what I'd do myself. I lived through most of the fourth Republic and the return of de Gaulle. I couldn't help but think of him as a nation saver. Generally I'm in a muddle about politics. Thomas used to try to comfort me by saying no one made as great a muddle as the French. He was in England during most of World War II as a member of de Gaulle's army. Sometimes his point of view was rather English."

Thomas . . . so that was his name. When he saw her again for the first time he'd asked what she'd done all those years abroad. She'd answered in her direct way, "I lived with a man I loved. He's dead now, and I've come home." But why had she chosen to speak of Thomas now? Maybe it was because they had been talking about politics. No matter. She had to say something about him eventually. There was no canceling out those years. His familiarity with grief made him certain of hers. It took people at the strangest times, with no warning. You could be looking at a kitchen door or walking down a street. Memory keeps no hours.

Rose turned her head to stare at the passing cars, but she refused to cry. In a moment she looked over at him and said in her normal voice, "I'm sure I'm insufferable, complaining about America so. Some days I think I have too much to remember."

Mr. Isaac smiled. "Better too many memories than too few."

The entrance to the theater was flooded with light. Posters advertising "My Fair Lady" promised song, dance, romance while intimating gaiety, renewal, forgetfulness. Mr. Isaac, collecting his change from the ticket seller, looked down at Rose's shoes beside his. They were pink, pink as the flowering peach blossoms in bloom now. Yes, of course, they matched her dress. What marvelous frivolity! Forgetting his timidity, he took her arm and guided her through the door to the lobby as if he were leading her into a grand ballroom.

❧ *Mark Van Doren* ❧

Mark Van Doren (1894–1973) was a noted American poet and critic, winning the Pulitzer Prize for his collected poems in 1939. He taught English at Columbia University for nearly forty years; he was literary editor of *The Nation*. This poem was taken from his last collection, *Good Morning*. Many of the poems in this volume allude to the final years of a lifetime and the pre-science of death.

OLD MAN, OLD WOMAN

Old man, if he cares much
When old woman is achesome, gives
No sign to strangers; even when
She staggers, seems not to notice

But does, and old woman knows it
In the odd way of animals
That watch each other incessantly.
Such tenderness is in these two,

Each of them sees everything
Outside, inside the other; old
Man, old woman suffer and then
Feel good together, their hearts equal,

Their eyes veteran, missing no
Least message, morning, or evening,
Winter or summer, during or after
Pain—oh, dear, plenty of that.

Free to Choose One's Life

"... one learns to walk alone, and that is one of the opportunities in age, a last chance to learn to be truly independent and free to choose one's life and interests and friends, enjoying them but not leaning on anyone. A state we dreamed of in adolescence but never quite found."

ANNE MORROW LINDBERGH
From a 1983 speech

"If one is not to please oneself in old age, when is one to please oneself?"

VITA SACKVILLE-WEST
All Passion Spent

German-born Eugen Berthold Friedrich Brecht, known to the world as Bertolt Brecht (1898–1956), playwright, poet, theatrical producer, theoretician, was considered one of the most influential dramatists of the twentieth century. His works often portray sinister capitalism corrupting the rich and brutalizing the poor. Lesser known are Brecht's short stories which he wrote on his travels throughout Europe. This one comes from a collection of stories written between 1921 and 1946.

THE UNSEEMLY OLD LADY

My grandmother was seventy-two years old when my grandfather died. He had a small lithographer's business in a little town in Baden and there he worked with two or three assistants until his death. My grandmother managed the household without a maid, looked after the ramshackle old house and cooked for the menfolk and children.

She was a thin little woman with lively lizard's eyes, though slow of speech. On very scanty means she had reared five of the seven children she had borne. As a result, she had grown smaller with the years.

Her two girls went to America and two of the sons also moved away. Only the youngest, who was delicate, stayed in the little town. He became a printer and set up a family far too large for him.

So after my grandfather died she was alone in the house.

The children wrote each other letters dealing with the problem of what should be done about her. One of them could offer her a home, and the printer wanted to move with his family into her house. But the old woman

From *Short Stories 1921-1946*.

turned a deaf ear to these proposals and would only accept, from each of her children who could afford it, a small monetary allowance. The lithographer's business, long behind the times, was sold for practically nothing, and there were debts as well.

The children wrote saying that, all the same, she could not live quite alone, but since she entirely ignored this, they gave in and sent her a little money every month. At any rate, they thought, there was always the printer who had stayed in the town.

What was more, he undertook to give his brothers and sisters news of their mother from time to time. The printer's letters to my father, and what my father himself learnt on a visit and, two years later, after my grandmother's burial, give me a picture of what went on in those two years.

It seems that, from the start, the printer was disappointed that my grandmother had declined to take him into the house, which was fairly large and now standing empty. He had four children and lived in three rooms. But in any case the old lady had only very casual relations with him. She invited the children for coffee every Sunday afternoon, and that was about all.

She visited her son once or twice in three months and helped her daughter-in-law with the jam-making. The young woman gathered from some of her remarks that she found the printer's little dwelling too cramped for her. He, in reporting this, could not forbear to add an exclamation mark.

My father wrote asking what the old woman was up to nowadays, to which he replied rather curtly: going to the cinema.

It must be understood that this was not at all the thing; at least, not in her children's eyes. Thirty years ago the cinema was not what it is today. It meant wretched, ill-ventilated premises, often converted from disused skittle-alleys, with garish posters outside displaying the murders and tragedies of passion. Strictly speaking, only adolescents went or, for the darkness, courting couples. An old woman there by herself would certainly be conspicuous.

And there was another aspect of this cinema-going to be considered. Of course, admission was cheap, but since the pleasure fell more or less into the category of self-indulgences it represented 'money thrown away'. And to throw money away was not respectable.

Furthermore, not only did my grandmother keep up no regular association with her son in town, but she neither invited nor visited any of her other acquaintances. She never went to the coffee-parties in the little town. On the other hand, she frequented a cobbler's workshop in a poor and even slightly notorious alley where, especially in the afternoon, all manner of none too reputable characters hung about: out-of-work waitresses and itinerant craftsmen. The cobbler was a middle-aged man who had knocked about the world and never made much of himself. It was also said that he drank. In any case, he was no proper associate for my grandmother.

The printer intimated in a letter that he had hinted as much to his mother and had met with a very cool reply. 'He's seen a thing or two,' she answered and that was the end of the conversation. It was not easy to talk to my grandmother about things she did not wish to discuss.

About six months after my grandfather's death the printer wrote to my father saying that their mother now ate at the inn every other day.

That really was news! Grandmother, who all her life had cooked for a dozen people and herself had always eaten up the leavings, now ate at the inn. What had come over her?

Shortly after this, my father made a business trip in the neighbourhood and he visited his mother. She was just about to go out when he turned up. She took off her hat again and gave him a glass of red wine and a biscuit. She seemed in a perfectly equable mood, neither particularly animated nor particularly silent. She asked after us, though not in much detail, and wanted principally to know whether there were cherries for the children. There she was quite her old self. The room was of course scrupulously clean and she looked well.

The only thing that gave an indication of her new life was that she did not want to go with my father to the churchyard to visit her husband's grave. 'You can go by yourself,' she said lightly. 'It's the third on the left in the eleventh row. I've got to go somewhere.'

The printer said afterwards that probably she had had to go to her cobbler. He complained bitterly.

'Here am I, stuck in this hole with my family and only five hours' badly-paid work, on top of which my asthma's troubling me again, while the house in the main street stands empty.'

My father had taken a room at the inn, but nevertheless expected to be invited by his mother, if only as a matter of form; however, she did not mention it. Yet even when the house had been full, she had always objected to his not staying with them and spending money on an hotel into the bargain.

But she appeared to have finished with family life and to be treading new paths now in the evening of her days. My father, who had his fair share of humour, found her 'pretty sprightly' and told my uncle to let the old woman do what she wanted.

And what did she want to do?

The next thing reported was that she had hired a brake and taken an excursion on a perfectly ordinary Thursday. A brake was a large, high-sprung, horse-drawn vehicle with a seating capacity for whole families. Very occasionally, when we grandchildren had come for a visit, grandfather had hired a brake. Grandmother had always stayed behind. With a scornful wave of the hand she had refused to come along.

And after the brake came the trip to K., a larger town some two hours' distance by train. There was a race-meeting there and it was to the races that my grandmother went.

The printer was now positively alarmed. He wanted to have a doctor called in. My father shook his head as he read the letter, but was against calling in a doctor.

My grandmother had not travelled alone to K. She had taken with her a young girl who, according to the printer's letter, was slightly feeble-minded: the kitchen-maid at the inn where the old lady took her meals every second day.

From now on this 'half-wit' played quite a part.

My grandmother apparently doted on her. She took her to the cinema and to the cobbler—who, incidentally, turned out to be a Social Demo-crat—and it was rumoured that the two women played cards in the kitchen over a glass of wine.

'Now she's bought the half-wit a hat with roses on it,' wrote the printer in despair. 'And our Anna has no Communion dress!'

My uncle's letters became quite hysterical, dealt only with the 'unseemly behaviour of our dear mother' and otherwise said nothing. The rest I know from my father.

The innkeeper had whispered to him with a wink: 'Mrs. B's enjoying herself nowadays, so they say.'

As a matter of fact, even in these last years my grandmother did not live extravagantly in any way. When she did not eat at the inn, she usually took no more than a little egg dish, some coffee and, above all, her beloved biscuits. She did, however, allow herself a cheap red wine, of which she drank a small glass at every meal. She kept the house very clean, and not just the bedroom and kitchen which she used. All the same, without her children's knowledge, she mortgaged it. What she did with the money never came out. She seems to have given it to the cobbler. After her death he moved to another town and was said to have started a fair-sized business in hand-made shoes.

When you come to think of it, she lived two lives in succession. The first one as daughter, wife and mother; the second simply as Mrs. B, an unattached person without responsibilities and with modest but sufficient means. The first life lasted some sixty years; the second no more than two.

My father learnt that in the last six months she had permitted herself certain liberties unknown to normal people. Thus she might rise in summer at three in the morning and take walks in the deserted streets of the little town, which she had entirely to herself. And, it was generally alleged, when the priest called on her to keep the old woman company in her loneliness, she invited him to the cinema.

She was not at all lonely. A crowd of jolly people forgathered at the cobbler's, it appears, and there was much gossip. She always kept a bottle of her red wine there and drank her little glassful whilst the others gossiped and inveighed against the town officials. This wine was reserved for her, though sometimes she provided stronger drink for the company.

She died quite suddenly on an autumn afternoon, in her bedroom, though not in bed but on an upright chair by the window. She had invited the 'half-wit' to the cinema that evening, so the girl was with her when she died. She was seventy-four years old.

I have seen a photograph of her which was taken for the children and shows her laid out.

What you see is a tiny little face, very wrinkled, and a thin-lipped, wide mouth. Much that is small, but no smallness. She had savoured to the full the long years of servitude and the short years of freedom and consumed the bread of life to the last crumb.

ᵉᔎ *Marilyn Zuckerman* ᔐᵉ

Marilyn Zuckerman (1925–   ) has had a long career as a
writer and publisher. In the 1970s, she received appointments in
the New Hampshire Council of the Arts' Poet-in-the-Schools
program and as poet Artist-in-Residence for the Massachusetts
Arts and Humanities Foundation.

AFTER SIXTY

The sixth decade is coming to an end
Doors have opened and shut
The great distractions are over—
passion . . . children . . . the long indenture of
marriage
I fold them into a chest
I will not take with me when I go

Everyone says the world is flat and finite
on the other side of sixty
That I will fall clear off the edge
into darkness
That no one will hear from me again
or want to

But I am ready for the knife slicing into the
future
for the quiet that explodes inside
to join forces with the strong old woman
to throw everything away and begin again

Now there is time to tell the story
—time to invent the new one
Time to chain myself to a fence outside the
missile base
To throw my body before a truck loaded with
phallic images
To write Thou Shalt Not Kill
on the hull of a Trident submarine
To pour my own blood on the walls of the
Pentagon
To walk a thousand miles with a begging bowl in
my hand

There are places on this planet
where women past the menopause
put on the tribal robes
smoke pipes of wisdom
—fly

Jon Godden (1906–1984) was born in Bengal, the eldest of four sisters, and spent many years of her life in India. Her sister, Rumer Godden, is the more prolific and well-known fiction writer. Jon was in her seventies when she wrote the novel *Ahmed and the Old Lady,* portraying eighty-year-old Leah Harding's freedom to pursue a long-held dream. In the novel, Leah, accompanied only by a young Indian servant, Ahmed, spends her last days on an arduous journey through the Indian mountains, totally absorbed in the beauty that surrounds her. This excerpt exposes some of her thoughts in the early days of her adventure.

from

AHMED AND THE OLD LADY

By mid-afternoon Leah had only reached the bend where the river turned towards the village and the road; the camp was still in sight, her tent a spot of white in the distance. She sat down on the grassy verge in the shade of a clump of trees, her feet on the river's strip of pebbly beach, and opened the satchel. She had been too absorbed in all she saw to think of stopping to eat; there were many wild flowers, birds she could not identify, butterflies; a lizard sunning itself on a stone had kept her motionless for minutes on end, watching the pulse beating in the pale throat, the diamond-shaped eyes, the flickering tongue. The river with its changing blues and greens, its varying surface, running smooth and shining in one stretch, broken and foaming in another, had accompanied her slow wander.

'What have I been doing all my life?' she asked herself as she unwrapped the sandwiches. 'What missing?' This power of seeing, really seeing, was something new to her. It was as if this land, so far from her own, had jerked her awake, pulled the veil of ignorance and indifference from her eyes, making her look, see, as she had never done before.

At the bottom of the satchel, under her spectacle case, was a letter from Hugh. It had arrived at the houseboat as she and Ahmed were leaving; she had read it, of course, in the car on their way, had put it in the satchel, and then had forgotten all about it, poor Hugh! And yet she was not an indifferent, careless grandmother. She loved Hugh with a deep, if often exasperated, love. Her son Paul, her only child, had been killed in his twenties in that other war, and his poor little widow had died in the flu epidemic, as so many had done, leaving the three-year-old boy to her and Geoffrey's care. She had devoted herself to Hugh, had hoped much of him. . . .

As he grew up, he had become more and more like his grandfather; in character, that is. In appearance he took after her, which was a pity; if it had been the other way round, would she have loved him more? She would certainly have liked him better, love and liking being very different feelings, as she had found. "How good your grandson is to you," her friends had often told her. "How lucky you are to have such a good steady boy!" Leah had, of course, always smilingly agreed, but sometimes she had found herself almost wishing for a bad grandson, a wild, gay, handsome, reckless grandson who would be exciting, interesting, even if he made her anxious, someone who would need her help and protection. Leah sighed and, putting on her spectacles, read the letter through again. It had been heavily censored, told her little. She knew, though, that Hugh was somewhere in North Africa and safe so far.

It was only when she came to Kashmir that she had been able to put the war out of her mind and she would not think of it now. "Why can't they all look, just look at the world, and enjoy it instead of destroying themselves and each other?" she asked the river and the hills. There was so much to see—a lifetime was not enough. . . .

Something was moving in the leaves above her head; she looked up as she heard the familiar cheerful notes. Small brown-crested birds such as these, bulbuls, with shining white cheeks and yellow undertails, had haunted the willows and orchards near the houseboat, even flying into the rooms. As she had expected, this pair readily took the crumbs she threw for them, only flying off when she went to wash her hands at the river's edge. The water was ice-cold even in the shallows; the colours of the submerged pebbles gleamed up at her.

The Baxters had told her that they had once taken a fishing boat on this same river, and now, for the first time, she wondered if she had a right to be here. When she and Ahmed had crossed the suspension bridge, she had seen a camp downstream and had glimpsed a fisherman casting a fly. Suppose such a fisherman should now appear on the path? She looked anxiously towards her camp. Was there someone coming up the river bank, someone tall, wearing a tweed jacket and a tweed hat, someone in waders, carrying a rod, a creel on his back, a landing net slung from his waist? It was Geoffrey, of course, as she had so often seen him, fishing the Scottish rivers he loved. Every spring or summer they had gone north and she had spent the long days as he expected and wished her to do, watching him fish.

The path was empty. She did not want to think of him or of her grandson. Surely she had earned the right to think for a while only of herself? As she walked on slowly, following the river upstream, and looking to the mountains at the head of the valley where tomorrow she would be journeying again, she remembered something she had read in the days soon after she arrived in India. It was something about the Hindu belief that in the last stage of life it is right and proper to forsake the world and concentrate on the soul's salvation—"to seek the Forest." Hinduism had defeated her—all those gods and goddesses and their innumerable names. Her mind was too direct and simple to grasp its convolutions and, she suspected, the core, the inner truth and meaning, had eluded her; but those words had remained in her mind, giving her a sense of peace each time she repeated them to herself. Well, in her way, that was what she, Leah, was doing— seeking the Forest—though she was not interested in the state of her soul. She was interested in this world, the physical, ever-present, many-coloured, natural world. More time on earth was all she asked.

Helen Hayes (1900–   ), American actress of stage, film, radio, and television, has been called "First Lady of the American Theatre" in honor of her long and outstanding acting career. Born in Washington, D.C., she made her debut on the Washington stage at the age of five. She won two Oscars, one in 1931 and another in 1970. The following was written when she was seventy-two years old. Her daughter had died years before of polio at age nineteen, and her husband had been dead for fifteen years. Her son had grown up and left home, and she had retired from her profession. In this selection, she comments on growing old, on living alone, and doing as she pleases, given the absence of her beloved family.

from

VOICES: AN EPILOGUE

Sometimes in the morning I pretend I'm still a great star of the theater and very carefully carry my breakfast to my room on a tray, using my best breakfast china and my best tray cloth. Everything is exquisite. Then I put it on the little table by my bed and crawl in, putting on a very pretty bed jacket, the tray on my lap—and I'm a star in bed having breakfast. It's fun, and it brings me back into the old rhythm and feeling. But usually I don't sleep late. I don't want to miss too much of the days that are left me—it isn't as wistful an idea as that—it's just that I love to be up and about, seeing the morning. I do bits and pieces around the house that need to be done. I do some writing, letters and things

From *The Woman Alone,* edited by Patricia O'Brian.

of that sort. That's another hour or two. Then in the summer and autumn, I have much to do in the garden. It is a very beautiful garden which I very much love and work in a lot.

As a matter of fact, since I've been alone and had fewer responsibilities and since I have, for sure, left my profession, I find the days are too short for me. Funny. Once in a while, I do a little television. When you've had a very active life, it is frightening to try to be inactive all at once. But being alone has its good points. I like coddling myself, thinking about me first, before anybody else. I don't know that I ever did that before. But it is pleasant, and aside from a few twinges of conscience—which happens once in a while—I'm living with that very well.

There were many times in my life, until I was left alone, that I wished for solitude. I now find that I love solitude. I never had the blessed gift of being alone until the last of my loved ones was wrested from me. Now I can go sometimes for days and days without seeing anyone. I'm not entirely alone, because I listen to the radio and read the newspapers. I love to read. That is my greatest new luxury, having the time to read. And oh, the little things I find to do that make the days, as I say, much too short.

Solitude—walking alone, doing things alone—is the most blessed thing in the world. The mind relaxes and thoughts begin to flow and I think that I am beginning to find myself a little bit.

I never had time for myself. I was always busy making the acquaintance of other people, and entertaining them in my home or in the theater . . . Now I have that time. I've found that though I have a lot of faults, and I am aware of them, I can live with myself. I've learned to forgive myself for some of the mistakes I've made. I've learned to tell myself that when I made mistakes, I had a good reason at the time, or thought I had, and that there couldn't have been any other way than the way it was. For instance, I've refused plays that I didn't like and they've turned out to be great successes. Instead of mourning that and blaming myself for having missed out, with another actress achieving that success, I say to myself, but it would have been so terrible not liking that play or that role if I had done it and it had been a success and I had been forced to play it every night for months.

Unfortunately, I know mostly women now. I like men better, but I am very happy with my women friends. One of the proud things in my life is that I know two women who have been my friends over sixty years. And I spent my seventy-first birthday with one of them on the tenth of October in New Hampshire. She also is a widow. My husband died fifteen years ago, and for two years I was just about as crazy as you can be and still be at large. I didn't have any really normal minutes during those two years.

It wasn't just grief. It was total confusion. A woman who loves a man, who has had the good fortune and good sense to marry a particularly bright one whom she trusts—I think she feels very helpless when he dies. I did. I've known other women, like Mrs. Wendell Willkie, who were terribly thrown by that loss when it came to them. I was frightened and alone. I felt unable to decide. Decisions were terrible—Charlie had always been watchful and supportive and protective about me in the theater. We don't all have a gift for being alone, living with ourselves. Some of us are afraid of ourselves. I don't know why. It must be something that goes way back, deep-seated in childhood. With some people it is so bad that they cannot trust themselves to be individuals and can only live as part of a group.

My great advantage was my career—it was there to protect me like a wonderful life preserver keeping me on top of it all, keeping me from sinking. A career is a good tranquilizer for the spirit when a woman is alone. I think it is good. But I've seen other women, without the advantage of a job or a career—the tranquilizers they choose are the more obvious ones, like the bottle or the bridge table.

After Charlie died, my friends finally persuaded me to do a picture, *Anastasia,* with Ingrid Bergman and Yul Brynner. I said, No, I can't, I haven't the will to do anything at the moment. They were so persistent, and they didn't realize I needed time to mend. I needed quiet time, apart time. Grief is a very feeling thing. If I had had a chance to sit still and indulge in grief, I think it would have made my time of recovery much quicker, shorter.

Instead I went over to England to do this film, and found myself doing the oddest things. I had always been so reliable and dependable, always on the job—a real trouper, they called me. Well, one time I took off, went to Brighton with a friend. I just took a fancy to go to Brighton and I went, and left no forwarding address at the hotel where I was living. Heavens, the picture company was beside itself. I had completely put it out of my mind that I was making a movie. Curious, isn't it?

That's a time I look back on and flinch to think of, because I was most unattractive. Unreliable and erratic. I squabbled with directors—I had never squabbled before. I took umbrage at nothing at all. I gave rather pompous and silly statements to the press. I was nutty, and that's the truth. How did I come out of it? I don't know, because I didn't know when I was in it that I was in it.

Now I look back and can see how my self-image had to change. Until

Charlie died, I was pretty darned arrogant. There was actually a time when I felt, why did God give me this gift of being so right so much of the time? Why should I be the one who always chooses the right play, the right line of action? I literally felt infallible. I don't any more. Unfortunately, today you have to be courageous to the point of audacity in the theater. It's one of the reasons I wanted to get away from it, get out of it, because I became too nervous and too frightened of my decisions. I told you I relied on Charlie. Really, he was making the decisions, but I wasn't recognizing it or acknowledging it to myself.

I think the problems of being an actress and finding myself alone have been no different from the problems of anyone else widowed or divorced. My private life has been far removed from my theater life. It was different for Katharine Cornell—at the time Guthrie McClintic died, a good ten or fifteen years ago, Kit walked off that stage and never walked on a stage again, never wanted to, never had the nerve to. And truly, I've been marking time since Charlie died. I haven't wanted, really, to be an actress since. Without his judgments.

I'm such a compulsive planner, now. I really bore myself with the way I fuss over plans. Every once in a while my companion will say, look it's six months off, Miss Hayes, can't we just wait? And I say, no, no, no, we have to straighten this out. It's a little crazy, I think, to make all these picky plans. I do it more than I ever did before, but of course, I depended on Charlie to do a lot of that. Not that he was much of a planner, but I would go along with him, and then we would just plunge ahead with whatever was to be done.

I'm seventy-two now, and I have to face up to some of the things that happen with age. I suppose I've tried to prove to myself and the world that I'm not getting old and deteriorated. My mind is as sharp as ever. I *can* remember things. I *can* think of the right word that I want to use. I *can* converse. The effort to prove all this makes me apt to overdo—trying to prove myself a little more than when I was young. It's nervousness about the deterioration of time—talking too much, trying to be funny too much. You have to face the idea that others have of you. As a dried-out lemon.

Oh, well, you just have to roll with the punches, to use the vernacular. For one thing, I used to take it for granted that if you were a celebrity, a star, you just walked into a room and things would happen, simply because it was you who walked in. Now I don't feel that. I take the back seat a lot, and that's a hard transition for someone who's been in the driver's seat through life.

Little things keep happening, and I'm startled. For example, there is a film I was asked to do by a producer recently. He and the writer were in love with it, and they were so eager for me to do it. They spent a year trying to raise the money to do that film in which I would have been the star. And they couldn't raise the money. That's a new thing for me—they couldn't raise the money for me to star. That means something extraordinary has happened. What do you do when you face that?

Well, I just told myself, all right, no more trying for star roles. If I want to be in the theater or films, I will play character roles, with young stars. There is nothing wrong with that. It's the general pattern of the great all-time stars. Youth should be served by age always. This is as it should be.

But this isn't the route for everyone. I remember Booth Tarkington years ago telling me about how he tried to get Maude Adams back on the stage when she had been gone many, many years. He wrote a play about an actress who was getting on and a young man who had a great feeling about this actress—two people, young and old, who come together. In the play, she taught him not to think of her age and he taught *her* not to think of it . . . but age, with capital letters, was the subject of the play. Poor Mr. Tarkington thought that was a graceful way to bring Maude Adams back. But she had been Peter Pan—how do you bring Peter Pan back as a middle-aged woman?

Well, she went to stay at his house, and he gave her the play in the evening to read. The next morning she came down and told him, "I don't understand this play at all. I couldn't possibly be in it, because I can't understand it." Puzzled, he said, "What's unclear about it?" And she said, "I have no realization of my age, I never think in terms of age. In going through this play, it is all about age. I have never aged."

And there it is. She was a little dumpy, she had lost a bit of her shape, but as far as she was concerned she had not aged. And she wasn't about to let anybody impose it on her. I wish it were possible for most of us to feel that way. Not that we would go gamboling about like lambs, but that we could stop trying to pretend we are young.

It's awfully hard to keep on remembering that I'm old. I'm as capable of romantic dreams as I have ever been in my life, but here in this country we have a sense of embarrassment about older people trying to enjoy some of the things they enjoyed in their youth. I knew a brilliant and attractive woman with money, widowed, very bright, and she was over sixty. We had supper one night in London, and she told me why she had moved there from the United States. She said, "I would have been covered with shame to be seen going out to dinner or to dance with a young man, but no one thinks anything of my doing it here in London. I don't have to be scorned for taking on a gigolo, as they call it." They were not gigolos, they were young friends. She likes to dance with young men, to be surrounded by young people, and she particularly likes having an escort.

There is nothing wrong with that woman. Her taste is impeccable. But here in the United States it would have looked atrocious, so she moved. It's almost an Oriental attitude. When I was in Korea I used to look at those elderly couples in their kind of uniforms—a gray Korean coat, the national dress, made exactly like the gay colored ones the young people wore, but gray. And their hats—the men look like old mother witch with those high-pointed crowns. All that gray stuff. They put on those uniforms when they reach a certain age, and that's that.

So here, women my age try to do the twist. Or they did—going down to the Peppermint Lounge in New York, trying to learn the twist. Why? Everybody over forty-five has a touch of arthritis and it must hurt to do the twist. That isn't natural. And it isn't natural for women whose shapes are changing—one's shape does change as one grows older—to put on mini-skirts and try to wear the things youngsters look so adorable in, with their coltish figures, and their long, straight, beautiful legs. Women my age, we should wear the things that look best on us. And stop carrying on like crazy. How silly it is—but it's the philosophy of this land, I suppose.

Anzia Yezierska (1885–1970), born in Russia, is best known for
her compassionate stories of Jewish immigrants, mostly women,
struggling to survive in New York's Lower East Side in the
1920s. Yezierska herself, born in a mud hut, coming to New
York at age sixteen, earned her living by working in sweat shops
and factories, sewing buttons on shirts. She was always fiercely
independent, and many of the stories Yezierska wrote when she
was in her eighties reflect her continuing free spirit.

A WINDOW FULL OF SKY

Afew blocks away from the room-
inghouse where I live is an old people's home. "Isle of the Dead," I used
to call it. But one day, after a severe attack of neuritis, I took a taxi to that
house of doom from which I had fled with uncontrollable aversion for years.
Cripples in wheelchairs and old men and women on benches stared into
vacancy—joyless and griefless, dead to rapture and despair. With averted
eyes I swept past these old people, sunning themselves like the timbers of
some unmourned shipwreck.

The hallman pointed out a door marked "Miss Adcock, Admissions."
I rapped impatiently. Almost as though someone had been waiting, the door
opened, and there was Miss Adcock trimly tailored with not a hair out of
place. Just looking at her made me conscious of my shabbiness, my un-
brushed hair escaping from under my crumpled hat, the frayed elbows of
my old coat. She pulled out a chair near her desk. Even her posture made
me acutely aware of my bent old age.

The conflict, days and nights, whether to seek admission to the home or
to die alone in my room, choked speech. A thin thread of saliva ran down
from the corner of my mouth. I tried to wipe it away with my fingers. Miss

Adcock handed me a Kleenex with a smile that helped me start talking.

"I've been old for a long, long time," I began, "but I never felt old before. I think I've come to the end of myself."

"How old are you?"

"Old enough to come here."

"When were you born?"

"It's such a long time ago. I don't remember dates."

Miss Adcock looked at me without speaking. After a short pause she resumed her probing.

"Where do you live?"

"I live in a roominghouse. Can anyone be more alone than a roomer in a roominghouse?" I tried to look into her eyes, but she looked through me and somehow above me.

"How do you support yourself?"

"I have a hundred dollars a month, in Social Security."

"You know our minimum rate is $280 a month."

"I've been paying taxes all my life. I understood that my Social Security would be enough to get me in here. . . ."

"It can be processed through Welfare."

I stood up, insulted and injured: "Welfare is charity. Why surrender self-respect to end up on charity?"

"Welfare is government assistance, and government assistance is not charity," Miss Adcock calmly replied. "I would like to explain this more fully when I have more time. But right now I have another appointment. May I come to see you tomorrow?"

I looked at Miss Adcock and it seemed to me that her offer to visit me was the handclasp of a friend. I was hungry for hope. Hope even made me forget my neuritis. I dismissed the thought of a taxi back to the rooming-house. I now had courage to attempt hobbling back with the aid of my cane. I had to pause to get my breath and rest on the stoops here and there, but in a way hope had cured me.

The prospect of Miss Adcock's visit gave me the strength to clean my room. Twenty years ago, when I began to feel the pinch of forced retirement, I had found this top-floor room. It was in need of paint and plumbing repairs. But the afternoon sun that flooded the room and the view across the wide expanse of tenement roofs to the Hudson and the Palisades beyond made me blind to the dirty walls and dilapidated furniture. Year after year the landlord had refused to make any repairs, and so the room grew dingier and more than ever in need of paint.

During my illness I had been too depressed to look at the view. But now I returned to it as one turns back to cherished music or poetry. The sky above the river, my nourishment in solitude, filled the room with such a great sense of space and light that my spirits soared in anticipation of sharing it with Miss Adcock.

When Miss Adcock walked into my room, she exclaimed: "What a nice place you have!" She made me feel that she saw something special in my room that no one else had ever seen. She walked to the window. "What a wonderful view you have here. I wonder if it will be hard for you to adjust to group living—eating, sleeping, and always being with others."

"I can no longer function alone," I told her. "At my age people need people. I know I have a lot to learn, but I am still capable of learning. And I feel the Home is what I need."

As if to dispel my anxiety, she said, "If you feel you can adjust to living with others, then of course the Home is the place for you. We must complete your application and arrange for a medical examination as soon as possible. By the way, wouldn't you like to see the room we have available right now? There are many applicants waiting for it."

"I don't have to see the room," I said in a rush.

She pressed my hand and was gone.

About two weeks later, Miss Adcock telephoned that I had passed the medical examination and the psychiatrist's interview. "And now," she said, "all that is necessary is to establish your eligibility for Welfare."

"Oh, thank you," I mumbled, unable to conceal my fright. "But what do you mean by eligibility? I thought I was eligible. Didn't you say . . . ?"

In her calm voice, she interrupted: "We have our own Welfare man. He comes to the Home every day. I'll send him to see you next Monday morning. As soon as I can receive his report, we can go ahead."

The Welfare man arrived at the appointed time.

"I'm Mr. Rader," he announced. "I am here to find out a few things to complete your application for the Home." The light seemed to go out of the room as he took possession of the chair. He was a thin little man, but puffed up, it seemed to me, with his power to give or withhold "eligibility." He put his attaché case reverently on the table, opened it, and spread out one closely printed sheet. "Everything you say," he cautioned, "will of course be checked by the authorities." He had two fountain pens in his breast pocket, one red and one black. He selected the black one. "How long have you lived here?"

"Twenty years."

"Show me the receipts." He leaned back in his chair and looked around the room with prying eyes. He watched me ruffling through my papers.

"I must have last month's receipt somewhere. But I don't bother with receipts. I pay the rent . . . they know me," I stammered. I saw him make rapid, decisive notations on his form.

"What are your assets?" he continued.

My lips moved but no words came out.

"Have you any stocks or bonds? Any insurance? Do you have any valuable jewelry?"

I tried to laugh away my panic. "If I had valuable jewelry, would I apply to get into the Home?"

"What are your savings? Let me see your bankbook." I stopped looking for the rent receipts and ransacked the top of my bureau. I handed him the bankbook. "Is that all your savings?" he asked. "Have you any more tucked away somewhere?" He looked intently at me. "This is only for the last few years. You must have had a bank account before this."

"I don't remember."

"You don't remember?"

Guilt and confusion made me feel like a doddering idiot. "I never remember where I put my glasses. And when I go to the store, I have to write a list or I forget what I came to buy."

"Have you any family or friends who can help you?" He glanced at his watch, wound it a little, and lit a cigarette, puffing impatiently. "Have you any professional diplomas? Do you go to a church or synagogue?"

I saw him making quick notes of my answers. His eyes took in every corner of the room and fixed on the telephone. He tapped it accusingly.

"That's quite an expense, isn't it?"

"I know it's a luxury," I said, "but for me it's a necessity."

He leaned forward. "You say you have no friends and no relatives. Who pays for it? Can you afford it?"

"I use some of my savings to pay for it. But I have to have it."

"Why do you have to have it?"

"I do have a few friends," I said impulsively, "but I'm terribly economical. Usually my friends call me."

I could feel my heart pounding. My "eligibility," my last stand for shelter, was at stake. It was a fight for life.

"Mr. Rader," I demanded, "haven't people on Social Security a burial allowance of $250? I don't want a funeral. I have already donated my body to a hospital for research. I claim the right to use that $250 while I am alive. The telephone keeps me alive."

He stood up and stared out the window. Then he turned to me, his forehead wrinkling: "I never handled a case like this before. I'll have to consult my superiors."

He wrote hastily for a few minutes, then closed the attaché case. "Please don't phone me. The decision rests in the hands of my superiors."

When the door closed, there was neither thought nor feeling left in me. How could Miss Adcock have sent this unseeing, unfeeling creature? But why blame Miss Adcock? Was she responsible for Welfare? She had given me all she had to give.

To calm the waiting time, I decided to visit the Home. The woman in charge took great pride in showing me the spacious reception hall, used on social occasions for the residents. But the room I was to live in was a narrow coffin, with a little light coming from a small window.

"I do not merely sleep in my room," I blurted out. "I have to live in it. How could I live without my things?"

She smiled and told me, "We have plenty of storage room in the house, and I'll assign space for all your things in one of the closets."

"In one of the closets! What earthly good will they do me there?" I suddenly realized that it would be hopeless to go on. Perhaps the coffin-like room and the darkness were part of the preparation I needed.

Back in my own place, the sky burst in upon me from the window and I was reminded of a long-forgotten passage in *War and Peace*. Napoleon, walking through the battlefield, sees a dying soldier and, holding up the flag of France, declaims: "Do you know, my noble hero, that you have given your life for your country?"

"Please! Please!" the soldier cries. "You are blotting out the sky."

⋖ *Marie Ponsot* ⋗

Marie Ponsot (1921–   ) was known as a translator and adapter of children's books before beginning her work as a poet in 1957. Having lived in both Europe and North Africa, Ponsot's poetry is full of rich worldly images. She is strongly feminist and her poems are noted for their wry, mischievous wit.

DISCOVERY

Though I sit here alone I
am smiling and
realize why as I find
that the answer (to my own
old poser of who will be
my magna mater) is clear;
I can even understand
her invisibility
for she, the grand
mother (I've always needed)
    is surely here
    too close to see
    for I am she.
Laughing she explains nothing.

My life is given back to me.

For we survived seedtime
(some seeds pop their pods and jump away;
some eased out of clumps by gold birds
float off, alight, and again drift;

some, deer after drinking drop
near a pleasant stream) we
survived and the winter
was kind to the seed
and now the winter has lifted;
I leave the season of need.

Daughter gone to lover of daughter,
sons to lovers of sons, all
have gone from me readily
with the extended almost soundless leap
of trust in genital clemency.
Left to myself I discover
that what had to spring together
has sprung together and the fields
are beds of blossoming,
the hollow meadows fill
again with blossoming.

Blessing the gardeners I do not doubt
the benefits the blessing yields
as daily less anxiously
I walk out among them
or windsoft beyond them
unheard unheeded
not lost not needed
reaching invisibly
for what is great yet proper to me
and cannot but mother me:
unconsidered liberty.

❧ *Katherine Anne Porter* ❧

Although Katherine Anne Porter (1890–1980) published comparatively little in her long life—a few books of short stories, several novellas, one novel, and one book of essays—she is considered to be one of America's most distinguished authors, a "writers' writer," and a consummate stylist. From her birth in a log cabin in Indian Creek, Texas, she rose to be a foremost figure in American literature, winning the Guggenheim Fellowship, the National Book Award, and the Pulitzer Prize. Many of her short stories are based on the facts of her early life in the South, transformed by her creative imagination into fiction.

THE LAST LEAF

Old Nannie sat hunched upon herself expecting her own death momentarily. The Grandmother had said to her at parting, with the easy prophecy of the aged, that this might be their last farewell on earth; they embraced and kissed each other on the cheeks, and once more promised to meet each other in heaven. Nannie was prepared to start her journey at once. The children gathered around her: "Aunt Nannie, never you mind! We love you!" She paid no attention; she did not care whether they loved her or not. Years afterward, Maria, the elder girl, thought with a pang, they had not really been so very nice to Aunt Nannie. They went on depending upon her as they always had, letting her assume more burdens and more, allowing her to work harder than she should have. The old woman grew silent, hunched over more deeply—she was thin and tall also, with a nobly modeled Negro face, worn to the bone and a thick fine sooty black, no mixed blood in Nannie—and her spine seemed suddenly to have given way. They could hear her groaning at night on her knees beside her bed, asking God to let her rest. When a black family moved out of a little cabin across the narrow creek, the first cabin empty for years, Nannie went down to look at it. She came back and asked Mister Harry, "Whut you aim to do wid dat cabin?" Mister Harry said, "Nothing," he supposed; and Nannie asked for it. She wanted a house of her own, she said; in her whole life she never had a place of her very own. Mister Harry said, of course she could have it. But the whole family was surprised, a little wounded. "Lemme go there and pass my last days in peace, chil'ren," she said. They had the place scrubbed and whitewashed, shelves put in and the chimney cleaned, they fixed Nannie up with a good bed and a fairly good carpet and allowed her to take all sorts of odds and ends from the house. It was astonishing to discover that Nannie had always liked and hoped to own certain things, she had seemed so contented and wantless. She moved away, and as the children said afterwards to each other, it was almost funny and certainly very sweet to see how she tried not to be too happy the day she left, but they felt rather put upon, just the same.

Thereafter she sat in the serene idleness of making patchwork and braiding woolen rugs. Her grandchildren and her white family visited her, and all kinds of white persons who had never owned a soul related to Nannie, went to see her to buy her rugs or leave little presents with her.

She had always worn black wool dresses, or black and white figured calico with starchy white aprons and a white ruffled mobcap, or a black taffety cap for Sundays. She had been finicking precise and neat in her ways, and she still was. But she was no more the faithful old servant Nannie, a freed slave: she was an aged Bantu woman of independent means, sitting on the steps, breathing the free air. She began wearing a blue bandanna wrapped around her head, and at the age of eighty-five she took to smoking a corncob pipe. The black iris of the deep, withdrawn old eyes turned a chocolate brown and seemed to spread over the whole surface of the eyeball. As her sight failed, the eyelids crinkled and drew in, so that her face was like an eyeless mask.

The children, brought up in an out-of-date sentimental way of thinking, had always complacently believed that Nannie was a real member of the family, perfectly happy with them, and this rebuke, so quietly and firmly administered, chastened them somewhat. The lesson sank in as the years went on and Nannie continued to sit on the doorstep of her cabin. They were growing up, times were changing, the old world was sliding from under their feet, they had not yet laid hold of the new one. They missed Nannie every day. As their fortunes went down, and they had very few servants, they needed her terribly. They realized how much the old woman had done for them, simply by seeing how, almost immediately after she went, everything slackened, lost tone, went off edge. Work did not accomplish itself as it once had. They had not learned how to work for themselves, they were all lazy and incapable of sustained effort or planning. They had not been taught and they had not yet educated themselves. Now and then Nannie would come back up the hill for a visit. She worked then almost as she had before, with a kind of satisfaction in proving to them that she had been almost indispensable. They would miss her more than ever when she went away. To show their gratitude, and their hope that she would come again, they would heap upon her baskets and bales of the precious rubbish she loved, and one of her great grandsons Skid or Hasty would push them away beside her on a wheelbarrow. She would again for a moment be the amiable, dependent, like-one-of-the-family old servant: "I know my chil'ren won't let me go away empty-handed."

UNCLE JIMBILLY STILL POTTERED around, mending harness, currying horses, patching fences, now and then setting out a few plants or loosening the earth around shrubs in the spring. He muttered perpetually to himself, his blue mouth always moving in an endless disjointed comment on things past and present, and even to come, no doubt, though there was nothing about him that suggested any connection with even the nearest future . . . Maria had not realized until after her grandmother's death that Uncle Jimbilly and Aunt Nannie were husband and wife . . . That marriage of convenience, in which they had been mated with truly royal policy, with an eye to the blood and family stability, had dissolved of itself between them when the reasons for its being had likewise dissolved . . . They took no notice whatever of each other's existence, they seemed to forget they had children together (each spoke of "my children"), they had stored up no common memories that either wished to keep. Aunt Nannie moved away into her own house without even a glance or thought for Uncle Jimbilly, and he did not seem to notice that she was gone . . . He slept in a little attic over the smoke-house, and ate in the kitchen at odd hours, and did as he pleased, lonely as a wandering spirit and almost as invisible . . . But one day he passed by the little house and saw Aunt Nannie sitting on her steps with her pipe. He sat down awhile, groaning a little as he bent himself into angles, and sunned himself like a weary old dog. He would have stayed on from that minute, but Nannie would not have him. "Whut you doin with all this big house to yoself?" he wanted to know. " 'Tain't no more than just enough fo' me," she told him pointedly; "I don' aim to pass my las' days waitin on no man," she added, "I've served my time, I've done my do, and dat's all." So Uncle Jimbilly crept back up the hill and into his smoke-house attic, and never went near her again . . .

ON SUMMER EVENINGS SHE sat by herself long after dark, smoking to keep away the mosquitoes, until she was ready to sleep. She said she wasn't afraid of anything: never had been, never expected to be. She had long ago got in the way of thinking that night was a blessing, it brought the time when she didn't have to work any more until tomorrow. Even after she stopped working for good and all, she still looked forward with longing to the night, as if all the accumulated fatigues of her life, lying now embedded in her bones, still begged for easement. But when night came, she remembered that she didn't have to get up in the morning until she was ready. So she would sit in the luxury of having at her disposal all of God's good time there was in this world.

Vita Sackville-West (1892–1962), British critic, novelist, poet, short story writer, biographer, and writer of gardening books and travel books, felt strongly that each human being should have a chance to develop his or her own interests and abilities. Her novel, *All Passion Spent,* reflects her philosophy. As the story begins, Lord Slane, a distinguished British public servant, former prime minister and viceroy of India, has just died at the age of ninety-four. His children, all elderly men and women over sixty years old, are discussing plans for their eighty-eight-year-old mother, Lady Slane. They have decided that she must live a few months of the year with each son or daughter, rotating from one to another.

from

ALL PASSION SPENT

Of course, she would not question the wisdom of any arrangements they might choose to make. Mother had no will of her own; all her life long, gracious and gentle, she had been wholly submissive—an appendage. It was assumed that she had not enough brain to be self-assertive. "Thank goodness," Herbert sometimes remarked, "Mother is not one of those clever women." That she might have ideas which she kept to herself never entered into their estimate. They anticipated no trouble with their mother. That she might turn round and play a trick on them—several tricks—after years of being merely a fluttering lovable presence amongst them, never entered into their calculations either. She was not a clever woman. She would be grateful to them for arranging her few remaining years.

After the funeral was over, everything at Elm Park Gardens subtly changed. Consideration towards Lady Slane was still observed, but a note of impatience crept in, a note of domination, held rather insistently by Herbert and Carrie. Herbert had become, quite definitely, the head of the family, and Carrie his support. They were prepared to take a firm though kind line with their mother. She could still be led to a chair, and, once lowered into it, could still be patted on the shoulder with a kindly protective gesture, but she must be made to understand that the affairs of the world were waiting, and that this pause of concession to death could not go on for ever. Like the papers in Lord Slane's desk, Lady Slane must be cleared up; then Herbert and Carrie could get back to their business. Nothing not put actually into words could have been conveyed more plainly.

Very quiet, very distinguished, very old, very frail, Lady Slane sat looking at her sons and daughters. Her children, who were accustomed to her, took her appearance for granted, but strangers exclaimed in amazement that she could not be over seventy. She was a beautiful old woman. Tall, slender, and pale, she had never lost her grace or her carriage. Clothes upon her ceased to be clothes and became draperies; she had the secret of line. A fluid loveliness ran over all her limbs. Her eyes were grey and deeply set; her nose was short and straight; her tranquil hands the hands of a Vandyck; over her white hair fell a veil of black lace, highly becoming. Her gowns for years past had always been soft, indefinite, and of unrelieved black. Looking at her, one could believe that it was easy for a woman to be beautiful and gracious, as all works of genius persuade us that they were effortless of achievement. It was more difficult to believe in the activity that Lady Slane had learned to pack into her life. Duty, charity, children, social obligations, public appearances—with these had her days been filled; and whenever her name was mentioned, the corollary came quick and slick, "Such a wonderful help to her husband in his career!" Oh yes, thought Edith, Mother is lovely; Mother, as Herbert says, is wonderful. But Herbert is clearing his throat. What's coming now?

"Mother, dear . . ." A form of address semi-childish, semi-conventional; Herbert putting his fingers into his collar. Yet she had once sat on the floor beside him, and shown him how to spin his top.

"Mother, dear. We have been discussing . . . we have, I mean, felt naturally troubled about your future. We know how devoted you were to Father, and we realise the blank that his loss must leave in your life. We have been wondering—and that is why we have asked you to meet us all here in the drawing-room before we separate again to our different homes—

we have been wondering where and how you will choose to live?"

"But you have decided it already for me, Herbert, haven't you?" said Lady Slane with the utmost sweetness.

Herbert put his fingers into his collar and peeked and preened until Edith feared that he would choke.

"Well! decided it for you, Mother, dear! decided is scarcely the word. It is true that we have sketched out a little scheme, which we could submit for your approval. We have taken your tastes into consideration, and we have realised that you would not like to be parted from so many interests and occupations. At the same time . . ."

"One moment, Herbert," said Lady Slane; "what was that you said about interests and occupations?"

"Surely, Mother, dear," said Carrie reproachfully, "Herbert means all your committees, the Battersea Club for Poor Women, the Foundlings' Ward, the Unfortunate Sisters' Organisation, the . . ."

"Oh yes," said Lady Slane; "my interests and occupations. Quite. Go on, Herbert."

"All these things," said Carrie, "would collapse without you. We realise that. You founded many of them. You have been the life of others. Naturally, you won't want to abandon them now."

"Besides, dear Lady Slane," said Lavinia—she had never unbent sufficiently to address her mother-in-law by any other name—"we realise how bored you would be with nothing to do. You so active, so energetic! Oh no, we couldn't visualise you anywhere but in London."

Still Lady Slane said nothing. She looked from one to the other with an expression that, in one so gentle, was surprisingly ironical.

"At the same time," Herbert proceeded, reverting to his original speech whose interruption he had endured, patient though not pleased, "your income will scarcely suffice for the expenses of a house such as you are entitled to expect. We propose, therefore . . ." and he outlined the scheme which we have already heard discussed, and may consequently spare ourselves the trouble of listening to again.

Lady Slane, however, listened. She had spent a great deal of her life listening, without making much comment, and now she listened to her eldest son without making any comment at all. He, for his part, was unperturbed by her silence. He knew that all her life she had been accustomed to have her comings and goings and stayings arranged for her, whether she was told to board a steamer for Capetown, Bombay, or Sydney; to transport her wardrobe and nursery to Downing Street; or to accompany her husband for the week-end to Windsor. On all these occasions she had obeyed her directions with efficiency and without surprise. Becomingly and suitably dressed, she had been ready at any moment to stand on quay or platform, waiting until fetched beside a pile of luggage. Herbert saw no reason now to doubt that his mother would dole out her time according to schedule in the spare bedrooms of her sons and daughters.

When he had finished, she said: "That's very thoughtful of you, Herbert. It would be very kind of you to put this house in the agents' hands to-morrow."

"Capital!" said Herbert; "I'm so glad you agree. But you need not feel hurried. No doubt some little time must elapse before the house is sold. Mabel and I will expect you at your convenience." And he stooped and patted her hand.

"Oh, but wait," said Lady Slane, raising it. It was the first gesture she had made. "You go too fast, Herbert. I don't agree."

They all looked at her in consternation.

"You don't agree, Mother?"

"No," said Lady Slane, smiling. "I am not going to live with you, Herbert; nor with you, Carrie; nor with you, William; nor with you, Charles, kind though you all are. I am going to live by myself."

"By yourself, Mother? It's impossible—and anyway, where would you live?"

"At Hampstead," replied Lady Slane, nodding her head quietly, as though in response to an inner thought.

"At Hampstead?—but will you find a house that will suit you; convenient, and not too dear?—Really," said Carrie, "here we are discussing Mother's house as though everything were settled. It is absurd. I don't know what has come over us."

"There is a house," said Lady Slane, again nodding her head; "I have seen it."

"But, Mother, you haven't been to Hampstead." This was intolerable. Carrie had known all her mother's movements day by day for the past fifteen years at least, and she revolted against the suggestion that her mother had visited Hampstead without her knowledge. Such a hint of independence was an outrage, almost a manifesto. There had always been so close and continuous a connection between Lady Slane and her eldest daughter; the plans for the day would always be arranged between them; Genoux would be sent round with a note in the morning; or they would telephone, at great length; or Carrie would come round to Elm Park Gardens after breakfast, tall, practical, rustling, self-important, equipped for the day with her gloves, her hat, and her boa, a shopping list slipped into her bag, and the agenda papers for the afternoon's committee, and the two elderly ladies would talk over the day's doings while Lady Slane went on with her knitting, and then they would go out together at about half-past eleven, two tall figures in black, familiar to the other old ladies of the neighbourhood; or if their business, for once, did not lie in the same direction, Carrie would at least drop into Elm Park Gardens for tea, and would learn exactly how her mother had spent her day. It was surely impossible that Lady Slane should have concealed an expedition to Hampstead.

"Thirty years ago," said Lady Slane. "I saw the house then." She took a skein of wool from her work-basket and held it out to Kay. "Hold it for me, please, Kay," and after first carefully breaking the little loops she began to wind. She was the very incarnation of placidity. "I am sure the house is still there," she said, carefully winding, and Kay with the experience of long habit stood before her, moving his hands rhythmically up and down, so that the wool might slip off his fingers without catching. "I am sure the house is still there," she said, and her tone was a mixture between dreaminess and confidence, as though she had some secret understanding with the house, and it were waiting for her, patient, after thirty years; "it was a convenient little house," she added prosaically, "not too small and not too large—Genoux could manage it single-handed I think, with perhaps a daily char to do the rough work—and there was a nice garden, with peaches against the wall, looking south. It was to be let when I saw it, but of course your father would not have liked that. I remember the name of the agent."

"And what," snapped Carrie, "was the name of the agent?"

"It was a funny name," said Lady Slane, "perhaps that's why I remember it. Bucktrout. Gervase Bucktrout. It seemed to go so well with the house."

"Oh," said Mabel, clasping her hands, "I think it sounds too delicious—peaches, and Bucktrout. . . ."

"Be quiet, Mabel," said Herbert. "Of course, my dear Mother, if you are set on this—ah—eccentric scheme, there is no more to be said about it. You are entirely your own mistress, after all. But will it not look a little odd in the eyes of the world, when you have so many devoted children, that you should elect to live alone in retirement at Hampstead? Far be it from me to wish to press you, of course."

"I don't think so, Herbert," said Lady Slane, and having come to the end of her winding, she said "Thank you, Kay," and making a loop on a long knitting needle she started on a fresh piece of knitting. "Lots of old ladies

live in retirement at Hampstead. Besides, I have considered the eyes of the
world for so long that I think it is time I had a little holiday from them.
If one is not to please oneself in old age, when is one to please oneself?
There is so little time left!"

"Well," said Carrie, making the best of a bad job, "at least we shall see
to it that you are never lonely. There are so many of us that we can easily
arrange for you to have at least one visitor a day. Though, to be sure,
Hampstead is a long way off, and it is not always easy to fit in the arrangements about the motor," she added, looking meaningly at her small husband, who quailed. "But there are always the great-grandchildren," she
said, brightening; "you'd like to have them coming in and out, keeping you
in touch; I know you wouldn't be happy without that."

"On the contrary," said Lady Slane, "that is another thing about which
I have made up my mind. You see, Carrie, I am going to become completely
self-indulgent. I am going to wallow in old age. No grandchildren. They
are too young. Not one of them has reached forty-five. No great-grandchildren either; that would be worse. I want no strenuous young people, who
are not content with doing a thing, but must needs know why they do it.
And I don't want them bringing their children to see me, for it would only
remind me of the terrible effort the poor creatures will have to make before
they reach the end of their lives in safety. I prefer to forget about them.
I want no one about me except those who are nearer to their death than
to their birth."

Herbert, Carrie, Charles, and William decided that their mother must
be mad. They took a step forward, and from having always thought her
simple, decided that old age had definitely affected her brain. Her madness,
however, was taking a harmless and even a convenient form. William
might be thinking rather regretfully of the lost subsidy to his house-books,
Carrie and Herbert might remain still a little dubious about the eyes of the
world, but, on the whole, it was a relief to find their mother settling her
own affairs. . . .

"About the house, Mother," began Carrie. "Would to-morrow suit you
to see it? I think I have a free afternoon," and she began to consult a small
diary taken from her bag.

"Thank you, Carrie," said Lady Slane, setting the crown upon the
surprises she had already given them, "but I have made an appointment to
see the house to-morrow. And, although it is very nice of you to offer, I
think I will go there alone."

IT WAS SOMETHING OF an adventure for Lady Slane to go alone to Hampstead, and she felt happier after safely changing trains at Charing Cross. An existence once limited only by the boundaries of Empire had shrunk since the era of Elm Park Gardens began. Or perhaps she was one of those people on whom a continuous acquaintance with strange countries makes little impression—they remain themselves to the end; or perhaps she was really getting old. At the age of eighty-eight one might be permitted to say it. This consciousness, this sensation, of age was curious and interesting. The mind was as alert as ever, perhaps more alert, sharpened by the sense of imminent final interruption, spurred by the necessity of making the most of remaining time; only the body was a little shaky, not very certain of its reliability, not quite certain even of its sense of direction, afraid of stumbling over a step, of spilling a cup of tea; nervous, tremulous; aware that it must not be jostled, or hurried, for fear of betraying its frail inadequacy. Younger people did not always seem to notice or to make allowance; and when they did notice they were apt to display a slight irritability, dawdling rather too markedly in order to keep pace with the hesitant footsteps. For that reason Lady Slane had never much enjoyed her walks with Carrie to the corner where they caught the bus. Yet, going up to Hampstead alone, she did not feel old; she felt younger than she had felt for years, and the proof of it was that she accepted eagerly this start of a new lap in life even though it be the last. Nor did she look her age, as she sat, swaying slightly with the rocking of the Underground train, very upright, clasping her umbrella and her bag, her ticket carefully pushed into the opening of her glove. It did not occur to her to wonder what her travelling companions would think, could they know that two days previously she had buried her husband in Westminster Abbey. She was more immediately concerned with the extraordinary sensation of being independent of Carrie.

The World
of Memory

So that we experience
       violently
            every day
two worlds
       one of which we share with the
       rose in bloom
            and one,
by far the greater,
       with the past,
            the world of memory
    WILLIAM CARLOS WILLIAMS
    "Shadows"

"I find my thoughts reverting more and more to days long passed.
I relive so many poignant experiences, brief and fleeting, the
imprints of which lie deep and clear in my heart."
    POLLY FRANCIS
    The Autumn of My Days

Sylvia Townsend Warner (1893–1978), English novelist, short story writer, and poet, was born at Harrow on the Hill. Although her father was a housemaster at Harrow School, she had no formal education. She worked in a munitions factory during World War II, and afterward, for ten years, was an editor of the ten-volume *Tudor Church Music* published by the Oxford University Press. A prolific writer of short stories, she was known for her elegant, graceful style and her witty, inventive tales. Her subject matter was usually the British middle class, although in her late years she wrote fairy tales about an imaginative elfin kingdom.

THE LISTENING WOMAN

It is common experience how the possessions of one's childhood vanish: the blue and white mug with D on it, picturing a dog and a duck and a dairymaid, and at the bottom when you have drunk up your milk, a daisy; the *ombres chinoises* marionettes, with strings attached to their joints—and if you pulled injudiciously, their elbows started up level with their ears, while their faces retained an impassive scornfulness for such mere contortions; the stuffed printed-cotton cat, on whose oval base were four mushroom-colored underpaws, a triumph of art and realism; the high chair, detestable because it was childish, but with a better side to its character since it raised you to the level whence you could see out of the window; the picture of Queen Victoria, and the watercolor landscape with the moon and the row of silhouetted fir trees which you privately connected with wolves and weren't easy about; and the carved wooden bear brought from Switzerland, and the red velvet pincushion, and the dolls' dinner service—all scattered, all gone, broken or left behind in house moving or given away. All gone from your ungrateful memory, too, forgotten for half a century or only brought to mind by something in a display cabinet; having emerged from neglect and oblivion as an antique, rare and costing a great deal of money.

And then, suddenly, when you are an old woman—though not in your case a rare and valued antique—they flock back; and as they reappear you discover that they are far more yours than you supposed—that you remember everything about them, the crack that ran through the dairymaid, the smell of the bear and of the pincushion, the rattle of the dolls' soup tureen because the lid didn't quite fit, the mild supportingness of the cat when used as a pillow. They are more faithful than you.

Mr. Collins, the assistant at the Abbey Antique Galleries, did not interrupt this train of thought which a thimble case had aroused in the old lady's mind. She was a Miss Mainwaring, and said by his employer, Mr. Edom, to be knowledgeable—high praise on those controlled lips. Mr. Edom did not acclaim this quality often—perhaps once a year or so. She was an aunt of Canon Balsam's, and visited. During those visits she would come to have a look round the Galleries, and this was what she was doing now. It was the first time Mr. Collins had been tête-à-tête with her; but her presence was so contained and her examination so unobtrusive—she was not one of those people who take things up or ask to have things taken down—that to all intents and purposes he might have been alone. Ultimately, she would buy something—if only for manners' sake. She was one of the old lot.

Mr. Edom was out, doing a valuation. That same morning he had come back from the auction rooms with a tea chest full of pewter—measures, platters, tankards, and tobacco boxes, collected by the late Randolph Fyffe-Randolph, M.F.H.—remarking that a good half of it was Britannia metal but the remainder not too bad. Mr. Collins was now peering into the remainder for touch marks. Touch marks are the devil, for pewterers had no conscience and stamped them here, there, and anywhere. He had settled a tankard—William Tomkins—and was thankfully putting it by when he happened to glance inside the lid. There, near the rim, was a different set of touch marks. He checked the second set of marks. If the lys was in fact a scepter and the mark like B face downward an elephant, the lid was David Oliphant, Anne and George I. A lid might have been wrenched off and replaced by an earlier lid; but the hinge showed no sign of this and the tankard, now that he came to look at it as a piece of pewter and not merely a field for touch marks, seemed a cut above William Tomkins, who supplied mostly pothouse stuff under George III. If William Tomkins had bought the tankard in a job lot—as he might well have done if he was short of stock just then—a begrimed David Oliphant tankard might have been handed to an apprentice for a rub-up, and the apprentice tempted to illicit sporting with the punches. Or was this being imaginative? Mr. Collins glanced at Miss Mainwaring and wondered if she was knowledgeable about pewter.

He saw her halt in front of a carved and gilded oblong frame. She was knowledgeable about frames, anyhow. He saw her look with a tranquil smile at the blackened oil painting on wood. He heard her say, "So here you are."

THE CANDLELIT WOMAN LEANING from the window was no darker than she had always been. If you were acquainted with her, you could distinguish the rim of her linen cap against the hooding shadow behind, and the hand holding the candlestick, and the other hand shielding the flame— the flame whose light shone gently and ruddily on the oval face, coloring the nearer cheek and the tip of the long nose and laying areas of shadow between the cheekbones and the rather small almond-shaped eyes. There she was. No restorer, no flaying turpentined hand, had come between them. Unchanged, she was still watching from her window, unalarmed, patient, and slightly amused; still, after more than half a century, waiting for Lucy Mainwaring to come into her grandfather's library.

She had watched several generations of Mainwarings. Grandfather's grandfather, a squire in Cambridgeshire, had taken her in quittance of a debt, together with a Watteau which turned out to be a Pater. They hung on either side of the fireplace, being much the same size. For a while the Watteau which turned out to be a Pater had been Lucy's preference: you could see more of it, and the lady had a lap dog. You could see more of it, and that was why after a year or two you saw there wasn't much in it. The lady sat propped against the balustrade like a doll, and the legs of the gentleman playing the mandolin were not a pair. But the other one, the older you grew and the oftener you looked at it, the more there was to see, to see into, to think about. So it came to be called Lucy's picture.

Time sweeps one on, sweeps one into the enthusiasms of one's adolescence and out of them into fresh enthusiasms. Lucy was sixteen and living for Botticelli when her grandfather died. The house was sold, the property distributed. Aunt Lalage, who lectured about Anglo-Saxons at Girton, went off with the library books, and with the books went the two pictures.

Mother resented this. It was such a beautiful old frame; Lalage had no
appreciation of antiques and would probably stick a fancy portrait of Beo-
wulf in it—the last thing in the world Grandfather had intended. And
whenever she and Lalage met—which was seldom—she would ask, "Have
you still got Lucy's picture?" Lucy saw her picture once or twice on
Lalage's wall. No, noted it: she did not see. By then she was living for
D'Annunzio, and for a young man called Dennis Macnamara, who thought
all that sort of thing great rot and died of dysentery in Mesopotamia. Lucy
remained a spinster. Aunt Lalage maturely married a don, who was Welsh
and made everyone read the Mabinogion. They retired to the land of his
fathers and Lucy's picture was lost in the mists of Snowdonia.

But here it was.

MR. COLLINS HAD HEARD her quiet exclamation. Obviously it had not
been addressed to him, since here he already was. But when a lady speaks,
especially such an old lady, it is manners to get up. He got up. Having got
up, he realized that it would not be manners to sit down again. Mr. Edom
had a particular way of approaching contemplative customers which Mr.
Collins in his clandestine heart called the Funeral Gondola. It was inimita-
ble, though no doubt part of it came by practice. Mr. Collins practiced a
few hushed strokes forward, and the old lady turned to him and said, "I
recognized it."

If she could do that through all those layers of varnish she was certainly
knowledgeable about the Dutch Masters.

"A Schalcken," he said.

She nodded.

"The frame is unusually fine," he continued. "It is contemporary. It was
probably made for that very picture."

"So I have always understood," said the old lady. "You see, it's my
picture." She turned back to the Schalcken and smiled at it.

Poor old thing, she must be a little mad. He must deal with her gently—
but he wished Mr. Edom would come back.

When people get up on your account, it is never easy to get them down
again. Lucy Mainwaring also wished that Mr. Edom would come back, and
faithful Ponto, his watchdog, return to those tankards. Instead, here he was,
lankly hovering. She would have to say something to him. What a pity,
when she had so much to say to the woman leaning out of the window; or
rather, so much to ask, for she herself had not very much to tell.

"Where did Mr. Edom get her?"

Mr. Collins did the best he could, which was to pretend he hadn't heard. For this was appalling—at any rate it was on the brink of becoming appalling. The poor old thing wasn't going to stop at being a little mad. She was going to work herself up, *idée fixe,* persecution mania, and all that. How on earth was he to deal gently with an elderly maniac, convinced that the Schalcken was her picture and had been stolen from her? He looked to see if she had an umbrella. She hadn't; but she could do a lot of execution with that handbag. If force of godless prayer could have fetched Mr. Edom back, Mr. Edom would have darkened the door at that same instant. Instead, it was a couple inflamed by a television series about adventures in finding unidentified antiques. Mr. Collins knew that kind at a glance— perhaps because there, but for the grace of God, he might have been adventuring himself.

"I don't suppose you've got any old books," said the lady.

So they were on the prowl for edgepaintings, were they? Mr. Collins had no patience with this craze for edgepaintings. He liked a handsome binding as well as any man; but with the spine of a book, and its sides, not to mention its interior, to be decorative on, tricking out its fore-edge—where at most a decent gilding should prevail—with esoteric views of St. Paul's or what not, was going too far.

He indicated a row of Surtees, a broken set of Migne's "Patrologiae," Hakluyt's "Navigations," and Bewick's "Birds." They took up each volume in turn, held it slantingly frontwise to the light, and spun the pages. "I'm afraid none of these are quite what we want," said the man. "Do you go in for Art Nouveau?" And the woman said, "Have you any old Victorian jewelry?"

THEY WERE NOT NICE people, but they were providential. Relieved of the necessity of throwing sticks for Mr. Edom's Ponto, Miss Mainwaring went on interrogating the woman at the window. Here she was—but how had she got here? Through what dusty auction rooms, unsurmisable owner-ships, perils? Lalage had died in 1942, with a small obituary in the *Times.* Her don survived her by six years, so earning a rather larger obituary, as by then there was more room for civilian demises. Nineteen years, then, had been spent by the candlelit lady in travelling from Merionethshire to Oxfordshire. But she might well have been blown out of her course. One of the unsurmisable owners, a bank manager, say, or a clergyman, powerless as a Jesuit under authority, could have been directed to a wider usefulness at Wolverhampton, from Wolverhampton to Brighton. Considered in that light, she had been expeditious; though she looked composed as ever, she might even be rather out of breath, having got to the Abbey Antique Galleries only just in time.

"Well, what about pictures? What's that old picture over there, for instance?"

They stood on her heels and, being polite, she moved aside. Trusty Ponto followed them, looking as if he might snap at any moment.

"It's quite interesting," said the man. "What you can see of it. What's it supposed to be?"

"Dutch School," said Mr. Collins, his eye resting on Miss Mainwaring.

"Ah! One sees a lot of that. What do you think of it, Freda?"

"I'm not all that set on pictures, as you know. They take up such a lot of wall space."

"This one wouldn't. It's a kit-cat. I must admit, I don't mind it. I believe I rather like it. It could come up a lot with cleaning."

"I quite like the frame," said the lady.

"Yes, you're right. It's a very handsome frame—or would be, with a regilding."

"But I can't say I'm drawn to the picture—what you can see of it. It strikes me as monotonous. And it would cost the earth to clean."

"We could have a bash at the cleaning ourselves," said the man. "Enough to get some idea what it's like. And then, if we didn't care for it, we could always take it out and use the frame for something else. Why not?"

"Have it your own way," said the lady.

The man pulled out a notecase. "How much?" he said.

"One thousand five hundred guineas," said Mr. Collins.

"No, thank you!" exclaimed the lady.

The man, assuming dignity, said he would think it over, and added, "Come on, Freda. There's nothing here."

BLITHELY PRECEDING THEM TO the door, Mr. Collins saw that Mr. Edom was standing just inside it. How much he had heard and what he thought of it could not be deduced. But Mr. Collins did not feel the relief he had anticipated. He hoped to feel it later on—which is a different sensation. "Miss Mainwaring is here, Mr. Edom."

Mr. Edom had already recognized the small figure at the end of the room. It struck him that Miss Mainwaring had aged since her previous visit—had aged quite surprisingly. If this was to be her last visit to the Galleries it was distressing that it should have exposed her to customers like those who had just gone out. She turned as he approached. Her face was deathly white. Her lips twitched. She should not have been left standing about while those barbarians were ravaging the shop. He handed her a chair, and she sat down like one utterly exhausted.

"I always think these unexpected returns of summer so late in the autumn are very trying," Mr. Edom said. "One isn't prepared for them."

There was something else Mr. Edom wasn't prepared for, thought Mr. Collins. She was quiet enough now—for which he took some credit to himself, since you would need to be uncommonly far out of your wits for the sum of one thousand five hundred guineas not to come as a quietener; it got rid of that clever couple fast enough. But though she was quiet, she was working herself up. He could feel it in the air. In another minute Mr. Edom would be blown out of his Indian summers by the knowledgeable Miss Mainwaring claiming the Schalcken as her own property and demanding to know how he came by it. If only he'd been able to slip in a word of warning!

Sure enough, she was beginning again. "Mr. Edom, I want the Schalcken."

Mr. Edom said there was no one he would rather see it go to. It was a very nice little bit of genre. He'd taken a fancy to it the moment he set eyes on it.

"I saw it before you did, though. It belonged to my grandfather. I haven't seen it for fifty years or so, but I recognized it."

"That doesn't surprise me, Miss Mainwaring. If I may say so, you've got an eye."

"I've left it a little late. But I must have it. I loved it very much. It was always spoken of as Lucy's picture. I even thought it was really mine. And now, after all these years . . ."

Years of forgetfulness, faithlessness, contempt, she thought; and years of faithful abidingness. Meanwhile Mr. Edom, his heart unbuttoning to romance, was saying that journeys end in lovers' meeting.

Mr. Collins felt an oncome of second thoughts. Nothing could be less like madness than Miss Mainwaring's request for a book to write on, to save getting up. She laid the book on her knee, spread open the checkbook, and began to write, frowning a little when it came to reducing the guineas to pounds, shillings, and pence.

"There!"

Some dealers in their arrogance affect not to look at checks. Mr. Edom always looked carefully at his. He did so now, and looked yet again. He coughed. "Miss Mainwaring. I'm sorry, but you haven't made this out right."

"Oh! Haven't I? How stupid of me. Well, tell me the amount, and I'll alter it."

"I paid eighty-five pounds for that picture," said Mr. Edom. Mr. Collins, wrenched from his second thoughts by total amazement, could hardly believe his ears. No reputable dealer discloses what he paid for a thing. To do so is unethical, strikes at the root of society, and lowers the tone of the trade. Yet here was Mr. Edom, that model of decorum, blurting out his eighty-five pounds without a decency-bit of "in the region of," and continuing, "If you will pay me a hundred guineas, I shall have made my profit. And we will both be pleased, I hope."

Such is human vanity that for a moment Lucy Mainwaring was extremely angry that her grandfather's Schalcken should have been bought for eighty-five pounds. She made out another check, and Mr. Edom receipted it. "But what I cannot understand," he exclaimed, "is how you got that other figure."

She saw Mr. Collins wishing the earth would swallow him up. "That man who left just as you came in was asking about it. I expect I misheard. I could easily have misheard. You see, I was so afraid he might get it." And seeing that Mr. Edom was not perfectly convinced, she added, "Now that she is mine, do tell me where you found her."

"I bought it from a publican in a village near Swindon. It was hanging in the snug."

She had an extraordinarily pretty laugh—a thing you don't often hear nowadays. But she was still looking white as a sheet, and her pretty laugh was like blossom on a winter bough. Having taken down the picture and set it on a level with Miss Mainwaring's view, Mr. Edom remarked, "As this is quite an occasion, I feel we should celebrate it." And going into his private room he returned with a bottle of hock and three glasses. "You too, Collins," he said, filling him the third glass. "And I suggest as a toast: All's well that ends well." His eye rested on Mr. Collins as he spoke, but blandly, and like an act of oblivion.

By the time Mr. Edom refilled her glass, Miss Mainwaring had begun to look more like herself. Still staring at the picture, she murmured, "I've made a discovery. I thought I knew everything about her, but I've made a discovery. She's not watching. She's listening." Mr. Edom took a careful scrutiny of the oval face. "Quite true. You're right, Miss Mainwaring. She's listening. Listening for a step she's waiting for, I should say."

"Come to that," added Mr. Collins, "you wouldn't see much on a dark night, holding a candle in front of your eyes like that. Schalcken liked his candlelight effects. But she's listening." For Mr. Collins felt he could rejoin society. It was true that he had misstated the price, but he was not the only person who had been unprofessional about his figures that afternoon.

Yes, she was listening. She was listening for a step in the darkness, the step of someone nearing the end of a journey, or the step of an approaching expected stranger; or for a last heartbeat.

❧ *Loren Eiseley* ❧

Loren Eiseley (1907–1977), naturalist, anthropologist, and author, is well known for his interpretation of scholarly, scientific subjects in a poetic, lyrical style. Born in Lincoln, Nebraska, he taught at the University of Kansas, at Oberlin, and at the University of Pennsylvania, and was Curator of Early Man at the University of Pennsylvania Museum.

THE BROWN WASP

There is a corner in the waiting room of one of the great Eastern stations where women never sit. It is always in the shadow and overhung by rows of lockers. It is, however, always frequented—not so much by genuine travelers as by the dying. It is here that a certain element of the abandoned poor seeks a refuge out of the weather, clinging for a few hours longer to the city that has fathered them. In a precisely similar manner I have seen, on a sunny day in midwinter, a few old brown wasps creep slowly over an abandoned wasp nest in a thicket. Numbed and forgetful and frost-blackened, the hum of the spring hive still resounded faintly in their sodden tissues. Then the temperature would fall and they would drop away into the white oblivion of the snow. Here in the station it is in no way different save that the city is busy in its snows. But the old ones cling to their seats as though these were symbolic and could not be given up. Now and then they sleep, their gray old heads resting with painful awkwardness on the backs of the benches.

Also they are not at rest. For an hour they may sleep in the gasping exhaustion of the ill-nourished and aged who have to walk in the night. Then a policeman comes by on his round and nudges them upright.

"You can't sleep here," he growls.

A strange ritual then begins. An old man is difficult to waken. After a muttered conversation the policeman presses a coin into his hand and passes fiercely along the benches prodding and gesturing toward the door. In his wake, like birds rising and settling behind the passage of a farmer through a cornfield, the men totter up, move a few paces, and subside once more upon the benches.

One man, after a slight, apologetic lurch, does not move at all. Tubercularly thin, he sleeps on steadily. The policeman does not look back. To him, too, this has become a ritual. He will not have to notice it again officially for another hour.

Once in a while one of the sleepers will not awake. Like the brown wasps, he will have had his wish to die in the great droning center of the hive rather than in some lonely room. It is not so bad here with the shuffle of footsteps and the knowledge that there are others who share the bad luck of the world. There are also the whistles and the sounds of everyone, everyone in the world, starting on journeys. Amidst so many journeys somebody is bound to come out all right. Somebody.

Maybe it was on a like thought that the brown wasps fell away from the old paper nest in the thicket. You hold till the last, even if it is only to a public seat in a railroad station. You want your place in the hive more than you want a room or a place where the aged can be eased gently out of the way. It is the place that matters, the place at the heart of things. It is life that you want, that bruises your gray old head with the hard chairs; a man has a right to his place.

But sometimes the place is lost in the years behind us. Or sometimes it is a thing of air, a kind of vaporous distortion above a heap of rubble. We cling to a time and a place because without them man is lost, not only man but life. This is why the voices, real or unreal, which speak from the floating trumpets at spiritualist seances are so unnerving. They are voices out of nowhere whose only reality lies in their ability to stir the memory of a living person with some fragment of the past. Before the medium's cabinet both the dead and the living revolve endlessly about an episode, a place, an event that has already been engulfed by time.

This feeling runs deep in life; it brings stray cats running over endless miles, and birds homing from the ends of the earth. It is as though all living creatures, and particularly the more intelligent, can survive only by fixing or transforming a bit of time into space or by securing a bit of space with its objects immortalized and made permanent in time. For example, I once saw, on a flower pot in my own living room, the efforts of a field mouse to build a remembered field. I have lived to see this episode repeated in a thousand guises, and since I have spent a large portion of my life in the shade of a nonexistent tree I think I am entitled to speak for the field mouse.

One day as I cut across the field which at that time extended on one side of our suburban shopping center, I found a giant slug feeding from a runnel of pink ice cream in an abandoned Dixie cup. I could see his eyes telescope and protrude in a kind of dim uncertain ecstasy as his dark body bunched and elongated in the curve of the cup. Then, as I stood there at the edge of the concrete, contemplating the slug, I began to realize it was like standing on a shore where a different type of life creeps up and fumbles tentatively among the rocks and sea wrack. It knows its place and will only creep so far until something changes. Little by little as I stood there I began to see more of this shore that surrounds the place of man. I looked with sudden care and attention at things I had been running over thoughtlessly for years. I even waded out a short way into the grass and the wild-rose thickets to see more. A huge black-belted bee went droning by and there were some indistinct scurryings in the underbrush.

Then I came to a sign which informed me that this field was to be the site of a new Wanamaker suburban store. Thousands of obscure lives were about to perish, the spores of puffballs would go smoking off to new fields, and the bodies of little white-footed mice would be crunched under the inexorable wheels of the bulldozers. Life disappears or modifies its appearances so fast that everything takes on an aspect of illusion—a momentary fizzing and boiling with smoke rings, like pouring dissident chemicals into a retort. Here man was advancing, but in a few years his plaster and bricks would be disappearing once more into the insatiable maw of the clover. Being of an archaeological cast of mind, I thought of this fact with an obscure sense of satisfaction and waded back through the rose thickets to the concrete parking lot. As I did so, a mouse scurried ahead of me, frightened of my steps if not of that ominous Wanamaker sign. I saw him vanish in the general direction of my apartment house, his little body quivering with fear in the great open sun on the blazing concrete. Blinded and confused, he was running straight away from his field. In another week scores would follow him.

I forgot the episode then and went home to the quiet of my living room. It was not until a week later, letting myself into the apartment, that I realized I had a visitor. I am fond of plants and had several ferns standing on the floor in pots to avoid the noon glare by the south window.

As I snapped on the light and glanced carelessly around the room, I saw a little heap of earth on the carpet and a scrabble of pebbles that had been kicked merrily over the edge of one of the flower pots. To my astonishment I discovered a full-fledged burrow delving downward among the fern roots. I waited silently. The creature who had made the burrow did not appear. I remembered the wild field then, and the flight of the mice. No house mouse, no *Mus domesticus,* had kicked up this little heap of earth or sought refuge under a fern root in a flower pot. I thought of the desperate little creature I had seen fleeing from the wild-rose thicket. Through intricacies of pipes and attics, he, or one of his fellows, had climbed to this high green solitary room. I could visualize what had occurred. He had an image in his head, a world of seed pods and quiet, of green sheltering leaves in the dim light among the weed stems. It was the only world he knew and it was gone.

Somehow in his flight he had found his way to this room with drawn shades where no one would come till nightfall. And here he had smelled green leaves and run quickly up the flower pot to dabble his paws in common earth. He had even struggled half the afternoon to carry his burrow deeper and had failed. I examined the hole, but no whiskered twitching face appeared. He was gone. I gathered up the earth and refilled the burrow. I did not expect to find traces of him again.

Yet for three nights thereafter I came home to the darkened room and my ferns to find the dirt kicked gaily about the rug and the burrow re-opened, though I was never able to catch the field mouse within it. I dropped a little food about the mouth of the burrow, but it was never touched. I looked under beds or sat reading with one ear cocked for rustlings in the ferns. It was all in vain; I never saw him. Probably he ended in a trap in some other tenant's room.

But before he disappeared I had come to look hopefully for his evening burrow. About my ferns there had begun to linger the insubstantial vapor of an autumn field, the distilled essence, as it were, of a mouse brain in exile from its home. It was a small dream, like our dreams, carried a long and weary journey along pipes and through spider webs, past holes over which loomed the shadows of waiting cats, and finally, desperately, into this room where he had played in the shuttered daylight for an hour among the green ferns on the floor. Every day these invisible dreams pass us on the street, or rise from beneath our feet, or look out upon us from beneath a bush.

Some years ago the old elevated railway in Philadelphia was torn down and replaced by a subway system. This ancient El with its barnlike stations containing nut-vending machines and scattered food scraps had, for generations, been the favorite feeding ground of flocks of pigeons, generally one flock to a station along the route of the El. Hundreds of pigeons were dependent upon the system. They flapped in and out of its stanchions and steel work or gathered in watchful little audiences about the feet of anyone who rattled the peanut-vending machines. They even watched people who jingled change in their hands, and prospected for food under the feet of the crowds who gathered between trains. Probably very few among the waiting people who tossed a crumb to an eager pigeon realized that this El was like a food-bearing river, and that the life which haunted its banks was dependent upon the running of the trains with their human freight.

I saw the river stop.

The time came when the underground tubes were ready; the traffic was transferred to a realm unreachable by pigeons. It was like a great river subsiding suddenly into desert sands. For a day, for two days, pigeons continued to circle over the El or stand close to the red vending machines. They were patient birds, and surely this great river which had flowed through the lives of unnumbered generations was merely suffering from some momentary drought.

They listened for the familiar vibrations that had always heralded an approaching train; they flapped hopefully about the head of an occasional workman walking along the steel runways. They passed from one empty station to another, all the while growing hungrier. Finally they flew away.

I thought I had seen the last of them about the El, but there was a revival and it provided a curious instance of the memory of living things for a way of life or a locality that has long been cherished. Some weeks after the El was abandoned workmen began to tear it down. I went to work every morning by one particular station, and the time came when the demolition crews reached this spot. Acetylene torches showered passers-by with sparks, pneumatic drills hammered at the base of the structure, and a blind man who, like the pigeons, had clung with his cup to a stairway leading to the change booth, was forced to give up his place.

It was then, strangely, momentarily, one morning that I witnessed the return of a little band of the familiar pigeons. I even recognized one or two members of the flock that had lived around this particular station before they were dispersed into the streets. They flew bravely in and out among the sparks and the hammers and the shouting workmen. They had returned—and they had returned because the hubbub of the wreckers had convinced them that the river was about to flow once more. For several hours they flapped in and out through the empty windows, nodding their heads and watching the fall of girders with attentive little eyes. By the following morning the station was reduced to some burned-off stanchions in the street. My bird friends had gone. It was plain, however, that they retained a memory for an insubstantial structure now compounded of air and time. Even the blind man clung to it. Someone had provided him with a chair, and he sat at the same corner staring sightlessly at an invisible stairway where, so far as he was concerned, the crowds were still ascending to the trains.

I have said my life has been passed in the shade of a nonexistent tree, so that such sights do not offend me. Prematurely I am one of the brown wasps and I often sit with them in the great droning hive of the station, dreaming sometimes of a certain tree. It was planted sixty years ago by a boy with a bucket and a toy spade in a little Nebraska town. That boy was myself. It was a cottonwood sapling and the boy remembered it because of some words spoken by his father and because everyone died or moved away who was supposed to wait and grow old under its shade. The boy was passed from hand to hand, but the tree for some intangible reason had taken root in his mind. It was under its branches that he sheltered; it was from this tree that his memories, which are my memories, led away into the world.

After sixty years the mood of the brown wasps grows heavier upon one. During a long inward struggle I thought it would do me good to go and look upon that actual tree. I found a rational excuse in which to clothe this madness. I purchased a ticket and at the end of two thousand miles I walked another mile to an address that was still the same. The house had not been altered.

I came close to the white picket fence and reluctantly, with great effort, looked down the long vista of the yard. There was nothing there to see. For sixty years that cottonwood had been growing in my mind. Season by season its seeds had been floating farther on the hot prairie winds. We had planted it lovingly there, my father and I, because he had a great hunger for soil and live things growing, and because none of these things had long been ours to protect. We had planted the little sapling and watered it faithfully, and I remembered that I had run out with my small bucket to drench its roots the day we moved away. And all the years since it had been growing in my mind, a huge tree that somehow stood for my father and the love I bore him. I took a grasp on the picket fence and forced myself to look again.

A boy with the hard bird eye of youth pedaled a tricycle slowly up beside me.

"What'cha lookin' at?" he asked curiously.

"A tree," I said.

"What for?" he said.

"It isn't there," I said, to myself mostly, and began to walk away at a pace just slow enough not to seem to be running.

"What isn't there?" the boy asked. I didn't answer. It was obvious I was attached by a thread to a thing that had never been there, or certainly not for long. Something that had to be held in the air, or sustained in the mind, because it was part of my orientation in the universe and I could not survive without it. There was more than an animal's attachment to a place. There was something else, the attachment of the spirit to a grouping of events in time; it was part of our mortality.

So I had come home at last, driven by a memory in the brain as surely as the field mouse who had delved long ago into my flower pot or the pigeons flying forever amidst the rattle of nut-vending machines. These, the burrow under the greenery in my living room and the red-bellied bowls of peanuts now hovering in midair in the minds of pigeons, were all part of an elusive world that existed nowhere and yet everywhere. I looked once at the real world about me while the persistent boy pedaled at my heels.

It was without meaning, though my feet took a remembered path. In sixty years the house and street had rotted out of my mind. But the tree, the tree that no longer was, that had perished in its first season, bloomed on in my individual mind, unblemished as my father's words. "We'll plant a tree here, son, and we're not going to move any more. And when you're an old, old man you can sit under it and think how we planted it here, you and me, together."

I began to outpace the boy on the tricycle.

"Do you live here, Mister?" he shouted after me suspiciously. I took a firm grasp on airy nothing—to be precise, on the bole of a great tree. "I do," I said. I spoke for myself, one field mouse, and several pigeons. We were all out of touch but somehow permanent. It was the world that had changed.

Julius Lester (1939–   ) is a writer of short stories and novels, a musician and folklorist. He currently teaches at the University of Massachusetts in the Department of Afro-American and Judaic Studies. *Do Lord Remember Me* is a novel of the final day of Reverend Joshua Smith, an old black minister. In this excerpt from the novel he is coming to terms with his life through the many memories which roll over him as he seemingly dozes in his recliner.

from

DO LORD REMEMBER ME

T*he Reverend Joshua Smith, Sr. was born November 5, 1900 in Ouichitta, Mississippi.*

He stared at what he'd written. It was a simple statement of fact. Or it was supposed to be. But it wasn't. Reverend Smith's eyes narrowed. Couldn't he remember even when he was born?

He rubbed his cheek as if it were a talisman that would yield the memory as elusive now as life itself was becoming, but his fingers found only the stubble of gray hair. His hands had trembled so that morning, he hadn't been able to hold the electric razor steady. Some mornings he steadied his wrist with his left hand, but not that morning. He preferred the clean stroke of a blade, but his hands shook so now that he couldn't put on shaving cream. The last time he had tried, more had gone on his lips than around them.

"What'd you do that for, Reverend Smith?" she'd asked from the door-way of the bathroom.

"I didn't do it on purpose," he snapped, not knowing she'd been there leaning on her cane.

"I wish you'd let me call the visiting nurse service and have them send somebody around every day to help you with things like that," she continued, concern in her voice.

"If you'd just let me alone, I'd be all right." He glared, a glob of shaving cream dropping from his upper lip onto the lapel of his bathrobe. He looked down at it and then at her. "I'm sorry," he mumbled.

She nodded, as if it were foolish to be sorry for what couldn't be helped. "Your breakfast is almost ready," she said, before turning and walking away.

It didn't matter now. Death had shown him its face twice and the last time it hadn't been so frightening or ugly. It was only his fear that had made Death ugly.

As if waking from a heavy sleep, he saw the sheet of paper at which his eyes were staring, and, for an instant, didn't recognize the handwriting, the words trembling on the page as if shaking in a cold wind.

He read the sentence again. It was wrong, but what was right? It was like that more and more, the seeing but not recognizing, the recognition without knowledge. There were old people, like her brother, Earl, who didn't know what year they were living in, didn't know that they were no longer who they had been.

With some effort he pushed the chair back from the desk and opened the center drawer. A manila folder lay atop a clutter of pads, pens, paper clips, and pencils and he placed it on the desk. Laboriously moving the chair forward, he opened the folder and looked at the first sentence of the obituary he'd written last week.

Reverend Joshua Smith was born November 5, 1900 in Ouichitta, Mississippi.

That was wrong, too. He read all three pages of the obituary and was pleased that everything else seemed correct. He turned the three stapled pages facedown on the empty side of the folder and looked at the next obituary, one he'd written last month.

The Reverend Joshua Smith, Sr. was born November 5, 1897 in Ouichitta, Mississippi.

He read the sentence again and nodded. That was right. He closed the folder of previously written obituaries and pushed it to the side. He drew a wavering line through "1900" and with an almost childlike intensity and concentration, wrote "1897" above, trying to make the lines and curves of the numbers as sturdy as youth. Shaking his head, he dropped the sheet of paper into the wastebasket beside his chair.

Opening the drawer to his right, he took another sheet of paper and wrote again:

The Reverend Joshua Smith, Sr. was born November 5, 1897 in Oui-chitta, Mississippi. . . .

He walked through the empty kitchen and not seeing her, assumed she was in the bedroom making the beds. He went into the living room where he sat down wearily in his leather recliner and was asleep, it seemed, before his eyes closed. But there was no clean separation between sleep and wakefulness any longer. Now that he was barred from the future, images of the past were freed from memory's prison and floated unbidden to the surface of his mind like corpses from undiscovered shipwrecks on the ocean's bottom. He watched them come, the faces, rooms, churches, highways, and he did not know if he was asleep and dreaming, or awake and remembering, or if each was the other and both one.

Since the stroke he had begun walking across the landscape of the past and the more he walked, the further away its horizon. The past seemed larger now than the future had appeared when he was young and possibility was all and the world was all possibility, even for one as black as him.

Why was the realm of the past vaster than future's sphere had been ever? Was it because possibility was an illusion of youth, while the past (when one had earned it) was like the curved dome of night into which he gazed in wonder and with awe? The past was an actuality whose detail and reality could not be seen and examined when it was present. Only now, when there was nothing but past, did it surface to be examined and lived truly for the first time.

The monumental contributions of Swiss psychiatrist Carl Gus-
tav Jung (1875–1961) to the subject of analytical psychology are
recorded in the twenty volumes of his collected works. *Memories, Dreams, Reflections* is his autobiography, begun in his
eighty-first year. He felt that the exterior events of his life, the
people he had known, the places he had visited, the things he had
done, were subordinate to his inner experiences. Consequently,
his autobiography concentrates on his inner life, his thoughts,
visions, and memories. "Retrospect" is the last chapter in the
book.

RETROSPECT

When people say I am wise, or a sage,
I cannot accept it. A man once dipped a hatful of water from a stream.
What did that amount to? I am not that stream. I am at the stream, but
I do nothing. Other people are at the same stream, but most of them find
they have to do something with it. I do nothing. I never think that I am
the one who must see to it that cherries grow on stalks. I stand and behold,
admiring what nature can do.

There is a fine old story about a student who came to a rabbi and said,
"In the olden days there were men who saw the face of God. Why don't
they any more?" The rabbi replied, "Because nowadays no one can stoop
so low."

One must stoop a little in order to fetch water from the stream.

The difference between most people and myself is that for me the
"dividing walls" are transparent. That is my peculiarity. Others find these

From *Memories, Dreams, Reflections.*

walls so opaque that they see nothing behind them and therefore think nothing is there. To some extent I perceive the processes going on in the background, and that gives me an inner certainty. People who see nothing have no certainties and can draw no conclusions—or do not trust them even if they do. I do not know what started me off perceiving the stream of life. Probably the unconscious itself. Or perhaps my early dreams. They determined my course from the beginning.

Knowledge of processes in the background early shaped my relationship to the world. Basically, that relationship was the same in my childhood as it is to this day. As a child I felt myself to be alone, and I am still, because I know things and must hint at things which others apparently know nothing of, and for the most part do not want to know. Loneliness does not come from having no people about one, but from being unable to communicate the things that seem important to oneself, or from holding certain views which others find inadmissible. The loneliness began with the experiences of my early dreams, and reached its climax at the time I was working on the unconscious. If a man knows more than others, he becomes lonely. But loneliness is not necessarily inimical to companionship, for no one is more sensitive to companionship than the lonely man, and companionship thrives only when each individual remembers his individuality and does not identify himself with others.

It is important to have a secret, a premonition of things unknown. It fills life with something impersonal, a *numinosum*. A man who has never experienced that has missed something important. He must sense that he lives in a world which in some respects is mysterious; that things happen and can be experienced which remain inexplicable; that not everything which happens can be anticipated. The unexpected and the incredible belong in this world. Only then is life whole. For me the world has from the beginning been infinite and ungraspable.

I have had much trouble getting along with my ideas. There was a daimon in me, and in the end its presence proved decisive. It overpowered me, and if I was at times ruthless it was because I was in the grip of the daimon. I could never stop at anything once attained. I had to hasten on, to catch up with my vision. Since my contemporaries, understandably, could not perceive my vision, they saw only a fool rushing ahead.

I have offended many people, for as soon as I saw that they did not understand me, that was the end of the matter so far as I was concerned. I had to move on. I had no patience with people—aside from my patients. I had to obey an inner law which was imposed on me and left me no freedom of choice. Of course I did not always obey it. How can anyone live without inconsistency?

For some people I was continually present and close to them so long as they were related to my inner world; but then it might happen that I was no longer with them, because there was nothing left which would link me to them. I had to learn painfully that people continued to exist even when they had nothing more to say to me. Many excited in me a feeling of living humanity, but only when they appeared within the magic circle of psychology; next moment, when the spotlight cast its beam elsewhere, there was nothing to be seen. I was able to become intensely interested in many people; but as soon as I had seen through them, the magic was gone. In this way I made many enemies. A creative person has little power over his own life. He is not free. He is captive and driven by his daimon.

> *Shamefully*
> *A power wrests away the heart from us,*
> *For the Heavenly Ones each demand sacrifice;*
> *But if it should be withheld*
> *Never has that led to good,*

says Hölderlin.

This lack of freedom has been a great sorrow to me. Often I felt as if I were on a battlefield, saying, "Now you have fallen, my good comrade, but I must go on." For "shamefully a power wrests away the heart from us." I am fond of you, indeed I love you, but I cannot stay. There is something heart-rending about that. And I myself am the victim; I *cannot* stay. But the daimon manages things so that one comes through, and blessed inconsistency sees to it that in flagrant contrast to my "disloyalty" I can keep faith in unsuspected measure.

Perhaps I might say: I need people to a higher degree than others, and at the same time much less. When the daimon is at work, one is always too close and too far. Only when it is silent can one achieve moderation.

The daimon of creativity has ruthlessly had its way with me. The ordinary undertakings I planned usually had the worst of it—though not always and not everywhere. By the way of compensation, I think, I am conservative to the bone. I fill my pipe from my grandfather's tobacco jar and still keep his alpenstock, topped with a chamois horn, which he brought back from Pontresina after having been one of the first guests at that newly opened *Kurort*.

I am satisfied with the course my life has taken. It has been bountiful, and has given me a great deal. How could I ever have expected so much? Nothing but unexpected things kept happening to me. Much might have been different if I myself had been different. But it was as it had to be; for all came about because I am as I am. Many things worked out as I planned them to, but that did not always prove of benefit to me. But almost everything developed naturally and by destiny. I regret many follies which sprang from my obstinacy; but without that trait I would not have reached my goal. And so I am disappointed and not disappointed. I am disappointed with people and disappointed with myself. I have learned amazing things from people, and have accomplished more than I expected of myself. I cannot form any final judgment because the phenomenon of life and the phenomenon of man are too vast. The older I have become, the less I have understood or had insight into or known about myself.

I am astonished, disappointed, pleased with myself. I am distressed, depressed, rapturous. I am all these things at once, and cannot add up the sum. I am incapable of determining ultimate worth or worthlessness; I have no judgment about myself and my life. There is nothing I am quite sure about. I have no definite convictions—not about anything, really. I know only that I was born and exist, and it seems to me that I have been carried along. I exist on the foundation of something I do not know. In spite of all uncertainties, I feel a solidity underlying all existence and a continuity in my mode of being.

The world into which we are born is brutal and cruel, and at the same time of divine beauty. Which element we think outweighs the other, whether meaninglessness or meaning, is a matter of temperament. If meaninglessness were absolutely preponderant, the meaningfulness of life would vanish to an increasing degree with each step in our development. But that is—or seems to me—not the case. Probably, as in all metaphysical questions, both are true: Life is—or has—meaning and meaninglessness. I cherish the anxious hope that meaning will preponderate and win the battle.

When Lao-tzu says: "All are clear, I alone am clouded," he is expressing what I now feel in advanced old age. Lao-tzu is the example of a man with superior insight who has seen and experienced worth and worthlessness, and who at the end of his life desires to return into his own being, into the eternal unknowable meaning. The archetype of the old man who has seen enough is eternally true. At every level of intelligence this type appears, and its lineaments are always the same, whether it be an old peasant or a great philosopher like Lao-tzu. This is old age, and a limitation. Yet there is so much that fills me: plants, animals, clouds, day and night, and the eternal in man. The more uncertain I have felt about myself, the more there has grown up in me a feeling of kinship with all things. In fact it seems to me as if that alienation which so long separated me from the world has become transferred into my own inner world, and has revealed to me an unexpected unfamiliarity with myself.

Freya Stark (1893–   ), British travel writer and authority on
the Near and Middle East, began her travels early; by the age
of three she had visited Italy, France, and many areas of her
native England, and by five years of age, she could speak three
languages. As a young woman, she learned Arabic, traveled to
the Arab world, entered into Arab life, living with the people in
Persia, Syria, Greece, and Turkey, and wrote books about her
travels. Not an ordinary traveler or travel writer, she approached
her subject with unusual openness and empathy, a philosophic
attitude, and a poetic turn of phrase, and has been called a "poet
of travels."

from
THE JOURNEY'S ECHO

Pictures of one's childhood are as frag-
mentary as the relics of the sailor's way which wanders through the south
of England; a stretch emerges here and there, though most of it has vanished
or been transformed. Amid these half-obliterated memories I can see, quite
sharply, my first meeting with the image of death.

I must have been about four years old and a nurse in our grandmother's
house was putting me to bed. It was a Victorian house where fireplaces had
tall brass fenders highly polished, and the black metal bed-rails ended in
knobs of brass; many pillows, beginning with bolsters, were piled up towards a chintz canopy from which curtains descended, securely lined
against draughts, tied with tasselled ropes of red and green. Standing there
on the eiderdown, being buttoned into a long nightgown that lay about my
feet, I asked if my mother would live for ever.

'No,' said nurse, 'not for ever; but for a long time.'

'How long?' said I. 'A thousand years?'

'No,' said nurse. 'Not a thousand years.'

The finality of Time was borne in upon me. Hours afterwards my parents, coming up to bed, found me half asleep but still sobbing at the top of the stairs, where I had crept a little nearer to those dear ones who in a thousand years would be dead.

This feeling has never really changed. If the world is not to last for ever, it seems to make no difference whether its time is to be counted in millions or billions of years; what matters is that there is an end. There can be no safe happiness until the fact has been faced and assimilated; and an absolute condition of all successful living, whether for an individual or a nation, is the acceptance of death.

GOOD DAYS ARE TO be gathered like sunshine in grapes, to be trodden and bottled into wine and kept for age to sip at ease beside his fire. If the traveller has vintaged well he need trouble to wander no longer; the ruby moments glow in his glass at will. He can still feel the spring in his step, and the wind on his face, though he sit in shelter: unless perhaps the sight of a long road winding, or the singing of the telegraph wires, or the wild duck in their wedges, or horses' hooves that clatter into distance, or the wayside stream—all with their many voices persuade him to try just one more journey before the pleasant world comes to an end.

ON THE WHOLE, AGE comes most gently to those who have some doorway into an abstract world—art, or philosophy, or learning—regions where the years are scarcely noticed and young and old can meet in a pale truthful light. We move there with increasing freedom as Time rubs out the illusions of possession, whose dark attendant, envy, fades away. The loss of our own things, or such we thought so, our faculties, our friends, our loves— makes us again receptive as in childhood, though now it is no human hand that gives. In our increasing poverty, the universal riches grow more apparent, the careless showering of gifts regardless of return; our private grasp lessens, and leaves us heirs to infinite loves in a common world where every joy is a part of one's personal joy. With a loosening hold returning towards acceptance, we prepare in the anteroom for a darkness where even this last personal flicker fades, and what happens will be in the Giver's hand alone.

THIS IS THE PROSPECT from the watershed, and when the traveller reaches it, it is a good thing to take an hour's leisure and look out on the visible portions of the journey, since never in one's life can one see the same view twice. I have placed my bundle beside me and found a flat stone and settled in the sun with my back to the road of my coming, and have looked as far as I can into the valley where the track is lost. And as the eye soon tires with so little detail to hold it, and the mist wreathes all in its timeless festoons, and no mortal inn is in sight—I have opened my bundle and sorted the few things collected and carried through the morning's climb, to count what personal oddments are there to help me on my way. This little book is the list of these things; and as it is a random assortment, not harvested from learning but from life and accident, it is probably just like the list of millions of other travellers, since the journey we make is the same. Who asks for originality in a soldier's kit-bag, or the knapsack of a mountaineer? Or who would not think it presumptuous in the snowflake to wish to be unique in its manner of falling to the ground? My hope is the very opposite; for we are all—unless suddenly cut off—bound to grow old; and as I am fortunate in looking to old age without either misgiving or regret, but with an interest of travel—I like to think that these stray reflections may not have been written for myself only, but for all who have climbed and crossed their ridges and are standing with me upon the verge of afternoon.

❧ Gwendolyn Brooks ❧

Gwendolyn Brooks (1917–   ), a native of Chicago, awarded the Pulitzer Prize for her poem *Annie Allen,* was the sixth woman ever to receive the Pulitzer Prize for Poetry and the first black poet to win that prize. She has been awarded two Guggenheim Fellowships, and in 1968 became Poet Laureate for Illinois. She has also written children's literature and novels, and is an editor and a professor.

THE BEAN EATERS

They eat beans mostly, this old yellow pair.
Dinner is a casual affair.
Plain chipware on a plain and creaking wood,
Tin flatware.

Two who are Mostly Good.
Two who have lived their day,
But keep on putting on their clothes
And putting things away.

And remembering . . .
Remembering, with twinklings and twinges,
As they lean over the beans in their rented back room that
        is full of beads and receipts and dolls and cloths,
        tobacco crumbs, vases and fringes.

❧

Poet, novelist, and essayist, Wendell Berry (1934–   ), a native Kentuckian, returned to a family farm in the northern Kentucky hills after several years in New York City. His move to the rural south has had a strong influence on his writing as he seeks to characterize the relationship between human values and the processes of nature. His novel *The Memory of Old Jack*, from which the following excerpt is taken, recounts one day in the life of a ninety-two-year-old farmer who is remembering and coming to terms with his life as a boy, husband, lover, farmer, father, and friend.

from

THE MEMORY OF OLD JACK

Since before sunup Old Jack has been standing at the edge of the hotel porch, gazing out into the empty street of the town of Port William, and now the sun has risen and covered him from head to foot with light. But not yet with warmth, and in spite of his heavy sheepskin coat he has grown cold. He pays that no mind. When he came out and stopped there at the top of the steps, mindful of the way the weight of his body is taking him, he propped it carefully with his cane and, in the way that has lately grown upon him, left it.

From the barn whose vaned cupola was visible over the house roof against the pale sky, Mat Feltner was calling his cows. Old Jack listened with an eagerness that carried him away from himself; for all his consciousness of where he was, he might have been asleep and dreaming. Mat waited, and called again. And then from the quietening of Mat's voice, Old Jack knew that the cows had come near and that Mat could see them moving up deliberative and shadowy out of the mists and the thinning darkness. And then he heard the barn doors slide open.

Except for the crowing now and then of roosters, the town and its outskirts were quiet. Old Jack's mind was with Mat there in the barn, stirring about the lives of animals. He knew the solitude that Mat had entered at the beginning of every workday since his son was killed in the war. He knew the stiffness and pain that the tobacco cutting had placed in Mat's back and shoulders and hands. He was aware of the deep somnolence of the hayricks in the loft of the barn.

Alert, absent in what he knew, the old man stood on the porch in the chill whitening of the dawn, empty of himself as a public statue, while all in him that had kept most alive lived there in the waking barn with Mat. And he has continued to stand there while the cries of roosters have flared and flared again across the ridges, and the daylight and then the sunlight have come. He has heard the waking of other farms, the summoning of stock from the pastures, the occasional bawling of a cow. He has heard the tractors start, the wagons lumbering to the fields.

Though tractors draw them now, not horses and mules, there is something in the sound of the wagons going out that is the same as always. Now there is the alien commotion of iron and fire, but within it or under it there is the old rattling and pounding of the empty wagon beds against the bolsters, hurrying out over the rough farm roads in the cool of the morning. As he listened there passed and passed again across the gaze of his memory a team of good mare mules that he bought as three-year-olds from Graham Foresee in the September of 1888.

They were a team of black, mealy-nosed mare mules with plenty of size and depth of body, with a lot of lift in their motion, matched well every way. Beck and Kate. As though the reins are in his hands, and he stands again on the rattling wagon, they are carrying him to the field. The sun is just coming up. It is the fall of the year. The mules are in good flesh, the hair glossy on them, and they are fresh from the night. They step together in the harness with an eager lightness that for a moment shortens his breath.

They were the first team of their quality that he ever owned. They were, maybe, an extravagance. He bought them because he needed a team, no question about that. But he bought as carefully as he did, and paid the price he paid, in a kind of celebration of himself. He had owned his place then—or owned the debt his father had left on it—for three years. And though he had not yet cleared the farm of debt, he was clearing it. He was going to clear it. There was no longer any doubt in him about his ability to do that. It had become plain to him that he was equal to what would be required of him, and to what he would require of himself. . . .

Though he stands leaning on his cane on the porch of the hotel in Port William, looking out into the first cool morning of September, 1952, he is not there. He is four miles and sixty-four years away, in the time when he had music in him and he was light. From the height of that time his mind comes down to him, a bird to the head of a statue, and another day of his old age lights the street. The chill has gone deep in him now. He will go down to Jasper Lathrop's store, where, though it is too early in the season yet to expect a fire, some of yesterday's warmth will have been held overnight. Smiting the edge of the porch sharply with his cane as if to set hard reality on the alert, taking careful sight on the stone steps, he lets himself heavily down. . . .

For a moment he attends to the sounds and smells around him there in the store. From the front come the voices of women, laughter. Beside him the talk of the men drones on—something he has passed through and beyond. He does not listen to the words. And his eyes keep their fixed gaze up on the windows straight in front of him. The glare of their morning light, like darkness, suits him as well now as sight. When he wants to, or needs to, he can still see well enough, but it has got so it takes an effort, as though to draw the world together; it seems less and less worth the trouble. His vision, with the finality of some physical change, has turned inward. More and more now the world as it is seems to him an apparition or a cloud that drifts, opening and closing, upon the clear, remembered lights and colors of the world as it was. This world as it is serves mostly to remind him, to turn him back along passages sometimes too well known into that other dead, mourned, unchangeable world that still lives in his mind. . . .

HE KNOWS TOO WELL the way his mind is taking him—his mind that, like a hunting dog backtracking through the country, keeps turning back and turning back, tracing out the way it has come. As if it will be any help to it to know. His mind, he thinks, would do well to settle down and be quiet, for pretty soon he is going up on the hill for the long sleep that most people he knows have already gone off to, and there is not a lot that a man's mind can do about that. He has no fear of death. It is coming, there is nothing to be done about it, and so he does not think about it much. It is the unknown, and he has come to the unknown before. Sometimes it has been very satisfying, the unknown. Sometimes not. Anyhow, what would a man his age propose to do instead of die? He has been around long enough to know that death is the only perfect cure for what ails mortals. After you have stood enough, you die, and that is all right.

And so he does not think of death more often than necessary, and he can quit thinking about it any time he wants to. He does not think of what lies ahead. He will leave that to the Old Marster. And there are days, less frequent now that he has so little will to attend to what is going on, when he lives caught up and enclosed in the present. He is like an old dog then—"Son," he said to Burley Coulter, who told Mat, "I'm just like an old dog. Got nothing on my mind but gravy, and now and then a fly"— sleeping a light sleep that allows him to remain aware of the warmth and comfort of whatever place he has come to, or waking and looking with idle and remote interest at the scene that his fading eyes have blurred and withdrawn from. Those are his best days, he knows, though they leave behind them a taint of idleness that troubles him and that has kept two such days from ever occurring together.

But the present is small and the future perhaps still smaller. And what his mind is apt to do is leap out of that confinement, like an old dog, still strong, that has been penned up and then let loose in the one countryside that it knows and that it knew for a long time. But it is like an old dog possessed by an old man's intelligent ghost that remembers all it has seen and done and all the places it has known, and that goes back to haunt and lurk in those places. Some days he can keep it very well in hand, just wandering and rummaging around in what he remembers. He is amazed at what he comes upon that he thought he had forgot. He can remember dates and names and prices and measures and dimensions of all kinds. He can remember the way men looked and the way they moved and how they worked and what they did. He can remember the faces and the bodies of women, and the playing of certain fiddlers; at times he can play a whole tune out in his head just like a Victrola. He can remember crops, their quality and weight and what they brought. He can remember the markings and the color and the conformation and the disposition and the gait of any number of horses and mules. He can remember, in detail down to the markings of their faces, bunches of cattle that he owned, and can move among them in his mind, looking them over. Sometimes he can recover a whole day, with the work he did in it, and the places and the animals and the people and even the words that belong to it.

And that is all right. But there have been some bad days in his life, too.

Plenty of them, and it is hard to keep his mind, ranging around the way it does, from crossing the track of his hard times. And though he would a lot rather let them lie still and be gone, once his mind strikes into his old troubles there is no stopping it; he is into his story then, watching, as he has helplessly done many times before, to see how one spell of trouble and sorrow led to another. Once he has started he has to go on, yet one more time, to the end.

Into
Another
Intensity

"We must be still and still moving into another intensity . . ."
T. S. ELIOT
"East Coker," The Four Quartets

*". . . it can't be categorically stated that death ends anything.
. . . The old man meets the young people and lives on."*
WILLIAM CARLOS WILLIAMS
I Wanted a Poem

*"What has happened has happened. The water
You once poured into the wine cannot be
Drained off again, but
Everything changes. You can make
A fresh start with your final breath."*
BERTOLT BRECHT
"Everything Changes"

William Butler Yeats (1865–1939), the great Irish lyric poet, was fascinated by the legends of Ireland and the occult. In his middle and late years he largely renounced his youthful interest in transcendentalism and dealt more with the material and realistic world and the polarity between the real and the spiritual. "Sailing to Byzantium," part of the longer work *The Tower*, published in 1928, was one of these later works. Yeats wrote that he used the image of Byzantium because he had read somewhere that in the Emperor's palace in Byzantium (now Istanbul) was a tree made of gold and silver and artificial birds that sang.

SAILING TO BYZANTIUM

I

That is no country for old men. The young
In one another's arms, birds in the trees,
—Those dying generations—at their song,
The salmon-falls, the mackerel-crowded seas,
Fish, flesh, or fowl, commend all summer long
Whatever is begotten, born, and dies.
Caught in that sensual music all neglect
Monuments of unageing intellect.

II

An aged man is but a paltry thing,
A tattered coat upon a stick, unless
Soul clap its hands and sing, and louder sing
For every tatter in its mortal dress,
Nor is there singing school but studying

Monuments of its own magnificence;
And therefore I have sailed the seas and come
To the holy city of Byzantium.

III

O sages standing in God's holy fire
As in the gold mosaic of a wall,
Come from the holy fire, perne in a gyre,
And be the singing-masters of my soul.
Consume my heart away; sick with desire
And fastened to a dying animal
It knows not what it is; and gather me
Into the artifice of eternity.

IV

Once out of nature I shall never take
My bodily form from any natural thing,
But such a form as Grecian goldsmiths make
Of hammered gold and gold enamelling
To keep a drowsy Emperor awake;
Or set upon a golden bough to sing
To lords and ladies of Byzantium
Of what is past, or passing, or to come.

◆§ *Philip Larkin* ३◆

Philip Larkin (1922–1985), poet, essayist, novelist, and music
critic, was also a librarian for most of his life. Educated at St.
John's College, Oxford, he became librarian of the Brynmor
Jones Library at the University of Hull in Yorkshire. Considered one of the finest poets of the twentieth century, he wrote
of the everyday, down-to-earth fears and concerns of ordinary
life, of disillusionment and disappointment, of love and death.
The poem "Aubade" is part of his *Collected Poems,* published
in 1988.

AUBADE

I work all day, and get half-drunk at night.
Waking at four to soundless dark, I stare.
In time the curtain-edges will grow light.
Till then I see what's really always there:
Unresting death, a whole day nearer now,
Making all thought impossible but how
And where and when I shall myself die.
Arid interrogation: yet the dread
Of dying, and being dead,
Flashes afresh to hold and horrify.

The mind blanks at the glare. Not in remorse
—The good not done, the love not given, time
Torn off unused—nor wretchedly because
An only life can take so long to climb
Clear of its wrong beginnings, and may never;
But at the total emptiness for ever,

The sure extinction that we travel to
And shall be lost in always. Not to be here,
Not to be anywhere,
And soon; nothing more terrible, nothing more true.

This is a special way of being afraid
No trick dispels. Religion used to try,
That vast moth-eaten musical brocade
Created to pretend we never die,
And specious stuff that says *No rational being*
Can fear a thing it will not feel, not seeing
That this is what we fear—no sight, no sound,
No touch or taste or smell, nothing to think with,
Nothing to love or link with,
The anaesthetic from which none come round.

And so it stays just on the edge of vision,
A small unfocused blur, a standing chill
That slows each impulse down to indecision.
Most things may never happen: this one will,
And realisation of it rages out
In furnace-fear when we are caught without
People or drink. Courage is no good:
It means not scaring others. Being brave
Lets no one off the grave.
Death is no different whined at than withstood.

Slowly light strengthens, and the room takes shape.
It stands plain as a wardrobe, what we know,
Have always known, know that we can't escape,
Yet can't accept. One side will have to go.
Meanwhile telephones crouch, getting ready to ring
In locked-up offices, and all the uncaring
Intricate rented world begins to rouse.
The sky is white as clay, with no sun.
Work has to be done.
Postmen like doctors go from house to house.

❧ *Dylan Thomas* ❧

Dylan Thomas (1914–1953), English poet and short story writer, born in Wales, was known for his exuberant style of writing and living. While still in school he began to write poetry, then worked as a journalist, and subsequently supported himself by writing film scripts and reading his poetry. He was thought of as a superb and careful craftsman, but his promising career was cut short by his death in New York City of acute alcoholism.

Do Not Go Gentle into That Good Night

Do not go gentle into that good night,
Old age should burn and rave at close of day;
Rage, rage against the dying of the light.

Though wise men at their end know dark is right,
Because their words had forked no lightning they
Do not go gentle into that good night.

Good men, the last wave by, crying how bright
Their frail deeds might have danced in a green bay,
Rage, rage against the dying of the light.

Wild men who caught and sang the sun in flight,
And learn, too late, they grieved it on its way,
Do not go gentle into that good night.

Grave men, near death, who see with blinding sight
Blind eyes could blaze like meteors and be gay,
Rage, rage against the dying of the light.

And you, my father, there on the sad height,
Curse, bless, me now with your fierce tears, I pray.
Do not go gentle into that good night.
Rage, rage against the dying of the light.

Arturo Vivante (1923–   ), poet, short story writer, novelist,
essayist, and translator, was born in Rome and grew up near
Siena. He spent the war years from 1938 on with his family, first
in England, and then in Canada, where he studied medicine at
McGill University. After the war, he returned to Italy, where
he received his degree in medicine, but soon gave it up to devote
himself to writing. He came to the United States in the '50s and
from 1968 to the present has been writer-in-residence at a number
of American colleges and universities. Seventy of his stories have
been published in *The New Yorker*.

LAST RITES

Better to die like the ancients," she
said. "A great high fever, and you are spirited away."

She must have had in mind the fever that had marked the beginning of
her illness, and that, without surgery, would indeed have spirited her away
in a few days. Instead, she had had all the "benefits" of modern medicine—
two major operations, sickening tests, transfusions, a cabinetful of drugs—
and after fourteen months she was still alive.

The first operation had broken the fever but not cured her. The second,
to which she had submitted at the doctors' insistence almost exactly a year
after the first, had revealed an incurable condition, and instead of seeing
fulfilled their promise that she would "get really well" she had seen strange
new medicines being brought into her room, medicines that were supposed
to retard the wild proliferation of the cells, and that the doctors, unwilling
to tell her what her illness was, tried to pass off as something else, until one
night, her pain keeping her awake, her suspicions fully aroused, and her
questions becoming more and more pressing, one of her sons, himself a

doctor, told her. All along, he had thought she should be told, believing that life might seem lighter to her and each moment of it have more meaning if she knew. Nor did it seem right that she, the most concerned, should be the least informed.

Fears confirmed will cause as much alarm as fears first stirred. Sitting up on her bed, leaning forward, her knees bent, she looked at him with eyes that welled with thought rather than with tears, and that her thinned, girlish look intensified so that they seemed even larger than they were. "Cancer . . . no less," she whispered. "Now let's just work on the pain—on the pain only—and never mind the rest."

It was April, in Siena, and outside in the garden a nightingale was singing. They listened in silence to the notes appealing, and he thought it would be good to die on such a night, and the verses of Keats came to his mind:

> *To cease upon the midnight with no pain,*
> *While thou art pouring forth thy soul abroad*
> *In such an ecstasy!*

He eyed the little bottle of opium drops on her night table. He would not remove it. He would not touch it. He would leave it there—though many mingled voices told him not to—within her reach, for her to empty "to the drains," if she so wished. He almost hoped—yes, *hoped*—that she would drink it.

But in the morning the bottle was still there—full, or nearly. The maid counted out the prescribed number of drops. Forty. But forty drops had not relieved the pain last night. Should she count more, the maid asked her.

"Oh, my dear, I wouldn't count them at all. I would pour it all out, except that I don't want to hurt you." She took the drops, and five more, then lay perfectly still and resigned, with her eyes closed and her arms at her sides, waiting with composure for the pain to go.

And she continued what her doctors called the "cure"—the new medicine from Switzerland. But she looked on it with scorn, as on something weak and ineffectual—the way a wine drinker looks on water at table.

One of the doctors, a small, sweet unpretentious man about her age, who had become very attached to her, was hopeful. He sat beside her and tried to cheer her.

"How long more do you think this can go on?" she asked him. "It can't go on much longer, can it, Doctor?"

"But, Madam, why do you say that? You can live for years."

"Years?"

"But certainly—five, six, seven, and perhaps even more."

It was just what she didn't want to hear. "If it were a question of weeks or months, I could bear it, but you talk of years. Imagine, years . . ."

The old doctor was wrong. After a few days, there came a crisis. Now the doctors multiplied their efforts, and though she was too ill to know what they were doing, more than once, with her hands, she tried to ward them off.

She came to an end six days later—not slowly, like a train arriving at a station, but swiftly and convulsively, like a train derailing. She died hard, because her roots were strong, and much more still than if she had gone gently was the final stillness that ensued.

The house had been geared for sickness so long, and now there was no sickness anymore—no one to take care of, or stay up for, or worry about. Now she was someone only to be missed. They began putting things away—cumbersome, ugly things of glass and white enamel, and boxes full of drugs. "Throw them away," one could almost hear her saying. "Clear out the cupboards. Open all the windows. Air, air the house." She had always been one for keeping things uncluttered, one for spring cleaning, and this was now her day.

Two days later, four men—by a happy chance, her favorite farmers from nearby—lifted the bier, bore it out into the sunny air, and laid it on the open hearse. Fronds brushed it as it passed down under a tunnel-like drive of ilex trees. On the highway, hedges and ditches were crowded with spring flowers. From the highway, the procession, on foot, turned left along an unpaved country road, and now there were fields of clover on each side, and vines in tender leaf, and olive trees with tiny yellow blossoms, and ripening peas and broad beans in their pods, and the wheat undulated by the wind— all things she loved, things she had tried to capture with her brush. "How surprised they would be," she once had said, "those people who praise me as a mother, if they knew that in my lifetime perhaps my children never gave me so much pleasure as the reflection that the sky makes on the leaves." The road climbed up through a wood. At first, there were acacias and honeysuckle on each side, then chestnut trees—great, ancient chestnut trees with hollow trunks and branches sprouting with the newest leaves. The procession took an even smaller road, which led to the brow of the hill up on the right. The slope above the road was a rock garden of wild and flowering plants whose leaves vied in beauty with the blossoms. On top of the hill, they came to four cypresses and to the tiny country cemetery enclosed by lichened walls. Her grave had been dug next to that of an old farmer who had died eight or nine years before. Small, witty, graceful, and a little quaint, he was remembered by everyone with pleasure.

She was laid in her grave. Though the parish priest was present, there was no service, tribute, or any kind of benediction, for she had never been baptized and didn't go to church. A mason—a skillful man, who did his work with intense passion, and whom she had known well, for he had recently restored part of her house—quickly covered the vault with terra-cotta tiles, laying them side by side with mortar. As usual, he worked with care and concentration. She would have admired him. At the end, he flicked the mortar off his trowel. That quick flicking of the trowel seemed to her son a kind of benediction, and the mortar that was flung from it holy water. She had never been fond of prayers, ceremonies, sermons; she had always been fond of watching skilled artisans at work. And this flipping of the trowel seemed so much more fitting, so much more to her taste, than any kind of religious benediction. It seemed to lend a touch of joy and freshness to the burial.

Afterward, the parish priest—a nice, if somewhat colorless, young man—said how sorry and embarrassed he was not to have given such a kind lady a blessing. He would have given it, he added, even though she was not religious, except that he thought she would not really have wanted it.

The grave was to be bordered by four bars of travertine. A stonecutter in town—a gentle little man, at the end of his career—advised her sons that if they wanted truly fine travertine and good cornices, they should go to a village twenty-odd miles away, where there were quarries of it. And there they went, and it was like some of the trips they had taken with her in her good days when, one or the other of them at the wheel, they would go out for long drives to some old village or country church and stop for coffee in the village square. They came back with four heavy cornices of travertine. The stonecutter engraved her name in marble, her name and dates—no mournful inscription, nothing else. He did his work by hand. "You won't find anyone else who does it by hand now. I am the only one in town," he said.

Certainly, her son thought, had she had a chance, she would have chosen this gentle man to carve her name. And it struck him that all during her illness and till the moment of her death she had had no say about what was done to her, that she had more or less given in to, reluctantly agreed with, anything the doctors ordered for her, but that from the moment of her death on everything that happened appeared to fall in with her wishes, though she had left none, though she had let none be known. It was, after so much dreariness, a pleasant observation: at last, it seemed to him, she had taken things in hand, in her own strong hands, and he could almost see them, those admirable hands, come alive again, directing, doing.

⋞ Anne Sexton ⋟

In *The Awful Rowing Toward God,* Pulitzer Prize–winning poet Anne Sexton's (1928–1974) eighth book of poetry, she grapples with the universal search for God. Sexton was born in Newton, Massachusetts, and taught at Boston University until her death.

COURAGE

It is in the small things we see it.
The child's first step,
as awesome as an earthquake.
The first time you rode a bike,
wallowing up the sidewalk.
The first spanking when your heart
went on a journey all alone.
When they called you crybaby
or poor or fatty or crazy
and made you into an alien,
you drank their acid
and concealed it.

Later,
if you faced the death of bombs and bullets
you did not do it with a banner,
you did it with only a hat to
cover your heart.
You did not fondle the weakness inside you
though it was there.
Your courage was a small coal

that you kept swallowing.
If your buddy saved you
and died himself in so doing,
then his courage was not courage,
it was love; love as simple as shaving soap.

Later,
if you have endured a great despair,
then you did it alone,
getting a transfusion from the fire,
picking the scabs off your heart,
then wringing it out like a sock.
Next, my kinsman, you powdered your sorrow,
you gave it a back rub
and then you covered it with a blanket
and after it had slept a while
it woke to the wings of the roses
and was transformed.

Later,
when you face old age and its natural conclusion
your courage will still be shown in the little ways,
each spring will be a sword you'll sharpen,
those you love will live in a fever of love,
and you'll bargain with the calendar
and at the last moment
when death opens the back door
you'll put on your carpet slippers
and stride out.

May Swenson (1919–1989) received nearly every award offered to a modern poet. Her work is often praised for its imagery, which is both exact and entrancing. Swenson said that her poetry was based on a "craving to get through the curtain of things as they *appear,* to things as they *are* and then into the larger, wilder space of things as they are *becoming."*

ENDING

Maybe there *is* a Me inside of me
and, when I lie dying, he
will crawl out. Through my toe.
Green on the green rug, and then
white on the wall, and then
over the windowsill, up the trunk
of the apple tree, he
will turn brown and rough and warty
to match the bark. But you'll be
able to see—(*who* will be
able to see?) his little jelly
belly pulsing with the heart inside
his transparent hide.
And, once on the top bough,
tail clinging, as well as "hands,"
he'll turn the purest blue
against the sky—
(say it's a clear day, and I don't die
at night). Maybe from there
he'll take wing—That's it!—

an ARCHAEOPTERYX! Endless,
the possibilities, my little Soul,
once you exit from my toe.
But, oh,
looking it up, I read:
"Archaeopteryx, generally considered
the first bird . . . [although]
closely related to certain small
dinosaurs . . . could not fly."
A pain . . . Oh, I
feel a pain in my toe!

Quaker Elizabeth Gray Vining (1902–   ), author of books
for both adults and children, including a John Newbery Medal
winner, *Adam of the Road,* was appointed tutor to Crown
Prince Akihito of Japan in 1946. When she left Japan in 1950
their majesties bestowed upon her the Third Order of the Sacred
Crown and celebrated with ceremonial parties. *Windows for the
Crown Prince* is her book about her experiences in Japan. In her
journal, *Being Seventy: The Measure of a Year,* she discusses
her emotions and observations about aging, and, in this excerpt,
her philosophy about living and dying.

from

BEING SEVENTY: THE MEASURE OF A YEAR

TUESDAY, MARCH 20

Chapel Hill was lovely this morning with redbud and daffodils blooming
everywhere. I drove along North Street past the little house that Morgan
and I built forty-three years ago. It stands among its trees (oaks, elms,
cedars) gray-shingled with white trim, with an air of elegance, tiny though
it is. All the other small houses built at the same time look shabby and tacky.
It was pain to see it—and joy. Those two golden young people who lived
there for three years belonged in another age, and perhaps to a fairy tale.

> *Fear no more the heat o' th' sun*
> *Nor the furious winter's rages;*
> *Thou thy worldly task hast done,*
> *Home art gone and ta'en thy wages.*

Golden lads and girls all must,
Like chimney-sweepers, come to dust.

These, I think, are some of the most beautiful lines ever written—and all with the simple words that everyone may use, but so fitted to the thought and the sound and to one another that together they take on a beauty and mystery far beyond their separate qualities.

She was young, Imogen, and actually not dead, only preserved by a potion until it was safe for her to live. But Arviragus and Guiderius, her brothers, thought that she was dead and said those perfect words over her as they strewed flowers on her body.

Thou thy worldly task hast done,
Home art gone and ta'en thy wages

expresses my fundamental conviction about death—and life. We each have some earthly task to do, and when it is done, we go home. When someone dies swiftly, of a heart attack, perhaps, full of years and honors, it is obvious that his time has come, his task done. But what of those who die young, like Morgan in full stride, his Ph.D. within his grasp? Or those who like Violet suffer year after year of strokes, living on, yet not really alive, to eighty-five or more?

The task, I think, is not an obvious one, not visible to the outward eye even of love. It must be some inner act of growth, some hidden contract to be met, some ripening to be accomplished. "Men must endure/their going hence," says Edgar in *King Lear,* "even as their coming hither;/ Ripeness is all." Some ripen young; some take a long time to it.

And how can I be so sure of this, without believing in an anthropomorphic god or a bookkeeper in heaven? Only because I know—I *know*—that there is meaning in the universe, not chaos, and that love is at the heart of it. . . .

WEDNESDAY, APRIL 11

The day before yesterday Howard Brinton died. He was eighty-nine, lame and blind, and he had for the last two or three years been a transparent shell through which the light shone. Up to the end he was dictating his articles on the early Friends, his mind clear and retentive, his spirit shining. More than anyone else, except possibly Rufus Jones, Howard Brinton has for me expressed the essence of Quakerism today. And as a person he was lovable, gentle, wise, humorous, clear-sighted. He had had a stroke a few days earlier and was in the hospital under oxygen; at the end his speech returned and his mind was clear. Yuki, his wife, was with him day and night. His death was a serene transition.

What makes one dying peaceful and another painful? I have been reading the last volume of Leon Edel's great biography of Henry James. "The Master" at seventy-three had a stroke. He had servants, nurses, a devoted secretary around him. His sister-in-law, his niece, and his nephew came from America to London to be with him and to take charge. It took him nearly three restless, uncomfortable, irritable months to die. During that time his mind was much occupied with that which had been the absorption of his life—writing. He dictated to his secretary letters to Napoleon and others, essays, many meaningless but beautifully worded paragraphs. On February 24, four days before the end, he spoke of having had a night of "horror and terror." Altogether it was a protracted and difficult dying.

Whittier died at eighty-four. He was staying with a friend and cousin, Sarah A. Gove, at her place, Elmfield, at Hampton Falls, New Hampshire. On September 3, 1892, he had a stroke. His much-loved niece, Elizabeth Pritchard, came from Portland to be with him. For the three days that he lived, he was full of acceptance—"It is all right. Everybody is so kind"— and of love. Over and over he said, "Love, love to all the world." On September 6, as the sun was rising, he died. It was a peaceful and beautiful dying, and brief.

Violet had two years of immobility and silence and apparently of unconsciousness after her last stroke, and then died alone in her room in the nursing home. I was not there. I could have been. I went to see her several times a week, but I did not know that the change was coming. This I can hardly bear, even now, after more than three years. Even if she knew nothing, I would have sat beside her. I would have been there.

Teilhard de Chardin prayed for a "good end" and died swiftly of a heart attack. Two years or so ago I wrote such a prayer for myself.

> O God our Father, spirit of the universe, I am old in years and in the sight of others, but I do not feel old within myself. I have hopes and purposes, things I wish to do before I die. A surging of life within me cries, "Not yet! Not yet!" more strongly than it did ten years ago, perhaps because the nearer approach of death arouses the defensive strength of the instinct to cling to life.

Help me to loosen, fiber by fiber, the instinctive strings that bind me to the life I know. Infuse me with Thy spirit so that it is Thee I turn to, not the old ropes of habit and thought. Make me poised and free, ready when the intimation comes to go forward eagerly and joyfully into the new phase of life that we call death.

Help me to bring my work each day to an orderly state so that it will not be a burden to those who must fold it up and put it away when I am gone. Keep me ever aware and ever prepared for the summons.

If pain comes before the end help me not to fear it or struggle against it but to welcome it as a hastening of the process by which the strings that bind me to life are untied. Give me joy in awaiting the great change that comes after this life of many changes, let my self be merged in Thy Self as a candle's wavering light is caught up into the sun.

This prayer, like many others, is really addressed more to myself than to God. And I am not at all sure that by the time one has reached seventy one can do anything at all about the manner of one's dying. Whittier and Teilhard de Chardin and Howard Brinton had won their way of dying by their way of living over the years before.

FRIDAY, AUGUST 5

Iris Murdoch is one of the few women novelists whom the critics take seriously. In *The Black Prince* she says, speaking in her own person as author, not as one of her characters: "Life is horrible, without metaphysical sense, wrecked by chance, pain and the close prospect of death."

She states this opinion with more pungency than most people, perhaps, but she is not alone in her view. Indeed it seems to me that it has become a modern cliché, with no more truth than most clichés. Unquestionably there is much pain, physical and mental, in the world. We can never forget the anguish of those who suffered in the German death camps, at Hiroshima and Nagasaki, in the villages of Vietnam: the three great crimes of the modern world. And pain goes on in prisons, ghettos, labor camps, in bombed villages and places where political prisoners are tortured. But pain is not cumulative. It is individual. When an individual has too much to bear, he is eased by death, which comes as a friend. And no one's life is wholly pain; each has some moments of beauty, of happiness.

To me it seems childish and churlish to say that life is horrible and without meaning. Life is a trust, given into our hands, to hold carefully, to use well, to enjoy, to give back when the time comes. Oh, I know I have been fortunate beyond most people and far beyond my deserts. Perhaps I lack that "tragic sense" which Europeans are said to have and in which Americans are reported to be deficient. I do not think that life lacks metaphysical sense, even if I cannot say explicitly what that sense is, and I am sure that life has meaning, that I have work to do, that when it is finished I shall abandon this body and enter the unknown.

Meanwhile there is the beauty of the sunrise, of a misty, salty sea coast with the bell buoy intoning, of a great pine tree against the sky. There is the deep joy of friendship, of human love, the challenge of writing, the excitement of watching the world careening on its way, the small steady comforts of cold water, of bed, of a shower bath, of a new laid egg, and hot coffee; the stimulus of books and reading and ideas that stir one to agreement or rejection or question.

Alice Walker (1944–   ) worked as an activist with voter registration and welfare programs in New York City before moving to the West Coast to pursue her writing. She has lived with families and groups in Kenya, Uganda, and the U.S.S.R. She is probably best known for her novel *The Color Purple*, which won an American Book Award and Pulitzer Prize before being made into a prize-winning movie. Her work has been characterized as "timid thunder," demonstrated by the following poem.

"Good Night, Willie Lee, I'll See You in the Morning"

Looking down into my father's
dead face
for the last time
my mother said without
tears, without smiles
without regrets
but with *civility*
"Good night, Willie Lee, I'll see you
in the morning."
And it was then I knew that the healing
of all our wounds
is forgiveness
that permits a promise
of our return
at the end.

As a self-educated novelist, Ellen Glasgow (1873–1945), who spent her life in Richmond, Virginia, gained renown as a writer of the Southern experience. She rebelled against the romantic depiction of the South so prevalent in the idealistic image portrayed by other writers of her day. Her autobiography, *The Woman Within*, reveals her private inner life as few autobiographies have done, and no one was allowed to read it until her death. In this excerpt she describes a near encounter with death after a massive heart attack.

from

THE WOMAN WITHIN

In the past few years I have made a thrilling discovery, and in the past year I have had an even more thrilling adventure. My discovery was that until one is over sixty one can never really learn the secret of living. My adventure led me to the utmost border of death ("the ragged edge of eternity," my doctor called it) and kept me lingering, wholly conscious, without fear or reluctance or hesitation, in the kind of peace (or was it spiritual affirmation?) that passes both understanding and misunderstanding.

With the sardonic twist of circumstance, so prevalent in human affairs, I had no sooner learned how to live than the threat of death struck me. Only an Act of God, I used to boast, could ever kill me; but the one end I had not ever foreseen (for I had always said jestingly that my heart was too hard and cold to give way) was now approaching. Pain was barbed with surprise, because this particular pain was the last thing I had ever expected. "You have had no mercy on your heart," the specialist remarked solemnly, and

I retorted, lightly, "My heart has never asked me for mercy."

It had taken me sixty years to discover that there was nothing to be done either about my own life or about the world in which I lived. All my fighting courage had brought to me was a badly damaged heart, yet a heart that was still undefeated. When the doctor told me this, I had a sudden uplifting sense of inward peace, of outward finality. I had done my best, and I could do nothing more. I had finished my course. I had kept the faith.

Youth is the season of tragedy and despair. Youth is the time when one's whole life is entangled in a web of identity, in a perpetual maze of seeking and of finding, of passion and of disillusion, of vague longings and of nameless griefs, of pity that is a blade in the heart, and of "all the little emptiness of love." Then the soul drifts on the shallow stream of personality, within narrow borders. Not until life has passed through that retarded channel out upon the wide open sea of impersonality, can one really begin to live, not simply with the intenser part of oneself, but with one's entire being. For sixty years, I was learning this elemental truth; and in the very moment of my discovery, I found also that the shadow I had imagined my own was the shadow of death. . . .

It is not possible to express, and especially to express in writing, the most profound experience that one has known:—the recognition of death as another aspect of life. Millions of words have been written of dying; yet it is beyond the power of speech or of intelligence to describe the indescribable. Never again can I come so near the end of life without passing on into death. For nearly half an hour the Maine doctor watched, with his finger on my pulse and his stethoscope on my heart, and for every minute of that time I was completely conscious, but too weak to move my lips or flutter my eyelashes. I could see, fading slowly away, features of a kindly Roman senator bending over me. I could hear the voice of Anne Virginia calling to hold me back. I could see the face of my sister Rebe between the bed and the window. I could see the doctor's lips whispering, and though I could not hear his words, I knew that he said: "She is on the ragged edge. All we can do is to wait." Afterwards, they told me he feared to give a second hypodermic, lest the shock of the needle might send me over that edge. . . . These things I remember or heard later; but these things are no more than the surface awareness, the thin shell of the moment. In my mind a single thought was repeated: If I cannot finish my book, I want to go quickly. After pain, there was no shadow of fear, of shrinking, or of reluctance. While an icy chill ran from my feet upward, it was, strangely enough, a chill that seemed the other side of a glow, of a warmth, as of an unutterable sense of fulfillment. I had never believed in a limited personal immortality, in a narrow margin of eternity, or of the separate ego. The peace I felt, was not the peace of possession. It was—the fleeting essence escapes whenever I try to confine it—a sense of infinite reunion with the Unknown Everything or with Nothing . . . or with God. But whether Everything or Nothing, it was surrender of identity. . . . By surrender, I do not mean extinction of identity. I mean, enlargement and complete illumination of being. In my death, as in my life, I was still seeking God, known or unknown. . . .

Days afterwards, I promised myself that I would never try to speak of what I could not put into words. All I knew was that I had looked at death, which is the other side of life, and that death was "lovely and soothing . . ." When I thought of dying, in those weary months of convalescence, it was not of dying as a cold negation, but as a warm and friendly welcome to the universe, to the Being beyond and above consciousness, or any vestige of self. . . . But to feel is one thing, and to write of feeling is yet another thing. Solemn words may wear on paper a look of shallowness and complete insincerity. . . .

FOR TWO MONTHS AFTER this I was not allowed to go downstairs, and all I saw of Maine that summer was a single tall pointed fir against a sky of crystal blue, or under swift scudding clouds. As soon as I was able to sit up, I went back to my book, for by this time I had reached very nearly the end of my second writing. At first I worked only fifteen minutes a day, but after six weeks I could hold out for half an hour. From far away the reverberations of war shocked my nerves; but the barbarians had not yet concentrated upon the British Isles, the spot of earth I loved most after my own country. . . .

In those weeks and months I never lost a piercing sense of unreality, as if the world around me, and even the thoughts in my own mind, were as insubstantial as mist, and might vanish at a breath, and leave me suspended in hollowness. Although I knew the sensation resulted from physical weakness alone, I seemed to be perpetually waiting for a distant call, or for the sound of a bell ringing somewhere, very far off, through the mist. To the people about me, the appearance was simply one of abstraction or absorption in work. But I could not rid myself of the feeling that there was some connection between my present detachment from living and that hour when I had hesitated, without fear, upon the brink of some deeper awakening. I had felt then that I was borne outward by a strong current, and I felt still the vague murmur of that tide as it receded.

Eleanor Roosevelt (1884–1962), wife of Franklin Delano Roosevelt, thirty-second president of the United States, was well known as America's "First Lady," as an advocate of the poor, the needy, and the discriminated against, and as a tireless investigator of social ills and concerns for her husband, who was confined to a wheelchair. After his death, in her old age, she became a world leader in her own right, her championship of human rights and her own humanitarianism earning for her the admiration and love of millions and the title of "First Lady" not just of the United States but of the entire world.

INTERVIEW WITH
ELEANOR ROOSEVELT

I don't know whether I believe in a future life. I believe that all that you go through here must have some value, therefore there must be some *reason*. And there must be some "going on." How exactly that happens I've never been able to decide. There is a future—that I'm sure of. But how, that I don't know. And I came to feel that it didn't really matter very much because whatever the future held you'd have to face it when you came to it, just as whatever life holds you have to face it in exactly the same way. And the important thing was that you never let down doing the best that you were able to do—it might be poor because you might not have much within you to give, or to help other people with, or to live your life with. But as long as you did the very best that you were able to do, then that was what you

Excerpt from *This I Believe,* edited by Edward P. Morgan.

were put here to do and that was what you were accomplishing by being here.

And so I have tried to follow that out—and not to worry about the future or what was going to happen. I think I am pretty much of a fatalist. You have to accept whatever comes and the only important thing is that you meet it with courage and with the best that you have to give.

Marianne Moore (1887–1972), distinguished poet, critic, prose writer, and editor, was well known for her witty, cerebral, original, and eloquent poetry. She is considered by many to be the foremost woman poet of this century, and has been awarded many prizes for her work, among them the Pulitzer Prize in 1951 for her *Collected Poems,* the National Medal for Literature, the Bollingen Prize, and the Poetry Society of America's Gold Medal for Distinguished Achievement, and from France, the Croix de Chevalier, Ordre des Arts et Lettres, for her translation of the fables of LaFontaine. Her poetry reflects her intense individuality and her vast range of interests from literature to nature to baseball.

WHAT ARE YEARS?

What is our innocence,
what is our guilt? All are
    naked, none is safe. And whence
is courage: the unanswered question,
the resolute doubt—
dumbly calling, deafly listening—that
in misfortune, even death,
        encourages others
        and in its defeat, stirs

    the soul to be strong? He
sees deep and is glad, who
    accedes to mortality
and in his imprisonment rises
upon himself as
the sea in a chasm, struggling to be

free and unable to be,
    in its surrendering
    finds its continuing.

  So he who strongly feels,
behaves. The very bird,
  grown taller as he sings, steels
his form straight up. Though he is captive,
his mighty singing
says, satisfaction is a lowly
thing, how pure a thing is joy.
    This is mortality,
    this is eternity.

❧ BIBLIOGRAPHY ❧

Bausch, Richard. "What Feels Like the World." In *Spirits and Other Stories.* New York: Simon and Schuster, 1987.

Baxter, Charles. "Fenstad's Mother." In *The Best American Short Stories 1989.* Selected by Margaret Atwood with Shannon Ravenel. Boston: Houghton Mifflin Company, 1989.

Berenson, Bernard. *Sunset and Twilight: From the Diaries of 1947–1958.* Edited by Nicky Mariano. New York: Harcourt, Brace & World, Inc., 1963.

Berry, Wendell. *The Memory of Old Jack.* San Diego: Harcourt, Brace, Jovanovich, 1974.

Brecht, Bertolt. *Short Stories 1921–1946.* Edited by John Willett and Ralph Mannheim. Translated by Yvonne Kapp, Hugh Rorrison and Anthony Tatlow. London: Methuen, 1983.

Brooks, Gwendolyn. *The World of Gwendolyn Brooks.* New York: Harper & Row, 1971.

Brown, Mary Ward. *Tongues of Flame.* New York: E. P. Dutton/Seymour Lawrence, 1986.

Canfield, Dorothy. *A Harvest of Stories.* New York: Harcourt, Brace & Co., 1956.

Carver, Raymond. *Where Water Comes Together with Other Water.* New York: Random House, 1984.

Coatsworth, Elizabeth. *Personal Geography: Almost an Autobiography.* Brattleboro, Vermont: The Stephen Greene Press, 1976.

Coles, Robert. "Una Anciana." In *Growing Old in America.* 2nd edition. Edited by Beth B. Hess. New Brunswick, New Jersey: Transaction Books, 1980.

Colette. *The Blue Lantern.* Translated by Roger Senhouse. New York: Farrar, Straus and Giroux, 1963.

Cousins, Norman. *Albert Schweitzer's Mission: Healing and Peace.* New York: W. W. Norton & Company, 1985.

Cowley, Malcolm. *The View from 80.* New York: The Viking Press, 1980.

Diehl, Digby. *Supertalk.* New York: Doubleday & Company, Inc., 1974.

Eberhart, Richard. *Collected Poems 1930–1976.* New York: Oxford University Press, 1976.

Eiseley, Loren. *The Night Country.* New York: Charles Scribner's Sons, 1971.

Fisher, M. F. K. *Sister Age.* New York: Alfred A. Knopf, 1983.

Glasgow, Ellen. *The Woman Within.* New York: Hill and Wang, 1954.

Godden, Jon. *Ahmed and the Old Lady.* New York: Alfred A. Knopf, 1976.

Goudeket, Maurice. *The Delights of Growing Old.* Translated by Patrick O'Brian. New York: Farrar, Straus and Giroux, 1966.

Hayes, Helen. "Voices: An Epilogue." In *The Woman Alone.* Edited by Patricia O'Brian. New York: Quadruple/The New York Times Book Co., 1973.

Helprin, Mark. *Ellis Island & Other Stories.* New York: Dell Publishing Co., Inc., 1981.

Jacobsen, Josephine. "Jack Frost." In *The Substance of Things Hoped For.* Edited by John B. Breslin, S.J. New York: Doubleday, 1987.

Kunitz, Stanley. *The Poems of Stanley Kunitz.* Boston: Little, Brown and Company, 1979.

Larkin, Philip. *Collected Poems.* Edited by Anthony Thwaite. New York: Farrar, Straus & Giroux, 1989.

Lessing, Doris. "Womb Ward." In *The New Yorker* December 7, 1989.

Lester, Julius. *Do Lord Remember Me.* New York: Holt, Rinehart and Winston, 1984.

Lindbergh, Anne Morrow. *The Unicorn and Other Poems: 1935–1955.* New York: Pantheon, 1956.

MacLeish, Archibald. *The Human Season: Selected Poems 1926–1972.* Boston: Houghton Mifflin Company, 1972.

Moore, Marianne. *The Complete Poems of Marianne Moore.* New York: The Macmillan Company/The Viking Press, 1967.

Moses, Anna Mary Robertson. *Grandma Moses: My Life's History.* Edited by Otto Kallir. New York: Harper & Brothers, 1952.

Myerhoff, Barbara. *Number Our Days.* New York: E. P. Dutton, 1978.

Neihardt, John G. *All Is But a Beginning: Youth Remembered, 1881–1901.* New York: Harcourt Brace Jovanovich, Inc., 1972.

Norris, Helen. *Water into Wine.* Urbana: University of Illinois Press, 1988.

Osborn, Carolyn. *Fields of Memory.* Bryan, Texas: Shearer Publishing, 1984.

Ponsot, Marie. *Admit Impediment.* New York: Alfred A. Knopf, 1981.

Porter, Katherine Anne. *The Leaning Tower: and Other Stories.* New York: Harcourt, Brace and Company, 1944.

Roethke, Theodore. *The Collected Poems of Theodore Roethke.* New York: Anchor Press/Doubleday, 1975.

Roosevelt, Eleanor. Interview in *This I Believe.* Edited by Edward P. Morgan. New York: Simon & Schuster, 1952.

Russell, Bertrand. *Portraits from Memory: and Other Essays.* London: George Allen & Unwin Ltd., 1956.

Sackville-West, Vita. *All Passion Spent.* London: Virago Press Ltd, 1983.

Sarton, May. *At Seventy: A Journal.* New York: W. W. Norton & Company, 1984.

Scott-Maxwell, Florida. *The Measure of My Days.* New York: Penguin Books, 1968.

Sexton, Anne. *The Awful Rowing Toward God.* Boston: Houghton Mifflin Company, 1975.

Shaw, Bernard. *Collected Letters: 1926–1950.* Edited by Dan H. Laurence. New York: Viking Penguin Inc., 1988.

Singer, Isaac Bashevis. *The Death of Methuselah and Other Stories.* New York: Farrar, Straus & Giroux, 1988.

Spender, Stephen. *Collected Poems: 1928–1985.* New York: Random House, 1986.

Stark, Freya. *The Journey's Echo.* London: John Murray, 1963.

Swenson, May. *New and Selected Things Taking Place: Poems by May Swenson.* Boston: Little, Brown and Company, 1954.

Tandy, Jessica and Hume Cronyn. Interview with Connie Goldman: "I'm Too Busy to Talk Now/Conversations with American Artists Over Seventy." 1985.

Thomas, Dylan. *The Collected Poems of Dylan Thomas.* New York: New Directions, 1957.

Van Doren, Mark. *Good Morning: Last Poems by Mark Van Doren.* New York: Hill and Wang/Farrar, Straus & Giroux, 1973.

Van Duyn, Mona. *Letters from a Father and Other Poems.* New York: Atheneum, 1982.

Vining, Elizabeth Gray. *Being Seventy: The Measure of a Year.* New York: The Viking Press, 1978.

Vivante, Arturo. *The Tales of Arturo Vivante.* New York: The Sheep Meadow Press, 1990.

Walker, Alice. *Good Night, Willie Lee, I'll See You in the Morning: Poems by Alice Walker.* San Diego: Harcourt Brace Jovanovich, 1975.

Warner, Sylvia Townsend. "The Listening Woman." In *The New Yorker* May 20, 1972.

Warren, Robert Penn. *New and Selected Poems: 1923–1985.* New York: Random House, 1985.

Wheelock, John Hall. "Song on Reaching Seventy." In *Twentieth-Century American Poetry.* New York: Modern Library, 1963.

White, Katharine S. *Onward and Upward in the Garden.* New York: Farrar, Straus & Giroux, 1979.

Williams, William Carlos. *The Collected Poems of William Carlos Williams: Volume II, 1939–1962.* Edited by Christopher MacGowan. New York: New Directions, 1954.

Yeats, W. B. *The Poems: A New Edition.* Edited by Richard J. Finneran. New York: Macmillan Publishing Company, 1983.

Yezierska, Anzia. *The Open Cage: An Anzia Yezierska Collection.* New York: Persea Books, 1979.

Zuckerman, Marilyn. "After Sixty." In *Ourselves, Growing Older.* Edited by Paula Brown Duren et al. New York: Simon and Schuster, 1987.

∙§ ACKNOWLEDGMENTS ⬥

Grateful acknowledgment is made to the following for permission to reprint previously published material:

ATHENEUM PUBLISHERS: "Letters from a Father" from *Letters from a Father and Other Poems* by Mona Van Duyn. Copyright © 1982 by Mona Van Duyn. Reprinted by permission of Atheneum Publishers, an imprint of Macmillan Publishing Company.

GWENDOLYN BROOKS: "The Bean Eaters" from *Blacks* by Gwendolyn Brooks. Copyright © 1987 by The David Company, Chicago. Reprinted by permission of Gwendolyn Brooks.

JONATHAN CLOWES LTD.: "Womb Ward" by Doris Lessing. Copyright © 1987 by Doris Lessing. First published in *The New Yorker*, December 1987. Reprinted by permission of Jonathan Clowes Ltd., London, on behalf of Doris Lessing.

NORMAN COUSINS: Excerpt from *Albert Schweitzer's Mission: Healing and Peace* by Norman Cousins, W.W. Norton & Co. © Norman Cousins.

LIZ DARHANSOFF LITERARY AGENCY: "Fenstad's Mother" by Charles Baxter. Copyright © 1988 by Charles Baxter. First published in *The Atlantic*.

DELACORTE PRESS/SEYMOUR LAWRENCE: "Palais de Justice" from *Ellis Island & Other Stories* by Mark Helprin. Copyright © 1978 by

Mark Helprin. Reprinted by permission of Delacorte Press/Seymour Lawrence, a division of Bantam Doubleday Dell Publishing Group, Inc.

DOUBLEDAY: Excerpts from *Supertalk* by Digby Diehl. Copyright © 1971, 1972, 1974 by Digby Diehl. Excerpts from *Goodnight Willie Lee, I'll See You in the Morning* by Alice Walker. Copyright © 1978 by Alice Walker. "Old Florist" from *The Collected Poems of Theodore Roethke.* Copyright 1946 by Harper & Brothers. Reprinted by permission of Doubleday, a division of Bantam Doubleday Dell Publishing Group, Inc. and William Heinemann Limited.

E.P. DUTTON: "The Amaryllis" from *Tongues of Flame* by Mary Ward Brown. Copyright © 1986 by Mary Ward Brown. Excerpts from *Number Our Days* by Barbara Myerhoff. Copyright © 1978 by Barbara Myerhoff. Reprinted by permission of the publisher, E.P. Dutton, an imprint of New American Library, a division of Penguin Books USA Inc.

ESTATE OF BERNARD BERENSON: Excerpt from *Sunset and Twilight: From the Diaries 1947–1958* by Bernard Berenson. Reprinted by permission of Sabina Anrep for the Estate of Bernard Berenson.

ESTATE OF RAYMOND CARVER: "Happiness in Cornwall" from *Where Water Comes Together with Other Water: Poems by Raymond Carver.* Copyright © 1984 by Raymond Carver. Reprinted by permission of Tess Gallagher for the Estate of Raymond Carver.

ESTATE OF SYLVIA TOWNSEND WARNER: "The Listening Woman" from *Selected Stories* by Sylvia Townsend Warner. Reprinted by permission of Chatto & Windus/The Hogarth Press on behalf of the Executors of the Estate of Sylvia Townsend Warner. THE ECCO PRESS: Excerpts from *The Journey's Echo* by Freya Stark. Copyright 1936, 1938, 1940, 1945, 1950, 1951, 1953, © 1958, 1959, 1961, 1963 by Freya Stark. First published by The Ecco Press in 1988. Reprinted by permission.

FARRAR, STRAUS & GIROUX, INC.: Excerpts from *The Blue Lantern* by Colette. Translation copyright © 1963 by Martin Secker and Warburg Ltd. "The Hotel" from *The Death of Methuselah* by Isaac Bashevis Singer. Copyright © 1971, 1974, 1978, 1985, 1986, 1988 by Isaac Bashevis Singer. "Old Man, Old Woman" from *Good Morning* by Mark Van Doren. Copyright © 1972, 1973 by the Estate of Mark Van

Doren. Excerpts from "Introduction" by E.B. White from *Onward and Upward in the Garden* by Katharine S. White. Introduction copyright © 1979 by E.B. White. Reprinted by permission of Farrar, Straus & Giroux, Inc. "Aubade" from *Collected Poems* by Philip Larkin. Copyright © 1988, 1989 by the Estate of Philip Larkin. Reprinted by permission of Farrar, Straus & Giroux, Inc. and Faber and Faber Ltd.

FLAMMARION: Excerpt from *The Delights of Growing Old* by Maurice Goudelet. Reprinted by permission of Flammarion.

JON GODDEN LITERARY FUND: Excerpt from *Ahmed and the Old Lady* by Jon Godden. Reprinted by permission of the Jon Godden Literary Fund.

CONNIE GOLDMAN: Excerpt from *I'm too Busy to Talk Now: Conversations with American Artists Over 70.* ® © Connie Goldman Productions, Inc.

GRANDMA MOSES PROPERTIES CO.: Excerpts from *My Life's History* by Grandma Moses. Copyright 1952, renewed 1980 by Grandma Moses Properties Co., New York.

HARCOURT BRACE JOVANOVICH, INC.: "The Last Leaf" from *The Leaning Tower and Other Stories* by Katherine Anne Porter. Copyright 1935 and renewed 1963 by Katherine Anne Porter. Excerpts from *The Memory of Old Jack* by Wendell Berry. Copyright © 1974 by Wendell Berry. "Sex Education" from *A Harvest of Stories* by Dorothy Canfield. Copyright 1945 by Dorothy Canfield Fisher. Copyright renewed 1973 by Sarah Fisher Scott. Excerpts from *The Woman Within* by Ellen Glasgow. Copyright 1954 and renewed 1982 by Harcourt Brace Jovanovich, Inc. Reprinted by permission of Harcourt Brace Jovanovich, Inc.

LOUISE LEVITAS HENRIKSEN: "A Window Full of Sky" by Anzia Yezierska from *How I Found America,* Persea Books, New York, 1991. Copyright Louise Levitas Henriksen.

HENRY HOLT AND COMPANY, INC.: Excerpts from *Do Lord Remember Me* by Julius Lester. Copyright © 1984 by Julius Lester. Reprinted by arrangement with Henry Holt and Company, Inc.

HOUGHTON MIFFLIN COMPANY: "Courage" from *The Awful Rowing Toward God* by Anne Sexton. Copyright © 1975 by Loring Conant,

Thomas. Reprinted by permission of New Directions Publishing Corp. and David Higham Associates Ltd.

THE NEW YORKER MAGAZINE: "Una Anciana" by Robert Coles. Copyright © 1973 by The New Yorker Magazine, Inc. Reprinted by permission.

W.W. NORTON & COMPANY, INC.: Excerpt from *At Seventy, A Journal* by May Sarton. Copyright © 1984 by May Sarton. Reprinted by permission of W.W. Norton & Co., Inc.

OXFORD UNIVERSITY PRESS, INC.: "Hardy Perennial" from *Collected Poems 1930–1976* by Richard Eberhart. Copyright © 1976 by Richard Eberhart. Reprinted by permission of Oxford University Press, Inc.

PANTHEON BOOKS: Excerpt from *Memories, Dreams, Reflections* by Carl G. Jung, edited by Aniela Jaffe, translated by Richard and Clara Winston. Translation copyright © 1961, 1962, 1963 by Random House, Inc. "Bare Tree" from *The Unicorn and Other Poems* by Anne Morrow Lindbergh. Copyright © 1955 by Anne Morrow Lindbergh. Reprinted by permission of Pantheon Books, a division of Random House, Inc.

RANDOM HOUSE, INC.: "After the Dinner Party" from *New and Selected Poems 1923–1985* by Robert Penn Warren. Copyright © 1985 by Robert Penn Warren. Reprinted by permission of Random House, Inc. "From My Diary" from *Collected Poems 1928–1985* by Stephen Spender. Copyright © 1986 by Stephen Spender. Reprinted by permission of Random House, Inc. and Faber and Faber Ltd.

ROUTLEDGE, CHAPMAN AND HALL AND METHUEN LONDON: "The Unseemly Old Lady" from *Short Stories 1921–1946* by Bertolt Brecht. Reprinted by permission of the publishers.

CHARLES SCRIBNER'S SONS: "Song on Reaching Seventy" from *This Blessed Earth* by John Hall Wheelock. Copyright © 1973, 1974, 1975, 1976 by John Hall Wheelock. "The Brown Wasps" from *The Night Country* by Loren Eiseley. Copyright © 1971 by Loren Eiseley. Reprinted by permission of Charles Scribner's Sons, an imprint of Macmillan Publishing Company.

THE SHEEP MEADOW PRESS: "Last Rites" from *The Tales of Arturo Vivante* by Arturo Vivante. © Arturo Vivante, The Sheep Meadow Press, 1990.

SIMON & SCHUSTER, INC.: "After Sixty" from *Ourselves, Growing Older* by Paula Brown Doress and Diana Laskin Siegal. Copyright © 1987 by Paula Brown Doress and Diana Laskin Siegal. Excerpt from *This I Believe* edited by Edward Morgan. Copyright 1952 by Help Inc. Copyright renewed 1980 by Edward P. Morgan.

THE SOCIETY OF AUTHORS: Twelve letters by Bernard Shaw from the 1926–1950 collection. Reprinted by permission of The Society of Authors on behalf of the Bernard Shaw Estate.

TIMES BOOKS: Excerpt from *The Woman Alone* by Patricia O'Brien. Copyright © 1973 by Patricia O'Brien. Reprinted by permission of Times Books, a division of Random House, Inc.

UNIVERSITY OF ILLINOIS PRESS: Excerpt from *Water into Wine* (Illinois Short Fiction Series, 1988) by Helen Norris. Copyright © 1988 by Helen Norris. Reprinted by permission of the author and the publisher.

UNIVERSITY OF NEBRASKA PRESS: Excerpt from *All Is But a Beginning: Youth Remembered 1881–1901* by John G. Neihardt. Copyright © 1972 by John G. Neihardt. Reprinted by permission of the University of Nebraska Press.

UNWIN HYMAN LTD.: Excerpt from *Portraits from Memory* by Bertrand Russell. Copyright © 1956 by George Allen & Unwin (Publishers) Ltd. Reprinted by kind permission of Unwin Hyman Ltd.

VIKING PENGUIN: Excerpts from *The View from 80* by Malcolm Cowley. Copyright © 1976, 1978, 1980 by Malcolm Cowley. Excerpt from *Personal Geography: Almost an Autobiography* by Elizabeth Coatsworth. Copyright © 1976 by Elizabeth Coatsworth Beston. Excerpts from *Being Seventy* by Elizabeth Gray Vining. Copyright © 1978 by Elizabeth Gray Vining. Reprinted by permission of Viking Penguin, a division of Penguin Books USA Inc.

VIRAGO PRESS LIMITED: Excerpt from *All Passion Spent* by Vita Sackville West. Copyright 1931 by Nigel Nicolson. Published by Virago Press Ltd. in 1983.

THE WASHINGTON POST: "The Autumn of My Life" by Polly Francis, The Washington Post, 1975. Reprinted by permission.

HARRIET WASSERMAN LITERARY AGENCY, INC.: "What Feels Like the World" by Richard Bausch. First published in *The Atlantic,* October 1985. Copyright © 1985 by Richard Bausch. Reprinted by permission of Harriet Wasserman Literary Agency, Inc., as agent for the author.